A BIOBIBLIOGRAPHY OF NATIVE AMERICAN WRITERS, 1772-1924

by

Daniel F. Littlefield, Jr.

and

James W. Parins

Native American Bibliography Series,
No. 2

THE SCARECROW PRESS, INC.
METUCHEN, N.J., & LONDON
1981

Library of Congress Cataloging in Publication Data

Littlefield, Daniel F.
  A biobibliography of native American writers,
1772-1924.

  (Native American bibliography series; no. 2)
  Includes index.
  1. Indians of North America--Bibliography.
2. American literature--Indian authors--
Bibliography. 3. United States--Imprints.
I. Parins, James W. II. Title. III. Series.
Z1209. 2. U5L57 [E77] 016. 973'0497   81-9138
ISBN 0-8108-1463-3   AACR2

CONTENTS

Editor's Foreword, by Jack W. Marken   iv

Preface   v

User's Note   ix

Introduction   xi

PART I: A Bibliography of Native American Writers   1

PART II: A Bibliography of Native American Writers
           Known Only by Pen Names   185

PART III: Biographical Notes   203

Index of Writers by Tribal Affiliation   315

Subject Index   328

iii

EDITOR'S FOREWORD

Just over a decade ago, Arlene Hirschfelder's small book entitled American Indian Authors: A Representative Bibliography was published. Since then many bibliographies of the American Indian have appeared, but no others have concentrated like Hirschfelder on writings by Indian authors until Daniel Littlefield and James Parins. Their bibliography is more selective than Hirschfelder's, however, because they have restricted eligibility for inclusion to writings done solely by Indian authors and have omitted material by Indian people but written down by non-Indians. For this reason, some users of this bibliography will note the omission of some books considered to be by Indians, particularly in the area of autobiography.

This bibliography covers the period from colonial times until the American Indian was granted citizenship. The over four thousand entries show that a large number of American Indians were active writers in a foreign language, English, during this century and a half. That the contributions are of so many different types in essay, fiction, and poetry shows that the writers had mastered various kinds of writing. The authors range from the obscure to the well-known. Comprising about a third of this book is the very interesting and useful section of biographical statements about the authors.

James Parins has had extensive experience in editing and textual analysis of literary works, and Daniel Littlefield has published widely in Native American studies. Their contribution of the second book in the Native American Bibliography Series is a significant addition to the bibliographical materials on the American Indian.

Jack W. Marken
Brookings, SD
June 1981

iv

PREFACE

This biobibliography is intended to provide information on a sizeable body of writing that has been largely overlooked by both scholars and the public. It includes works written in English by Native Americans, excluding those from Canada, from Colonial times to 1924. Not strictly literary in scope, this book lists works of some very different sorts: political essays and addresses, satirical pieces written in various dialects, myths and legends, original poetry and fiction, published letters, historical works, personal reminiscences, and other genres. However, all works included here have in common the fact that they were written with an audience in mind, usually a public one. Furthermore, most were written for publication; those that were not but were subsequently published were published because of their merit or because of the public issues they addressed.

The wide spectrum of writing represented here, we believe, will be useful to those seeking to understand the opinions, attitudes, and concerns of the Native Americans during some of the most crucial and chaotic years in their history. Our purpose is to add to the body of knowledge concerned with Native American culture and history. We believe that any study of American ethnic history is incomplete without the expressions of self-concept like those of writers identified in the present work.

The bibliography includes works published between 1772 and the end of 1924. We realize that we have cut off some writers in the middle of their careers, but we would have done the same had we chosen a closing date earlier than 1924. We realize, too, that the selection of any closing date besides the present would be somewhat arbitrary. A closing date of the present would result in a multivolume product, which practical considerations of time required us to forgo. Therefore, in selecting a closing date, we chose 1924 because in many ways it was a signal year in Native American affairs. Congress granted U.S. citizenship to all native-born Native Americans who had not been granted citizenship before that date; with citizenship, an old era in Native American affairs ended and a new one began. The new spirit of the times was reflected in the passage of the Pueblo Lands Act that same year. The victory that the bill represented for Native Americans was the result of renewed national interest in Native affairs that led shortly to the Meriam Report and a few years later to the Indian Reorganization Act and the Native American's New Deal.

One of the major problems encountered in compiling this book was identifying the writers. For purposes of this work, we have defined a Native American as a person who had tribal affiliation or maintained tribal ties and who was recognized by his contemporaries as a Native American. Writers were identified in a number of ways, such as inclusion on tribal rolls, attendance at government schools that were limited to Native Americans, and various kinds of publication data. In compiling the main bibliography, we at no time identified a writer solely on the basis of a personal claim of Native citizenship; if corroboration was not available, we did not include the writer's works. Fortunately, we were able to find corroborating evidence for or against the claim of nearly every writer. However, Part II is a bibliography of writers who are known to us only by their pen names. Those writers were included primarily on the basis of self-identification and the contents of the works.

Sources of information for this biobibliography include, of course, standard bibliographic tools such as the Readers' Guide to Periodical Literature, the International Index, and the National Union Catalog of Pre-1956 Imprints. But most periodical works by Native Americans appear in periodicals that are not indexed in the standard periodical indices. Therefore, we consulted publications by and for Native Americans as well as records, documents, and publications of various agencies, organizations, educational institutions, and re-

ligious groups. For biographical information, we inspected tribal
rolls from the Federal Records Center at Fort Worth, Texas, and
the Wisconsin Historical Society. Besides tribal histories, helpful
published material was found in Handbook of American Indians North
of Mexico (Washington, 1907-1910) and Frederick J. Dockstader's
Great North American Indians (New York, 1977) as well as in biographical dictionaries such as Who Was Who and Dictionary of American Biography. We also used the resources of the Oklahoma Historical Society, the Wisconsin Historical Society, the Bacone College
Library, and the Muskogee Public Library. Additional information
was gathered through interlibrary loan from the University of Oregon
Library, the Minnesota Historical Society, the Library of Congress,
and other institutions.

The use of the collections of all of these institutions not only
provided data for the present work, but actually enlarged its scope
as we became more aware of the dimensions of the project. As the
work progressed, we became cognizant of the mass of Native American writing and realized the likelihood that much more material
exists. But accessibility is a major problem, particularly regarding
periodical materials. Extant issues are scattered, and few are indexed, requiring that the researcher look at each issue, when he
can obtain access to it. Newspaper material is particularly difficult
to get at because of incomplete runs and the lack of access to small
newspapers in the geographical region where each writer lived. Any-
thing approaching a complete survey of the existing newspaper resources would be too time-consuming, if not physically impossible.
Thus we confess that this book is only the beginning of a thorough
examination of the subject. There is undoubtedly more material to
be gathered when resources become more generally accessible. We
hope that this work will serve as a starting point for others who
wish to join us in an exploration of this important part of American
culture.

Of the many people and organizations that assisted us in our
work, we wish especially to acknowledge the help of Steve Domjan-
ovich of the Bacone College Library and the staffs of the Oklahoma

Historical Society, the Wisconsin Historical Society, and the Muskogee Public Library. For their interlibrary loan assistance, we thank the librarians of the University of Oregon Library and the Minnesota Historical Society.

Daniel F. Littlefield, Jr.
James W. Parins

USER'S NOTE

Users of this bibliographic guide will discover some bibliographic nightmares: weeklies that occasionally or for several months running issued a monthly in the place of a weekly issue; volume numbers out of order; the same volume sequences of the same title, published at different times by the same organization, but without a series designation; and several periodicals with the same title, but published by different organizations. We have retreated to common sense in dealing with those matters.

We have taken certain steps to assist the user. First, we have arranged the entries for each writer in chronological order. We assumed that the user will not be familiar with most of the work included and that a chronological arrangement would reflect a writer's range and development much better than would an alphabetical listing of his work.

Second, the writers are listed in alphabetical order, and after each name is a tribal designation. For those users who are interested in tribal groups or tribal literatures, the first Index is a list of writers according to their tribal affiliation. In listing their affiliation, we have used the designations that the writers or their publishers used in identifying them. If the information was available, we have further identified the band, tribal division, or reservation of members of large or scattered groups such as the Sioux and Chippewas. Further information on the writers and their backgrounds appears in the biographical notes in Part III. However, the reader should realize that these are simply notes and are not offered as complete biographical statements.

Third, each entry in the bibliography is preceded by a number, after which appears a letter that designates the general genre category into which the work fits. Following is a key to the genre designations:

A = Address   M = Myths or legends
C = Collections and compilations   N = Nonfiction prose
D = Drama   P = Poetry
E = Edition   S = Sermon
F = Fiction   T = Translation into English
L = Letter

Last, for those users who are interested in themes, ideas, or subjects, the Subject Index is a general guide to the bibliographic entries.

INTRODUCTION

Publication in 1946 of Margot Astrov's anthology The Winged Serpent (New York, 1946) brought Native American prose and poetry to widespread attention. The collection consisted of translations of traditional songs, chants, prayers, and tales collected during the preceding five or six decades by anthropologists and ethnologists such as Ruth Benedict, Franz Boaz, Daniel G. Brinton, Ruth Bunzel, Frances Densmore, Alice Fletcher, and others. Astrov's volume had not been the first such anthology. Natalie (Curtis) Burlin's anthology of chants and songs, The Indian Book (New York, 1904), was reprinted in 1923 and 1935; and George W. Cronyn edited a similar anthology called The Path of the Rainbow (New York, 1918), which was republished in 1934. Burlin and Cronyn, like Astrov, relied on the work of the anthropologists and ethnologists. But it was Astrov's work that caught the public attention. It was republished as American Indian Prose and Poetry (New York, 1962), and with that publication a new dimension was opened in Native American literary studies.

The past decade has witnessed the publication of numerous such volumes, including a republication of Cronyn's anthology as American Indian Poetry (New York, 1973). The underlying rationale of these anthologies is the historical consideration of the Native American as a maker of songs, chants, tales, and myths, and his creations are offered to the reader in translation. In later anthologies, such as Literature of the American Indian (New York, 1973) by Thomas E. Sanders and Walter W. Peek and American Indian Literature (Norman, 1979) by Alan R. Velie, editors added sections containing representative pieces written by contemporary Native Americans. Others, such as Terry Allen's The Whispering Wind (New York, 1972), John Milton's Four Indian Poets (Vermillion, 1974), and, more recently, Geary Hobson's The Remembered Earth (Albuquerque, 1979), are anthologies of writings by contemporary writers. The latter anthologies reflect the tremendous vitality of Native American literature during the last decade.

In his introduction, Milton writes, "Very recently, really in the past ten years, and with a noticeable growth in only the past five years, contemporary Indians have been writing poetry in English, so that there is no need for translation and rewriting. Perhaps, for this reason, the poetry is purer. In any case, no one stands between the poetry and the reader. The communication is direct" (p. 9). Milton's statement points out a significant problem relating to

editions of translated traditional chants, songs, tales, and speeches.
For over a century, while recognizing the value and beauty of translations, writers have also recognized the problems of aesthetic response and critical evaluation posed by them.[1] Although some of
the translations in the anthologies were done by anthropologists who
were native speakers, such as Ella Deloria, Archie Phinney, and
Francis LaFlesche, the perceptive reader puts aside a volume of
translations with some doubts. Astrov aptly points out that the reader
must consider the effect of the translator's personality in the translation. "For translation is," she says, "if not creative, then re-
creative work. It is surely a high art" (pp. 4-5). How much of the
songs, chants, or tales as we see them reprinted, one asks, belongs
to the original maker? Most pieces were passed down by oral tradition from generation to generation before the collectors recorded
them; each work no doubt changed more or less as it was passed
down. Finally, one must ultimately ask how much of the song or
chant belongs to the native informant and how much belongs to the
translator.

By communicating directly, as Milton has pointed out, writing
in English by Native Americans stands in sharp contrast to translations. It involves oral traditions only insofar as they appear in the
contents of the works. The works appear in the language in which
they were originally conceived. But more important, they were
written down by the writers who conceived them. As a result, response to and evaluation of them can be much more definitive. But
Milton's language suggests that literary production in English is rel-
atively new to Native Americans, while Charles R. Larson pushes
back the beginnings of Native American fiction only a few decades
in his American Indian Fiction (Albuquerque, 1978).

Unfortunately, the scope of some anthologies and such critical
studies as Larson's has tended to reinforce the idea that there was
a limited literary production until well into this century; in fact,
from the late eighteenth century until the early years of the twentieth,
a large number of native writers wrote verse and prose in English
and published it widely. Only Hobson (p. 5) has indicated that a
sizeable body of Native American literature existed in the nineteenth
century. If other editors and scholars have been aware of that production, they have unfortunately chosen heretofore to ignore it, for
upon close examination, the body of English writings by Native Americans from 1772 to 1924 is likely to arrest, for a number of reasons,
the attention of not only the scholar but the casual reader as well.

First, one is struck by the quantity of the writing. Hundreds,
perhaps thousands, of writers produced thousands of works. They
have been identified in sufficient numbers to justify certain generali-
zations. An obvious one is that literary production in English is a
direct indication of the degree of acculturation of the tribes and reflects the impact of assimilationist policies upon them. Most Native
Americans who wrote in English before the Civil War, for example,
belonged to tribes who had been displaced by non-Native populations
in the eastern part of the nation or had been forced, as a result of

federal policy, to remove to lands farther west. Cut off from their traditional life styles or homelands, they were forced to acculturate in order to survive. Samson Occom, who began writing in the years just before the Revolutionary War, was from the Mohegan tribe that had early felt the impact of European civilization. In the first half of the nineteenth century, there was literary activity among the rapidly acculturating Cherokees in the South and the Six Nations and Chippewas of the Great Lakes region. Prominent among the latter was George Copway, who wrote prolifically, traveled widely, and edited a newspaper, Copway's American Indian, for a short time. The differences between the pre-Civil War writers and their native counterparts farther west are sharply brought into focus by the fact that a posthumous volume of poetry by the Cherokee poet John Rollin Ridge was published in 1868, the year of the last treaty negotiated with a Native American tribe in the United States, preceding by several years the great wars in the West. Later, as the western tribes were forced to acculturate, literacy levels rose, and their members, too, like their eastern counterparts decades earlier, began to write in English. The result was a great body of writing in English, writing that varies widely in form, technique, and quality and provides valuable insights into the Native American's self-concept throughout the decades.

Many of these writers achieved national reputations. Among them were Charles A. Eastman and Gertrude Simmons Bonnin, who were well known for their autobiographical works, John Oskison for his fiction, Will Rogers for his humor, Rolla Lynn Riggs for his drama, Charles Curtis and Robert Latham Owens for their political writings, and Francis La Flesche, Arthur C. Parker, John N. B. Hewitt, and William Jones for their anthropological and ethnological studies.

The extent of the writings and the exact number of Native American writers may never be known because of the publication outlets sought by the writers. Before the Civil War, the outlets were limited. Writers sometimes published their works themselves, but often, because they were oddities, their works were printed by commercial presses, and national newspapers and journals sometimes published their shorter works. The Native Americans established their own outlets for their writing during the first half of the century. The establishment of The Cherokee Phoenix newspaper in 1828 was a great step forward for English literacy among the Cherokees and the editors published the writings of Cherokee citizens. The same was true of its successor in the West, The Cherokee Advocate, founded in 1844. Another notable newspaper of the pre-Civil War days was Copway's American Indian, mentioned above, founded in 1851. Indian writers occasionally published, as well, in mission-supported publications such as the Cherokee Messenger, printed at Baptist Mission, Cherokee Nation, and the Indian Advocate published at Louisville, Kentucky.

After the Civil War, publications accepting Indians' work multiplied. Various newspapers of the Indian Territory served writers

there, and in the last two decades of the last century and the first
two decades of this, mission-based publications and Indian-owned
newspapers in the Upper Midwest and Plains states and territories
proliferated. Among the latter were the White Earth Progress,
founded in 1887, the White Earth Tomahawk, founded in 1903, and
the Odanah Star, founded in 1913. Also important as publishers of
Indian writing during this time were the weekly and monthly publications of Hampton Institute and the government schools such as Carlisle, Haskell, Chilocco, Genoa, Phoenix, and Chemawa. Near the
end of the period under consideration, politically oriented journals
edited by Native Americans began to appear, notably the American
Indian Magazine and Wassaja. Finally, by the turn of the century,
commercial presses more readily accepted Indians' work as did national magazines such as Harper's and the Atlantic Monthly.

For such publication outlets, Native writers produced works
as varied in form as their backgrounds. There are novels, short
stories, prose narratives, lyric and narrative poetry, addresses, animal fables, romances, legends, histories, political memorials, political epistles, political essays, dialect poetry and fiction, familiar
essays, and linguistic, anthropological, religious, and ethnological
tracts. The works vary in tone from serious to humorous and in
purpose from propaganda to sheer entertainment. In most respects,
they reflect the trends in popular writing among non-Indians of their
times. The early poetry reflects the Romantic and Victorian traditions, while some later works reflect trends in poetry during the late
nineteenth century. Much of John Rollin Ridge's poetry, for instance,
is highly derivative and smacks of Neo-Classical and Romantic influ-
ences, while the dialect poetry of Alexander Posey and Bertrand N.
O. Walker makes those writers the Native American counterparts of
James Whitcomb Riley, who wrote for the Hoosiers, or Paul Lau-
rence Dunbar, who wrote for the Blacks. In short fiction, Posey,
Walker, John Oskison, and William Jones made use of dialect in
much the same ways that the non-Native writers Charles Chesnutt,
Hamlin Garland, and George Washington Cable used it in their works.
The humorous letters of many writers, particularly those from the
Indian Territory, fit squarely into the tradition of the professional
humorists of the pre-Civil War years or the "Phunny Phellows" and
other humorists of the last three decades of the century. There is
a noticeable absence of drama by Native writers, but the absence is
not surprising in light of the fact that drama was not a dominant literary form in nineteenth-century America and that little drama of
quality was produced in the larger society.

Despite their acculturation, some of the writers evidently did
not find literary production easy. Creek poet Alexander Posey put it
as follows:

> The Indian talks in poetry; poetry is his vernacular--not
> necessarily the stilted poetry of books, but the free and un-
> trammeled poetry of Nature, the poetry of the fields, the
> sky, the river, the sun and the stars. In his own tongue
> it is not difficult for the Indian to compose,--he does it

instinctively; but in attempting to write in English he is handicapped. Words seem hard, form mechanical, and it is to these things that I attribute the failure of the civilized Indian to win fame in poetry.[2]

According to Sanders and Peek (pp. 449-450) this tension is still felt by some contemporary Native writers who experience "the problems inherent in conveying cultural awareness in a language antithetical to the culture's survival."

If much of the writing is derivative or conforms in mode to the popular literary tastes of the day, what then distinguishes the English writing of Native Americans from other writing of the nineteenth and early twentieth century and therefore makes it worth studying? Although the fact that it was produced by Native Americans is remarkable, that is not enough. It is therefore necessary for the reader to look for something distinctive in the works themselves. While he is struck by the extent to which most of the works conform to popular literary standards of the day, the discerning reader at the same time notes evidence that its production results from the writer's particular racial, cultural, and social background. Despite the degree of acculturation that their writing displays, most Native American writers made some use of their native backgrounds. Of particular interest to them were the stresses and pressures placed upon the native population by the expansion of the non-Native society in America.

The century and a half preceding 1924 was perhaps the most dramatic in Native American history. By 1824, when the Bureau of Indian Affairs was established, the tribes indigenous to lands east of the Appalachian chain had been destroyed, contained on small tracts, or pushed westward, and white settlements were pressing the tribes of the old Northwest and old South and Southwest. However, many of the tribes east of the Mississippi and most of those west of the river still occupied at least a part of the lands they claimed as theirs and that were recognized as such by the United States, the Spanish, or the British. A century later, Natives within the boundaries of the United States either lived on no tribal land whatsoever or occupied reservation lands designated by the federal government, lands that might or might not be ancestral lands. The intervening century was one of extreme social discontinuity, which was accompanied by dispossession, bitterness, tragedy, and sometimes violence.

Among the tribes that bore the brunt of removal policy, social discontinuity was extreme. Although they were cut off from their ancestral lands, some factions in each tribe tried to reestablish and maintain the old ways on western soil, but the prevailing trend was toward emulating the white man's ways as a means to survival.

Further inroads into tribal independence and autonomy were made during the time commonly known as the "reservation period" and the second removal period. Forced changes in life styles, pressure from the westward migration of whites, and enforcement of reservation policy led to the Modoc, Sioux, Comanche, Paiute, and Apache wars. The government's ultimate step in destruction of some tribal land titles was the General Allotment Act of 1887, which forced the members of many tribes to give up the traditional communal ownership of land and to accept titles to individual tracts. At the same time, there was a movement to give all Indians "American" names. Both allotment and renaming struck deeply at the Indian's concept of himself and of the tribal community.

The enforced state of poverty, disease, demoralization, and dependency upon the federal government that resulted from removal, reservation policy, and allotment was bolstered by the government's "civilization" programs. Since colonial times, missionaries had been active among the native population. Their activities increased greatly in the early nineteenth century, and, in general, conversion was more successful as the tribal structures broke down and cultural discontinuity became complete. The missions strongly emphasized education and their influence is pronounced in the works of early writers such as Samson Occom, William Apes, Elias Boudinot, and George Copway. The government's "civilization" policy, which was well under way by the nineteenth century, also focused on education, but it was most successful after the Civil War. By that time, some tribes such as the Cherokees and Choctaws had their own well-established educational systems. Perhaps the most significant step in education was the system of the off-reservation schools, begun with the establishment of the school at Carlisle Barracks, Pennsylvania, in 1879. Carlisle and other schools established elsewhere in the country aimed at breaking the ties of Native youth with the reservation and at helping them enter the white society by providing education, mainly vocational in thrust, beyond the grammar school level. As a result of the policies of the missions and of the federal government throughout the century and a half preceding 1924, large numbers of Native Americans became literate in English.

Federal policy and Native-white relations furnished not only the means but quite frequently the substance for the Native American writing in English. For all intents, most traditional life ways of most tribes indigenous to the lands east of the Mississippi existed only in memory by 1850, and those of the tribes in the West existed only in memory by 1890, except perhaps among some of the Pueblos in the Southwest. It is not surprising, then, that a major--if not the major--theme in Native American writing in English is what was variously called "the Indian problem" or "the plight of the Red Man," that is, the condition of Native Americans in white society. Writers responded to it differently in different historical periods. Early writers asserted the importance of Christianity in the Native's life. Near the end of the reservation period, Native American writers recognized the significance of the extinction of the old tribal life ways. They sought to preserve as much of their national identity, language, and culture as possible. Much of their efforts were turned toward recording the ways of the "old people"--the social and religious practices, the culinary arts, the crafts, the myths, the superstitions, and the language. Thus, among their numbers can be found journalists, folklorists, oral historians, and formally trained ethnologists. After Indian Service schools began to implement the Americanization policy of Secretary of the Interior Thomas J. Morgan, writers espoused the virtues of vocational education. In the first and second decades of the twentieth century, writings took a nostalgic turn, and soon the nostalgia turned to political aggression as writers such as Carlos Montezuma, Arthur C. Parker, and Sherman Coolidge debated the value of the Bureau of Indian Affairs and the pros and cons of disbanding it. Other writers such as Gertrude Bonnin persistently urged the recognition of Native American rights. Still others debated the issue of U. S. citizenship. In general, most writers exhibit a racial or cultural self-consciousness that results in a large part from the peculiarities of Native American history of the nineteenth and early twentieth centuries.

Thus, even a cursory survey of works by the Native Americans during this period reveals several significant points. First, Native Americans wrote extensively in English, which fact necessitates reevaluation of writing by Native Americans during recent decades; the prolixity of early writers gives to recent writing more of the character of a renascence than of a beginning as some editors and scholars have described it. Second, while in many respects Native American writers of the earlier period produced works that were derivative and contained themes and modes of expression typical of the popular writing of the dominant society, all writers were concerned to some degree with the condition of the Native American. Third, their writing provides those interested in Native American studies with an excellent gauge against which to measure the degree of acculturation of some Native Americans during the historical period covered here. Fourth, and perhaps most significant, in most works there is a racial and cultural consciousness and many present, from the Indian's perspective, the results of the confrontation of their cultures with that of the dominant society, a confrontation everpresent in the history of the New World since 1492.

Notes

1. For some early writers who recognized the problems of translations, see J. S. Brisbin, "The Poetry of Indians," Harper's New Monthly Magazine, 57 (June, 1878), 104-108, and Charles G. Leland, "The Edda Among the Algonquin Indians," Atlantic Monthly, 54 (August, 1884), 222-234. For comments of writers in this century, see Mary Austin's introduction to Cronyn's anthology and the introduction to the anthology edited by Gloria Levitas, et al., American Indian Prose and Poetry (New York, 1974). See also the introduction to In the Trail of the Wind (New York, 1971), edited by John Bierhorst.

2. The Poems of Alexander Posey (Topeka: Crane & Company, Printers, 1910), p. 62.

PART I

A BIBLIOGRAPHY OF NATIVE AMERICAN WRITERS

ADAIR, B. K. (Cherokee)
  1L   "Letter from Mr. Adair," Indian Chieftain, July 25, 1889.
  2L   "Falling into Line," Indian Chieftain, April 2, 1891.

ADAIR, HUGH MONTGOMERY (Cherokee)
  3N   "Salutatory," Cherokee Advocate, November 18, 1891.
  4N   "Interview with Chief Harris," Cherokee Advocate, June 1, 1892.
  5N   "Valedictory," Cherokee Advocate, November 18, 1893.

ADAIR, J. W. (Cherokee)
  6N   "Things Proposed for Legislation," Indian Chieftain, December 10, 1885.
  7L   "Cherokee Affairs," Indian Chieftain, February 18, 1886.
  8L   "Who Owns the Cherokee Nation," Indian Chieftain, March 11, 1886.
  9L   "Hon. J. H. Beck," Indian Chieftain, May 27, 1886.
  10L   "Mr. Beck," Indian Chieftain, July 29, 1886.
  11N   "Delaware District Alliance," Indian Chieftain, April 30, 1891.
  12N   "The Cow Law," Indian Chieftain, May 7, 1891.
  13L   "Monopoly," Indian Chieftain, December 3, 1891.
  14L   "Why Action Is Demanded," Indian Chieftain, February 23, 1893.
  15N   "Cherokee Reservees," Indian Chieftain, March 30, 1893.

ADAIR, JOHN LYNCH (Cherokee)
  16N   With William Penn Adair, Rufus O. Ross, and Daniel H. Ross. "To the Congress of the United States," Cherokee Advocate, June 16, 1876.
  17P   "Hec Dies: An Imitation," Cherokee Advocate, June 13, 1877.
  18C   Compiled Laws of the Cherokee Nation, Published by Authority of the National Council. Tahlequah, Ind. Terr.: National Advocate Print, 1881.
  19N   "Salutatory," Indian Chieftain, December 24, 1885.
  20P   "Joy Returneth with the Morning," Indian Chieftain, February 14, 1889.
  21L   "Measures before the Territorial Committee," Indian Chieftain, January 16, 1890.
  22L   "Indian Affairs Brightening," Indian Chieftain, January 23, 1890.

23L   "Two Weeks' Letters, " Indian Chieftain, February 6, 1890.
24L   "Our Special Washington Correspondence, " Indian Chieftain, February 20, 1890.
25L   "Our Special Washington Correspondence, " Indian Chieftain, February 27, 1890.
26L   "Washington's Birthday Celebration, " Indian Chieftain, March 6, 1890.
27L   "A Cessation of Hostilities, " Indian Chieftain, March 13, 1890.
28L   "Our Special Washington Correspondence, " Indian Chieftain, March 20, 1890.
29L   "Our Special Washington Correspondence, " Indian Chieftain, April 10, 1890.
30L   "Our Special Washington Correspondence, " Indian Chieftain, April 24, 1890.
31L   "Our Special Washington Correspondence, " Indian Chieftain, May 8, 1890.
32L   "Our Special Washington Correspondence, " Indian Chieftain, May 15, 1890.
33L   "Our Special Washington Correspondence, " Indian Chieftain, June 5, 1890.
34L   "Our Special Washington Correspondence, " Indian Chieftain, June 12, 1890.
35L   "Our Special Washington Correspondence, " Indian Chieftain, July 3, 1890.
36N   "A Protest against Senate Joint Resolution 114, and against House Joint Resolution 193, " Cherokee Advocate, August 6, 1890.
37L   Letter, Cherokee Advocate, August 6, 1890.
38N   "Versus Monopoly, " Cherokee Advocate, August 31, 1892.
39N   "Last Hit at Monopoly, " Cherokee Advocate, October 26, 1892.
40P   "Joy Returneth with the Morning. " In H. F. and E. S. O'Beirne. The Indian Territory: Its Chiefs, Legislators and Leading Men. St. Louis: C. B. Woodward Company, 1892, pp. 266-267.
41P   "Hec Dies. " In H. F. and E. S. O'Beirne. The Indian Territory: Its Chiefs, Legislators and Leading Men. St. Louis: C. B. Woodward Company, 1892, pp. 267-268.
42C   Constitution and Laws of the Cherokee Nation. Published by an Act of the National Council. Parsons, KS: The Foley R'y Printing Co., 1893.
43P   "Joy Returneth with the Morning, " Indian Chieftain, October 29, 1896.

ADAIR, LENA HARNAGE (Cherokee)
44P   "A Campaign Song, " Muskogee Times Democrat, August 27, 1907.
45P   "Tahlequah, " Tahlequah Arrow, February 19, 1916.

ADAIR, WALTER (Cherokee)
46L   Letter, Cherokee Phoenix & Indians' Advocate, January 1, 1831.

ADAIR, WALTER THOMPSON (Cherokee)
47L "From the Seminary," Cherokee Advocate, April 4, 1877.
48L "To the People," Cherokee Advocate, February 26, 1879.
49L "'W. T. A.' Replies to 'L.,'" Indian Journal, May 5, 1881.
50L "Bread Money," Cherokee Advocate, March 3, 1882.
51L "Bread Money," Cherokee Advocate, May 12, 1882.
52N "'Sunta' Brewer Murdered," Cherokee Advocate, May 12, 1882.

ADAIR, WASHINGTON (Cherokee)
53N "Politics," Indian Chieftain, February 10, 1887.
54N "West of 96 Degrees and the Valiant Pack," Indian Chieftain, April 7, 1887.
55L "The Lease," Indian Chieftain, September 27, 1888.
56N "The Outlet," Indian Chieftain, April 11, 1889.
57N "The Allotment," Indian Chieftain, November 13, 1890.

ADAIR, WILLIAM PENN (Cherokee)
58L "The Cherokee Resolutions," Arkansian, September 7, 1860.
59L "The Cherokee Resolutions [second]," Arkansian, September 7, 1860.
60N With Elias C. Boudinot. Reply of the Southern Cherokees to the Memorial of Certain Delegates from the Cherokee Nation, Together with the Message of John Ross, Ex-Chief of the Cherokees, and Proceedings of the Council of the "Loyal Cherokees," Relative to the Alliance with the So-Called Confederate States. Washington, DC: McGill and Witherow, 1866.
61L Letter, Cherokee Advocate, October 15 and 22, 1870.
62N Protest of W. P. Adair, Chairman Cherokee Delegation, against the Right Claimed by the United States to Exact Licenses from Adopted Cherokees, under the Intercourse Act of 1834, to Trade in the Indian Country, and for Other Purposes. Washington, DC: Joseph L. Pearson, 1870.
63L With C. N. Vann, Samuel Smith, George W. Scraper, and Lewis Downing. "Letter from the Cherokee Delegation," Cherokee Advocate, April 1, 1871.
64C With C. N. Vann. History of the Claim of the Texas Cherokees. New York, 1873.
65N With Will P. Ross, Rufus O. Ross, and D. W. Bushyhead. "Memorial of Cherokee Delegation Protesting against Senate Bill No. 505," Cherokee Advocate, March 28, 1874.
66N With Will P. Ross, D. W. Bushyhead, and Rufus O. Ross. "Report of the Cherokee Delegates, 1873-4," Cherokee Advocate, December 26, 1874.
67A Remarks of W. P. Adair, Cherokee Delegate, in Relation to the Expediency and Legality of Organizing the Indian Country into a Territory of the United States, to be Called the Territory of "Ok-la-ho-ma," Made before the Committee on Territories, of the House of Representatives of the United States, January 31, 1876. N. p., 1876?

68L   Letter, Cherokee Advocate, March 25, 1876.

69L   Letter, Cherokee Advocate, June 3, 1876.

70N   With Daniel H. Ross, John L. Adair, and Rufus O. Ross. "To the Congress of the United States," Cherokee Advocate, June 16, 1876.

71L   Letter, Cherokee Advocate, October 7, 1876.

72L   Letter, Cherokee Advocate, November 4, 1876.

73L   Letter, Cherokee Advocate, April 18, 1877.

74L   With Daniel H. Ross. Letter, Cherokee Advocate, January 12, 1878.

75N   With Daniel H. Ross. "Objections of the Cherokee Delegation to Bill S. No. 230 and Bill H. R. No. 228, and Similar Measures Pending before the 1st Session, 45th Congress, Authorizing the So-called 'Eastern Band' of the Cherokees (Citizens of North Carolina,) to Sue the Cherokee Nation, &c.," Cherokee Advocate, April 6, 1878.

76N   With Daniel H. Ross. "Official Statement of the Cherokee Delegation in Regard to the Expenditure of Cherokee Funds and the Financial Condition of the Cherokee Nation, and in Relation to the Educational Situation of Said Nation," Cherokee Advocate, April 20, 1878.

77A   "Speech of W. P. Adair, of the Cherokee Nation, Delivered Oct. 4th, 1878, before the Indian International Fair, or Agricultural Association, at Muskogee, Indian Territory, at Its Fifth Annual Meeting," Cherokee Advocate, October 12, 1878.

78A   "Address of Hon. W. P. Adair, before the Indian International Agricultural Society and Fair at Muskogee, October 3d, 1878," Indian Journal, October 9 and 16, 1878.

79N   Objections of the Cherokee Delegation to Bill S. No. 230 and Bill H. R. No. 228, and Similar Measures Pending before the 1st. Session, 45th. Congress. n. p., 1878?

80L   With Daniel H. Ross. "To the People of the Cherokee Nation," Cherokee Advocate, July 30, 1879, and August 6 and 13, 1879.

81N   With Will P. Ross, Samuel Smith, and Daniel H. Ross. "Report of the Delegation," Cherokee Advocate, October 13, 1880.

82N   Memorial of Indian Delegates, Petitioning for the Forfeitures of Land Grants of the Indians Claimed by Railroad Corporations. Washington, DC: n. p., 1880.

ADAMS, ALEX (Pawnee)

83N   "The Indian in the Print Shop," Chilocco Annual. Chilocco, OK: Chilocco Indian School, 1920, p. 27.

ADAMS, RICHARD CALMIT (Delaware)

84M   A Delaware Indian Legend and the Story of Their Troubles. Washington, 1899.

85N   A Brief Sketch of the Sabine Land Cession in Texas ... Made by the Republic of Texas, to the Cherokees, Delawares, Shawnees and Associated Bands, Made by Treaty and Signed ... February 23, 1836, under Authority of "the Consultation of Texas, in General Convention Assembled," Nov. 13th, 1835. And under Authority of the Resolutions of the General Council of the Provisional Government of Texas of December 22, 1835, and December 28, 1835. Washington, DC: J. Byrne & Co., [c1901].

86N Memorial of the Delaware Indians ... Residing in the Cherokee Nation, Praying Relief Relative to Their Rights in and Ownership of Certain Lands within the Boundaries of Said Nation. Washington, DC: Government Printing Office, 1903.

87N The Ancient Religion of the Delaware Indians and Observations and Reflections. Washington, DC: The Law Reporter Printing Co., 1904.

88P To the Delaware Indians. Washington? 1904?

89M Legends of the Delaware Indians and Picture Writing. Washington, 1905.

90N A Brief History of the Delaware Indians. Washington, DC: Government Printing Office, 1906.

91N Delaware Indians. Mr. Clark, of Wyoming, Presented the Following Memorial and Accompanying Papers Praying That Such Legislation Be Enacted as Will Provide for the Issuing to the Delaware Indians and Their Descendants Land Warrants as Bounties, Etc. Washington, DC: Government Printing Office, 1909.

92N Just a Few Thoughts. N. p., c1909.

93N Claims of Delaware Indians ... Memorial of the Delaware Indians, Known as the "Head of the Algonquin Confederation," in Support of a Bill (S. 6940) to Compensate the Delaware Indians for Services Rendered by Them to the United States in Various Wars. Washington, DC: Government Printing Office, 1910.

94N Claims of Indian Tribes ... Letters Relating to Claims of Various Indian Tribes for Losses Sustained During the War of the Rebellion. Washington, DC: Government Printing Office, 1911?

95N The Adoption of Mew-seu-qua, Tecumseh's Father, and the Philosophy of the Delaware Indians, with Unpolished Gems. Washington, DC: The Crane Printing Company, 1917.

96N Claims of the Delaware Indians; Memorial of the Delaware Tribe of Indians, Showing the Services Rendered by Them to the United States in Various Wars. June 24, 1921. Memorial of the Delaware Tribe of Indians, by Richard C. Adams, in Support of Senate Bill 663 and H. R. 6051. Washington, DC: [Government Printing Office?], 1921.

AGOSA, ROBERT D. (Chippewa)
97N "An Indian's Career," Indian Leader, March 4 and 11, 1910.

AITSAN, LUCIUS BEN (Kiowa)
98N The Story of My Life. Chicago, n. d.

ALBERTY, ELIAS CORNELIUS (Cherokee)
  99L "To the Cherokee People," Cherokee Advocate, April 20,
      1901.
  100L "Questions of the Day," Cherokee Advocate, September 27,
      1902.
  101L "Politics," Cherokee Advocate, October 11, 1902.
  102N "The Cherokee Orphan Asylum," Vinita Weekly Chieftain,
      July 23, 1903.
  103L "The Orphan Asylum," Vinita Indian Chieftain, December
      24, 1903.

ALBERTY, JOHN WRIGHT (Cherokee)
  104L Letter, Cherokee Advocate, February 28, 1877.

ALEXANDER, JACOB (Creek)
  105M "The Origin of Stones," Bacone Chief. Bacone, OK: Ba-
      cone College, 1924, pp. 86-87.

ALEXANDER, JOHN C. (Choctaw)
  106N "Historical," Bacone Chief. Bacone, OK: Bacone College,
      1921, pp. 48-53.

ALFORD, THOMAS WILDCAT (Absentee Shawnee)
  107A "Graduating Address," Southern Workman, 11 (July, 1882),
      78.
  108L Letter, Southern Workman, 12 (July, 1883), 80.
  109L Letter, Southern Workman, 13 (June, 1884), 74.
  110L Letter, Southern Workman, 13 (December, 1884), 129.
  111L "From an Indian Graduate," Southern Workman, 15 (Decem-
      ber, 1886), 8.
  112L Letter, Southern Workman, 16 (May, 1887), 57.
  113L "Advice to Returning Students," Southern Workman, 17 (De-
      cember, 1888), 129.
  114L "A Unique Christmas Tree," Southern Workman, 18 (March,
      1889), 34.
  115L "Making Excuses for the Government," Southern Workman,
      18 (April, 1889), 45.
  116L "Shawnee Allotments," Southern Workman, 18 (September,
      1889), 97.
  117A "The Shawnees of the Present," Southern Workman, 32
      (August, 1903), 385-386.

ALIS, HERMAN (Mission)
  118N "The Painter's Trade," Native American, June 5, 1909.

ALLEN, JOSIAH (Pima)
  119A "Reality, Not a Dream," Native American, June 3, 1905.

ANDERSON, ALICE (Choctaw)
  120N "Education for the Indian," Indian Leader, May, 1915.

ANDERSON, ARTHUR (Yokaia)
  121N "Duties of Indian Graduates," Native American, May 22,
      1909.

ANDERSON, HELLEN REBECCA (Cherokee)
122P "The Unruly Pigs," Twin Territories, 5 (April, 1903), 136.

ANDERSON, MABEL WASHBOURNE (Cherokee)
123L "From Eureka Springs," Indian Chieftain, September 1, 1887.
124N "On Mrs. Thompson's Death," Indian Chieftain, November 1, 1894.
125N "The Board of Education Condemned," Weekly Capital, January 24, 1896.
126P "To Auld Lang Syne," Indian Chieftain, July 2, 1896.
127N "An Osage Niobe," Tahlequah Arrow, May 17, 1900. Reprinted from St. Louis Globe-Democrat.
128P "Nowita, Sweet Singer," Indian Chieftain, August 23, 1900.
129N "Nowita, Sweet Singer," Indian Chieftain, August 23, 1900.
130N "In Memoriam," Indian Chieftain, February 14, 1901.
131N "Echo of a Sermon," Indian Chieftain, March 28, 1901.
132N "Miss Vinnie Ream," Indian Chieftain, April 4, 1901.
133N "Love of the Beautiful," Indian Chieftain, April 11, 1901.
134N "Love of the Beautiful," Twin Territories, 3 (April, 1901), 72.
135N "Some of the Children of Charles Dickens' Fancy," Twin Territories, 3 (June, 1901), 103.
136N "Old Fort Gibson on the Grand," Twin Territories, 4 (September, 1902), 249-255.
137P "Nowita, the Sweet Singer," Twin Territories, 5 (January, 1903), 1-2.
138N "United Daughters of the Confederacy," Vinita Weekly Chieftain, March 5, 1903.
139N "Edward Pason Washbourne," Vinita Weekly Chieftain, September 3, 1903.
140N "Father of his Country," Vinita Weekly Chieftain, February 23, 1905.
141N "Old Fort Gibson," Sturm's Statehood Magazine, 1 (November, 1905), 89-92.
142N "Nowita, the Sweet Singer, a Romantic Tradition of Spavinaw, Indian Territory," Sturm's Statehood Magazine, 1 (January, 1906), 86-89.
143N "Sketches of Famous Indians," Sturm's Oklahoma Magazine, 2 (July, 1906), 90-91.
144N "Old Fort Gibson on the Grand," Indian Advocate, 18 (December, 1906), 396-400.
145N "The Southern Artist," Sturm's Oklahoma Magazine, 4 (June-July, 1907), 5-7.
146N "The Cherokee Poet and 'Mt. Shasta,'" Sturm's Oklahoma Magazine, 6 (March, 1908), 23-25.
147F "Joe Jamison's Sacrifice," Sturm's Oklahoma Magazine, 6 (July, 1908), 44-48.
148N "Easter and Nature in Happy Harmony," Sturm's Oklahoma Magazine, 12 (April, 1911), 8-9.
149N Life of General Stand Watie, the Only Indian Brigadier General of the Confederate Army and the Last General to Surrender. Pryor, OK: Mayes County Republican, c1915. Reprinted in 1931.

ANDERSON, PASQUALA (Mission)
    150N "The Use of Difficulties," Red Man, 15 (March, 1900), 3.

ANDERSON, PHENIA (Concow, or Konkau)
    151F "Why the Ground Mole Is Blind," Indian Craftsman, 2 (January, 1910), 27.

ANTON, FLORENCE (Pima)
    152M "How the Indians Came into This Country," Native American, June 15, 1907.

ANTON, WALLACE (Pima)
    153N "Care of Teeth," Native American, May 1, 1915.

ANTONE, LOLA (Pima)
    154N "How a Woman Can Help on the Farm," Native American, May 23, 1908.

ANTONIO, HAL (Pima)
    155M "Pima Story of the Deluge," Native American, February 18, 1905.

ANTONIO, JOSE (Papago)
    156M With Pablo Narcho and Jose Lewis. "The Papago Legend of the Formation of the Earth," Indian Leader, October, 1917.
    157M With Pablo Narcho and Jose Lewis. Indian Legends and Superstitions. Lawrence, KS: Haskell Institute, 1917.

APACHE, ANTONIO (Apache)
    158A Address, Red Man, 13 (March, 1896), 5.
    159A Address at Carlisle Commencement, Red Man, 14 (April, 1897), 3.

APES, WILLIAM (Pequot)
    160N A Son of the Forest. The Experience of William Apes, A Native of the Forest. New York: The Author, 1829. 2nd rev. ed., 1831.
    161S The Increase of the Kingdom of Christ, A Sermon. New York: The Author, 1831.
    162N The Experiences of Five Christian Indians of the Pequod Tribe. Boston: J. B. Dow, 1833. 2nd ed., 1837.
    163N Indian Nullification of the Unconstitutional Laws of Massachusetts, Relative to the Marshpee Tribe; or, the Pretended Riot Explained. Boston: J. Howe, 1835.
    164N Eulogy on King Philip: As Pronounced at the Odeon, in Federal Street, Boston. Boston: The Author, 1836. 2nd ed., 1837.
    165P "Indian Hymn," Red Man, 9 (June, 1889), 1.

ARCASA, ALEXANDER (Colville)
    166N "How Christmas Is Spent at My Home," Carlisle Arrow, December 27, 1912.

ARCHAMBEAU, LORENA (Sioux)
  167A "Nursing as a Vocation for Indian Girls," Indian Leader,
        June 13-20, 1924.

ARCHIQUETTE, MARTIN (Oneida)
  168N "Interesting Mishaps of an Indian Boy's First Farm Experi-
        ence," Red Man, 8 (November, 1888), 8.
  169A "Modes and Tenses," Red Man, 10 (June, 1891), 5.

ARROW, ARTHUR (Sioux)
  170M "Legend about Black Hills, South Dakota," Indian Leader,
        May, 1915.

ARTESHAW, MARIE (Chippewa)
  171N "Crawling Stone Lake," Red Man, 3 (October, 1910), 80.

ASHMUN, H. C. (Chippewa)
  172N "Indian of Yesterday Today and Tomorrow," Odonah Star,
        March 25, 1916, and April 8, 1916.

AVALOS, CIPRIANA (Pueblo)
  173N "The Heroes of Today," Native American, March 17, 1900.

AVALOS, JUAN B. (Pueblo)
  174N "Thomas A. Edison," Native American, April 14, 1900.

AVELINE, FRANK D. (Miami)
  175N "Which Profession Is Best for the Indians?" Morning Star,
        5 (August, 1884), 4.

AXTELL, OBED (Nez Percé)
  176N "Christmas Among My People," Carlisle Arrow, December
        18, 1914.

AZURE, OVILLA (Chippewa)
  177F With Michael Wilkie. "The Boys of Carlisle '15 Twenty-
        five Years Hence," Carlisle Arrow, June 4, 1915.
  178N "Opportunity," Carlisle Arrow, June 4, 1915.

BAGNELL, AMY T. (Rogue River, or Tututni)
  179N "The Original Easter," Native American, April 21, 1900.
  180N "Send Out Thy Light," Native American, May 24, 1902.
  181N "Reminiscences of the Class of 1902," Native American,
        May 24, 1902.

BAKER, LILLIE (Navajo)
  182N "The Navajo, a Different People," Chilocco Annual. Chiloc-
        co, OK: Chilocco Indian School, 1920, p. 34.

BALDWIN, MARIE L. B. (Chippewa)
  183N "John N. B. Hewitt, Ethnologist," Quarterly Journal of the

Society of American Indians, 2 (April-June, 1914), 146-
150.
184N Modern Home-Making and the Indian Woman. Columbus,
Ohio? 1911?

BALENTI, MICHAEL R. (Cheyenne)
185N "History from an Indian Pen," Indian's Friend, 21 (November, 1908), 10.
186N "The Comanche Tribe," Indian Craftsman, 1 (February,
1909), 29-30.
187N "Indian Basketry and Pottery," Indian Craftsman, 2 (September, 1909), 26-30.
188N "History of the Kiowas," Indian Craftsman, 2 (January,
1910), 25-26.

BALENTI, WILLIAM M. (Cheyenne)
189M "The Origin of the Iroquois Nation," Indian Craftsman, 2
(November, 1909), 26-29.

BALL, JOSEPH (Klamath)
190N "The Sign of Equality," Native American, May 30, 1903.

BALLARD, W. H. (Cherokee)
191N "The Night Hawk Society," Tahlequah Arrow, July 14, 1906.

BAPTISTE, JOHN (Winnebago)
192N "Our National Progress," Red Man, 11 (March-April, 1893),
3.

BARADA, MITCHELL (Omaha)
193A "Citizenship of the Omaha Indians," Red Man, 14 (February,
1897), 5.
194N "Has Citizenship Proved a Failure Among the Omaha Indians?" Red Man, 14 (March, 1898), 5.

BARNABY, JOSEPHINE (Omaha)
195N The Present Condition of My People. New York: American
Missionary Association, 1880?
196N "Coming Home," Southern Workman, 14 (November, 1885),
116.
197L Letter, Southern Workman, 18 (November, 1889), 116-117.
198N The Present Condition of My People. New York: American
Missionary Association, 190-?

BARSE, ALCESTA (Sioux)
199N "Education for the Indians," Indian Leader, April, 1916.

BASKIN, SAMUEL (Sioux)
200A "What the White Man Has Gained from the Indian," Red
Man, 13 (May-June, 1896), 8.

BASTIAN, JOHN (Puyallup)
201M "The Story of the Bluejay," Red Man, 3 (January, 1911),
211-212.

202M "Indian Legend of the Bluejay," <u>Indian Leader</u>, November
24, 1911.

BATTICE, CORA MELBOURNE (Sac and Fox)
203F "The Book of Fate," <u>Carlisle Arrow</u>, June 4, 1915.

BATTICE, WALTER C. (Sac and Fox)
204L "Home to Indian Territory and Back," <u>Southern Workman</u>,
15 (December, 1886), 128.
205A "Commencement Address of Walter Battice," <u>Southern Work-
man</u>, 16 (July, 1887), 79.
206L "Some Old Traditions," <u>Southern Workman</u>, 17 (Mav, 1888),
57-58.
207N "A Reservation School," <u>Red Man</u>, 9 (June, 1889), 6.

BEALE, GRACE HENRIETTA (Navajo)
208N "My People," <u>Indian Leader</u>, June 8-22, 1923.

BEAN, J. S. (Cherokee)
209L "Why He Changes," <u>Indian Chieftain</u>, March 31, 1887.

BEAR, JOHN (Winnebago)
210N "How John Bear Got Here," <u>Southern Workman</u>, 17 (July,
1888), 80.

BEAR, JOHNSON (Cherokee)
211N "The Farmer of Today," <u>Chilocco Annual</u>. Chilocco, OK:
Chilocco Indian School, 1920, pp. 21-22.

BEAR, JOSEPH L. (Sioux)
212M "Legend of Elk Horn Butte," <u>Red Man</u>, 3 (September, 1910),
27-28.

BEAR, STELLA V. (Arickara)
213M "Ghost-Bride Pawnee Legend," <u>Indian Craftsman</u>, 2 (January, 1910), 24-25.
214M "Indian Legend--Creation of the World," <u>Red Man</u>, 2 (April,
1910), 47-48.
215M "Indian Legend--How the World Was Peopled," <u>Indian's
Friend</u>, 23 (December, 1910), 7-8.

BEARFACE, ROSA (Sioux)
216N "Visit from Miss Dawes," <u>Southern Workman</u>, 17 (April,
1888), 46.

BEARSKIN, CORA (Seneca)
217N "An Indian Custom," <u>Indian Leader</u>, September, 1915.

BEAULIEU, C. H. (Chippewa)
218N "A Trip to La Point, Wisconsin," <u>Tomahawk</u>, October 26
and November 2, 9, 16, and 23, 1916.
219N "Les Roys," <u>Tomahawk</u>, December 7 and 14, 1916.
220N "Incidents of Old Crow Wing and Northern Minnesota: Major
James Whitehead," <u>Tomahawk</u>, January 4 and 11, 1917.

221N "A Statement," Tomahawk, August 23, 1917.
222N "Pacifism," Tomahawk, October 31, 1918.
223L "Bureaus in the Making," Tomahawk, November 28, 1918.
224L "A Communication," Tomahawk, April 3, 1919.
225L "A Communication," Tomahawk, June 12, 1919.
226L "A Communication," Tomahawk, August 14, 1919.
227N "85-Year-Old Chippewa Chief Who Still Joins in Dances,"
      Tomahawk, September 18, 1919. Reprinted from Sun-
      day Pioneer Press, August 24, 1919.
228L "A Communication," Tomahawk, October 23, 1919.
229L "A Communication," Tomahawk, May 1, 1924.

BEAULIEU, CLARENCE R. (Chippewa)
230L "Defends the Indians," Tomahawk, May 22, 1919. Reprinted
      from Minneapolis Tribune.

BEAULIEU, GUSTAVE H. (Chippewa)
231N "Might Is Not Right," Tomahawk, September 10, 1903.
232N "Posthumous Notes," Tomahawk, December 13, 1917.

BEAULIEU, IRENE CAMPBELL (Sioux)
233M "Origin of the Buffalo: A Dakotah Legend." In Tributes to
      a Vanishing Race. Comp. Irene C. Beaulieu and Kath-
      leen Woodward. Chicago: Privately Printed, 1916, pp.
      48-49.
234C With Kathleen Woodward. Tributes to a Vanishing Race.
      Chicago: Privately Printed, 1916.
235P "Poor Lo." In Tributes to a Vanishing Race. Comp. Irene
      C. Beaulieu and Kathleen Woodward. Chicago: Privately
      Printed, 1916, p. 55.

BEAULIEU, THEODORE (Chippewa)
236N "The Ojibways, Their Customs and Traditions as Handed
      Down for Centuries from Father to Son," Tomahawk,
      May 7 and 14, June 3, July 2 and 23, August 20, and
      October 1, 1903.
237N "White Cloud--Wah-Bon-Ah-Quod," Tomahawk, March 10,
      1904.
238N "May-Zhuck-Ke-Ge-Shig, Hereditary Chief of the Minnesota
      Chippewas," Tomahawk, March 17, 1904.
239N "The General Council, Minnesota Chippewas," Tomahawk,
      April 28, 1921.

BEAUREGARD, MARGARET (Chippewa)
240N "The Indian Girl as a Homemaker," Indian School Journal,
      10 (June, 1910), 51-52.
241N "An Indian Girl on Wifehood," Indian's Friend, 23 (October,
      1910), 11.

BEBEAU, GENEVIEVE (Chippewa)
242M "The Origin of Thunder," Red Man, 3 (April, 1911), 340.
243M "The Origin of Thunder," Native American, April 1, 1911.

BECK, JOHN H. (Cherokee)
244L   "A Greater Question Than a Sale of the Outlet," Indian
     Chieftain, July 30, 1885.
245L   "Cherokee Citizenship," Indian Chieftain, January 14, 1886.
246L   "As Native Born Cherokees," Indian Chieftain, February 11,
     1886.
247L   "Answer to Adair," Indian Chieftain, March 18, 1886.
248L   "Sequoyah," Indian Chieftain, April 8, 1886.
249L   "Mr. Beck to Mr. Adair," Indian Chieftain, June 24, 1886.
250L   "Beck to Adair," Indian Chieftain, August 12, 1886.
251L   "Our 'Sovereignty'," Indian Chieftain, August 12, 1886.
252L   "The Shawnees, Delawares, Negroes and Adopted Citizens,"
     Indian Chieftain, September 16, 1886.
253L   "Hon. Joel B. Mayes," Indian Chieftain, October 28, 1886.
254L   "The Course to Pursue," Indian Chieftain, January 6, 1887.
255L   "The Downing Platform," Indian Chieftain, April 7, 1887.
256L   "The Platforms," Indian Chieftain, April 28, 1887.
257L   "The Platforms," Indian Chieftain, May 5, 1887.
258L   "The Platforms," Indian Chieftain, May 12, 1887.
259L   "The Platforms," Indian Chieftain, May 19, 1887.
260L   "Industry Necessary to Form the Orator," Telephone, May
     16, 1888.
261L   "West of 96," Indian Chieftain, September 5, 1889.
262L   "Beck Denies the Charges," Cherokee Telephone, July 2,
     1891.
263L   "J. H. Beck and Cherokee Citizenship," Indian Chieftain,
     November 5, 1891.
264L   "Beck Replies," Cherokee Telephone, June 23, 1892.

BECK, STACY (Cherokee)
265N   "The Custom of Scalping," Indian's Friend, 20 (August,
     1908), 7.
266M   "The Thunder Tradition," Red Man, 2 (March, 1910), 30-35.

BELL, LUCIEN BURR (Cherokee)
267L   "Shaky and Uncertain," Vindicator, March 22, 1876.
268N   "Hooley Bell on Politics," Muskogee Times Democrat, Sep-
     tember 18, 1906.

BELL, MATTIE (Cherokee)
269N   "Words," Cherokee Advocate, July 4, 1877.

BELL, OREGONIA (Cherokee)
270N   "Life Is What We Make It," Cherokee Advocate, June 9,
     1882.

BELL, WILLIAM WATIE (Cherokee)
271L   "Watie Bell Replies," Indian Chieftain, July 11, 1889.
272L   "Watie and the Telephone," Indian Chieftain, August 1, 1889.

BELLANGER, ALICE (Chippewa)
273N   "Home-making," Indian Leader, June, 1915.

274N "Making Maple Sugar in Minnesota," Indian Leader, May, 1916.

BELLECOURTE, CHARLES JAMES (Chippewa)
275N "Indian Trail," Tomahawk, March 1, 22, and 29, and April 12 and 19, 1923.

BENDER, CHARLES A. (Chippewa)
276N "What Holds the Indians Back?" Red Man and Helper, February 14, 1902.

BENDER, FRED (Chippewa)
277N "Higher Academic Training for Indians," American Indian Magazine, 5 (April-June, 1917), 103-106.

BENGE, SAMUEL HOUSTON (Cherokee)
278N With Pleasant Porter and W. P. Ross. "Memorial of the Grand Council of Nations of the Indian Territory," Cherokee Advocate, June 18, 1870.

BISHOP, ALBERT (Seneca)
279N "Why Are We Here?" Red Man, 11 (May, 1890), 3.

BISHOP, B. FRANKLIN (Seneca)
280N "Lack of Indian Leaders," Indian School Journal, 8 (September, 1908), 25-26. Reprinted from Southern Workman.

BISHOP, WILLIAM C. (Cayuga)
281M "The Old Man of the Sky," Indian Craftsman, 1 (February, 1909), 28.
282M "An Iroquois Legend," Indian Craftsman, 1 (March, 1909), 29.
283N "The Origin of the Turtle Clan," Indian's Friend, 24 (April, 1912), 10.

BLACKBEAR, JOSEPH (Cheyenne)
284N "The Ration System," Red Man, 14 (March, 1898), 4-5.

BLACKBEAR, THOMAS (Sioux)
285N "The Friends and the Indians," Red Man, 12 (December, 1893), 7.

BLACKBIRD, ANDREW J. (Ottawa)
286N History of the Ottawa and Chippewa Indians of Michigan. Ypsilanti, MI: Ypsilanti Job Printing House, 1887.
287N "Twenty-one Precepts of the Ottawa Indians," Journal of American Folklore, 5 (October, 1892), 332-334.
288N Complete Both Early and Late History of the Ottawa and Chippewa Indians, of Michigan, a Grammar of Their Language, Personal and Family History of Author. Harbor Springs, MI: Babcock and Darling, 1897.
289N The Indian Problem, from the Indian's Viewpoint. Philadelphia: National Indian Association, 1900.

BLACKWOOD, MARGARET O. (Chippewa)
290N "The Klamaths and Modocs," Indian Craftsman, 2 (September, 1909), 31-32.
291F "The Naming of a Town," Red Man, 2 (June, 1910), 40-41.
292N "Beliefs of the Chippewas," Red Man, 3 (September, 1910), 28.

BLUESKY, BERTRAM (Seneca)
293N "Higher Education in Public Schools and Colleges for the Indian," Quarterly Journal of the Society of American Indians, 2 (January-March, 1914), 75-76.

BLUESKY, LOUISE (Chippewa)
294N "Possibilities of Spare Moments," Carlisle Arrow, May 22, 1914.

BOND, T. J. (Choctaw)
295N "Let Us Progress," Vindicator, March 27, 1875.
296L Letter, Vindicator, April 10, 1875.
297L ["Education Among the Choctaws,"] Vindicator, April 17, 1875.
298L Letter, Vindicator, June 19, 1875.
299L Letter, Vindicator, June 26, 1875.
300L ["Choctaw Schools,"] Vindicator, July 10, 1875.
301L ["Choctaw Education,"] Vindicator, July 31, 1875.
302L "The Education of the People," Vindicator, June 14, 1876.

BONNIN, GERTRUDE SIMMONS (Sioux)
303N "Impressions of an Indian Childhood," Atlantic, 85 (January, 1900), 37-47.
304N "School Days of an Indian Girl," Atlantic, 85 (February, 1900), 185-194.
305N "An Indian Teacher Among Indians," Atlantic, 85 (March, 1900), 381-386.
306F "Soft-Hearted Sioux," Harper's, 102 (March, 1901), 505-508.
307F "Trial Path: An Indian Romance," Harper's, 103 (October, 1901), 741-744.
308M Old Indian Legends, Retold by Zitkala-Sa; With Illustrations by Angel de Cora (Hinook-Mahiwi-Kilinaka). Boston: Ginn & Company, 1901.
309N ["The Indian Dance,"], Red Man and Helper, August 22, 1902.
310F "Warrior's Daughter," Everybody's, 6 (April, 1902), 346.
311M "Iya, the Camp-eater, from 'Old Indian Legends,'" Twin Territories, 4 (September, 1902), 274-276.
312N "Why I Am a Pagan," Atlantic, 90 (December, 1902), 801-803.
313P "The Indian's Awakening," American Indian Magazine, 4 (January-March, 1916), 57-59.
314N "A Year's Experience in Community Service Work Among the Ute Tribe of Indians," American Indian Magazine, 4 (October-December, 1916), 307-310.
315P "The Red Man's America," American Indian Magazine, 5 (January-March, 1917), 64.

316N "Chipeta, Widow of Chief Ouray," American Indian Magazine, 5 (July-September, 1917), 168-170.

317P "A Sioux Woman's Love for Her Grandchild," American Indian Magazine, 5 (October-December, 1917), 230-231.

318N "Mrs. Bonnin Speaks," Tomahawk, December 6, 1917.

319N "Indian Gifts to Civilized Man," Indian Sentinel, 1 (July, 1918), 13-14.

320N "Editorial Comment," American Indian Magazine, 6 (July-September, 1918), 113-114.

321N "Indian Gifts to Civilized Man," American Indian Magazine, 6 (July-September, 1918), 115-116.

322N "America, Home of the Red Man," American Indian Magazine, 6 (Winter, 1919), 165-167.

323N "The Coronation of Chief Powhatan Retold," American Indian Magazine, 6 (Winter, 1919), 179-180.

324N "Editorial Comment," American Indian Magazine, 6 (Winter, 1919), 161-162.

325L "Letter to the Chiefs and Head Men of the Tribes," American Indian Magazine, 6 (Winter, 1919), 196-197.

326N "Editorial Comment," American Indian Magazine, 7 (Spring, 1919), 5-9.

327N "Indian Gifts to Civilized Man," Tomahawk, July 17, 1919.

328N "America's Indian Problem," Edict, 2 (December, 1921), 1-2.

329F American Indian Stories. Washington, DC: Hayworth, 1921.

330N "An Indian Praying on the Hilltop," American Indian Advocate, 4 (Winter, 1922), 1.

331N With Charles H. Fabens and Matthew K. Sniffin. Oklahoma's Poor Rich Indians, an Orgy of Graft and Exploitation of the Five Civilized Tribes, Legalized Robbery. Philadelphia: Office of the Indian Rights Association, 1924.

BONSER, HARRY (Sioux)

332N "American Citizenship," Carlisle Arrow and Red Man, November 2, 1917.

BOUDINOT, ELIAS (Cherokee)

333F Poor Sarah; or Religion Exemplified in the Life and Death of an Indian Woman. Mount Pleasant, OH: Elisha Bates, 1823. Reprinted in 1833.

334A An Address to the Whites. Delivered in the First Presbyterian Church on the 26th of May, 1826. Philadelphia: William F. Geddes, 1826.

335N "Prospectus for Publishing at New Echota, in the Cherokee Nation, a Weekly Newspaper, to be Called the Cherokee Phoenix." Broadside, 1827.

336N "To the Public," Cherokee Phoenix, February 21, 1828.

337N "Prospectus," Cherokee Phoenix, February 28, 1828.

338N ["Valedictory,"] Cherokee Phoenix, December 3, 1828.

339N "To the Public," Cherokee Phoenix, December 29, 1828.

340N "Cherokee Phoenix, and Indians' Advocate," Cherokee Phoenix, and Indians' Advocate, February 11, 1829.

341N "National Academy," Cherokee Phoenix, and Indians' Advocate, February 18, 1829.

342N   "Indian Clans," Cherokee Phoenix, and Indians' Advocate,
       February 18, 1829.

343N   "Examination of the School at Brainerd," Cherokee Phoenix,
       and Indians' Advocate, August 12, 1829.

344N   "Intruders," Cherokee Phoenix, and Indians' Advocate, March
       24, 1830.

345N   "Intruders," Cherokee Phoenix, and Indians' Advocate, April
       7, 1830.

346N   "An Interesting Trial," Cherokee Phoenix, and Indians' Ad-
       vocate, November 20, 1830.

347N   ["Georgia Laws,"] Cherokee Phoenix & Indians' Advocate,
       March 19, 1831.

348N   "Georgia and the Missionaries," Cherokee Phoenix & Indi-
       ans' Advocate, July 2, 1831.

349N   "To the Readers of the Cherokee Phoenix," Cherokee Phoe-
       nix & Indians' Advocate, August 27, 1831.

350N   Editorial, Cherokee Phoenix & Indians' Advocate, September
       17, 1831.

351N   "Indian Emigration," Cherokee Phoenix & Indians' Advocate,
       February 18, 1832.

352N   "Remarkable Fulfillment of Indian Prophecy," Cherokee
       Phoenix & Indians' Advocate, June 28, 1832.

353N   Letters and Other Papers Relating to Cherokee Affairs; Be-
       ing in Reply to Sundry Publications Authorized by John
       Ross. By E. Boudinot, Formerly Editor of the Chero-
       kee Phoenix. Athens, GA: Southern Banner, 1837.

354N   Documents in Relation to the Validity of the Cherokee Treaty
       of 1835 ... Letters and Other Papers Relating to Chero-
       kee Affairs: Being a Reply to Sundry Publications Au-
       thorized by John Ross. Washington, DC: Blair & Rives,
       [1838].

BOUDINOT, ELIAS CORNELIUS (Cherokee)

355L   "Correspondence," Arkansian, May 21, 1859.

356L   "Correspondence," Arkansian, June 4, 1859.

357L   "Correspondence," Arkansian, June 4, 1859.

358L   "Correspondence," Arkansian, June 4, 1859.

359N   "The Letter to Col. Hindman," Arkansian, October 14,
       1859.

360N   "'One of the 35'--Again," Arkansian, December 16, 1859.

361N   "To the Readers of the Arkansian," Arkansian, February
       24, 1860.

362N   "Valedictory," Arkansian, May 11, 1860.

363N   "The Protestation of the Would Be Democracy of Benton
       County," Arkansian, May 25, 1860.

364N   "Salutatory," Arkansas True Democrat, June 16, 1860.

365N   "Personal," Arkansas True Democrat, July 21, 1860.

366N   "Personal," Arkansian, August 4, 1860.

367N   With William Penn Adair. Reply of the Southern Cherokees
       to the Memorial of Certain Delegates from the Cherokee
       Nation, Together with the Message of John Ross, Ex-
       Chief of the Cherokees, and Proceedings of the Council
       of the "Loyal Cherokees," Relative to the Alliance with

the So-Called Confederate States. Washington, DC: McGill and Witherow, 1866.

368N Memorial of Elias C. Boudinot, a Cherokee Indian, to the Senate and House of Representatives of the United States. Can a Bureau or Department Annul the Stipulations of a Treaty? What is the Money Value of the Honor of a Nation Solemnly Pledged? Washington? 1870.

369N Speech on the Indian Question, Delivered at Vinita, Cherokee Nation. September 21. Terre Haute, IN: Journal Office Print., 1871.

370A Speech of Elias C. Boudinot, a Cherokee Indian, on the Indian Question, Delivered at Vinita, Cherokee Nation, the Junction of the Atlantic and Pacific, and the Missouri, Kansas, and Texas Railroads, September 21, 1871. Washington, DC: McGill & Witherow, 1872.

371A Speech of Elias C. Boudinot, a Cherokee Indian, Delivered before the House Committee on Territories, February 7, 1872, in Behalf of a Territorial Government for the Indian Territory, in Reply to Wm. P. Ross, a Cherokee Delegate, in His Argument Against Any Congressional Action upon the Subject. Washington, DC: McGill & Witherow, 1872.

372A Speech of Elias C. Boudinot, of the Cherokee Nation, Delivered before the House Committee on Territories, March 5, 1872, on the Question of a Territorial Government for the Indian Territory, in Reply to the Second Argument of the Indian Delegations in Opposition to Such Proposed Government. Washington, DC: McGill & Witherow, 1872.

373N The Manners, Customs, Traditions, and Present Condition of the Civilized Indians of the Indian Territory. n. p., 1872?

374N "The Indian Territory and Its Inhabitants," Geographical Magazine, 1 (June, 1874), 92-95.

375N Remarks of Elias C. Boudinot, of the Cherokee Nation, in Behalf of the Bill to Organize the Territory of Oklahoma, before the House Committee on Territories, May 13, 1874. Washington, DC: McGill and Witherow, [1874].

376N Division of Lands, United States Courts, and a Delegate in Congress for the Civilized Indians of the Indian Territory. Speech of E. C. Boudinot, of the Cherokee Nation, Delivered at Vinita, Indian Territory, August 29th, 1874. St. Louis: Barns & Beynon, 1874.

377N A Territorial Government for the Civilized Indians of the Indian Territory: If They Must Be Subjected to the Responsibilities of Citizens of the United States, They Should Have Their Privileges Also. n. p., 1874.

378L ["Territorial Government,"] Vindicator, May 1, 1875.

379L "Letter from Col. Boudinot," Vindicator, September 25, 1875.

380N "Prospectus of the Indian Progress," Vindicator, October 2, 1875.

381L "Letter from Col. Boudinot," Indian Progress, February 4, 1876.

382L   "Col. Boudinot's Answer to the Open Letter," Indian Prog-
      ress, February 18, 1876.
383L   "Washington," Indian Progress, February 25, 1876.
384L   "Washington," Indian Progress, March 3, 1876.
385L   Letter, Indian Progress, March 17, 1876.
386A   "Oklahoma," Indian Progress, March 17 and 24, 1876.
387A   Oklahoma: An Argument by E. C. Boudinot, of the Chero-
      kee Nation, Delivered before the House Committee on
      Territories, February 3, 1876. Washington, DC: Mc-
      Gill and Witherow, 1876.
388N   The Memorial of Elias C. Boudinot to the Congress of the
      United States. Washington? 1877.
389N   Oklahoma. Argument of Col. E. C. Boudinot before the
      Committee on Territories, January 29, 1878. The Com-
      mittee Having under Consideration H. R. Bill No. 1596.
      Alexandria, VA: G. H. Ramey & Sons, 1878.
390N   Indian Territory: Argument Submitted to the Senate Com-
      mittee on Territories, January 17, 1879, the Committee
      Having under Consideration the Resolutions of D. W.
      Voorhees, Relating to the Indian Territory. Washington,
      DC: T. McGill, 1879.
391N   "The Ceded Lands West," Indian Journal, August 26, 1880.
392L   "A Communication from Col. Boudinot," Indian Chieftain,
      July 16, 1885.
393L   "Our Western Lands," Indian Chieftain, September 3, 1885.
394L   "Not Parallel Cases," Indian Chieftain, September 10, 1885.
395L   "Tom Howie," Indian Chieftain, September 10, 1885.
396L   "Letter from Col. Boudinot," Indian Chieftain, July 1, 1886.
397L   "An Interesting Communication," Indian Journal, November
      18, 1886.
398L   "The Right of Way Question," Indian Chieftain, July 7, 1887.
399P   "The Rose, the Bird and the Bride," Southern Workman, 16
      (December, 1887), 128.
400A   With Ridge Paschal and Jesse Cochran. "The Concluding
      Speeches of the Debates on the Lease of the Strip West
      of 96 Degrees Made by Col. E. C. Boudinot, Ridge
      Paschal and Jesse Cochran, February 1, 1888," Chero-
      kee Advocate, March 7, 1888.
401L   "Letter from Washington," Indian Chieftain, April 19, 1888.
402L   "White Citizens Have Equal Rights," Indian Chieftain, Octo-
      ber 24, 1889.

BOUDINOT, ELIAS CORNELIUS, JR. (Cherokee)
403L   "From Washington," Cherokee Telephone, April 28, 1892.

BOUDINOT, FRANKLIN JOSIAH (Cherokee)
404L   "Mineral Lease Clause," Tahlequah Arrow, March 23, 1901.
405L   "Boudinot Is Opposed," Indian Chieftain, April 4, 1901.
406N   "Buffington's Protest," Tahlequah Arrow, January 24, 1903.
407A   "Message of Chief Boudinot," Tahlequah Arrow, November
      25, 1905.

BOUDINOT, WILLIAM PENN (Cherokee)
408P   "Life's Phantom," Arkansian, April 2, 1859.

409C   Laws of the Cherokee Nation, Passed During the Years
        1839-1867, Compiled by Authority of the National Coun-
        cil. St. Louis: Missouri Democrat Print, 1868.

410L   Letter, Cherokee Advocate, May 30, 1874.

411C   Constitution and Laws of the Cherokee Nation. Published
        by Authority of the National Council. St. Louis: R. &
        T. A. Ennis, 1875.

412N   "The Second Cherokee Phoenix," Cherokee Advocate, March
        1, 1876.

413L   "The Old Settler Claim," Cherokee Advocate, April 11, 1884.

414C   Laws and Joint Resolutions of the Cherokee Nation, Enacted
        by the National Council, During the Regular and Extra
        Sessions of 1884-5-6. Published by Authority of the
        National Council. Tahlequah, I. T.: E. C. Boudinot,
        Jr., 1887.

415L   Letter, Cherokee Advocate, April 4, 1888.

416L   Letter, Cherokee Advocate, May 23, 1888.

417L   "From Delegate Boudinot," Indian Chieftain, August 9, 1888.

418L   "Delegate Boudinot," Indian Chieftain, August 30, 1888.

419P   "The Spectre," Red Man, 9 (May, 1889), 1. Reprinted
        from Indian Missionary.

420L   "Monopoly of Improvements," Cherokee Advocate, August
        31, 1892.

421L   "Monopoly of Lands," Cherokee Advocate, September 21,
        1892.

422L   "Monopoly of Lands," Cherokee Advocate, October 26, 1892.

423N   "Sketch of D. W. Bushyhead's Public and Private Life,"
        Tahlequah Arrow, February 19, 1898.

424P   "The Spectre," Muskogee Phoenix, February 14, 1899.

425P   "The Spectre," Twin Territories, 1 (July, 1899), 166.

BOURASSA, ROSA (Chippewa)

426N   "Not Who, But What," Red Man, 10 (May, 1890), 2.

BOUTWELL, LEON (Chippewa)

427N   "My First Christmas," Carlisle Arrow, December 18, 1914.

BOW, CLAUDE (Sioux)

428F   "A Fairy Tale," Southern Workman, 17 (July, 1888), 80.

BOWKER, MABEL (Sioux)

429F   "The Indian Boy Who Lived with Toads," Indian Leader,
        May, 1915.

BRACKLIN, EDWARD (Chippewa)

430N   "Christmas for the Indian Youth," Carlisle Arrow, Decem-
        ber 27, 1912.

431M   "The Legend of the Thunderbird," Red Man, 6 (February,
        1914), 238.

432M   "The Legend of the Thunderbird," Carlisle Arrow, March
        13, 1914.

433M   "The Legend of the Thunderbird," Indian's Friend, 26 (May,
        1914), 10.

BRADLEY, ESTELLE (Chippewa)
    434N "Campus Animals I Have Known," <u>Carlisle Arrow</u>, May 16, 1913.
    435N "Na-Ne-Bosho's Air Flight," <u>Red Man</u>, 5 (June, 1913), 469-470.

BRAVE, BENJAMIN (Sioux)
    436L "Brotherhood of Christian Unity at Lower Brule," <u>Southern Workman</u>, 16 (July, 1887), 80.
    437L "A Young Catechist," <u>Southern Workman</u>, 18 (July, 1889), 82.
    438A "The Old and the New," <u>Southern Workman</u>, 26 (April, 1897), 72-73.

BRAZZANOVICH, FLORA (Paiute)
    439F "A Christmas Story," <u>Indian Leader</u>, December, 1918.

BRECKINRIDGE, JOHN C. (Pima)
    440N "The Indian As He Is," <u>Native American</u>, May 25, 1912.

BRECKINRIDGE, MARY (Pima)
    441N "The Pima Indians," <u>Native American</u>, May 25, 1912.

BRESETTE, FRANCIS (Chippewa)
    442N "About Sugar Bush," <u>Red Man</u>, 8 (July-August, 1888), 8 and 8 (September, 1888), 2.

BREWER, ELLA L. (Puyallup)
    443N "Hampton Ideals," <u>Quarterly Journal of the Society of American Indians</u>, 1 (April, 1913), 60.

BROKER, FREDERICK (Chippewa)
    444N With Myrtle Thomas. "Class History," <u>Carlisle Arrow</u>, May 22, 1914.

BROKER, JOSEPH HENRY (Chippewa)
    445N "Home Building for Indians," <u>Carlisle Arrow</u>, May 16, 1913.

BROWN, DAVID J. (Cherokee)
    446P "Sequoyah," <u>Cherokee Advocate</u>, February 26, 1879.
    447P "Sequoyah," <u>Indian Chieftain</u>, March 25, 1886.
    448P "Kee-Too-Whah," <u>Telephone</u>, July 26, 1889.
    449P "Sequoyah," <u>Twin Territories</u>, 2 (June, 1900), 113.

BROWN, HARRY (Sioux)
    450L "From the Indians," <u>Southern Workman</u>, 10 (April, 1881), 47.

BROWN, IRENE M. (Sioux)
    451N "The Passing Earth Lodge," <u>Indian Craftsman</u>, 1 (February, 1909), 31-32.

BROWN, JOHN F. (Seminole)

452N   With Daniel H. Ross, R. M. Wolfe, William L. Byrd, and
          Pleasant Porter. "Supplement to Memorial of April 6th,
          on Railroad Question," Cherokee Advocate, May 5, 1882.
453L   Letter to the Editor of the Catholic Columbian, Indian Jour-
          nal, June 16, 1887.

BROWN, MARGARET JEANE (Alaskan Native)
454N   "My Message to Garcia," Carlisle Arrow, June 4, 1915.

BRUCE, LOUIS (Mohawk)
455A   Commencement Address, Carlisle Indian School, April 2,
          1913, Red Man, 5 (May, 1913), 416-420.

BRUNETT, JOSEPH M. (Menominee)
456N   "Higher Education for the Indian: The Appeal of the Young
          Indian," Quarterly Journal of the Society of American
          Indians, 1 (July-September, 1913), 285-286.

BRUNETTE, CECILIA (Menominee)
457F   "Ma-na-posh's Christmas Adventure," Indian Leader, De-
          cember, 1915.
458N   "The Red Cross Christmas Roll Call," Indian Leader, De-
          cember, 1918.

BRUNETTE, WILLIAM A. (Chippewa)
459N   "Let's Have Facts About the Indians, and Not Fiction,"
          Tomahawk, December 11, 1924.

BRYANT, CHARLIE (Cherokee)
460F   "Mr. Brown's Hunt," Twin Territories, 3 (March, 1901),
          62.

BUCK, GEORGE (Sioux)
461N   "Industrial Education, the Salvation of the Indian Youth,"
          Red Man, 12 (February, 1895), 3.

BUCK, MABLE (Sioux)
462N   ["The Maple Tree,"] Red Man, 12 (May, 1895), 4.

BUFFINGTON, EZEKIEL (Cherokee)
463L   Letter, Cherokee Advocate, May 6, 1876.
464L   "Indian Rights," Cherokee Advocate, August 5, 1876.

BUFFINGTON, THOMAS MITCHELL (Cherokee)
465A   "Chief's Message," Tahlequah Arrow, November 18, 1899.
466A   "The Chief's Message," Wagoner Record, November 23,
          1899.
467A   "The Chief's Message," Indian Chieftain, November 23,
          1899.
468A   "Annual Message Delivered November 7, 1900, by Honorable
          T. M. Buffington, Principal Chief of the Cherokee Na-
          tion," Cherokee Advocate, November 10, 1900.
469A   Second Annual Message of T. M. Buffington, Principal Chief

of the Cherokee Nation, Delivered Wednesday, November 7, 1900, at Tahlequah, Indian Territory. Tahlequah, I. T.: The Sentinel Publishing Co., 1900.

470A   "Chief's Message," Daily Chieftain, November 8, 9, 11, 12, and 13, 1901.

471A   "Chief's Message," Indian Chieftain, November 14, 1901.

472N   ["Thanksgiving Proclamation,"] Daily Chieftain, November 14, 1901.

473A   "Chief's Message," Cherokee Advocate, November 16, 1901.

474A   "Annual Message," Cherokee Advocate, November 8, 1902.

475A   "Chief Buffington's Fourth Annual Message," Tahlequah Arrow, November 8, 1902.

476N   A Proclamation. Tahlequah, I. T., n. p., 1902. Broadside.

BURKE, JOSEPH (Pima)

477N   "How My People Spend Christmas at Home," Native American, December 25, 1909.

478N   "Panama Canal," Native American, May 23, 1914.

BURKE, ROBERT (Pima)

479A   "Salutatory," Native American, May 16, 1914.

BURNEY, BENJAMIN CROOKS (Chickasaw)

480A   "Message of Gov. B. C. Burney to the Chickasaw Legislature," Cherokee Advocate, September 24, 1879.

BUSCH, ELMER (Pomo)

481A   "Acorn Bread," Red Man, 5 (September, 1912), 24.

BUSH OTTER, GEORGE (Sioux)

482N   "My New Thoughts," Southern Workman, 10 (June, 1881), 67.

483A   "George Bush Otter's Address," Southern Workman, 14 (January, 1885), 7.

484N   "General Sherman Not Right," Morning Star, 7 (November, 1886), 3.

BUSHYHEAD, DENNIS WOLFE (Cherokee)

485N   With R. O. Ross, W. P. Adair, Will P. Ross. "Memorial of Cherokee Delegation Protesting Against Senate Bill No. 505," Cherokee Advocate, March 28, 1874.

486N   With W. P. Ross, Rufus O. Ross, and W. P. Adair. "Report of the Cherokee Delegates, 1873-4," Cherokee Advocate, December 26, 1874.

487A   "Speech of the Hon. D. W. Bushyhead at Schrimsher's Springs, near Tahlequah, Cherokee Nation, July 19th, 1879," Indian Journal, July 31, 1879.

488N   "Thanksgiving Proclamation!" Cherokee Advocate, November 26, 1879.

489A   "First Annual Message of Hon. D. W. Bushyhead, Principal Chief of the Cherokee Nation," Cherokee Advocate, November 26, 1879.

490A "First Annual Message of D. W. Bushyhead, Chief of the
      Cherokee Nation," Indian Journal, November 27, 1879.

491A First Annual Message of Hon. D. W. Bushyhead, Principal
      Chief of the Cherokee Nation. Tahlequah, I. T., n. p.,
      1879.

492A "First Annual Message of Hon. D. W. Bushyhead, Principal
      Chief of the Cherokee Nation," Cherokee Advocate, Octo-
      ber 13, 1880.

493A "Second Annual Message of Hon. D. W. Bushyhead, Princi-
      pal Chief of the Cherokee Nation," Indian Journal, No-
      vember 11, 1880.

494L "A Defense of the Cherokee Indians," Cherokee Advocate,
      April 13, 1881.

495A "Third Annual Message of Hon. D. W. Bushyhead, Principal
      Chief of the Cherokee Nation," Cherokee Advocate, No-
      vember 9, 1881.

496N "Thanksgiving Proclamation by His Excellency D. W. Bushy-
      head, Principal Chief," Cherokee Advocate, November
      16, 1881.

497A "Fourth Annual Message of Hon. D. W. Bushyhead, Princi-
      pal Chief, Cherokee Nation," Cherokee Advocate, Novem-
      ber 10, 1882.

498A "Appendix to Message," Cherokee Advocate, November 17,
      1882.

499N "Thanksgiving Proclamation," Cherokee Advocate, November
      24, 1882.

500N "Thanksgiving Proclamation," Cherokee Advocate, November
      16, 1883.

501N With J. G. Schrimsher, L. B. Bell, Is-pa-he-che, Samuel
      Checote, D. M. Hodge, G. W. Grayson. "Protest of
      D. W. Bushyhead, Principal Chief, and Other Cherokee
      and Creek Indians, Against the Passage of Senate Bill
      No. 50 and House Bill No. 3961," Cherokee Advocate,
      March 28, 1884.

502A "Second Annual Message," Indian Chieftain, November 13,
      1884.

503A "Message of Chief Bushyhead," Indian Journal, November
      13, 1884.

504N "Thanksgiving Proclamation," Indian Journal, November 27,
      1884.

505L With H. T. Landrum and Richard M. Wolfe. "Has the Red
      Man Rights?" Cherokee Advocate, March 27, 1885.

506L "To the Cherokee and Other Indians," Indian Chieftain, Au-
      gust 6, 1885.

507A "Remarks of Chief Bushyhead," Cherokee Advocate, August
      14, 1885.

508A "Message of D. W. Bushyhead," Indian Journal, November
      12, 1885.

509A Sixth Annual Message of Hon. D. W. Bushyhead, the Senate
      and Council of the Cherokee Nation. n. p., 1885.

510L Letter, Cherokee Advocate, April 2, 1886.

511A "Fourth Annual Message, [Second Term] of Hon. D. W.
      Bushyhead, Principal Chief of the Cherokee Nation,"
      Cherokee Advocate, November 3, 1886.

512A   Fourth Annual Message of Hon. D. W. Bushyhead, Principal Chief of the Cherokee Nation, I. T., Delivered at Tahlequah, Cherokee Nation, November 2nd, 1886. Tahlequah, I. T.: Advocate Job Office, 1886.
513L   "Letter of Acceptance," Muskogee Phoenix, May 28, 1891.
514L   "View on the Liberal Party Platform," Cherokee Telephone, June 18, 1891.

BUSSELL, CLARA (Klamath)
515F   "A Stolen Girl," Native American, June 15, 1907.

BUTLER, GEORGE O. (Cherokee)
516N   "To Our Readers," Cherokee Advocate, November 25, 1893.
517N   "Salutatory," Cherokee Advocate, November 23, 1901.

BUTTERFIELD, ANGELINE (Chippewa)
518L   "Bayfield Party Flays Peavy," Odanah Star, February 4, 1916.

BYRD, WILLIAM LEANDER (Chickasaw)
519N   With Daniel H. Ross, R. M. Wolfe, John F. Brown, and Pleasant Porter. "Supplement to Memorial of April 6th, on Railroad Question," Cherokee Advocate, May 5, 1882.
520A   Address and Policy of William L. Byrd. Delivered at Ardmore, Pickens County, Chickasaw Nation, on Monday, June 18, 1888. N. p., 1888.
521A   "Annual Message," Indian Citizen, September 15, 1892.

CAIN, ARCHIBALD (Creek)
522N   "Agriculture," Bacone Chief. Bacone, OK: Bacone College, 1924, p. 104.

CAJUNE, FRANK (Chippewa)
523A   "Sketch of Senator Dawes," Red Man, 14 (February, 1897), 5.

CALAC, CLAUDINA (Mission)
524A   "Class President's Address," Native American, May 30, 1903.

CALAC, GEORGIA E. (Mission)
525N   "A Festival Among Mission Indians," Indian Leader, May, 1915.

CALLAHAN, SOPHIA ALICE (Creek)
526F   Wynema: A Child of the Forest. Chicago: H. J. Smith & Co., 1891.

CAMPBELL, JOSEPH (Wichita)
527F   "A Man Who Became an Owl," Indian Leader, May, 1915.

CAREY, JAMES (Cherokee)

528N Memorial of John Rogers, Principal Chief, and James Carey
      and Thomas L. Rodgers, Chiefs and Headmen, Being
      Members of a Committee on Behalf of the Cherokee Old
      Settlers West of the Mississippi, for Themselves and
      Their People. April, 1844. Washington, DC: Blair
      & Rives, 1844.

CARLIN, WALTER (Sioux)
529M "Legend of the Man Who Became a Fish," Indian Leader,
      March 29, 1912.

CARR, ROBERT L. (Creek)
530N "The Indian Stamp Dance," Indian Leader, January, 1916.

CARTER, CALEB (Nez Percé)
531N "An Indian Thanksgiving," Indian Leader, November 27, 1908.
532N "A Christmas at My Home," Indian Leader, December 25,
      1908.
533N "Christmas Among the Nez Percés," Red Man, 3 (February,
      1911), 252-254.
534N "How the Nez Percés Trained for Long Distance Running,"
      Red Man, 4 (September, 1911), 15-16.
535M "The Coyote and the Wind," Red Man, 5 (January, 1913),
      208.
536M "The Coyote and the Wind," Carlisle Arrow, February 7,
      1913.
537M "The Feast of the Animals," Red Man, 5 (June, 1913), 467-
      468.

CARTER, CHARLES D. (Chickasaw)
538N "Indian Progress as Viewed by an Indian," Indian Craftsman,
      1 (May, 1909), 12-18.

CARTER, MINOT (Sioux)
539P "Fancies," Indian Leader, November 10, 1922.
540P "Raindrops," Indian Leader, November 10, 1922.

CASH, A. WARREN (Sioux)
541N "How Will Membership Help?" American Indian Advocate,
      4 (Winter, 1922), 8.

CASWELL, BENJAMIN (Chippewa)
542N "True Civilization," Red Man, 11 (May, 1892), 3-4.
543A Address at Carlisle Commencement, Red Man, 15 (February-
      March, 1899), 10.

CETAN SAPA (Sioux)
544N "The Yankton Sioux of South Dakota," Twin Territories, 3
      (August, 1902), 241-242.

CHAPMAN, ARTHUR (Chippewa)
545P "Indians in Khaki," Tomahawk, September 11, 1919.
546P "The White Man's Road," Tomahawk, August 4, 1921.

CHASE, HIRAM (Omaha)
547L "A Letter from an Omaha," Southern Workman, 16 (May, 1887), 59.
548N "Indian Blames Uncle Sam," Indian School Journal, 9 (May, 1909), 23. Reprinted from Indian News.
549N "The Law and the American Indian in America," Ohio Law Reporter, 9 (October 30, 1911), 245-349.

CHASE, HIRAM, JR. (Omaha)
550N "My Trip to Kansas City," Carlisle Arrow, January 23, 1914.
551A "Valedictory," Carlisle Arrow, June 4, 1915.

CHECOTE, SAMUEL (Creek)
552A "Address of Samuel Checote, Muscogee Chief," Cherokee Advocate, June 8, 1870.
553A "Chief Sam'l Checote's Message to the Creek Council at Okmulgee," Indian Journal, October 19, 1882.
554A "Chief Checote's Message," Indian Journal, October 18, 1883.
555A Address to Carlisle Students, Morning Star, 4 (January, 1884), 3.

CHEERLESS, LUCIANA (Pima)
556M "A Pima Legend," Native American, November 14, 1908.
557N "A Veteran Missionary and His Work," Indian's Friend, 21 (March, 1909), 10.

CHICKENEY, CHARLES W. (Menominee)
558N "Paternalism Does Not Promote Progress," Quarterly Journal of the Society of American Indians, 2 (October-December, 1914), 300-302.

CHIEFCHILD, DELIA (Crow)
559N "Indian Customs," Indian Leader, October 23, 1908.

CHILDERS, ELLIS BUFFINGTON (Creek)
560L ["The Outlook for Indian Legislation in Washington,"] Muskogee Phoenix, February 27, 1896.

CHILDERS, ROBERT C. (Creek)
561L "Honest Indian Views," Muskogee Phoenix, April 9, 1891.
562L "Statehood Convention," Muskogee Phoenix, September 17, 1891.
563L "Communication from R. C. Childers," Muskogee Phoenix, February 8, 1894. Reprinted from Tulsa Review.

CHOATE, ROBERT M. (Cherokee)
564N "The Fight Against Alcohol," Indian Leader, June, 1915.

CHOORO, EMMA (Hopi)
565N "Hopi Superstition," Native American, December 12, 1908.

CHOOROMI, JOHN (Hopi)
566N "Life Among the Hopi," Native American, April 18, 1903.
Reprinted from Talks and Thoughts.

CHOTEAU, LUZENA (Wyandot)
567N "Use and Improve or Lose," Red Man, 11 (May, 1892), 2.

CHOUTEAU, EDMOND (Cherokee)
568N "Work," Indian Chieftain, May 9, 1889.

CLARK, EMMA P. (Pima)
569N "Cause, Prevention, and Treatment of Tuberculosis," Native American, June 29, 1912.

CLARKE, FRANCIS (Walapai)
570N "Review of the Car," Native American, May 30, 1903.

CLARKE, MALCOLM (Piegan)
571N "The Reasons Why," Red Man, 11 (March-April, 1893), 2.

CLARKE, PETER DOOYENTATE (Wyandot)
572N Origin and Traditional History of the Wynadotts, and Sketches of Other Indian Tribes of North America. True Traditional Stories of Tecumseh and His League, in the Years 1811 and 1812. Toronto: Hunter, Rose & Co., 1870.

CLEMENTS, LUTHER (Michopdo)
573M "How Death Came to the Red Man," Indian Leader, May, 1915.

CLINTON, MARY L. (Modoc)
574M "How the Owl Came to Hoot," Native American, June 15, 1907.

CLOUD, BENEDICT D. (Sioux)
575M "How the Great Spirit Taught the Dakotas to Pray," Red Man, 4 (December, 1911), 165-166.
576M "How the Great Spirit Taught the Dakotas to Pray," Indian's Friend, 24 (March, 1912), 8.

CLOUD, ELIZABETH BENDER (Chippewa)
577A "A Hampton Graduate's Experience," Southern Workman, 45 (February, 1916), 109-112.

CLOUD, HENRY ROE (Winnebago)
578A "An Appeal to the Christian People of America," Indian's Friend, 23 (November, 1910), 9-10.
579N "A Brave Indian Superintendent," Native American, December 24, 1910.
580A "An Appeal to Christian People," Indian School Journal, 11 (December, 1910), 6-7.
581A "The Indian of To-Day," Southern Workman, 39 (December, 1910), 688-690.

582N   "A Brave Indian Superintendent," Indian Leader, January 13, 1911.

583N   "Some Social and Economic Aspects of the Reservation," Southern Workman, 42 (February, 1913), 72-77.

584N   "Some Social and Economic Aspects of the Reservation," Quarterly Journal of the Society of American Indians, 1 (April, 1913), 149-155.

585N   "Education of the American Indian," Quarterly Journal of the Society of American Indians, 2 (July-September, 1914), 203-209.

586N   "A Timely Plea," Indian's Friend, 27 (October, 1914), 9.

587N   "Education of the American Indian," Southern Workman, 44 (January, 1915), 12-16.

588N   "The Home Problem of the Indian," Red Lake News, February 15, 1915. Reprinted from Southern Workman.

589F   "Give Me This Mountain," Indian Leader, April 2, 1915.

590N   "From Wigwam to Pulpit: A Red Man's Own Story of His Progress from Darkness to Light," Missionary Review of the World, 38 (May, 1915), 328-339.

591N   "Alfred Longley Riggs, D. D.," American Indian Quarterly, 4 (April-June, 1916), 180-182.

592N   "From Wigwam to Pulpit," Southern Workman, 45 (July, 1916), 400-406.

593A   "Baccalaureate Address," Indian Leader, June, 1917.

594A   "A Master Builder," Southern Workman, 46 (November, 1917), 634.

595N   "Future of the Red Men in America," Missionary Review of the World, 47 (July, 1924), 529-532.

COACHMAN, WARD (Creek)

596A   "Message of Chief Ward Coachman to the Muskoke Council," Indian Journal, October 3, 1878.

COCHRAN, JESSE (Cherokee)

597A   "The Concluding Speeches of the Debates on the Lease of the Strip West of 96° Made by Col. E. C. Boudinot, Ridge Paschal and Jesse Cochran, February 1, 1888," Cherokee Advocate, March 7, 1888.

598L   "Mr. Cochran's Views," Indian Chieftain, March 27, 1890.

COFFEY, ROBERT (Comanche)

599N   "The Purpose of the Peyote Club," Bacone Chief. Bacone, Okla.: Bacone College, 1922, 103.

COLBERT, BEN H. (Choctaw)

600N   "Events of Three Generations," New-State Tribune, July 26, 1906.

COLBERT, DAUGHERTY [WINCHESTER] (Chickasaw)

601N   Address by P. P. Pitchlynn, Principal Chief of the Choctaw Nation, and Winchester Colbert, Governor of the Chickasaw Nation, to the Choctaws and Chickasaws: Explanatory of the Circumstances under Which the Treaty with

the United States, Concluded April 28, 1866, Was Nego-
tiated, and of the More Important Stipulations Contained
Therein, with Suggestions as to the Policy Proper to Be
Pursued Hereafter by the Two Nations. Washington, DC:
Joseph L. Pearson, 1866.

COLBERT, HUMPHREY (Chickasaw)
  602L ["Sunday Schools,"] Vindicator, October 13, 1875.

COLE, COLEMAN (Choctaw)
  603L "Removal of the Chief's Office," Vindicator, September 4,
      1875.
  604L "From Governor Cole," Vindicator, March 29, 1876.
  605L "Letter from Gov. Cole," Vindicator, April 5, 1876.
  606L "Constitutional Amendment Again," Vindicator, May 10, 1876.
  607A "Message of Coleman Cole," Indian Journal, October 12,
      1876.
  608A "Annual Message of Coleman Cole, Principal Chief, Choctaw
      Nation," Vindicator, October 18, 1876.
  609N "Memorial," Indian Journal, April 26, 1877.
  610A "To the Hard Working Community at Large," Indian Journal,
      June 21, 1877.
  611L "Gov. Cole's Defense," Atoka Independent, September 7,
      1877.
  612L "Gov. Cole's Defense," Cherokee Advocate, September 12,
      1877.
  613A "Governor Cole's Message," Atoka Independent, October 12,
      1877.
  614A "Gov. Cole's Message," Cherokee Advocate, October 17,
      1877.
  615N "What Is a Gentleman. Proverbs by Gov. Cole," Atoka In-
      dependent, January 11, 1878.
  616N "Contributed by Gov. Cole," Atoka Independent, March 8,
      1878.
  617L "Gov. Cole and the Washington Post," Indian Journal, June
      19, 1878.
  618L "To the Aborigines of the Western Continent," Indian Jour-
      nal, April 24, 1879.

COLEMAN, CHARLES F. (Mission)
  619N "The Mission Indians of California," Red Man and Helper,
      February 14, 1902.

COLT, LEWIS (Pima)
  620A "What Some of the Returned Students Are Doing," Native
      American, April 1, 1916.

COMINGDEER, JOHN (Cherokee)
  621N "Egotism," Indian Sentinel, November 3, 1898.
  622N "A Vacant Chair at Home," Tahlequah Arrow, January 12,
      1901.

COMPLAINVILLE, LILLIAN T. (Nez Percé)

623N "How Many Steps in the Rear?" Red Man, 14 (March,
       1898), 5.

CONGER, LUCILLE (Sioux)
624N "A Step Forward," Southern Workman, 31 (December, 1902),
       687-689.

CONLAN, CZARINA M. (Choctaw)
625N "Fourth Annual Report: The Oklahoma Historical Society,"
       Indian School Journal, 24 (December, 1924), 67-69.

CONROY, HARRY (Sioux)
626N "My Happiest Christmas," Carlisle Arrow, December 27,
       1912.

COOCHASNEMA, JESSIE (Hopi)
627A "When I Return to My People," Native American, June 16,
       1906.

COODEY, WILLIAM SHOREY (Cherokee)
628N "Memorial of the Delegates from the Cherokee Indians,"
       Cherokee Phoenix & Indians' Advocate, March 5, 1831.
629N With John Martin and John Ridge. "Cherokee Memorial,"
       Cherokee Phoenix & Indians' Advocate, March 24, 1832.
630L "To the Editors," Cherokee Phoenix & Indians' Advocate,
       May 26, 1832. Reprinted from National Intelligencer.

COOK, CHARLES SMITH (Sioux)
631N "The Oglalas," Red Man, 10 (April, 1890), 8. Reprinted
       from Southern Workman.
632N "Indian Names for Indians," Southern Workman, 19 (October,
       1890), 106-107.

COOK, WILLIAM TUTTLE (Cherokee)
633L "Bill Cook's Letter," Telephone, April 5, 1895.
634L "Penitent Bill Cook," Indian Chieftain, April 11, 1895.

COOKE, CLIFFORD (Ottawa)
635N "Patriots All--A True Story," Indian Leader, May, 1915.
636N "A Fable, a la George Ade," Indian Leader, May, 1915.

COOKSON, EDLEY LEVI (Cherokee)
637L "Appointed Time," Indian Chieftain, September 12, 1901.
638N "Real Indian Sentiment," Indian Journal, October 4, 1901.
639L "That 'Nigger' Steal," Vinita Weekly Chieftain, July 30,
       1903.
640L "To the Public," Vinita Daily Chieftain, July 28, 1903.
641L "Another One Nailed," Tahlequah Arrow, August 1, 1903.

COOLIDGE, SHERMAN (Arapaho)
642L "The Prophet of Light," Southern Workman, 19 (July, 1890),
       82.
643N "Indian as a Soldier," Review of Reviews, 7 (June, 1893), 597.

644A "The American Indian--His Duty to His Race and to His Country, the United States of America," Quarterly Journal of the Society of American Indians, 1 (April, 1913), 20-24.

645N "The American Indian of Today," Quarterly Journal of the Society of American Indians, 2 (January-March, 1914), 33-35.

646N "American Indians for the Honor of Their Race," Red Man, 6 (March, 1914), 251-255.

647N "The Function of the Society of American Indians," Quarterly Journal of the Society of American Indians, 2 (July-September, 1914), 186-190.

648N With Arthur C. Parker. "Proclamation," Indian Leader, October, 1915.

649A "Opening Address of the President," Quarterly Journal of the Society of American Indians, 4 (July-September, 1916), 227-229.

650A "American Indian Day Address," American Indian Advocate, 4 (Winter, 1922), 3.

COOPER, ELECTA (Oneida)
651N "Things I Like at Haskell," Indian Leader, May, 1915.

COOPER, STELLA (Potawatomi)
652N "What the Government Has a Right to Expect of the Educated Indian Girl," Indian School Journal, 11 (June, 1911), 37-38.

COPWAY, GEORGE (Chippewa)
653N The Life, History, and Travels, of Kah-ge-ga-gah-bowh (George Copway), a Young Indian Chief of the Ojebwa Nation, a Convert to the Christian Faith, and a Missionary to His People for Twelve Years; With a Sketch of the Present State of the Ojebwa Nation, in Regard to Christianity and Their Future Prospects. Also an Appeal; With All the Names of the Chiefs Now Living, Who Have Been Christianized, and the Missionaries Now Laboring Among Them. Written by Himself. Albany: Weed and Parsons, 1847.

654N The Life, History, and Travels of Kah-ge-ga-gah-bowh, (George Copway) a Young Indian Chief of the Ojebwa Nation, a Convert to the Christian Faith, and a Missionary to His People for Twelve Years; With a Sketch of the Present State of the Objebwa [sic] Nation, in Regard to Christianity and Their Future Prospects. Also, an Appeal; With All the Names of the Chiefs Now Living, Who Have Been Christianized, and the Missionaries Now Laboring Among Them. Written by Himself. 2nd ed. Philadelphia: J. Harmstead, 1847.

655N The Life, History, and Travels of Kah-ge-ga-gah-bowh, (George Copway) a Young Indian Chief of the Ojebwa Nation, a Convert to the Christian Faith, and a Missionary to His People for Twelve Years; With a Sketch of the Present State of the Objebwa [sic] Nation, in Regard to

Christianity and Their Future Prospects. Also, an Appeal; With All the Names of the Chiefs Now Living, Who Have Been Christianized, and the Missionaries Now Laboring Among Them. Written by Himself. 6th ed. Philadelphia: J. Harmstead, 1847.

656N   "The American Indians," American Review, n.s. 3 (June, 1849), 631-637.

657N   "The Lectures of Kah-ge-ga-gah-bowh (or G. Copway, the Indian Chief) ... on Monday, Feb. 26, and on Wednesday, Feb. 28, 1849." Circular, with autograph letter of G. Copway on the back. Boston, 1849.

658N   The Life, Letters and Speeches of Kah-ge-ga-gah-bowh, or, G. Copway, Chief Ojibway Nation. New York: S. W. Benedict, 1850.

659P   The Ojibway Conquest; A Tale of the Northwest. New York: G. P. Putnam, 1850.

660N   Organization of a New Indian Territory, East of the Missouri River. Arguments and Reasons Submitted to the Honorable the Members of the Senate and House of Representatives of the 31st Congress of the United States: By the Indian Chief Kah-ge-gah-bowh, or Geo. Copway. New York: S. W. Benedict, 1850.

661N   Recollections of a Forest Life; or, The Life and Travels of Kah-ge-ga-gah-bowh, or George Copway, Chief of the Ojibway Nation. London: C. Gilpin, 1850? 2nd. 1851.

662N   The Traditional History and Characteristic Sketches of the Ojibway Nation. London, C. Gilpin, 1850.

663N   "Brief Memorandum of Topics," Copway's American Indian, July 10, 1851.

664N   "European Observations," Copway's American Indian, July 10, 1851.

665N   "Medicine Men in Broadway," Copway's American Indian, July 10, 1851.

666N   "Plain Talk to the Wise," Copway's American Indian, July 10, 1851.

667N   "The Pleasures of a Country Ramble," Copway's American Indian, July 10, 1851.

668A   "Speech," Copway's American Indian, July 10, 1851.

669N   "Storm at Sea," Copway's American Indian, July 10, 1851.

670N   "Sun Painting," Copway's American Indian, July 10, 1851.

671N   "Cooper," Copway's American Indian, July 19, 1851.

672N   "The Doom of the World," Copway's American Indian, July 19, 1851.

673N   "Influence on Dreams," Copway's American Indian, July 19, 1851.

674M   "Legend No. 1: Origin of Death and Medicine Worship," Copway's American Indian, July 19, 1851.

675N   "Plays and Exercises," Copway's American Indian, July 19, 1851.

676N   "Causes Not Always Apparent; Or, Horse Radish and Religion," Copway's American Indian, July 26, 1851.

677M   "Legend II: The Star and the Lily," Copway's American Indian, July 26, 1851.

678N "Mind," Copway's American Indian, July 26, 1851.
679N "The Wars Between the Iroquois and Western Hurons, Terminating in the Wars Between the Ojibways and Iroquois in Canada West," Copway's American Indian, July 26, 1851.
680N "Can Such Things Be?" Copway's American Indian, August 2, 1851.
681M "Legend III: The First Murder Caused by Alcoholic Drink," Copway's American Indian, August 2, 1851.
682N "Query," Copway's American Indian, August 2, 1851.
683N "Flowers," Copway's American Indian, August 9, 1851.
684N "Indian Treaties," Copway's American Indian, August 9, 1851.
685M "Legend IV: The Thunder's Nest," Copway's American Indian, August 9, 1851.
686N "Scenes of the West. Death of Tecumseh," Copway's American Indian, August 9, 1851.
687N "The Fine Arts; An Indication," Copway's American Indian, August 16, 1851.
688N "From the Editor's Note Book of Travel," Copway's American Indian, August 16, 1851.
689M "Legend Fourth: The Two Cousins," Copway's American Indian, August 16, 1851.
690N "The Potency of the Pen," Copway's American Indian, August 16, 1851.
691N "So Dies a Wave along the Shore," Copway's American Indian, August 16, 1851.
692N "The Confederation of the Indian Tribes," Copway's American Indian, August 23, 1851.
693F "Intellect in Rags; A Tale," Copway's American Indian, August 23, 1851.
694M "Legend Sixth: The Long Chase," Copway's American Indian, August 23, 1851.
695N "The Pen," Copway's American Indian, August 23, 1851.
696N "Cuba," Copway's American Indian, August 30, 1851.
697N "The Farmer's Greatest Enemy," Copway's American Indian, August 30, 1851.
698N "The Light Literature of the Present Age," Copway's American Indian, August 30, 1851.
699N "Peace," Copway's American Indian, August 30, 1851.
700N "The Chippeways on Their Way to Minnesota," Copway's American Indian, September 13, 1851.
701N "Our Album," Copway's American Indian, September 13, 1851.
702N "Death of James Fennimore [sic] Cooper," Copway's American Indian, September 20, 1851.
703N "Missionary Labor among the Indians," Copway's American Indian, September 20, 1851.
704N "Our Album," Copway's American Indian, September 20, 1851.
705F "The Hunter's Wife," Copway's American Indian, September 27, 1851.
706F "The Indian's Reproof," Copway's American Indian, September 27, 1851.

707N   "Our Album," Copway's American Indian, September 27, 1851.

708N   "Success in Life," Copway's American Indian, September 27, 1851.

709N   "Women as They Might Be, and as They Are," Copway's American Indian, September 27, 1851.

710N   Running Sketches of Men and Places, in England, France, Germany, Belgium, and Scotland. New York: J. C. Riker, 1851.

711N   The Traditional History and Characteristic Sketches of the Ojibway Nation. Boston: B. F. Mussey & Co., 1851.

712N   The Traditional History and Characteristic Sketches of the Ojibway Nation. Boston: Sanborn, Carter, Bazin & Co., [1855].

713N   Indian Life and Indian History, by an Indian Author. Embracing the Traditions of the North American Indians Regarding Themselves, Particularly of That Most Important of All the Tribes, the Ojibways. Boston: A. Colby & Co., 1858.

714N   "The American Indians," Red Man, 9 (May, 1889), 7.

CORNELIUS, BRIGMAN (Oneida)
715A   "Wherein the Dawes Bill Has Been a Disappointment to Its Advocates," Red Man, 14 (February, 1897), 4-5.

716N   "The Advancement of the Indian," Red Man, 14 (April, 1897), 8.

CORNELIUS, CHESTER POE (Oneida)
717A   "The Harvest Is Ready," Morning Star, 7 (July, 1887), 7.

718N   "Life in the Logging Region," Red Man, 8 (February, 1888), 2.

CORNELIUS, E. L. (Oneida)
719N   "Indian Education," Red Man and Helper, July 4, 1902. Reprinted from Progress.

CORNELIUS, ELECTA (Oneida)
720N   "New Year's Day among the Oneidas," Indian Leader, December 28, 1906.

CORNELIUS, LILLY (Oneida)
721A   "Push On! Keep Moving!" Red Man, 9 (June, 1889), 1.

CORNELIUS, NANCY O. (Oneida)
722A   Address, Red Man, 11 (January-February, 1893), 4. Reprinted from Indian Bulletin.

723A   Address Before the Mohonk Conference, 1894, Red Man, 12 (December, 1894-January, 1895), 7.

CORNPLANTER, EDWARD (Seneca)
724M   "Origin of the Little Water Medicine Society," Quarterly Journal of the Society of American Indians, 3 (January-March, 1915), 49-52.

725M   "The Turtle's War Party: A Seneca Legend," Quarterly

Journal of the Society of American Indians, 5 (July-
September, 1917), 195-197.

COSAR, GALVOS (Creek)
  726M "An Indian Tale," Bacone Chief. Bacone, OK: Bacone Col-
      lege, 1922, p. 64.
  727M "An Indian Legend," Indian Leader, May 4, 1923.
  728N "History of the American Indian's Participation in the Civil
      War," Bacone Chief. Bacone, OK: Bacone College,
      1923, p. 79.

COSTO, MARTIN (Mission)
  729N "Indians of Southern California," Red Man and Helper, Feb-
      ruary 20-27, 1903.

COSTO, NATTIE (Mission)
  730N "Indian Festival," Indian Leader, September 4, 1908.

CRABTREE, MARY (Little Lake, or Mitomkai Pomo)
  731N "Class History, 1908," Native American, May 23, 1908.

CROTZER, GRACE (Wyandot)
  732N "The Value of Thorough Domestic Training," Indian Leader,
      June 9, 1911.

CROWE, JANIE (Seneca)
  733N "Iroquois New Year's Festival," Indian Leader, May, 1915.

CRUTCHFIELD, JOSEPH VANN (Cherokee)
  734L "Generalities and Specialities," Cherokee Advocate, March
      31, 1882.

CUNNINGHAM, JETER THOMPSON (Cherokee)
  735L "Objects to Springer's Bill," Indian Chieftain, April 5, 1888.
  736L "The Issues of To-Day," Indian Chieftain, April 12, 1888.
  737L "Where the Trouble Lies," Indian Chieftain, May 5, 1888.
  738L "How to Dispose of Our Surplus Grass Money," Indian Chief-
      tain, May 31, 1888.
  739L "Are We Really Bankrupt?" Indian Chieftain, January 9,
      1890.
  740L "The Chief Always Right," Indian Chieftain, February 20,
      1890.
  741N With E. E. Starr and Colonel J. Harris. "Report of the
      Late Delegation to Washington, to Negotiate a Loan on
      the Strip Debt," Cherokee Advocate, June 17, 1893.

CURTIS, CHARLES (Kansa)
  742A Charges of Fraud Made Against Pensioners Are Untrue.
      Speech of Charles Curtis of Kansas, in the House of
      Representatives, January 19, 1900. Washington, DC:
      Government Printing Office, 1900.
  743N Agreement with the Choctaw and Chickasaw Tribes ... Re-
      port. Washington, DC: Government Printing Office,
      1902.

744N Territories. Meeting of the Committee on Territories, March 29, 1904. Washington, DC: Government Printing Office, 1904.

745N Delegate from Indian Territory. Committee on Territories ... February 6, 1905. Statement of Hon. Charles Curtis. Washington, DC: Government Printing Office, 1905.

746N Loaning Money in the District of Columbia ... Report. Washington, DC: Government Printing Office, 1911. Reprinted in 1912.

747N Service Pension. Report of the Committee on Pensions, Together with the Views of a Minority, on H. R. 1, an Act Granting a Service Pension to Certain Defined Veterans of the Civil War and the War with Mexico. Washington, DC: Government Printing Office, 1912.

748N Duty on Laboratory Glassware and Surgical and Scientific Instruments ... Report. Washington, DC: Government Printing Office, 1920.

749N Duty on Magnesite Ores ... Report. Washington, DC: Government Printing Office, 1920.

CUSHING, GEORGE (Alaskan Native)
750N "My Summer Outing," Carlisle Arrow and Red Man, December 7, 1917.

CUSICK, DAVID (Tuscarora)
751N David Cusick's Sketches of Ancient History of the Six Nations:--Comprising--First--A Tale of the Foundation of the Great Island; (Now North America,) the Two Infants Born, and the Creation of the Universe. Second--A Real Account of the Early Settlers of North America, and Their Dissentions. Third--Origin of the Kingdom of the Five Nations, Which Was Called a Long House; The Wars, Fierce Animals, &c. Lewiston, NY: The Author, 1827.

752N David Cusick's Sketches of Ancient History of the Six Nations:--Comprising--First--A Tale of the Foundation of the Great Island, (Now North America,) the Two Infants Born, and the Creation of the Universe. Second--A Real Account of the Early Settlers of North America, and Their Dissentions. Third--Origin of the Kingdom of the Five Nations, Which Was Called a Long House: The Wars, Fierce Animals, &c. 2d ed. Of 7000 Copies. --Embelished with 4 Engravings. Tuscarora Village (Lewiston, Niagara Co.). Lockport, NY: Cooley & Lothrop, Printers, 1828.

753N David Cusick's Sketches of Ancient History of the Six Nations, Comprising First--A Tale of the Foundation of the Great Island, (Now North America,) the Two Infants Born, and the Creation of the Universe. Second--A Real Account of the Early Settlers of North America, and Their Dissensions. Third--Origin of the Kingdom of the Five Nations, Which Was Called a Long House: The Wars, Fierce Animals, &c. 3rd ed. Lockport, NY: Turner & McCollum, Printers, 1848.

754N "David Cusick's Sketches of Ancient History of the Six Na-
tions, Comprising First--A Tale of the Foundation of the
Great Island, (Now North America), the Two Infants
Born, and the Creation of the Universe. Second--A Real
Account of the Early Settlers of North America, and
Their Dissensions. Third--Origin of the Kingdom of the
Five Nations, Which Was Called a Long House: The
Wars, Fierce Animals, &c.," in William M. Beauchamp,
The Iroquois Trail, Fayetteville, NY: Recorder Print,
1892, pp. 1-38.

DAGENETT, CHARLES EDWIN (Peoria)
755N "The Life of an Indian Pony," Red Man, 8 (June, 1888), 8.
756A "Hand and Mind Culture," Red Man, 10 (June, 1891), 1.
757N "Chilocco Indian Industrial School Commencement," Red
Man, 13 (July, 1895), 5.
758A "The Indian as a Master Workman," Quarterly Journal of
the Society of American Indians, 1 (April, 1913), 56-57.
759N "Returned Students," Red Man, 6 (June, 1914), 421-426.

DALE, WILLIAM (Caddo)
760M "An Indian Legend of the Sun," Indian Craftsman, 2 (November, 1909), 29-30.
761M "A Legend of the Sun," Indian's Friend, 22 (June, 1910), 11.

DAMON, NELLIE (Navajo)
762N "Indian Dances," Indian Leader, September 11, 1908.

DAVIDSON, HAL O. (Mohave)
763M "The Story of the Creation (As Told by the Mohave)," Native American, June 15, 1907.

DAVIS, GILBERT (Apache)
764A "Some Things Necessary for Success," Native American,
April 1, 1916.

DAVIS, OSCAR DE FOREST (Chippewa)
765N "Striking a Balance," Red Man and Helper, February 20-27,
1903.

DAVIS, RICHARD (Cheyenne)
766N "Story of My Life," Morning Star, 6 (December, 1885), 5.
767A "Indian Citizenship," Red Man, 11 (January-February, 1893),
1.

DAVIS, SAMUEL G. (Haida)
768N "The Totem and the Potlach," Indian's Friend, 24 (November, 1911), 9. Reprinted from Home Mission Monthly.

DAWSON, ANNA (Arickara)
769N "A Dakota Blizzard," Southern Workman, 26 (February,
1897), 30-31.

770N "A Christmas Stocking," Southern Workman, 27 (March, 1898), 54.

DE CORA, ANGEL (Winnebago)
771N "The Native American Art," Indian School Journal, 7 (July, August, September, 1907), 44-45.
772N "Native Indian Art," Native American, August 31, 1907.
773N "Native Indian Art," Indian's Friend, 20 (October, 1907), 8, 11.
774N "Native Indian Art," Southern Workman, 36 (October, 1907), 527-528.
775N "Native Indian Art," National Education Association of the United States. Journal of Proceedings and Addresses, 1907, pp. 1005-1007.
776N "An Autobiography," Red Man, 3 (March, 1911), 279-285.
777N "Fourth Annual Conference of Society of American Indians," Carlisle Arrow, October 30, 1914.
778N "My People," Southern Workman, 26 (June, 1897), 115-116.

DEDRICK, EDITH (Klamath)
779N "From Greenville to Phoenix," Native American, July 8, 1905.

DE FOND, SAMUEL C. (Sioux)
780N "Old Indian Ways," Southern Workman, 16 (January, 1887), 8. Reprinted from Talks and Thoughts.
781N "The Indian Brave of the Future," Southern Workman, 16 (April, 1887), 45.
782L Letter, Southern Workman, 19 (February, 1890), 23.

DE GRASSE, ALFRED (Mashpee)
783P "Our Trees," Carlisle Arrow, April 11, 1911.
784M "The Legend of the Red Eagle," Red Man, 3 (March, 1911), 297-298.
785M "The Legend of the Red Eagle," Indian's Friend, 23 (August, 1911), 10.

DEITZ, ANGEL DE CORA (Winnebago)
See DE CORA, ANGEL.

DEITZ, WILLIAM (Sioux)
786N "The Indian in Art," Indian's Friend, 24 (February, 1912), 2. Reprinted from New York Sun.

DELORIA, ELLA CARA (Sioux)
787N "Health Education for Indian Girls," Southern Workman, 53 (February, 1924), 63-68.

DEMARRIAS, FRANCES (Sioux)
788N "An Indian Christmas Celebration," Indian Leader, December, 1915.
789N "The Haskell Exposition," Indian Leader, June, 1916.
790N "Woman's Part in the World Conflict," Indian Leader, June, 1918.

DENETSOUENBEGA, MANUELITO (Navajo)
791M "A Legend of Shiprock," Indian Leader, March, 1916.

DENOMIE, ANTOINE (Chippewa)
792N "Answers Tomahawk Score," Odanah Star, November 26,
1913.

DENOMIE, S. F. (Chippewa)
793N "Report of the Delegates," Odanah Star, July 18, 1913.

DENOMIE, WILLIAM H. (Chippewa)
794N "Something Yet to be Attained," Red Man, 12 (January-
February, 1894), 3.

DE PELTQUESTANQUE, ESTAIENE M. (Kickapoo)
795N "Indian Nurses and Nursing Indians," American Indian Magazine, 3 (July-September, 1915), 169-174.

DICK, COFFEE (Cherokee)
796L "From the Cherokee Nation," Arkansian, October 7, 1859.
797L "From the Cherokee Nation," Arkansian, October 14, 1859.
798L "From the Cherokee Nation," Arkansian, November 18, 1859.
799L "From the Cherokee Nation," Arkansian, December 23, 1859.
800L "Review of Letter No. 2, of 'Slick Skin,'" Arkansian, March
2, 1860.
801L "Review of Letter No. 3," Arkansian, March 9, 1860.

DICK, JOHN HENRY (Cherokee)
802N "Will Make Changes," Indian Sentinel, June 22, 1900.

DODSON, JOHN (Shoshoni)
803A "Get Ready for the Place Above You," Native American,
June 11, 1904.

DOHERTY, JOHN J. (Chippewa)
804L "Talks on Village and River Improvements," Odanah Star,
January 1, 1915.
805N "Should Build Roads Thro' Reservation," Odanah Star, January 15, 1915.
806L "Communication," Odanah Star, September 24, 1915.
807L "Road Appropriation Much Needed," Odanah Star, November
19, 1915.
808L "Should Enforce Treaty," Odanah Star, November 19, 1915.
809L "To My Indian Friends," Odanah Star, July 7, 1916.
810N "What the Indian Did for Democracy," Tomahawk, July 3,
1919.

DOOLITTLE, OTTOWELL (Little Lake, or Mitomkai Pomo)
811N "Essay on the Life of George Washington," Native American, February 28, 1903.

DORCHESTER, DANIEL (Yuma)
812A "Looking Forward," Native American, June 11, 1904.

DOWNING, LEWIS (Cherokee)
813N "A Day of Fasting and Prayer [a Proclamation]," Cherokee Advocate, October 22, 1870.
814N "Protest of the Cherokee Nation Against a Territorial Government," Cherokee Advocate, March 18, 1871.
815L With W. P. Adair, C. N. Vann, Samuel Smith, and George W. Scraper. "Letter from the Cherokee Delegation," Cherokee Advocate, April 1, 1871.

DOXON, CHARLES (Onondaga)
816A "Charles Doxon's Speech," Southern Workman, 16 (May, 1887), 56.
817A "Speech of Charles Doxon," Southern Workman, 16 (August, 1887), 89.
818N "An Indian as a Mechanic," Southern Workman, 34 (September, 1905), 503-505.
819N "Moral Influence of Industrial Education," Missionary Review of the World, 29 (December, 1906), 896-898.
820N "An Indian's Accomplishments," Indian Outlook, 1 (January, 1907), 2.
821A "Industrial Education for the Indian," Native American, February 2, 1907.
822N "Industrial Education for the Indians," Southern Workman, 36 (August, 1907), 427-429.
823A "Address by Mr. Charles Doxon," Red Man, 5 (May, 1913), 423-426.
824N "The Onondaga Indian Welfare Society and Its Work," Carlisle Arrow and Red Man, January 4, 1918.

DOXTATOR, MARGARET (Oneida)
825N "The Importance of Making the Home Attractive," Indian Leader, June, 1914.

DOYETO, MORRIS (Kiowa)
826N "Religious Department," Bacone Chief. Bacone, OK: Bacone College, 1924, p. 80.

DRAPEAU, AGNES (Sioux)
827M "Legend of Girl with Golden Arm," Indian Leader, May, 1915.

DREW, HARVEY (Klamath)
828A "The Building of a Class," Native American, June 3, 1905.

DU BRAY, JOSEPH (Sioux)
829N "We Had an Opportunity to See the Civilized Country," Southern Workman, 20 (October, 1891), 237.

DUCKWORTH, M. ZOE (Delaware)
830P "'Wahoma' (A Lament) Song of the Dying Nations," Muskogee Phoenix, September 7, 1905.
831P "Wahoma," Southwesterner, September 9, 1905.

DUNCAN, DE WITT CLINTON (Cherokee)

832L Letter, Cherokee Advocate, August 23, 1873.

833L Letter, Cherokee Advocate, July 1, 1876. Signed in Cherokee script.

834L Letter, Cherokee Advocate, July 22, 1876. Signed in Cherokee script.

835N "Our Indian Policy," Cherokee Advocate, October 21, 1876.

836L Letter, Cherokee Advocate, December 23, 1876.

837L Letter, Cherokee Advocate, October 19, 1878.

838N "The Oklahoma Question," Indian Journal, January 6, 1881.

839L Letter, Cherokee Advocate, February 9, 1881.

840L Letter, Cherokee Advocate, June 15, 1881.

841L Letter, Cherokee Advocate, July 27, 1881.

842L Letter, Cherokee Advocate, August 31, 1881.

843L Letter, Cherokee Advocate, September 28, 1881.

844L "The Cherokees' Chain of Title," Cherokee Advocate, December 23, 1881.

845L "Cherokee Land Patent," Cherokee Advocate, February 3, 1882.

846L "Our National Patent," Cherokee Advocate, March 31, 1882.

847N "Story of the Cherokees," Cherokee Advocate, October 6, 13, 20, and 27, 1882. Reprinted from Weekly Magazine. Also published separately, n. p., n. d.

848L Letter, Cherokee Advocate, January 26, 1883.

849N "The Statehood of the Indian Territory," Cherokee Advocate, March 16 and 23, 1883.

850L "What Is the Matter?" Cherokee Advocate, April 27, 1883.

851N "A Novelty in Cherokee Literature," Indian Chieftain, January 21, 1886.

852N "The Cherokee Outlet," Andover Review, 16 (October, 1891), 342-351.

853N "The Cherokee Outlet," Lend a Hand, 7 (October, 1891), 257-258.

854L "Old Settler Money," Cherokee Advocate, July 11, 1894.

855L "The Final Wind-up," Arrow, June 7, 1895.

856N "'Too-qua-stee' on Monopoly," Arrow, July 14, 1895.

857L "Allotment," Indian Chieftain, September 5, 1895.

858L "'Too-Qua-stee' on Monopoly," Indian Chieftain, September 19, 1895.

859L "Unpatriotic Politics," Arrow, September 12, 1896.

860L "Not Adopted Citizens," Indian Chieftain, September 3, 1896.

861L "Difficulties Galore," Indian Chieftain, January 28, 1897.

862L "All Individual Rights Denied," Indian Chieftain, May 13, 1897.

863L "Those Townsites Again," Indian Chieftain, May 20, 1897.

864L "A Halt Suggested," Indian Chieftain, May 20, 1897.

865L "Too-qua-stee at Tahlequah," Indian Chieftain, May 27, 1897.

866L "Reasons for Not Treating," Indian Chieftain, June 10, 1897.

867L "More Townlot Talk," Indian Chieftain, June 17, 1897.

868L "A Momentous Occasion," Indian Chieftain, June 24, 1897.

869L "Our Status after January, 1898," Indian Chieftain, July 8, 1897.

870L "A Society Problem Essayed," Indian Chieftain, July 29, 1897.
871L "Cherokee Protection," Indian Chieftain, August 26, 1897.
872L "Coming Senate Committee," Indian Chieftain, August 26, 1897.
873L "History Repeats Itself," Indian Chieftain, August 26, 1897.
874N "The Creek Agreement," Indian Chieftain, October 7, 1897.
875L "The Delaware Claim," Indian Chieftain, October 28, 1897.
876L "The Citadel Invaded," Indian Chieftain, November 25, 1897.
877L "Who Holds Our Lands," Indian Chieftain, December 2, 1897.
878L "A Friendly Criticism," Indian Chieftain, December 16, 1897.
879L "Too-qua-stee Has Read the Bill," Indian Chieftain, January 20, 1898.
880N "Tom Starr," Indian Chieftain, January 27, 1898.
881L "An Open Letter to Hon. Charles Curtis," Indian Chieftain, February 17, 1898.
882L "The Townlot Problem," Indian Chieftain, February 24, 1898.
883L "'Too-qua-stee' in Washington (two letters)," Indian Chieftain, March 31, 1898.
884L "'Too-qua-stee' in Washington," Indian Chieftain, April 14, 1898.
885L "View of the Delegates," Indian Chieftain, April 21, 1898.
886L "'Too-qua-stee' in Washington," Indian Chieftain, April 21, 1898.
887N "The Indian's Hard Lot," Indian Chieftain, June 2, 1898.
888L "Admission of the Government's Bad Faith with the Cherokees," Indian Chieftain, July 7, 1898.
889N "A Great Injustice," Indian Sentinel, July 15, 1898.
890L "Evils of the Curtis Bill," Indian Chieftain, July 21, 1898.
891L "Too-qua-stee's Rejoinder," Indian Chieftain, August 4, 1898.
892L "Conscience Set Aside," Indian Chieftain, August 18, 1898.
893L "The Mineral Outrage," Indian Chieftain, August 25, 1898.
894L "Unjust Treatment," Indian Chieftain, September 1, 1898.
895L "Too-qua-stee's Criticisms," Indian Chieftain, September 8, 1898.
896L "Townsite Matter Discussed," Indian Chieftain, September 15, 1898.
897L "The Curtis Law Is a Calamity," Indian Chieftain, September 29, 1898.
898L "Coercive Throughout," Daily Chieftain, October 3, 1898.
899L "Coercive Throughout," Indian Chieftain, October 6, 1898.
900L "No Remedy Probable," Daily Chieftain, October 7, 1898.
901L "No Remedy Probable," Indian Chieftain, October 13, 1898.
902L "The Town Lots," Indian Chieftain, October 20, 1898.
903L "Indian Treaties," Daily Chieftain, October 27, 1898.
904L "Indian Treaties," Indian Chieftain, November 3, 1898.
905L "Cannot Be Abolished," Daily Chieftain, November 17, 1898.
906L "Cannot Be Abolished," Indian Chieftain, November 24, 1898.

907N   "Absence from Church," Indian Chieftain, December 15, 1898.

908L   "An Opinion Reviewed," Daily Chieftain, December 23, 1898.

909L   "An Opinion Reviewed," Indian Chieftain, December 29, 1898.

910L   "Too-qua-stee on the Agreement," Indian Chieftain, January 19, 1899.

911L   "The Agreements," Indian Chieftain, January 26, 1899.

912L   "Hark, from the Tomb," Indian Chieftain, March 2, 1899.

913L   "Monument to Sequoyah," Indian Chieftain, March 9, 1899.

914P   "The White Man's Burden," Daily Chieftain, March 27, 1899.

915P   "The White Man's Burden," Indian Chieftain, March 30, 1899.

916P   "The Dead Nation," Daily Chieftain, April 24, 1899.

917P   "The Dead Nation," Indian Chieftain, April 27, 1899.

918L   "Purely Legal Question," Indian Chieftain, June 8, 1899.

919L   "National vs. Downing," Daily Chieftain, June 13, 1899.

920L   "National vs. Downing," Indian Chieftain, June 15, 1899.

921L   "National Consistency," Indian Chieftain, June 29, 1899.

922N   "A Hard Problem Indeed," Indian Chieftain, July 20, 1899.

923L   "Platform Reviewed," Indian Chieftain, July 27, 1899.

924P   "A Vision of the End," Indian Chieftain, August 3, 1899.

925L   "Indian Education," Indian Chieftain, August 31, 1899.

926L   "Tooquastee Maligned," Indian Chieftain, September 7, 1899.

927L   "Our Noble Statesmen?" Indian Chieftain, September 14, 1899.

928L   "Methods of 1835," Indian Chieftain, September 21, 1899.

929L   "The $4,000,000 Claim," Indian Chieftain, September 28, 1899.

930N   "No Agreement," Indian Chieftain, November 30, 1899.

931L   "Anent the Agreement," Indian Chieftain, November 30, 1899.

932F   "Magnificent Tom, or a Brave Girl's Fate," Indian Chieftain, December 21, 1899.

933L   "Anent Judge Springer," Indian Chieftain, January 25, 1900.

934L   "History Repeats Itself," Daily Chieftain, February 26, 1900.

935L   "History Repeats Itself," Indian Chieftain, March 1, 1900.

936L   "History Repeats Itself," Cherokee Advocate, March 10, 1900.

937L   "Too-qua-stee Talks," Daily Chieftain, May 8, 1900.

938L   "Too-qua-stee Talks," Indian Chieftain, May 10, 1900.

939L   "Unjust Tyranny," Daily Chieftain, June 1, 1900.

940L   "Curtis' 'Wormwood' Likened unto 'Mercury' of Mythology," Daily Chieftain, June 5, 1900.

941L   "Curtis' 'Wormwood,'" Indian Chieftain, June 7, 1900.

942L   "How Indian Legislation Is Effected in Congress," Daily Chieftain, June 11, 1900.

943L   "Strikes the Keynote," Indian Chieftain, June 14, 1900.

944L   "Passage of the Curtis Bill," Daily Chieftain, June 16, 1900.

945N   "Indian Rights Disregarded," Cherokee Advocate, June 16, 1900.

946L   "History Repeats Itself," Daily Chieftain, June 21, 1900.

947L   "Passage of the Curtis Bill," <u>Indian Chieftain</u>, June 21, 1900.

948L   "How Indian Legislation Is Effected in Congress," <u>Cherokee Advocate</u>, June 23, 1900.

949L   "History Repeats Itself," <u>Indian Chieftain</u>, June 28, 1900.

950L   "Flag and Constitution," <u>Indian Chieftain</u>, July 5, 1900.

951L   "Monetary Legislation," <u>Indian Chieftain</u>, July 19, 1900.

952L   "Imperialism," <u>Indian Chieftain</u>, August 9, 1900.

953L   "Carpetbag Sermon," <u>Indian Chieftain</u>, September 6, 1900.

954P   "Cherokee Memories," <u>Indian Chieftain</u>, October 4, 1900.

955P   "The Angel of Hope," <u>Indian Chieftain</u>, October 11, 1900.

956L   "Their Day in Court," <u>Indian Chieftain</u>, October 18, 1900.

957L   "Violated Treaties," <u>Indian Chieftain</u>, October 25, 1900.

958L   "The $4,000,000 Claim," <u>Indian Chieftain</u>, November 8, 1900.

959P   "Truth Is Mortal," <u>Indian Chieftain</u>, February 7, 1901.

960L   "Treaty Provisions," <u>Indian Chieftain</u>, February 21, 1901.

961L   "Anent the Towns," <u>Daily Chieftain</u>, March 4, 1901.

962L   "Anent the Towns," <u>Indian Chieftain</u>, March 7, 1901.

963L   "Anent Owen," <u>Indian Chieftain</u>, March 14, 1901.

964L   "Address to Cherokees," <u>Indian Chieftain</u>, March 28, 1901.

965L   "In Reply to Owen," <u>Indian Chieftain</u>, April 4, 1901.

966L   "Cherokees Beware," <u>Indian Chieftain</u>, April 18, 1901.

967L   "Rejoinder to Judge Springer," <u>Indian Chieftain</u>, May 9, 1901.

968L   "Wants No Agreement," <u>Indian Chieftain</u>, May 30, 1901.

969L   "Why Make a Treaty?" <u>Indian Chieftain</u>, June 6, 1901.

970L   "Against a Treaty," <u>Indian Chieftain</u>, June 13, 1901.

971L   "Nature's Forum," <u>Indian Chieftain</u>, August 8, 1901.

972L   "Freedman Citizenship," <u>Daily Chieftain</u>, September 10, 1901.

973L   "Freedman Citizenship," <u>Indian Chieftain</u>, September 12, 1901.

974L   "Defends His Name," <u>Indian Chieftain</u>, April 10, 1902.

975L   "The Railroad Claim," <u>Indian Chieftain</u>, July 17, 1902.

976L   "Who Are the Croakers?" <u>Indian Chieftain</u>, July 17, 1902.

977L   "Against Agreement of 1902," <u>Cherokee Advocate</u>, July 26, 1902.

978N   "Skill Is Education," <u>Vinita Weekly Chieftain</u>, January 1, 1903.

979L   "Nuts to Crack," <u>Vinita Weekly Chieftain</u>, January 8, 1903.

980L   "An Empty Victory," <u>Vinita Daily Chieftain</u>, February 5, 1903.

981L   "Intermarried Citizens," <u>Vinita Weekly Chieftain</u>, March 19, 1903.

982L   "'Them' Two Speeches," <u>Vinita Weekly Chieftain</u>, July 23, 1903.

983N   "The Story of Allotment," <u>Vinita Weekly Chieftain</u>, September 3, 1903.

984L   "The Railroad Land Claim," <u>Vinita Daily Chieftain</u>, September 5, 1903.

985L   "The Railroad Land Claim," <u>Vinita Weekly Chieftain</u>, September 11, 1903.

986L   "Surplus Lands of Cherokees," Vinita Weekly Chieftain, November 19, 1903.

987L   "Wants Double Statehood," Vinita Daily Chieftain, May 6, 1904.

988P   "Good Manners," Vinita Weekly Chieftain, May 19, 1904.

989P   "A Christmas Song," Vinita Weekly Chieftain, December 17, 1903.

990P   "Sequoyah," Vinita Weekly Chieftain, June 2, 1904.

991P   "Dignity," Vinita Weekly Chieftain, August 11, 1904.

992P   "Indian Territory at World's Fair," Vinita Weekly Chieftain, September 29, 1904.

993P   "Indian Territory at World's Fair," Muskogee Democrat, October 1, 1904.

994P   "Thanksgiving," Vinita Weekly Chieftain, November 24, 1904.

995L   "Interesting Cherokee History," Vinita Daily Chieftain, September 8, 1905.

996N   "Passing of the Tribal Governments," Tahlequah Arrow, March 3, 1906.

997L   "The Whiskey Agency," The Weekly Chieftain, July 3, 1908.

DUNCAN, EMMA (Cherokee)
998N   "Bells," Children's Play Ground, August 9, 1881.

DUNCAN, J. C. (Cherokee)
999P   "The Red Man's Burden: Parody on Kipling's Poem," Indian Sentinel, March 30, 1899.

DUNCAN, JAMES W. (Cherokee)
1000N   "Our School Law," Indian Chieftain, November 19, 1885.

1001N   "Some Geology of the Cherokee Nation," Cherokee Advocate, December 2, 1891.

1002N   "Our Land Tenure," Indian Chieftain, August 25, 1892.

1003L   "Answers Springer," Indian Chieftain, April 11, 1901.

1004N   "The 'Unsettled Condition,'" Indian Chieftain, April 18, 1901.

1005N   "Important Meeting of Ketoowahs," Tahlequah Arrow, May 16, 1912.

DUNCAN, JENNIE (Cherokee)
1006N   "The Fallen Tree," Children's Play Ground, August 9, 1881.

DUNCAN, WALTER ADAIR (Cherokee)
1007L   "Cherokee Resolutions," Arkansian, August 17, 1860.

1008L   "Cherokee Orphan Asylum," Cherokee Advocate, August 24, 1872.

1009L   "Cherokee Orphan Asylum, No. 2," Cherokee Advocate, September 7, 1872.

1010N   "Nature of the Cherokee Orphan Asylum," Cherokee Advocate, August 12, 1876.

1011N   "Indian International Fair," Indian Journal, August 17, 1876.

1012N   "Cherokee Orphan Asylum," Cherokee Advocate, August 26, 1876.

1013N   "The Indian Question," Indian Journal, September 7, 1876.

1014N   "Education, or Watch the Future," Cherokee Advocate, September 26, 1877.

1015N   "Education, or Watchword for the Future--Advance," Cherokee Advocate, October 24, 1877.

1016N   "Educational," Cherokee Advocate, June 11, 1879.

1017L   "Education and Labor," Cherokee Advocate, July 30, 1879.

1018N   "For the Advocate," Cherokee Advocate, June 9, 1880.

1019N   "The Fair," Indian Journal, September 30, 1880.

1020N   "Sehon Chapel," Cherokee Advocate, March 16, 1883.

1021N   "Educational," Cherokee Advocate, July 27, 1883.

1022N   "Sky Sketches," Cherokee Advocate, October 12, 1883.

1023N   "Cherokee Antiquities," Cherokee Advocate, April 25, 1884.

1024L   ["National Education Association"], Indian Journal, July 24, 1884.

1025N   "Mormonism," Cherokee Advocate, February 23, 1887.

1026N   "Mormonism," Cherokee Advocate, May 4, 1887.

1027N   "The Lease Question Again," Telephone, September 13, 1888.

1028N   "Worth of Grass," Cherokee Advocate, September 26, 1888.

1029N   "To Sell or Not to Sell," Telephone, April 19, 1889.

1030L   "What Shall We Do?" Telephone, October 3, 1889.

1031N   Claim of the Cheyennes and Arapahoes to Certain Cherokee Lands, Considered in the Light of Facts. Tahlequah, I. T.: n. p. 1889.

1032N   "How Now?" Cherokee Telephone, April 21, 1892.

1033N   "Allotment of Land," Cherokee Advocate, September 21, 1892.

1034L   "Theosophy," Cherokee Advocate, September 21, 1892.

1035L   "Allotment," Muskogee Phoenix, September 29, 1892.

1036L   "Allotment 5," Cherokee Advocate, October 26, 1892.

1037L   "Allotment," Muskogee Phoenix, October 27, 1892.

1038L   "Allotment," Muskogee Phoenix, December 1, 1892.

1039L   "Home Scraps," Muskogee Phoenix, February 16, 1893.

1040L   "Home Rule and Statehood," Muskogee Phoenix, March 2, 1893.

1041L   "Cherokee Bonds," Muskogee Phoenix, August 24, 1893.

1042L   "The National Debt," Cherokee Advocate, August 26, 1893.

1043N   "Monopoly: Status of Delaware Citizens," Cherokee Advocate, September 2, 1893.

1044N   "The Schools," Cherokee Advocate, September 9, 1893.

1045L   "Cherokee Bonds," Muskogee Phoenix, September 14, 1893.

1046L   "Statehood," Cherokee Advocate, September 16, 1893.

1047L   "The Strip Money," Cherokee Advocate, September 30, 1893.

1048N   "Statehood," Cherokee Advocate, October 14, 1893.

1049N   "Strip Money," Cherokee Advocate, October 21, 1893.

1050N   "Status of Cherokee Nation--Some Propositions," Cherokee Advocate, October 28, 1893.

1051N   "In the Great Debate," Muskogee Phoenix, November 2, 1893.

1052N   "No Statehood," Cherokee Advocate, December 9, 1893.

1053L   Letter, Cherokee Advocate, February 28, 1894.

1054L   "No Territorial Government," Muskogee Phoenix, March 15, 1894.

1055L   "No Territorial Government," Indian Citizen, March 22, 1894.

1056L   Letter, Cherokee Advocate, May 16, 1894.

1057N   "On Exit of Mrs. Carrie Ross," Indian Arrow, July 7, 1894.

1058L   "Senator Platt on the Treaties," Muskogee Phoenix, July 26, 1894.

1059L   "Worship in Washington," Muskogee Phoenix, August 30, 1894.

1060L   "From Delegate Duncan," Muskogee Phoenix, December 22, 1894.

1061L   "He's Said to Be a Preacher," Indian Chieftain, January 28, 1895.

1062N   "As It Seems to Me," Cherokee Advocate, February 6, 1895.

1063N   "The Platt Amendment," Muskogee Phoenix, June 4, 1896.

1064L   "What He Says Now," Arrow, July 26, 1895.

1065L   "Scores the Cherokee Advocate," Tahlequah Arrow, March 12, 1898.

1066N   "Rogers, Gill and Thomas," Cherokee Advocate, September 22, 1900.

1067N   "Notes on the Agreement," Cherokee Advocate, April 20, 1901.

1068N   "Why I Will Not Vote for the Agreement," Cherokee Advocate, April 27, 1901.

1069N   "Some Notes on the Curtis Act," Cherokee Advocate, May 4, 1901.

1070N   "Mineral and Oil Leases," Cherokee Advocate, May 11, 1901.

1071N   "Mineral Leases," Cherokee Advocate, May 18, 1901.

1072N   "What Next?" Cherokee Advocate, June 29, 1901.

1073N   "What About Those Leases?" Cherokee Advocate, August 17, 1901.

1074N   "Several Things," Tahlequah Arrow, May 30, 1903.

1075N   "Law Not Enforced," Tahlequah Arrow, July 4, 1903.

1076N   "That Ten Acres," Tahlequah Arrow, July 11, 1903.

1077N   "That Lease Deal," Tahlequah Arrow, August 15, 1903.

1078N   "The Excluded Cherokees," Tahlequah Arrow, September 12, 1903.

1079N   "That Fort Smith Strip," Tahlequah Arrow, September 26, 1903.

1080N   "The Law and the Construction Put Upon It," Tahlequah Arrow, October 3, 1903.

1081N   "Worth Contending For," Tahlequah Arrow, October 17, 1903.

1082N   "A Nation's Death," Tahlequah Arrow, December 26, 1903.

1083N   "The Facts About Sequoyah," Tahlequah Arrow, January 9, 1904.

1084N   "Sequoyah vs. Cadmus," Tahlequah Arrow, January 30, 1904.

1085N "As to Statehood," Tahlequah Arrow, October 8, 1904.
1086N "The Indian Question," Tahlequah Arrow, October 29, 1904.
1087N "Prefers Arkansas to Single Statehood," Tahlequah Arrow,
       November 12, 1904.
1088N "That Ten Acres of Land," Tahlequah Arrow, March 4,
       1905.
1089N "Unjust to Citizens," Tahlequah Arrow, March 11, 1905.
1090N "What Constitutes Citizenship," Tahlequah Arrow, March
       18, 1905.
1091N "The Lost Cherokees," Tahlequah Arrow, April 1, 1905.
1092N "Power of the Dawes Commission," Tahlequah Arrow,
       April 8, 1905.
1093N "The Profit and Loss," Tahlequah Arrow, April 22, 1905.
1094N "Grafting," Tahlequah Arrow, April 29, 1905.
1095N "Agreed Facts," Tahlequah Arrow, June 24, 1905.
1096N "Some Mistakes," Tahlequah Arrow, June 17, 1905.
1097N "No Compromise," Tahlequah Arrow, July 22, 1905.
1098N "The Right Should Prevail," Tahlequah Arrow, July 29,
       1905.
1099L "Against Statehood," Vinita Weekly Chieftain, August 3,
       1905.
1100N "Territorial Government," Tahlequah Arrow, August 12,
       1905.
1101N "The Retort Courteous," Tahlequah Arrow, August 26,
       1905.
1102N "Worse Than at First," Tahlequah Arrow, September 9,
       1905.
1103N "Now, What!" Tahlequah Arrow, December 16, 1905.
1104N "In Doubtful Mood," Tahlequah Arrow, March 10, 1906.
1105N "Some Cherokee History," New-State Tribune, April 5,
       1906.
1106N "Which the Indian's Friend?" Tahlequah Arrow, June 30,
       1906.
1107N "Coming Events," Tahlequah Arrow, August 11, 1906.
1108L "Old School Affairs and Sequoyah," New-State Tribune,
       August 30, 1906.
1109N "The White Man Case," Tahlequah Arrow, December 1,
       1906.
1110N "The White Man Case Again," Tahlequah Arrow, April 27,
       1907.

DURANT, WILL (Choctaw)
1111A "A Choctaw Roasts Hitchcock," New-State Tribune, August
       30, 1906.

DYE, BERTHA E. (Seneca)
1112N "Tales of My Grandfather," Red Man, 15 (February-March,
       1899), 2.

EASCHIEF, ANNIE (Pima)
1113N "Peaches," Native American, March 3, 1917.

1114N "How We Can Save Clothing," <u>Native American</u>, April 20, 1918.

1115N "Utilization of Left-Overs," <u>Native American</u>, September 6, 1919.

EASCHIEF, MANUEL (Pima)
1116N "Painting," <u>Native American</u>, June 15, 1907.

EASCHIEF, OLDHAM (Pima)
1117N "A Short History of the Phoenix Indian School," <u>Native American</u>, April 4, 1908.

EASTMAN, CHARLES ALEXANDER (Sioux)
1118A "An Indian Collegian's Speech," <u>Southern Workman</u>, 17 (December, 1888), 128.

1119N "Sioux Mythology," <u>Popular Science</u>, 46 (November, 1894), 88-91.

1120A Address at Carlisle Commencement, <u>Red Man</u>, 15 (February-March, 1899), 9.

1121F "The Making of a Prophet," <u>Red Man</u>, 15 (December, 1899), 2.

1122N "Notes of a Trip to the Southwest," <u>Red Man</u>, 16 (May, 1900), 4.

1123F "An Indian Festival," <u>Red Man</u>, 16 (June, 1900), 2.

1124N "A True Story with Several Morals," <u>Red Man</u>, 16 (June, 1900), 8.

1125N "The Story of the Little Big Horn," <u>Chautauquan</u>, 31 (July, 1900), 353-358.

1126F "A Chipmunk Hunt," <u>Red Man and Helper</u>, September 7, 1900. Reprinted from <u>St. Nicholas</u>.

1127N <u>Indian Boyhood</u>. New York: McClure, Phillips & Co., 1902. Reprinted in 1907 and 1908.

1128F "Hakadah's First Offering," <u>Current Literature</u>, 34 (January, 1903), 29-32.

1129A "Indian Traits," <u>Southern Workman</u>, 32 (April, 1903), 225-227.

1130F "The Great Cat's Nursery," <u>Harper's Monthly Magazine</u>, 107 (November, 1903), 939-946.

1131N "First Impressions of Civilization," <u>Harper's Monthly Magazine</u>, 108 (March, 1904), 587-592.

1132F "The Gray Chieftain," <u>Harper's Monthly Magazine</u>, 108 (March, 1904), 882-887.

1133F <u>Red Hunters and the Animal People</u>. New York: Harper & Brothers, 1904. Reprinted in 1905.

1134F "The Madness of Bald Eagle," <u>Southern Workman</u>, 34 (March, 1905), 141-143.

1135N "Indian Handicrafts," <u>Craftsman</u>, 8 (August, 1905), 658-662.

1136F "Grave of the Dog," <u>Metropolitan Magazine</u>, 23 (February, 1906), 569.

1137N "Dr. Eastman's Hiawatha," <u>Indian School Journal</u>, 6 (April, 1906), 59-60.

1138N "Re-Naming the Indians," <u>Indian School Journal</u>, 6 (July, 1906), 31-32.

1139F "War Maiden of the Sioux," Ladies Home Journal, 23 (August, 1906), 14.

1140F "Rain-in-the-face: The Story of a Sioux Warrior," Outlook, 84 (October 27, 1906), 507-512.

1141N "The School Days of an Indian," Outlook, 85 (April 13 and 20, 1907), 851-856, 894-899.

1142F Old Indian Days. New York: McClure Company, 1907.

1143F With Elaine Goodale Eastman. Wigwam Evenings; Sioux Folk Tales Retold by Charles A. Eastman (Ohiyesa) and Elaine Goodale Eastman. Boston: Little, Brown, and Company, [1909]. Reprinted in 1919, 1922, and 1932.

1144N "Adventures of My Uncle," Indian School Journal, 10 (October, 1910), 38-43.

1145N "A Winter's Camp," Indian School Journal, 11 (December, 1910), 11-14.

1146N Indian Boyhood. Garden City: Doubleday, Page & Company, 1910. Reprinted in 1914.

1147F Old Indian Days. New York: Doubleday, Page & Co., 1910.

1148M With Elaine Goodale Eastman. Smoky Day's Wigwam Evenings; Indian Stories Retold. Boston: Little, Brown, and Company, 1910. Reprinted in 1917 and 1920.

1149N "The Indian and the Moral Code," Outlook, 97 (January 7, 1911), 30-34.

1150N "A Canoe Trip Among the Northern Ojibways," Red Man, 3 (February, 1911), 235-244.

1151N "Indian Code of Honor," Indian School Journal, 11 (May, 1911), 44-46.

1152N "Life and Handicrafts of the Northern Ojibwas," Southern Workman, 40 (May, 1911), 273-278.

1153N "The Wild Rice Harvest," Indian Leader, October 27, 1911.

1154N The Soul of the Indian; An Interpretation. Boston: Houghton Mifflin Company, 1911.

1155N "Education without Books," Craftsman, 21 (January, 1912), 372-377.

1156N "The Last of the Algonquins," Travel, 18 (January, 1912), 19-22.

1157N Indian Child Life. Boston: Little, Brown, and Company, 1913. Reprinted in 1914, 1925, and 1926.

1158F Indianerdrengen Ohiyesa; Barndomserindringer. København: V. Prior, 1913.

1159F Ohijesa; Jugenderinnerungen eines Sioux-Indianers. Hamburg: Agentur des Rauhen Hauses, 1913.

1160N "My People: The Indians' Contribution to the Art of America," Craftsman, 27 (November, 1914), 179-186.

1161N "'My People:' The Indians' Contribution to the Art of America," Red Man, 7 (December, 1914), 133-140.

1162N "The Indian in School," Journal of Education, 80 (December 31, 1914), 653-654.

1163N Indian Scout Talks; A Guide for Boy Scouts and Campfire Girls. Boston: Little, Brown, and Company, 1914. Reprinted in 1915.

1164N "The Indian as a Citizen," Lippincott's, 95 (January, 1915), 70-76.

1165N   "The Indian's Health Problem," Popular Science Monthly, 86 (January, 1915), 49-54.

1166N   "The Indian's Gifts to the Nation," Quarterly Journal of the Society of American Indians, 3 (January-March, 1915), 17-23.

1167N   "The Indian's Health Problem," Review of Reviews, 51 (February, 1915), 240-241.

1168N   The Indian To-day; The Past and Future of the First American. Garden City, NY: Doubleday, Page & Company, 1915.

1169N   "The Indian's Health Problem," American Indian Magazine, 4 (April-June, 1916), 139-145.

1170N   From the Deep Woods to Civilization; Chapters in the Autobiography of an Indian. Boston: Little, Brown, and Company, 1916. Reprinted in 1920 and 1925.

1171N   "The Language of Footprints," St. Nicholas, 44 (January, 1917), 267-269.

1172N   "The Sioux of Yesterday and Today," American Indian Magazine, 5 (October-December, 1917), 233-239.

1173N   Indian Heroes and Great Chieftains. Boston: Little, Brown, and Company, 1918. Reprinted in 1924.

1174N   "The American Eagle an Indian Symbol," American Indian Magazine, 7 (Spring, 1919), 89-96.

1175N   "Justice for the Sioux," American Indian Magazine, 7 (Spring, 1919), 79-81.

1176N   "The Indian's Plea for Freedom," American Indian Magazine, 6 (Winter, 1919), 162-165.

1177N   "A Review of the Indian Citizenship Bills," American Indian Magazine, 6 (Winter, 1919), 181-183.

1178N   "What Can the Out-of-doors Do for Our Children?" Education, 41 (May, 1921), 599-605.

1179N   Indian Boyhood. Boston: Little, Brown, and Company, 1922. Reprinted in 1924, 1927, 1929, 1930, and 1933.

1180N   "The Indian Family Altar," Indian, October, 1922.

1181F   With Elaine Goodale Eastman. Vecery ve wigwamu; Povidky Siouxského kmene vypravované Karlen A. Eastmanem (Ohiyesa) a Helenou Goodale Eastmanovou. Praze: J. Laichter, 1922.

1182F   Ohijesa; Jugenderinnerungen eines Sioux-Indianers. Hamburg: Ernte-Verlag, [1923].

EASTMAN, PETER (Sioux)

1183N   "Farming," Carlisle Arrow, May 16, 1913.

1184N   "The Skating Pond," Carlisle Arrow, May 16, 1913.

EATON, RACHAEL CAROLINE (Cherokee)

1185N   John Ross and the Cherokee Indians. Menasha, WI: George Banta Publishing Company, 1914.

1186N   John Ross and the Cherokee Indians. Muskogee, OK: Star Printery, Inc., 1921.

EDDLEMAN, ORA V. (Cherokee)
See REED, ORA V. EDDLEMAN

EDMONDSON, BULA (Cherokee)
1187A "Our Alma Mater," Tahlequah Arrow, June 7, 1902.

ELLIS, ESTELLA W. (Sac and Fox)
1188M "The Raccoon and the Opossum," Red Man, 3 (April, 1911), 344.

ELM, CORA (Oneida)
1189M "The Creation of the Earth," Carlisle Arrow, February 14, 1913.
1190F With Iva Metoxen. "First Book of the Chronicles of the Class of 1913," Carlisle Arrow, May 16, 1913.
1191N "My Outing," Carlisle Arrow, May 16, 1913.
1192M "The Creation of the Earth," Red Man, 6 (September, 1913), 30.

EMERSON, CALVIN (Pima)
1193A "The Returned Students' Failure," Native American, April 1, 1916.

ENAS, LASALLE (Pima)
1194N "Health in the Home," Native American, May 20, 1911.

ENMEGAHBOWH (Chippewa)
1195L The Church and the Indians ... Letter from the Rev. J. J. Enmegahbowh [on] the Death of Chief I. H. Tuttle. New York: Office of the Indian Commissioner, Protestant Episcopal Church, [1874?].
1196N En-me-gah-bowh's Story. An Account of the Disturbances of the Chippewa Indians at Gull Lake in 1857 and 1862, and Their Removal in 1868. Minneapolis: Woman's Auxiliary, St. Barnabas Hospital, 1904.

ENOS, JOHNSON (Pima)
1197M "A Pima Indian Legend," Red Man, 3 (October, 1910), 75-76.
1198M "A Pima Indian Legend," Native American, November 5, 1910.
1199N "Advantages of Indians Being Farmers," Native American, May 24, 1913.

ESTES, JOSEPH FOLSOM (Sioux)
1200N "Indian Debating Society," Southern Workman, 13 (April, 1884), 42.

ETHELBA, KAY (Apache)
1201N "Growth," Native American, May 24, 1902.

ETTAWAGESHIK, J. WILLIAM (Ottawa)
1202M "The Maple Sugar Sand," Red Man, 3 (January, 1911), 206-207.
1203N "The 'White House,'" Carlisle Arrow, April 21, 1911.
1204F "An Indian Practical Joke," Indian's Friend, 23 (June, 1911), 11.

1205M "The Formation of Gold," Red Man, 4 (September, 1911), 26.

1206M ["The Origin of Gold,"] Indian's Friend, 24 (September, 1911), 3.

EUBANKS, WILLIAM (Cherokee)

1207L "Magnetism--What Is It?" Cherokee Advocate, January 19, 1883.

1208N "The Celestial Stranger--No. 1," Cherokee Advocate, January 11, 1884.

1209N "The Celestial Stranger--No. 2," Cherokee Advocate, January 18, 1884.

1210N "Meteorites Nothing but Terrestrial Products," Cherokee Advocate, March 7, 1884.

1211N "Is the Universe of Stars a Piece of Limestone or Is It a Celestial Mud Puddle," Cherokee Advocate, April 18, 1884.

1212L "What Does It Mean?" Indian Chieftain, April 7, 1887.

1213L "'Theosophy' or Wisdom Religion and Its Opponents," Cherokee Advocate, October 26, 1892.

1214T Constitution and Laws of the Cherokee Nation. Published by an Act of the National Council, 1892. n. p., 1893.

1215N "The Seed of the Plant and the Spirit of Man," Cherokee Advocate, January 17, 1894.

1216N "The Red Race," Cherokee Advocate, January 12, 1901.

1217N "The New Age," Cherokee Advocate, January 19, 1901.

1218M "Cherokee Legend of the Son of Man," Wagoner Record, January 24, 1901. Reprinted from Cherokee Advocate.

1219N "Destruction of the Cherokee People in 1901," Cherokee Advocate, April 20, 1901.

FERRIS, GEORGE (Klamath)

1220N "Evolution of Indian Education," Red Man and Helper, March 22, 1901.

FIELDS, ARTHUR (Pawnee)

1221N "Calisthenics," Bacone Chief. Bacone, OK: Bacone College, 1924, p. 128.

1222N "Science Department," Bacone Chief. Bacone, OK: Bacone College, 1924, p. 108.

FIELDS, RICHARD (Cherokee)

1223L Letter, Cherokee Phoenix and Indians' Advocate, September 9, 1829.

FIELDS, RICHARD H. (Cherokee)

1224L Letter, Cherokee Advocate, March 31, 1882.

1225L Letter, Cherokee Advocate, April 20, 1883.

1226N "Contentment," Cherokee Advocate, August 17, 1883.

1227N "Starting in Life," Cherokee Advocate, August 24, 1883.

1228N "The Honor of Filling Well One's Station in Life," Cherokee Advocate, August 31, 1883.

1229N   "Retrospection," Cherokee Advocate, November 30, 1883.
1230N   "The Annual Fair," Cherokee Advocate, September 12, 1884.
1231N   "By No Means High Standing," Cherokee Advocate, September 19, 1884.
1232N   "Cherokee Orphan Asylum," Indian Chieftain, June 25, 1885.
1233L   "What Is That to Be?" Indian Chieftain, September 29, 1885.
1234N   "Christmas," Indian Chieftain, December 17, 1885.
1235N   "Practical Talents," Cherokee Advocate, February 5, 1886.
1236L   "The Negro," Cherokee Advocate, May 12, 1886.
1237N   "Slander and Prejudice," Indian Chieftain, September 2, 1886.
1238L   "Political," Indian Chieftain, November 4, 1886.
1239L   "Political Dots from Saline," Telephone, August 2, 1889.
1240N   "Honorable Joel B. Mayes," Cherokee Advocate, February 10, 1892.
1241N   "Living Temples," Cherokee Advocate, December 9, 1893.
1242N   "In Memoriam," Indian Sentinel, February 18, 1898.
1243N   "In Memory of Brice Adair," Indian Sentinel, June 10, 1898.
1244L   "Advice to Young Men," Indian Sentinel, November 24, 1898.
1245N   "Read for a Purpose," Indian Sentinel, February 23, 1899.

FINLEY, MINNIE (Caddo)
1246N   "Out of the Bay into the Ocean," Red Man, 15 (February-March, 1899), 3.

FIRE THUNDER, ELLA (Sioux)
1247N   "An Indian Childhood," Southern Workman, 26 (February, 1897), 29-30.
1248N   "To Hampton and Back," Southern Workman, 26 (April, 1897), 71.

FISH, CHARLES L. (Sioux)
1249N   "The Stone Arrow Heads," Red Man, 3 (March, 1911), 298-299.

FISHER, HENRY CLAY (Creek)
1250L   ["Education"], Indian Journal, March 3, 1881.
1251L   Letter, Cherokee Advocate, April 11, 1884.

FISHER, WILLIAM (Creek)
1252L   "School Matters," Muskogee Phoenix, June 21, 1888.

FLAME, SYLVESTER (Yuma)
1253A   "The Desert," Native American, June 3, 1905.

FLOOD, HENRY J. (Sioux)
1254A   "Haskell Business Graduate's Idea of Debit and Credit," Indian Leader, June, 1914.

FOLSOM, DON D. (Choctaw)

1255L "A Choctaw's Views," Indian Chieftain, March 29, 1894.
1256N "Allotment," Wagoner Record, April 6, 1894.

FOLSOM, ISRAEL (Choctaw)
1257P "Lo! The Poor Indian's Hope," Vindicator, May 1, 1875.
1258N "Choctaw Traditions," Vindicator, November 3, 10, 17, 24, and December 1, 8, and 22, 1875.
1259N "Choctaw Traditions," Indian Journal, October 4, 1883.

FOLSOM, JOSEPH P. (Choctaw)
1260C Constitution and Laws of the Choctaw Nation. New York: W. P. Lyon & Son, 1869.
1261L "The Tax Law," Vindicator, June 14, 1876.

FONTENELLE, EUGENE (Omaha)
1262N "Our Summer Out," Southern Workman, 17 (January, 1888), 8.

FOREMAN, HARRISON (Cherokee)
1263L "After the Judge," Indian Chieftain, September 10, 1890.

FOREMAN, STEPHEN (Cherokee)
1264N "'Set de Furder, Set de Furder,'" Cherokee Advocate, October 12, 1878.
1265N "Forty Years Ago," Cherokee Advocate, September 17, 1879.
1266N "Green Leaf," Cherokee Advocate, January 7, 1880.

FOSTER, WIMMIE (Paiute)
1267N "Agriculture and Nature Study," Native American, June 15, 1907.

FRECHETTE, JULIA (Chippewa)
1268N "My Trip to Carlisle," Carlisle Arrow, June 4, 1915.

FREEMAN, ALBERT B. (Sioux)
1269A "The American Indian's Appeal," American Indian Magazine, 5 (April-June, 1917), 89-92.

FREEMAN, THEODORE R. (Creek)
1270A "Salutatory," Senior Class Annual. Chilocco, OK: Chilocco Indian School, 1924.

FREEMONT, HENRIETTA R. (Omaha)
1271N "Specialties," Red Man, 12 (February, 1895), 4.

FRENCH, WILLIAM (Cherokee)
1272N "Going to School," Children's Play Ground, August 9, 1881.

FRIDAY, MOSES (Arapaho)
1273M "Arapaho Tradition of Creation," Red Man, 3 (January, 1911), 209-210.
1274F "The Morning and Evening Star," Red Man, 3 (January, 1911), 202-203.
1275N "The Cave," Carlisle Arrow, April 11, 1911.

FROST, ALICE (Crow)
1276N   "Minnehaha Literary Society," <u>Bacone Chief</u>. Bacone, OK:
        Bacone College, 1924, p. 82.
1277F   "We-ja-ka-chaw's Hunting Trip," <u>Bacone Chief</u>. Bacone,
        OK: Bacone College, 1924, p. 84.

FULLER, ELSIE (Omaha)
1278P   "A New Citizen," <u>Talks and Thoughts of the Hampton Indi-</u>
        <u>an Students</u>, 2 (April, 1887), 1.
1279P   "I'm a Citizen," <u>Southern Workman</u>, 16 (May, 1887), 56.

FULWILDER, PENROSE (Little Lake, or Mitomkai Pomo)
1280N   "My People," <u>Native American</u>, May 15, 1909.

GABRIEL, CHRISTIANA (Serrano)
1281N   "The Fiestas of the Seranno [sic] Indians," <u>Red Man</u>, 3
        (February, 1911), 254-255.
1282N   "Stories of the Serrano," <u>Red Man</u>, 4 (October, 1911), 82.

GADDY, VIRGINIA (Delaware)
1283N   "The Adoption Dance," <u>Red Man</u>, 4 (January, 1912), 210.

GANSWORTH, HOWARD (Tuscarora)
1284A   Address at Carlisle Commencement, <u>Red Man</u>, 15 (February-
        March, 1899), 10.
1285A   "The American Indian," <u>Red Man and Helper</u>, September 7,
        1900.
1286L   In Michigan, <u>Red Man and Helper</u>, October 24, 1902.
1287A   Address Before the Wilmington, Delaware, Young Men's
        Christian Association, <u>Red Man and Helper</u>, January 16,
        1903.

GANSWORTH, LEANDER (Tuscarora)
1288P   ["Come Now Thou Bright and Sunny Spring,"] <u>Red Man</u>, 12
        (May, 1895), 5.

GARDNER, LUCIE (Sioux)
1289N   "Value of Domestic Training," <u>Indian Leader</u>, July 4, 1902.

GAREN, MARY (Iroquois)
1290N   "Good Bread and Butter," <u>Chilocco Annual</u>. Chilocco, OK:
        Chilocco Indian School, 1920, p. 38.

GARLOW, WILLIAM (Tuscarora)
1291N   "Possibilities in Spare Moments," <u>Carlisle Arrow</u>, May 16,
        1913.

GARVIE, JAMES WILLIAM (Sioux)
1292P   "The Broad Highway," <u>Carlisle Arrow</u>, June 4, 1915.
1293N   "Room No. 14," <u>Carlisle Arrow</u>, June 4, 1915.

GARVIN, ISAAC L. (Choctaw)
   1294A "Message of I. L. Garvin, Principal Chief of the Choctaw
         Nation, to the National Council," Indian Journal, Novem-
         ber 13, 1879.

GASHOIENIM, NORA (Hopi)
   1295F "A Hopi Indian Story," Native American, June 15, 1907.

GEORGE, DAHNEY E. (Cherokee)
   1296N "The Origin of Some Indian Mounds," Red Man, 15 (February-
         March, 1899), 6.

GEORGE, LEWIS (Klamath)
   1297M "Tradition of the Crows," Red Man, 2 (June, 1910), 42.
   1298M "Tradition of the Crows," Indian's Friend, 22 (June, 1910),
         5.
   1299M "Tradition of the Crows," Southern Workman, 44 (June,
         1915), 334.

GIBBS, ADIN C. (Delaware)
   1300P "The Cornwall Seminary," Indian Chieftain, May 6, 1886.

GIBSON, CHARLES (Creek)
   1301N "Last Rebel Shot," Muskogee Phoenix, November 28, 1895.
   1302N "A 'Medicine Man's Examination,'" Twin Territories, 1
         (December, 1899), 13.
   1303N "Creek Indian Traditions," Cherokee Advocate, September
         29, 1900. Reprinted from Indian Journal.
   1304N "An Indian Pow-Wow," Indian Journal, December 7, 1900.
   1305N "A Creek Camp Hunt," Indian Journal, January 4, 1901.
   1306N "The Indians' Christmas," Indian Journal, January 4, 1901.
   1307N "Some Indians Have No Christmas Day," Wagoner Record,
         January 10, 1901.
   1308N "How Lo, the Poor Indian Does It," Indian Journal, Janu-
         ary 11, 1901.
   1309N "Old-Time Camp Hunts of the Creek Indians," Wagoner
         Record, January 17, 1901.
   1310N "Kee-to-wah," Indian Journal, January 18, 1901.
   1311N "The Kee-too-wahs," Wagoner Record, January 24, 1901.
   1312N "The Kee-to-wahs," Tahlequah Arrow, January 26, 1901.
   1313N "The Is-Spo-Ko-Kee Creek," Twin Territories, 3 (March,
         1901), 49-50.
   1314N "The Indian Clown," Indian Journal, March 22, 1901.
   1315N "Indian Tradition," Indian Journal, March 29, 1901.
   1316N "Who Are the Philippinos?" Indian Journal, April 5, 1901.
   1317N "An Old Curio," Indian Journal, May 3, 1901.
   1318N "Happiness," Indian Journal, May 10, 1901.
   1319N "Did You Ever Think of It?" Indian Journal, May 24, 1901.
   1320N "Whiskey Robs Indians of Their Self-Respect," Red Man
         and Helper, May 31, 1901. Reprinted from Indian Jour-
         nal.
   1321N "More Indian Tradition," Indian Journal, June 7, 1901.
   1322N "Passing of Creek Lands," Indian Journal, June 21, 1901.

1323M "The Sky Cha-Cul-La," Indian Journal, June 28, 1901.

1324N "The Creek Treaty," Twin Territories, 3 (July, 1901), 136.

1325N ["Removal of the Creeks,"] Times-Record (Blackwell), March 5, 1903. Reprinted from Kansas City Journal.

1326N "Old Fashion Creek Hunt," Indian Journal, July 7, 1901.

1327N "American Grit," Indian Journal, July 19, 1901.

1328N "Indian Festivities," Indian Journal, July 19, 1901.

1329N "Where Our Lands Are Gone," Indian Journal, July 26, 1901.

1330N "Indian Bugaboo," Indian Journal, August 2, 1901.

1331N "His Glory Gone," Indian Journal, August 16, 1901.

1332N "Water Works," Indian Journal, August 23, 1901.

1333N "They Like Muskmelons," Indian Journal, August 23, 1901.

1334N "Centipede War," Indian Journal, August 23, 1901.

1335N "Creek Lands," Indian Journal, August 23, 1901.

1336N "The Younger Bend Again," Indian Journal, August 23, 1901.

1337N "The Would-be and the Has-been's," Indian Journal, August 30, 1901.

1338N "The Younger Bend Again," Muskogee Daily Phoenix, August 30, 1901.

1339N "Supplementary Treaty," Indian Journal, September 6, 1901.

1340N "The Indian Schools," Indian Journal, September 13, 1901.

1341N "The Horse Thief Harbor," Indian Journal, September 27, 1901.

1342N "Creek Law of Descent," Indian Journal, September 27, 1901.

1343N "The Big Indian," Indian Journal, September 27, 1901.

1344M "Where the Creeks Came From," Indian Journal, September 27, 1901.

1345N "The School Question," Indian Journal, September 27, 1901.

1346N "Creek Land Deeds," Indian Journal, November 8, 1901.

1347N "Creek Towns," Indian Journal, November 22, 1901.

1348N "A Good Move," Indian Journal, November 22, 1901.

1349N "Some Peculiarities of an Indian," Indian Journal, November 22, 1901.

1350N "Lasting Friendship," Indian Journal, November 22, 1901.

1351N "How the Creek Indian Used to Raise His Children," Indian Journal, November 29, 1901.

1352N "Creek Deeds Again," Indian Journal, November 29, 1901.

1353N "Mr. Indian Must Work," Indian Journal, December 6, 1901.

1354F "The Indian and the Devil," Indian Journal, December 20, 1901.

1355N "The Passing of the Indian," Indian Journal, January 3, 1902.

1356F "The Colored Man's Story of Providence," Indian Journal, January 17, 1902.

1357F "David and Jonathan," Indian Journal, January 17, 1902.

1358F "How Se-Mah-Tee Conquered," Indian Journal, January 17, 1902.

1359N "Old Land-Marks of Eufaula," Indian Journal, January 24, 1902.

1360N   "Creek War Whoop," Indian Journal, January 31, 1902.

1361M   "The Dwarf or Charmed Deer," Indian Journal, January 31, 1902.

1362N   "An Indian Funeral," Indian Journal, February 7, 1902.

1363N   "The Old Haunts by Moonlight," Indian Journal, February 7, 1902.

1364N   "Another Indian Funeral," Indian Journal, February 14, 1902.

1365N   "Government Offices," Indian Journal, February 14, 1902.

1366N   "What a Change," Indian Journal, February 21, 1902.

1367N   "Pluck or Luck, Honesty or Cowardice," Indian Journal, February 28, 1902.

1368F   "A Creek Fable," Twin Territories, 4 (March, 1902), 63-65.

1369N   "That United States Flag," Indian Journal, March 7, 1902.

1370N   "An Unrecorded Run for a Home in Oklahoma," Indian Journal, March 14, 1902.

1371F   "Why a Coon Is So Black Around His Eyes," Indian Journal, March 14, 1902.

1372N   "About an Indian," Indian Journal, March 21, 1902.

1373N   "Don't All Speak at Once," Indian Journal, March 21, 1902.

1374N   "The Passing of the Creek Dirt Dauber," Indian Journal, March 21, 1902.

1375F   "The Story of the Dead Wife," Indian Journal, March 28, 1902.

1376N   "About an Indian," Tahlequah Arrow, March 29, 1902.

1377N   "The Passing of the Indian," Twin Territories, 4 (April, 1902), 93-94.

1378N   "About an Indian," Chickasaw Enterprise, April 3, 1902.

1379N   "Education of the Indian," Indian Journal, April 4, 1902.

1380F   "The Old Gent's Conversion," Indian Journal, April 11, 1902.

1381N   "Insane Asylum for Indians," Indian Journal, April 18, 1902.

1382N   "Snake Root," Indian Journal, April 18, 1902.

1383N   "Creek Indian Lands," Native American, April 19, 1902.

1384N   "Bad Roads," Indian Journal, April 25, 1902.

1385N   "Game Protection," Indian Journal, April 25, 1902.

1386N   "Creek Buffalo Hunt," Indian Journal, May 9, 1902.

1387N   "Our Raid," Indian Journal, May 9, 1902.

1388N   "The Indian: His Past," Indian Journal, May 16, 1902.

1389N   "The Indian--His Present," Indian Journal, May 23, 1902.

1390N   "The Indian--His Future," Indian Journal, June 6, 1902.

1391N   "Ye Old Tyme Indian," Tahlequah Arrow, June 7, 1902.

1392N   "A Yamping Scrape," Indian Journal, June 13, 1902.

1393N   "A Dream of Creek Deeds," Indian Journal, June 20, 1902.

1394N   "We Have Been There," Indian Journal, June 20, 1902.

1395N   "The Indian's Future," Tahlequah Arrow, June 21, 1902.

1396N   "Creek Summer Resorts," Indian Journal, June 27, 1902.

1397N   "The Indian a Genius," Indian Journal, June 27, 1902.

1398N   "The Indian--His Present," Red Man and Helper, July 4, 1902.

1399N   "Teddy," Indian Journal, July 4, 1902.

1400N "The Way of the Spokogee," Indian Journal, July 4, 1902.
1401N "The Indian's Land Deals," Indian Journal, July 11, 1902.
1402N "Not in It," Indian Journal, July 11, 1902.
1403N "Red Whiskey," Indian Journal, July 18, 1902.
1404N "An Incident of the Rebellion," Indian Journal, July 18, 1902.
1405N "More About the Spokogees," Indian Journal, July 25, 1902.
1406F "Old Hickory," Indian Journal, July 25, 1902.
1407N ["Uncle Dick,"] Tahlequah Arrow, July 26, 1902.
1408N "Passing of the Indian's Religion," Indian Journal, August 1, 1902.
1409N "Raising the Dead," Indian Journal, August 1, 1902.
1410N "A Relic of Other Days," Indian Journal, August 1, 1902.
1411N "The Spokogees," Tahlequah Arrow, August 2, 1902.
1412N "As It's Done in the B. I. T.," Indian Journal, August 15, 1902.
1413N "Wakachee," Indian Journal, August 15, 1902.
1414N "The Red Stick War," Indian Journal, August 22, 1902.
1415N "'All's Well That Ends Well,'" Indian Journal, September 5, 1902.
1416N "An Indian's Revenge," Indian Journal, September 5, 1902.
1417N "Council Ground Hill," Indian Journal, September 12, 1902.
1418N "The Creek Five Merchants," Indian Journal, September 12, 1902.
1419N "When Sow Bosom Was Dear," Indian Journal, September 12, 1902.
1420N "Observation," Indian Journal, September 19, 1902.
1421N "Stan Watie," Indian Journal, September 19, 1902.
1422N "Telling It 'Scarery,'" Indian Journal, September 19, 1902.
1423N "The Promised Land," Indian Journal, September 26, 1902.
1424N "Things That Move at Night," Indian Journal, September 26, 1902.
1425F "Wild Cat's Long Swim," Twin Territories, 4 (October, 1902), 300-301.
1426N "The Creek Deeds," Indian Journal, October 3, 1902.
1427N "When Ft. Smith Was Boss," Indian Journal, October 3, 1902.
1428N "The Indian's Beliefs and Disbeliefs," Indian Journal, October 10, 1902.
1429N "An Indian Advises the Indians," Indian Journal, October 17, 1902.
1430N "As Charles Gibson Saw It," Indian Journal, October 17, 1902.
1431F "Wild Cat's Long Swim," Indian Journal, October 17, 1902.
1432N "The Indian's Beliefs and Disbeliefs," Tahlequah Arrow, October 18, 1902.
1433N "Indian Beliefs," Chickasaw Enterprise, October 23, 1902.
1434N "The Big Powwow," Indian Journal, October 24, 1902.
1435N "The Dependent Indian," Indian Journal, October 24, 1902.
1436N "Died with Their Boots On," Indian Journal, October 24, 1902.
1437N "The Indian's Notion About the Soul," Indian Journal, October 24, 1902.

1438N   "Lost: Three Thousand Deeds," Indian Journal, October 24, 1902.

1439N   "A Seminole," Indian Journal, October 24, 1902.

1440N   "How the Mighty Have Fallen," Indian Journal, October 31, 1902.

1441N   "The Indian's Rumination," Indian Journal, October 31, 1902.

1442N   "Should Pass a Stock Law," Indian Journal, November 7, 1902.

1443N   "A Slight Touch of Civilization," Indian Journal, November 7, 1902.

1444N   "A Dream," Indian Journal, November 14, 1902.

1445N   "The Great Physician," Indian Journal, November 14, 1902.

1446N   "What We Saw Last Saturday," Indian Journal, November 14, 1902.

1447N   "About Fish Killing," Indian Journal, November 21, 1902.

1448N   "As to Statehood," Indian Journal, November 21, 1902.

1449N   "Hard Luck," Indian Journal, November 28, 1902.

1450N   "The Great Powwow," Indian Journal, December 5, 1902.

1451N   "The Indian and the Water," Indian Journal, December 12, 1902.

1452N   "Through the Land of the Longhorns," Indian Journal, December 12, 1902.

1453N   "What the Wild Waves Said," Indian Journal, December 12, 1902.

1454N   "A Three Cornered Fight," Indian Journal, December 19, 1902.

1455N   "The Creek Deeds," Indian Journal, December 19, 1902.

1456N   "Indeed Monstrous," Indian Journal, December 19, 1902.

1457N   "And It Rained," Indian Journal, December 26, 1902.

1458N   "Another Ramble," Indian Journal, December 26, 1902.

1459N   "As to Statehood Again," Indian Journal, December 26, 1902.

1460N   "Isparhecher's Anecdote," Indian Journal, January 2, 1903.

1461N   "The Other Side," Indian Journal, January 2, 1903.

1462N   "Prophet Wachache," Indian Journal, January 2, 1903.

1463N   "Dustin, I. T.," Indian Journal, January 9, 1903.

1464N   "Looking Backward," Indian Journal, January 9, 1903.

1465N   "Loss of Domains," Indian Journal, January 9, 1903.

1466F   "An Indian Squirrel Hunt," Indian Journal, January 16, 1903.

1467N   "The Indian Victimized," Indian Journal, January 16, 1903.

1468N   "Looking Backward," Indian Journal, January 16, 1903.

1469N   "What We Saw on a Hunt," Cherokee Advocate, January 31, 1903.

1470F   "Why the Lion Eats His Meat Raw," Twin Territories, 5 (February, 1903), 61-62.

1471N   "The Creek Deeds," Indian Journal, February 13, 1903.

1472N   "The Future of the Creek Nation," Indian Journal, February 20, 1903.

1473N   "Enterprise of Eufaula," Indian Journal, February 27, 1903.

1474N   "Indian Land Claimants," Indian Journal, February 27, 1903.

1475N   "Pocahontas Was a Creek," Tahlequah Arrow, February 28, 1903.

1476N   "Indian Proverb," Twin Territories, 5 (March, 1903), 115.

1477N   "The Rebellion of 1860," Indian Journal, March 6, 1903.

1478N   "Capache Ematha," Red Man and Helper, March 13, 1903.

1479N   "Is Life Worth Living?" Indian Journal, March 13, 1903.

1480N   "A Sure Thing," Indian Journal, March 13, 1903.

1481N   "Indian Proverbs," Indian Journal, March 20, 1903.

1482N   "No One to Lend a Hand," Indian Journal, March 27, 1903.

1483N   "Ispaheche," Indian Journal, April 3, 1903.

1484N   "Cutting and Slashing," Indian Journal, April 10, 1903.

1485N   "Ispaheche's War Story," Cherokee Advocate, April 11, 1903.

1486N   "Who Cares?" Indian Journal, April 17, 1903.

1487N   "Eufaula, I. T.," Indian Journal, April 24, 1903.

1488N   "Sacred Relics," Indian Journal, May 1, 1903.

1489N   "Now and Then," Indian Journal, May 8, 1903.

1490N   "Exacting Leases," Indian Journal, May 15, 1903.

1491N   "Too Much Expected of Him," Indian Journal, May 29, 1903.

1492N   "Our Country as a State," Indian Journal, June 5, 1903.

1493N   "Some More Creek Relics," Indian Journal, June 5, 1903.

1494N   "Paying Dirt," Indian Journal, June 12, 1903.

1495N   "About Anybody's Politics," Indian Journal, June 26, 1903.

1496N   "Luck," Indian Journal, August 14, 1903.

1497N   "An Indian's View of Indians," Chilocco Farmer and Stock Grower, 3 (July, 1903), 482.

1498F   ["The Wolf and the Rabbit,"] Twin Territories, 5 (July, 1903), 255-257.

1499N   "The Last on Earth," Indian Journal, September 4, 1903.

1500F   "A Creek Fable," Muskogee Phoenix, September 10, 1903.

1501N   "A Creek Custom," Red Man and Helper, January 22, 1904.

1502N   "The Indian's Religion," Cherokee Advocate, August 13, 1904.

1503N   "The Indian's Religion," Muskogee Democrat, August 15, 1904.

1504N   "Gibson's Indian Lore: Unpublished History by Charles Gibson," Cherokee Advocate, August 20, 1904.

1505N   "Reminiscent," Muskogee Democrat, August 22, 1904.

1506N   "Gibson's Rifle Shots," Cherokee Advocate, September 10, 1904.

1507N   "Gibson's Rifle Shots," Muskogee Democrat, September 12, 1904.

1508N   "Dog Feast," Indian Journal, September 16, 1904.

1509N   "Gibson's Indian Lore [Dog Feast]," Cherokee Advocate, September 24, 1904.

1510N   "The Way of the Indian," Muskogee Democrat, September 26, 1904.

1511N   ["Future of the Indian,"] Indian Journal, October 7, 1904.

1512N   "School Money," Cherokee Advocate, October 29, 1904.

1513N   "The Creek a Transgressor," Indian Journal, November 11, 1904.

1514N   "How It Feels to Have Them Taken Off," Indian Journal, November 18, 1904.

1515N   "Charles Gibson's Lore," Indian Journal, November 25, 1904.

1516N   "The State of Bone," Indian Journal, December 16, 1904.

1517N   "Gibson's Rifle Shots," Indian Journal, January 20, 1905.

1518N   "Practice on Territory," Tahlequah Arrow, January 21, 1905.

1519N   "The Indian and His Ways," Tahlequah Arrow, January 28, 1905.

1520F   "An Indian Fable," Indian Journal, February 3, 1905.

1521N   "The Red Man and Politics," Indian School Journal, 5 (September, 1905), 23.

1522F   "A Creek Indian Fable," Sturm's Statehood Magazine, 1 (October, 1905), 88-90.

1523N   "The Indian--His Long Trip," Indian Journal, October 6, 13, 20, and 27, 1905.

1524N   "The Native Indian," Indian Journal, December 1, 1905.

1525F   "Gibson's Indian Lore," Muskogee Phoenix, December 28, 1905.

1526N   "A Few More Lone Moons Then Alas for Poor Lo," Muskogee Democrat, January 9, 1906.

1527N   "How the War God Swept Creeks into Famous 'Green Peach' War," Muskogee Democrat, January 15, 1906.

1528N   "Gibson's Rifle Shots," Indian Journal, January 19, 1906.

1529N   "Gibson's Rifle Shots," Indian Journal, January 26, 1906.

1530M   "A Subterranean World," Sturm's Statehood Magazine, 1 (February, 1906), 89-90.

1531N   "Gibson's Rifle Shots," Indian Journal, February 16, 1906.

1532N   "Gibson's Rifle Shots," Indian Journal, February 23, 1906.

1533F   "Wild Cat's Long Swim," Sturm's Statehood Magazine, 2 (March, 1906), 84-85.

1534N   "Some Thirty Years Ago," Muskogee Phoenix, March 1, 1906.

1535N   "Gibson's Rifle Shots," Indian Journal, March 2, 1906.

1536N   "One Thing and Another," Indian Journal, March 9, 1906.

1537N   "Gibson's Indian Lore," Muskogee Phoenix, March 15, 1906.

1538N   "An Indian's Incompetency," Indian Journal, March 16, 1906.

1539N   "In a 25 Pound Flour Sack," Indian Journal, March 16, 1906.

1540N   "Government Guardianship of Lo," New-State Tribune, March 22, 1906.

1541N   "Creek Council," Indian Journal, March 30, 1906.

1542N   "His Days Ended," Indian Journal, March 30, 1906.

1543N   "The Old Song," Indian Journal, May 4, 1906.

1544N   "Why We Are All Full Bloods," Indian Journal, May 4, 1906.

1545N   "Make Your Will," Indian Journal, May 25, 1906.

1546N   "Our Trip to Chicago," Indian Journal, June 1, 1906.

1547N   "Sacred to the Memory," Indian Journal, June 8, 1906.

1548N   "The Full Blooded Indian," New-State Tribune, July 12, 1906.

1549N   "The Indian and Strong Drink," New-State Tribune, July 19, 1906.

1550N "Gibson's Rifle Shots," Indian Journal, June 22, 1906.
1551N "Leap in the Dark," Indian Journal, July 13, 1906. Reprinted from Kansas City World.
1552T "A Full Blood Indian's Story of the Encroachments of the White Man," by Lahta Yahola, Indian Journal, July 20, 1906.
1553N "Gibson's Rifle Shots," Indian Journal, July 27, 1906.
1554N "Something New Under the Sun," Indian Journal, June 28, 1907.
1555N "From the Red Man's Viewpoint," Indian Advocate, 19 (September, 1907), 299-301. Reprinted from Indian School Journal.
1556N "Gibson Talks County Seat," Indian Journal, January 17, 1908.
1557N "Gibson under Statehood," Indian Journal, April 10, 1908.
1558N "Collecting the Price," Indian Journal, April 17, 1908.
1559N "Spring," Indian Journal, April 17, 1908.
1560F "Luck and Last Confederate Gun," Indian Journal, April 24, 1908.
1561N "Este Charte," Indian Journal, May 1, 1908.
1562N "Ready to Make Their Wills," Indian Journal, May 1, 1908.
1563N "Ah-pus-kee," Indian Journal, May 8, 1908.
1564F "An Indian Thinks," Indian Journal, May 8, 1908.
1565N "The Skunk," Indian Journal, May 8, 1908.
1566N "Some Interesting Spots," Indian Journal, May 8, 1908.
1567N "Whence Comes the Snake Indian," Indian Journal, May 15, 1908.
1568N "The Happy Hunting Ground," Indian Journal, May 22, 1908.
1569N "Snakes Without Booze," Indian Journal, June 4, 1908.
1570N "Gone Over to See," Indian Journal, June 5, 1908.
1571N "Tribute to Alex Posey," Muskogee Times Democrat, June 9, 1908.
1572N "We Fear," Indian Journal, June 26, 1908.
1573F "The Indian on the Trail," Indian Journal, July 10, 1908.
1574N "Innocents Imposed Upon," Indian Journal, July 31, 1908.
1575N "Again and Again," Indian Journal, August 14, 1908.
1576N "Lo, the Poor Indian," Indian Journal, September 4, 1908.
1577F "Statehood Among the Indians," Indian Journal, September 25, 1908.
1578N "An Aged Creek Passed Away," Indian Journal, October 9, 1908.
1579N "Thanksgiving," Indian Journal, November 27, 1908.
1580N "The Indian Is Dissatisfied," Indian Journal, February 26, 1909.
1581N "History Repeats Itself," Indian Journal, April 16, 1909.
1582N "One More Appeal," Indian Journal, June 18, 1909.
1583N "How Would It Work?" Indian Journal, April 1, 1910.
1584N "The Mound Builders," Indian Home and Farm, May 14, 1910.

GILMORE, GUS (Apache)
1585A Address, Native American, May 27, 1905.

GIVEN, JOSHUA H. (Kiowa)
1586A "We Come to Tell You," Morning Star, 7 (July, 1887), 7.

GOODY, IDA (Apache)
1587N "Geronimo," Native American, June 16, 1923.

GORDON, JANE ZANE (Wyandot)
1588N "Will Indians Give up Tribal Independence for Newly [sic]
       American Citizenship?" Indian Tepee, 6 (August, 1924),
       2-3.

GORDON, PHILIP B. (Chippewa)
1589N "The Remnants of Powhatan's Tribe," Indian Leader, Sep-
       tember, 1915.
1590N "Catholic Indians to the Fore," War-Whoop, 1 (January,
       1916), 4.
1591N "The Editor's Preliminary Bow," War-Whoop, 1 (January,
       1916), 2.
1592N "The War-Whoop," War-Whoop, 1 (January, 1916), 1-3.
1593N "The Remnants of the Powhatan Tribe," American Indian
       Magazine, 4 (January-March, 1916), 54-56. Reprinted
       from the Missionary.
1594A "Opposition to the Indian Bureau," American Indian Maga-
       zine, 4 (July-September, 1916), 259-260.
1595N "Bishop Baraga," Anishinabwe Enamiad, 1 (April, 1918),
       4.
1596N "The Chippewa Indians," Anishinabwe Enamiad, 1 (April,
       1918), 1.
1597N "Dedication," Anishinabwe Enamiad, 1 (April, 1918), 1.
1598N "Extension of Democracy to the American Indian," Anishin-
       abwe Enamiad, 1 (April, 1918), 5-6.
1599N "Forgiving and Forgetting," Anishinabwe Enamiad, 1 (April,
       1918), 7.
1600N "Introductory," Anishinabwe Enamiad, 1 (April, 1918), 1.
1601N "My Neighbor," Anishinabwe Enamiad, 1 (April, 1918), 7.
1602N "Pointed Paragraphs," Anishinabwe Enamiad, 1 (April,
       1918), 6-7.

GOUGE, JOSEPH J. (Chippewa)
1603N "Our Nation's Demand," Red Man, 15 (February-March,
       1899), 2.

GOULETTE, EMMA D. JOHNSON (Potawatomi)
1604N "Discussion," Native American, January 17, 1903.
1605N "Common School Education for the Indian Child," Quarterly
       Journal of the Society of American Indians, 1 (July-
       September, 1913), 300-304.
1606N "Higher Standards in Civil Service for the Indian School
       Employee," Quarterly Journal of the Society of American
       Indians, 3 (April-June, 1915), 98-103.
1607N "The Returned Girl Student," American Indian Magazine,
       4 (April-June, 1916), 134-138.

GOURD, LOUIS B. R. (Cherokee)
    1608N "The Native American in the World War," Indian Leader,
           June, 1918.

GOYITNEY, ANNIE (Pueblo)
    1609N "What Should Be the Aim of a Carlisle Indian Girl?" Red
           Man and Helper, March 22, 1901.

GRAY, STAND WATIE (Cherokee)
    1610L Letter, Cherokee Advocate, April 4, 1888.

GRAYSON, GEORGE WASHINGTON (Creek)
    1611A "Speech of Hon. G. W. Grayson, Delivered at the Barbe-
           cue Held near Rev. J. M. Perryman's, July 9th," Indi-
           an Journal, August 7, 1879.
    1612N "A Talk on the 'White Settler' Question," Indian Journal,
           June 2, 1881.
    1613L "An Apology," Indian Journal, July 7, 1881.
    1614A Address, Cherokee Advocate, July 20, 1881.
    1615N "Touch Not, Taste Not," Indian Journal, June 7, 1883.
    1616L "From a Voter," Indian Journal, September 20, 1883.
    1617L "The New Orleans Exposition," Indian Journal, April 10,
           1884.
    1618L "The Indian Question," Indian Journal, March 19, 1885.
    1619L "Protest from the Creek Delegation," Indian Journal, Janu-
           ary 5, 1887.
    1620N "Make Haste Slowly," Muskogee Phoenix, October 3, 1889.
    1621L "Statements Are Misleading," Tahlequah Arrow, August 12,
           1905.

GRAYSON, GEORGE WASHINGTON (Creek)
    1622M "The Story of the Tosas," Bacone Chief (Bacone, Okla.:
           Bacone College, 1922), 65-66.

GREEN, FLORA (Cherokee)
    1623N "A Dream," Wreath of Cherokee Rose Buds, August 2,
           1854.

GREEN, TZULKO (Navajo)
    1624N "Home of Lincoln," Native American, February 15, 1908.
    1625N "The Home of Lincoln," Indian's Friend, 21 (October,
           1908), 2.

GREENBRIER, ADELINE (Menominee)
    1626M "The Legend of Pond Lilies," Red Man, 2 (April, 1910), 48.

GREENBRIER, CARLYSLE (Menominee)
    1627F "The Beaver Medicine," Indian Craftsman, 2 (January,
           1910: 17-24.
    1628M "An Indian Story from an Indian Pen," Indian's Friend, 22
           (March, 1910), 8.
    1629M "The Flying Canoe Legend," Red Man, 3 (September, 1910),
           24-25.

GREENSKY, NAOMI EVELYN (Chippewa)
1630N "Our Skating Pond," Carlisle Arrow, June 4, 1915.

GREENWAY, MINNIE (Cherokee)
1631N "Much in Little," Cherokee Advocate, June 23, 1882.

GREGG, CLARK (Assiniboin)
1632N "The Course of Indian Empire Must Be Eastward," Red
     Man, 12 (February, 1895), 5.

GREGORY, JAMES ROANE (Euchee)
1633L "Replies to McKellop," Muskogee Phoenix, April 14, 1892.
1634L "Remarks from Mr. Gregory," Muskogee Phoenix, May 12,
     1892.
1635P "Otheen, Okiyetos," Wagoner Record, June 21, 1895.
1636P "Ram," Wagoner Record, June 21, 1895.
1637P "Home's Chief," Wagoner Record, July 12, 1895.
1638N "Hurrah for Espehecher!" Wagoner Record, July 12, 1895.
1639P A Poem, Entitled Lucy's-Poney. Wagoner, Indian Terri-
     tory: Record Print, 1895.
1640L "Communicated," Muskogee Evening Times, January 20,
     1898.
1641N "Early Creek History," Twin Territories, 1 (November,
     1899), 236-237.
1642N "The Seminoles of Florida," Twin Territories, 2 (February,
     1900), 30-31.
1643L "A New Creed," Wagoner Record, May 10, 1900.
1644L "Beware of the Breakers," Wagoner Record, May 24, 1900.
1645P "The Green Corn Dance," Wagoner Record, August 9, 1900.
1646P "Nineteenth Century Finality," Wagoner Record, August 9,
     1900.
1647P "Life," Wagoner Record, August 16, 1900.
1648N "Cherokee War Magic," Wagoner Record, November 22,
     1900.
1649N "Creek Indian Philosopher," Wagoner Record, November
     29, 1900.
1650N "Some Early History of the Creek Nation," Wagoner Rec-
     ord, January 24, 1901.
1651N "Traditions of the Creek," Indian Journal, February 22,
     1901.
1652N "Historic Numerals of the Creek Indians," Wagoner Rec-
     ord, February 7, 1901.
1653N "Some Creek History of the Civil War," Wagoner Record,
     March 7, 1901.
1654N "Early History of the Creek Nation," Indian Journal, March
     8, 1901. Reprinted from the Star.
1655N "Pawnee Wars," Indian Journal, March 8, 1901.
1656N "Some Creek History of the Civil War," Indian Journal,
     March 15, 1901.
1657N "Meaning of Is-po-ko-kees," Indian Journal, March 15,
     1901.
1658N "The Hee-chee-tees of the Creeks," Indian Journal, April
     19, 1901.

1659N "Euchees of the Creeks," Indian Journal, April 26, 1901.
1660N "The Cherokee Indians," Cherokee Advocate, June 8, 1901.
      Reprinted from Wagoner Record.
1661N "Early Creek History," Sturm's Statehood Magazine, 1
      (October, 1905), 86-87.

GRITTS, DANIEL (Cherokee)
  1662L "Mr. Gritts' Utterances," Indian Chieftain, June 9, 1887.

GRUMBOISE, EMMA (Chippewa)
  1663N "My Experience at a Camp Fire Meeting," Carlisle Arrow,
      October 3, 1913.

GUY, JAMES HARRIS (Chickasaw)
  1664L "A Chickasaw Gives the Facts in the Case," Indian Cham-
      pion, January 10, 1885.
  1665P "Fort Arbuckle." In H. F. O'Beirne, Leaders and Lead-
      ing Men of the Indian Territory. Chicago: American
      Publishers' Association, 1891, p. 213.

HALF BREED, RICHARD (Cherokee)
  1666L "Spring Has Come," Cherokee Advocate, May 4, 1870.

HAMILTON, JOSEPH H. (Piegan)
  1667N "What Is Wrong with the World," Red Man, 11 (May, 1892),
      2.

HAMILTON, ROBERT J. (Piegan)
  1668N "The Picnic," Red Man, 11 (June and July, 1892), 3.
  1669N "The Backbone of Indian Civilization," Montanian, July 24,
      1896.

HAMLIN, GEORGE (Chippewa)
  1670N "Along New Trails," Southern Workman, 33 (January, 1904),
      52-54.

HAMMOND, JAMES P. (Yuma)
  1671N "Homes and Health," Native American, February 14, 1903.
  1672A "Out of the Depths," Native American, June 11, 1904.

HARDY, JAMES ORA (Seneca)
  1673N "Salutatory," Chilocco Senior Class Annual. Chilocco, OK:
      Chilocco Indian School, 1920, pp. 15-16.
  1674N "School Athletics," Chilocco Senior Class Annual. Chiloc-
      co, OK: Chilocco Indian School, 1920, p. 37.

HARDY, PERCY (Seneca)
  1675N "The Aeroplane," Chilocco Senior Class Annual. Chilocco,
      OK: Chilocco Indian School, 1920, p. 28.

HARE, DE WITT (Sioux)

1676P "The Mighty Rivers," American Indian Magazine, 7 (Fall, 1919), 137.

HARKINS, GEORGE W. (Chickasaw)
1677L "To the American People," Cherokee Phoenix & Indians' Advocate, January 28, 1832. Reprinted from New York Observer.
1678L ["Okmulgee Council,"] Vindicator, September 4, 1875.
1679N Argument of George W. Harkins, Delegate of the Chickasaw Nation, in Opposition to the Bill Introduced by Mr. Springer to Provide for the Organization of the Territory of Oklahoma, and for Other Purposes. Washington, DC: Gibson Brothers, 1888.

HARRIS, ARTHUR T. (Mohave-Apache)
1680N "An Indian's Way of Training a Child," Native American, May 14, 1910.

HARRIS, COLONEL JOHNSON (Cherokee)
1681L "To the Cherokee People," Cherokee Advocate, September 21, 1892.
1682N With E. E. Starr and J. T. Cunningham. "Report of the Late Delegation to Washington to Negotiate a Loan on the Strip Debt," Cherokee Advocate, June 17, 1893.
1683L "To the Cherokee People," Cherokee Advocate, September 16, 1893.
1684A "Annual Message," Indian Chieftain, November 9, 1893.
1685A "Message," Cherokee Advocate, November 11, 1893.
1686A "Special Message," Cherokee Advocate, November 25, 1893.
1687A "Special Message," Cherokee Advocate, April 18, 1894.
1688A "The Chief's Message," Indian Chieftain, April 26, 1894.
1689L "To the Cherokee People," Cherokee Advocate, May 30, 1894.
1690A "The Third Annual Message of Hon. C. J. Harris, Principal Chief C. N.," Cherokee Advocate, November 7, 1894.
1691N "Thanksgiving Proclamation by the Chief," Cherokee Advocate, November 11, 1894.
1692A "Third Annual Message of Hon. C. J. Harris, Principal Chief, C. N., Delivered November 6, 1894," Muskogee Phoenix, November 14, 1894.
1693A "Chief Harris' Message," Indian Chieftain, November 15, 1894.
1694A Third Annual Message of C. J. Harris, Principal Chief. Tahlequah, I. T., 1894.
1695N An Appeal by the Delegates of the Five Civilized Nations of Indians to the Congress of the United States for Justice. n. p. [1895 or 1895?]
1696A "Chief Harris' Message to the National Council in Extra Session September 11, 1895," Muskogee Phoenix, September 19, 1895.
1697A "Chief Harris' Message," Indian Chieftain, September 19, 1895.

1698N   "Early Cherokee History," <u>Indian Chieftain</u>, August 16, 1900.

1699N   "Old Cherokee Laws and Treaties," <u>Tahlequah Arrow</u>, March 9, 1907.

1700N   "Some Cherokee History," <u>Indian School Journal</u>, 11 (June, 1911), 25-26.

HARRIS, CYRUS (Chickasaw)
1701A   "Message of Governor Harris," <u>Vindicator</u>, September 14, 1872.

HARRIS, DAVID A. (Catawba)
1702N   "History of the Catawbas," <u>Indian School Journal</u>, 5 (September, 1905), 20.

HARRIS, FRANCES (Sac and Fox)
1703N   "Voices Calling," <u>Red Man</u>, 15 (March, 1900), 2.

HARRIS, GEORGE (Cherokee)
1704N   "The Discouraged Man," <u>Bacone Chief</u>. Bacone, OK: Bacone College, 1917, pp. <u>46-47</u>.

HARRIS, ROBERT MAXWELL (Chickasaw)
1705A   "Governor Harris' Message," <u>Muskogee Phoenix</u>, July 29, 1897.

1706A   "Governor Harris' Message," <u>Purcell Register</u>, September 16, 1897.

HARRIS, WILLIAM (Creek)
1707N   "Can Real Progress Be Made under Autocracy," <u>Indian Progress</u>, 21 (June, 1918), 23.

HART, HOMER (Cheyenne)
1708M   "The Thunder Bird," <u>Indian Leader</u>, May, 1915.

HASTINGS, WILLIAM WIRT (Cherokee)
1709L   "Would Not Sectionize," <u>Indian Chieftain</u>, October 2, 1890.
1710A   "Cherokee Affairs Discussed," <u>Tahlequah Arrow</u>, July 19, 1902.
1711N   "Agent Should Be Appointed," <u>Tahlequah Arrow</u>, September 22, 1906.
1712N   With E. M. Landrum. <u>Sequoyah, the Cherokee Cadmus; The Greatest Genius of All American Indians. (With: The Cherokees</u>, by W. T. Hutchings; <u>History of the Cherokee Nation</u>, and, <u>Hymns</u>.) Tahlequah, I. T.: The Sequoyah Association, [1906?]
1713N   William Brown and Levi B. Gritts. <u>Memorial of William W. Hastings, National Attorney for the Cherokee Nation, Remonstrating Against the Passage of the Bill (S. 10575) to Authorize William Brown and Levi B. Gritts to Institute and Prosecute Suits in the Court of Claims in a Certain Case</u>. Washington, DC: Government Printing Office, 1911.

1714N   "Indian Funds Are Not Being Dissipated," Weekly Chieftain, March 22, 1912.

1715A   "Address of Hon. William W. Hastings of Oklahoma," Congressional Record, July 16, 1917.

1716A   "Address of Hon. William W. Hastings of Oklahoma," Native American, October 6, 1917.

HAUSER, ANNA (Cheyenne)

1717F   "The Indian's Gift," Carlisle Arrow, February 7, 1913.

1718F   "The Indian's Gift," Red Man, 5 (February, 1913), 263.

1719N   "Salutatory," Carlisle Arrow, May 16, 1913.

1720N   "A Summer at Ocean City," Carlisle Arrow, May 16, 1913.

1721F   "The Indian's Gift," Indian's Friend, 25 (September, 1913), 8.

HAWKINS, EDNA (Cheyenne)

1722P   "Class Song: To Beethoven's Minuet in G, No. 2," Chilocco Senior Class Annual. Chilocco, OK: Chilocco Indian School, 1920, p. 40.

1723N   "An Up-To Date [sic] Bungalow," Chilocco Senior Class Annual. Chilocco, OK: Chilocco Indian School, 1920, p. 22.

HAWKINS, KISH (Cheyenne)

1724L   "Sentiments of an Indian Boy," Cheyenne Transporter, July 15, 1885.

1725A   "Five Years at Carlisle," Red Man, 9 (June, 1889), 1.

HAWLEY, ALVIN (Sioux)

1726N   "The Development of Industrial Education," Indian Leader, June, 1916.

HAYES, HENRY HORACE (Creek)

1727N   "Our Annual Debate," Carlisle Arrow, June 4, 1906.

HAYES, JOSEPH WILLIAM (Chickasaw)

1728N   "Valedictory," Senior Class Annual. Chilocco, OK: Chilocco Indian School, 1923, p. 222-224.

HAYES, NOAH (Nez Percé)

1729N   "The Advancement of the Indian," Chilocco Senior Class Annual. Chilocco, OK: Chilocco Indian School, 1920, p. 46.

HAZEN, BESSIE (Chippewa)

1730N   "Important Training for the Indian," Indian Leader, November, 1915.

1731N   "Wool," Indian Leader, May, 1916.

HAZLETT, MALCOLM (Caddo)

1732N   "The National Game," Chilocco Senior Class Annual. Chilocco, OK: Chilocco Indian School, 1920, p. 16.

HENDERSON, KATE (Sioux)
  1733A "The Woman with the Pretty Hands," Southern Workman,
         20 (August, 1891), 221.

HENDERSON, WILLIAM PENN (Cherokee)
  1734L "Sheriff Henderson's Views," Indian Chieftain, March 21,
         1889.
  1735N "Mr. Henderson and the Advocate," Indian Chieftain, April
         11, 1889.

HENDRICKS, GEORGE (Cherokee)
  1736N "Football," Bacone Chief. Bacone, OK: Bacone College,
         1924, p. 110.

HENDRICKS, WILLIAM (Cherokee)
  1737L With J. M. Bryan and William Wilson. "What the Old
         Settlers Say," Cherokee Advocate, May 2, 1877.

HERROD, MARY L. (Creek)
  1738N "Public School," Indian Journal, July 21, 1881.

HEWITT, JOHN NAPOLEON BRINTON (Tuscarora)
  1739N "Iroquoian Etymologies; Reply to H. Hale," Science, 17
         (April 17, 1891), 217-220. Correction: 17 (April 24,
         1891), 234.
  1740N "Etymology of the Two Iroquoian Compound Stems, -skĕń-
         ra-keǫ-tê and -ndu-ta-keǫ-te," Science, 19 (April 1,
         1892), 190-192.
  1741N Polysynthesis in the Languages of the American Indians.
         Washington, DC: Judd and Detweiler, 1893.
  1742N "Era of the Formation of the Historic League of the Iro-
         quois," American Anthropologist, 7 (January, 1894), 61-
         67.
  1743N Era of the Formation of the Historic League of the Iro-
         quois. Washington, DC: Judd and Detweiler, 1894.
  1744N "Iroquoian Concept of the Soul," Journal of American Folk-
         lore, 8 (April, 1895), 107-116.
  1745N The Cosmogonic Gods of the Iroquois. Philadelphia? 1895.
  1746N The Name Cherokee and Its Derivation. New York: G. P.
         Putnam's Sons, 1900.
  1747N Orenda and a Definition of Religion. New York: G. P.
         Putnam's Sons, 1902.
  1748N "Iroquoian Cosmology; First Part." In U.S. Bureau of
         American Ethnology, Twenty-first Annual Report, 1899-
         1900. Washington, DC: Government Printing Office,
         1903.
  1749N Iroquoian Cosmology (First Part). Washington, DC: Gov-
         ernment Printing Office, 1904. Extract from the Twenty-
         first Annual Report of the Bureau of American Ethnology.
  1750N With Cyrus Thomas. "Xuala and Guaxule: Indian Villages
         Mentioned in De Soto's Chronicles," Science, n. s. 21
         (July 2, 1905), 863-867.

1751N   Various entries in Handbook of American Indians North of
         Mexico. Ed. Frederick Webb Hodge. 2 Pts. Washing-
         ton, DC: Government Printing Office, 1907-1910. En-
         tries: Adoption, Atrakwaye, Attacapa, Beothucan Family
         (with Albert S. Gatschet), Cabbasagunti, Calumet, Cana-
         joharie, Canadaigua, Caneadea, Canienga, Carcajon,
         Catherine's Town, Caughnawaga, Cayuga (with James
         Mooney), Chaunis Temoatan, Chiefs, Clan and Gens,
         Conestoga, Confederation, Coreorgonel, Cotechney, Dance,
         Dayoitgao, Dekanawida, Erie, Family, Fetish, Goiogouen,
         Government, Hagonchenda, Hens, Hiawatha, Hochelaga,
         Houattaehronen, Huron, Iroquoian Family, Iroquois, Je-
         dakne, Jonondes, Juraken, Kachnawaacharege, Kagough-
         sage, Kahendohon, Kanagaro, Kanghsaws, Kanatiochtiage,
         Kaneenda, Kanesodageh, Karaken, Karhationni, Karhawen-
         radonh, Khioetoa, Kinship (with John R. Swanton), Kon-
         tareahronon, Mahusquechikoken, Maskasinik, Mohawk,
         Nadowa, Nanabozho, Nescopeck, Neutrals, Newtychanning,
         Nikikouek, Oneida (tribe), Oneida (village), Onekagoncka,
         Ongniaahra, Onkwe Iyede, Onnahee, Onnontioga, Onondaga
         (tribe), Onondaga (town), Onondaghara, Onontatacet, Ont-
         waganha, Orenda, Ossewingo, Ossossané, Oswegatchie,
         Otkon, Otskwirackeron, Ottawa (with James Mooney), Ou-
         enrio, Owego, Oyaron, Pocahontas (with Alexamder F.
         Chamberlain), Potawatomi (with James Mooney), Punxsu-
         tawny, Red Jacket, Sainte Antoine, Sauk, Sault au Recol-
         let, Seneca, Shikellamy, Skaniadariio, Solocka, Squawki-
         how, Susquehanna, Tasqui, Thayendanegea, Tiosahrondi-
         on, Tribe, Tsaganha, Tuscarora (tribe), Tuscarora (vil-
         lage), Wampum, White Dog Sacrifice, Eleazer Williams,
         Women.
1752N   "The Teaching of Ethnology in Indian Schools," Quarterly
         Journal of the Society of American Indians, 1 (April,
         1915), 30-35.
1753E   With Jeremiah Curtin. Seneca Fiction, Legends, and
         Myths. In U.S. Bureau of American Ethonology, Thirty-
         second Annual Report, 1910-1911. Washington, DC: Gov-
         ernment Printing Office, 1918.
1754E   With Jeremiah Curtin. Introduction to Seneca Fiction,
         Legends, and Myth, Collected by Jeremiah Curtin and
         J. N. B. Hewitt; Ed. by J. N. B. Hewitt. Washington,
         DC: Government Printing Office, 1919.
1755N   A Constitutional League of Peace in the Stone Age of Amer-
         ica. The League of the Iroquois and Its Constitution. In
         Smithsonian Institution, Annual Report, 1918. Washing-
         ton, DC: Government Printing Office, 1920.

HEYL, RICHARD D. (Apache)
1756L   "The Last and Only Condition," Red Man and Helper, Octo-
         ber 10, 1902.
1757L   "Go Thou and Do Likewise," Red Man and Helper, October
         24, 1902.
1758A   Address Before the Wilmington, Delaware, Young Men's

Christian Association, Red Man and Helper, January 16, 1903.

HICKS, CLARA (Cherokee)
1759N "'Act Well Your Part,'" Cherokee Advocate, July 4, 1877.

HICKS, ELIJAH (Cherokee)
1760N With John Ross, George Lowrey, Major Ridge. Memorial of John Ross, George Lowrey, Major Ridge, and Elijah Hicks, Delegates from the Cherokee Nation of Indians, April 16, 1824. Washington, DC: Gales and Seaton, 1824.
1761A "An Address to the Citizens of Coosewatee District," Cherokee Phoenix, July 21, 1828.
1762L "Georgia and the Cherokees," Cherokee Phoenix & Indians' Advocate, May 19, 1832.
1763L "Humane Policy of President Jackson," Cherokee Phoenix & Indians' Advocate, April 14, 1832.
1764L "For the Cherokee Phoenix," Cherokee Phoenix & Indians' Advocate, May 19, 1832.
1765N "Salutatory," Cherokee Phoenix & Indians' Advocate, September 8, 1832.

HICKS, WILLIAM (Cherokee)
1766A With John Ross. "Message of the Principal Chiefs," Cherokee Phoenix, October 22, 1828.
1767L Letter, Cherokee Phoenix, and Indians' Advocate, July 8, 1829.

HIGHEAGLE, ROBERT P. (Sioux)
1768N "Indian Day Schools: Their Purpose," Southern Workman, 33 (October, 1904), 554.

HILL, JESSE (Seneca)
1769N "My Medicine Man," Southern Workman, 28 (February, 1899), 73.

HILLMAN, LEVI (Oneida)
1770N "Desirable Objects of Attainment," Native American, December 10, 1909. Reprinted from Carlisle Arrow.
1771N "The Walking Purchase," Red Man, 3 (November, 1910), 125-126.
1772M "One of the Seneca Stories," Red Man, 3 (February, 1911), 251.

HODGE, DAVID MCKILLOP (Creek)
1773A Remarks ... Delegate of the Musgogee Nation of Indians Against the Establishment by Congress of a United States Government over the Indian Country Without the Consent of the Indians. Delivered Before the Committee on Territories of the House of Representatives of the United States, April 22, 1876. Washington, DC: Government Printing Office, 1876.

1774A Remarks of D. M. Hodge, Delegate of the Muskogee Nation of Indians, Against the Establishment by Congress of a United States Government over the Indian Country Without the Consent of the Indians. Washington, DC: Gibson Brothers, 1878.

1775N Argument of David M. Hodge ... Before the Committee on Indian Affairs of the U.S. Senate, March 10, 1880, in Support of Senate Bill No. 1145, Providing for the Payment of Awards Made to Creek Indians Who Enlisted in the Federal Army, Loyal Refugees and Freedmen. Washington? 1880?

1776N With Robert McGill Loughridge. English and Muskogee Dictionary. St. Louis: J. T. Smith, 1890. Reprinted 1964.

HODJKISS, WILLIAM D. (Sioux)
1777P "Song of the Storm-Swept Plain," Indian School Journal, 13 (March, 1913), 332.

HOLMES, FRANK (Chippewa)
1778N "Senior Problems," Carlisle Arrow, May 22, 1914.

HOPKINS, SARAH WINNEMUCCA (Paiute)
See WINNEMUCCA, SARAH

HOWARD, BARNEY (Pima)
1779N "In the Bakeshop," Native American, June 15, 1907.

HOXIE, SARA (Noamlaki)
1780N "The American Indian," Indian Craftsman, 2 (December, 1909), 29-30.

HOXIE, WILLIAM (Mission)
1781N "The Indian May Solve the Problem Thru [sic] Industry," American Indian Magazine, 4 (January-March, 1916), 19-24.

HUDSON, FRANK (Pueblo)
1782P ["'Tis Not Strong in Limb as Yonder Oak,"] Red Man, 12 (May, 1895), 5.

HUGHES, EULA (Chickasaw)
1783N "What a 1920 Girl Should Wear," Chilocco Annual. Chilocco, OK: Chilocco Indian School, 1920, p. 33.

1784P With Florence Holland. "Class Song: To Rose Marie," Chilocco Annual. Chilocco, OK: Chilocco Indian School, 1920, p. 43.

HUGHES, MARTHA (Pima)
1785N "Bread Making," Native American, May 16, 1914.

HUNT, EVELYN (Pueblo)
1786N "The Co-ze-na Dance," Indian Leader, March, 1917.

HUNTER, LUCY E. (Winnebago)
    1787N   "The Nebraska Winnebagoes," Southern Workman, 42 (April, 1913), 217-221.
    1788N   "The Value and Necessity of Higher Academic Training for the Indian Student," Quarterly Journal of the Society of American Indians, 3 (January-March, 1915), 11-15.
    1789N   "Higher Academic Training for the Indian," Southern Workman, 44 (March, 1915), 139-143.

IGNATIUS, JOE MACK (Potawatomi)
    1790A   "My Heart Talks to My People," Quarterly Journal of the Society of American Indians, 1 (April, 1913), 47-49.
    1791N   "I Make Talk to White Man, His Government," Quarterly Journal of the Society of American Indians, 2 (April-June, 1914), 151.

INGALLS, SADIE M. (Sac and Fox)
    1792M   "Why Crows Are Black," Red Man, 5 (January, 1913), 207.
    1793M   "Why Crows Are Black," Carlisle Arrow, February 7, 1913.
    1794N   "My Trip to Gettysburg," Carlisle Arrow, May 16, 1913.

ISHAM, IRA O. (Chippewa)
    1795A   "The Case of the Lac Court D'Oreilles Chippewas," Quarterly Journal of the Society of American Indians, 4 (July-September, 1916), 248-252.

ISRAEL, ELLA (Cherokee)
    1796N   "Good Manners," Carlisle Arrow, June 4, 1915.

IVEY, AUGUSTUS E. (Cherokee)
    1797L   "A Communication," Indian Chieftain, February 26, 1885.
    1798L   "Gus Ivey, Cherokee Journalist, Supports W. W. Hastings," Muskogee Times Democrat, May 2, 1914. Reprinted from Tahlequah Arrow.

JACKSON, ALFRED (Pima)
    1799N   "The First Christmas," Native American, December 26, 1914.
    1800N   "Agriculture and School Gardens," Native American, May 22, 1915.

JACKSON, BERNARD S. (Yuma)
    1801N   "Steam Boilers and Pumps," Native American, May 23, 1908.

JACKSON, CHARLES (Chippewa)
    1802N   "A Communication," Tomahawk, November 13, 1919.

JACKSON, EMMA (Klamath)

1803A   "Thrums from the Class of 1904," <u>Native American</u>, June 11, 1904.

JACKSON, HELEN (Pima)
1804A   "Forecast of the Class of 1905," <u>Native American</u>, June 3, 1905.

JACKSON, ROBERT (Chehalis)
1805N   "Our Todays," <u>Red Man</u>, 13 (March, 1896), 1-2.

JACKSON, THOMAS F. (Pima)
1806N   "Progress Among the Pimas," <u>Native American</u>, June 16, 1923.

JAEGER, AGNES R. (Yuma)
1807A   "Snap Shots of the Class of 1905," <u>Native American</u>, June 3, 1905.

JAMES, ALICE (Choctaw)
1808N   "The Fate of the Old Maple," <u>Twin Territories</u>, 3 (March, 1901), 62.

JAMES, FREMONT (Digger)
1809N   "How the California Indians Spend Their Christmas," <u>Native American</u>, December 25, 1909.
1810N   "Mariposa Grove of Big Trees," <u>Native American</u>, April 16, 1910.
1811N   "The Digger Indians," <u>Native American</u>, May 14, 1910.

JAMES, JULIA (Oneida)
1812N   "Visit in Asia," <u>Red Man</u>, 11 (May-June, 1893), 4.

JAMES, OTWIN (Potawatomi-Kansa)
1813N   "Description of the Old and New Kaw Reservation," <u>Morning Star</u>, 5 (August, 1884), 4.

JAMISON, JACOB M. (Seneca)
1814N   "Indians as Allies of the United States," <u>Red Man</u>, 14 (March, 1898), 4.

JEROME, ELMIRA (Chippewa)
1815M   "A Legend of the Pottawatomi," <u>Indian Craftsman</u>, 1 (March, 1909), 17-18.
1816N   "A Sketch of the Munsee Indians," <u>Indian Craftsman</u>, 1 (June, 1909), 32-33.

JEROME, MARCELLE (Chippewa)
1817N   "Business Training for the Indian," <u>Indian Leader</u>, June 9, 1911.

JOCKS, JOSEPH (Mohawk)
1818N   "Canadian Winter Sports," <u>Carlisle Arrow</u>, May 22, 1914.
1819M   "The Origin of Races," <u>Carlisle Arrow</u>, May 29, 1914.

1820M "The Origin of Races," Indian's Friend, 27 (December, 1914), 7.

JOHNS, DELLA MAY (Seneca)
1821N "Inauguration of Domestic Science Course," Carlisle Arrow, June 4, 1915.

JOHNS, LILLIAN (Maricopa)
1822N "Sometime," Native American, June 3, 1905.

JOHNSON, A. ELLA (Seneca)
1823N "The Indian Medicine Man," Red Man, 4 (December, 1911), 166.

JOHNSON, ELIAS (Tuscarora)
1824M Legends, Traditions and Laws, of the Iroquois, or Six Nations, and History of the Tuscarora Indians. Lockport, NY: Union Printing and Publishing Co., 1881.

JOHNSON, ELIZA (Pima)
1825N "The Casa Grande Ruin," Native American, May 16, 1914.

JOHNSON, JOHN (Chippewa)
See ENMEGAHBOWH

JOHNSON, RUTH ADELIA (Seneca)
1826N "Where I Like to Browse," Chilocco Annual. Chilocco, OK: Chilocco Indian School, 1920, p. 31.

JOHNSON, S. ARTHUR (Wyandot)
1827N "Gates and Gateways," Red Man, 11 (March-April, 1893), 3-4.

JOHNSON, VICTOR H. (Dalles)
1828N "Assimilation, as Illustrated by the Dalles Tribe," Red Man and Helper, February 26-March 4, 1904.
1829P "The Brook," Indian's Friend, 20 (September, 1907), 7. Reprinted from Dartmouth Magazine.
1830P "The Brook," Southern Workman, 39 (December, 1910), 649.

JOHNSTON, DOUGLAS HENRY (Chickasaw)
1831A "Governor Johnson's [sic] Message," New-State Tribune, September 6, 1906.
1832N Argument on Behalf of the Chickasaw Nation Against the Reopening of the Choctaw and Chickasaw Citizenship Rolls. Washington, DC: Government Printing Office, 1910.

JONES, FLORA E. (Munsee)
1833M "A Seneca Indian Legend of True Friendship," Red Man, 5 (December, 1912), 173-174.

JONES, FRANK (Sac and Fox)

1834A   "The Result of the Dawes Bill," <u>Red Man</u>, 14 (February, 1897), 4.

1835N   "The Conqueror's Debt to the Conquered," <u>Red Man</u>, 14 (April, 1897), 7.

JONES, JOHN (Creek)
1836N   "'A Pull,'" <u>Indian Scout</u>, 2 (June, 1916), 10.

JONES, STEPHEN (Sioux)
1837N   "Reservation Leaders, the Good and the Bad," <u>American Indian Magazine</u>, 4 (January-March, 1916), 34-37.

1838N   "Urges Indians to Obtain Education," <u>Indian Leader</u>, February 21, 1919.

JONES, WILLIAM (Sac and Fox)
1839N   "Frederic Remington's Pictures of Frontier Life," <u>Harvard Monthly</u>, 27 (February, 1899), 186-190.

1840F   "An Episode of the Spring Round-Up," <u>Harvard Monthly</u>, 28 (April, 1899), 46-53.

1841F   "Anoska Nimiwina," <u>Harvard Monthly</u>, 28 (May, 1899), 102-111.

1842F   "Lydie," <u>Harvard Monthly</u>, 28 (July, 1899), 194-201.

1843F   "Anoska Nimiwina," <u>Southern Workman</u>, 28 (August, 1899), 298-303.

1844N   "Osakie Legend of the Ghost Dance," <u>Journal of American Folklore</u>, 12 (October, 1899), 284-286.

1845F   "Chiky," <u>Harvard Monthly</u>, 29 (November, 1899), 59-65.

1846F   "In the Name of His Ancestor," <u>Harvard Monthly</u>, 29 (December, 1899), 109-115.

1847F   "The Usurper of the Range," <u>Harvard Monthly</u>, 30 (March, 1900), 13-22.

1848F   "The Heart of the Brave," <u>Harvard Monthly</u>, 30 (May, 1900), 99-106.

1849F   "A Lone Star Ranger," <u>Harvard Monthly</u>, 30 (June, 1900), 154-161.

1850N   "Episodes in the Culture-Hero Myth of the Sauks and Foxes," <u>Journal of American Folklore</u>, 14 (October, 1901), 225-239.

1851N   <u>Some Principles of Algonquian Word-Formation</u>. Lancaster, PA: The New Era Printing Company, 1904.

1852N   "Algonkin Manitou," <u>Journal of American Folklore</u>, 18 (July, 1905), 183-190.

1853N   <u>The Algonkin Manitou</u>. Boston, 1905.

1854T   <u>Fox Texts</u>. Leyden: E. J. Brill, 1907.

1855N   Various entries in <u>Handbook of American Indians North of Mexico</u>. Ed. Frederick Webb Hodge. 2 Pts. Washington, DC: Government Printing Office, 1907-1910. Entries: Keokuk, Kickapoo (with James Mooney), Makwisuchigi, Minnehaha, Mokohoko, Mythology, Oshkushi, Oueschekagamiouilimy, Outchichagami, Pamissouk, Poweshiek.

1856N   "Notes on the Fox Indians," <u>Journal of American Folklore</u>, 24 (April, 1911), 209-237.

1857N   Algonquian (Fox), an Illustrative Sketch.   Rev. Truman
       Michelson.   Washington, DC: Government Printing Of-
       fice, 1911.
1858N   "Notes on the Fox Indians," Iowa Journal of History and
       Politics, 10 (January, 1912), 70-112.
1859N   "Kickapoo Ethnological Notes," American Anthropologist,
       15 (April, 1913), 332-335.
1860C   Kickapoo Tales Collected by William Jones.   Tr. Truman
       Michelson.   Leydon: E. J. Brill, 1915.
1861F   "Ojibway Tales from the North Shore of Lake Superior,"
       Journal of American Folklore, 29 (July, 1916), 368-391.
1862C   Ojibwa Texts Collected by William Jones.   Ed. Truman
       Michelson.   2 vols.   Leyden: E. J. Brill, 1917-1919.

JORDAN, JOHN W. (Cherokee)
  1863L   "Canadian District," Cherokee Advocate, August 5, 1876.
  1864A   "Speech on Statehood in Convention," Muskogee Phoenix,
        February 8, 1894.

JORDAN, PETER JOSEPH (Chippewa)
  1865N   "Reminiscences," Carlisle Arrow, May 22, 1914.
  1866M   "A Pawnee Legend of the Corn," Carlisle Arrow, Novem-
        ber 20, 1914.
  1867M   "A Pawnee Legend of the Corn," Carlisle Arrow and Red
        Man, November 2, 1917.

JOSE, MAGELA (Papago)
  1868N   "How My People Live," Native American, May 14, 1910.
  1869N   "Papago Girl Tells of Hopi Snake Dance," Native American,
        October 8, 1910.

JUAN, JOSE (Pima)
  1870N   "My Allotment," Native American, June 15, 1918.

KAH-GE-GA-GAH-BOWH (Chippewa)
See COPWAY, GEORGE

KAH O SED, E. C. (Chippewa)
  1871L   "A Communication," Tomahawk, March 13, 1924.

KAKAQUE, MARY (Potawatomi)
  1872N   "The Indians' Protection from Injury by Storms," Indian
        Leader, November, 1915.

KALAMA, FRANCIS (Puyallup)
  1873N   "Citizenship," Indian Leader, June, 1915.

KALKA, JOSE (Pima)
  1874N   "An Officer's Outing," Native American, October 14, 1905.

KANARD, BETTIE (Creek)

1875N "Indian Dishes and Drinks," Bacone Chief. Bacone, OK: Bacone College, 1917, pp. 35-38.

KATE, CLARA M. (Hopi)
1876N "The Hopi Indians," Native American, June 27, 1908.

KEALEAR, CHARLES H. (Sioux)
1877N "Conditions at Wind River Reservation, Wyoming," Quarterly Journal of the Society of American Indians, 1 (April, 1913), 58-59.
1878N "Reservation Management," Quarterly Journal of the Society of American Indians, 1 (April, 1913), 158-161.
1879N "What the Indian Can Do for Himself," Quarterly Journal of the Society of American Indians, 2 (January-March, 1914), 41-42.
1880N "Arapaho Indians Drunk at Dance," Carlisle Arrow, February 6, 1914. Reprinted from Cheyenne State Leader.
1881N "An Appeal from Wyoming," Quarterly Journal of the Society of American Indians, 3 (October-December, 1915), 265-269.

KELLOGG, LAURA MINNIE CORNELIUS (Oneida)
1882N ["Indian Public Opinion,"] Red Man and Helper, October 10, 1902.
1883P "A Tribute to the Future of My Race," Red Man and Helper, March 13, 1903. Reprinted from Riverside Daily Press.
1884N "Some Facts and Figures on Indian Education," Quarterly Journal of the Society of American Indians, 1 (April, 1913), 36-46.

KELTON, HOMER (Mohave)
1885F "The Wise Fox and the Foolish Fox," Red Man and Helper, May 10, 1901.

KENDALL, HENRY J. (Pueblo)
1886N "Why Is It That Some of the Whites Hate the Indians?" Morning Star, 3 (July, 1883), 4.

KENNAWA, HERB (Mohave)
1887N ["Customs and Beliefs of the Mohaves,"] Red Man, 14 (July-August, 1897), 3.

KENNEDY, ALVIN (Seneca)
1888N "The Senecas' Green Corn Dance," Red Man, 3 (October, 1910), 77-78.
1889M "The Keepers of the West Door of the Lodge," Red Man, 3 (January, 1911), 208-209.
1890N "The Coming of the New Year," Red Man, 3 (June, 1911), 454.
1891N "Salutatory," Carlisle Arrow, April 21, 1911.

KENNEY, LOUISA (Klamath)

1892M "Why the Rabbit Is Timid," Red Man, 2 (April, 1910), 27.
1893F "An Indian's Power of Observation," Indian's Friend, 21
(October, 1908), 2. Reprinted from Carlisle Arrow.

KEOKUK, FANNIE (Sac and Fox)
1894N "The Croatan Indians," Indian Craftsman, 2 (September,
1909), 22.
1895N "The Medicine Dance," Red Man, 2 (April, 1910), 46-47.
1896N "Moses Keokuk, Chief of the United Sacs and Foxes," Indian's Friend, 22 (June, 1910), 10.
1897N "Chief Keokuk, the Sac and Fox," Red Man, 3 (September,
1910), 25-26.

KERSHAW, WILLIAM J. (Menominee)
1898P "The Indian's Salute to His Country," Indian Leader, October, 1915.
1899N "Looking Backward," Quarterly Journal of the Society of
American Indians, 2 (January-March, 1914), 36-38.
1900N "The Red Man's Appeal: Being an Address to the President of the United States," Quarterly Journal of the Society of American Indians, 2 (October-December, 1914),
275-276.
1901P "The Indian's Salute to His Country," American Indian Magazine, 4 (January-March, 1916), 66.

KESHENA, ELIZABETH (Menominee)
1902M "Legend of the Catfish," Red Man, 3 (February, 1911),
256.
1903M "How the Hunter Punished the Snow," Red Man, 3 (April,
1911), 342-343.

KEWAYGESHIK, MARY WONITA (Ottawa)
1904M "The Legend of Meno," Carlisle Arrow, June 4, 1915.

KE-WA-ZE-ZHIG (Chippewa)
1905A An Address Delivered in Alston Hall, Boston, February 26,
1861, Before a Convention Met to Devise Ways and Means
to Elevate and Improve the Conditions of the Indians of
the United States. By Ke-wa-ze-zhig, a Son of the Chief
of the Chippeways. With a Report of the Proceedings of
the Convention, and a Poem by a Friend. Boston: The
Author, 1861.

KING, BIRDIE (Oneida)
1906N "The Best Training for the Indian," Indian Leader, May,
1915.

KING, INEZ M. (Stockbridge)
1907N "Beyond the 'Three R's'," Red Man and Helper, February
14, 1902.

KING, JOHN (Absentee Shawnee)
1908N "Carpenter Shop," Southern Workman, 13 (April, 1884), 43.

KING, KENNETH (Sioux)
  1909N "The Trip to Harrisburg," Carlisle Arrow, November 6,
    1914.

KING, LOUIS (Chippewa)
  1910N "Commerce and Culture, Not Antagonistic," Indian Leader,
    July 4, 1902.
  1911N "Sequoyah Literary Society," Bacone Chief. Bacone, OK:
    Bacone College, 1915, p. 27.

KING, MARIE (Oneida)
  1912N "Cotton," Indian Leader, May, 1916.

KINGSLEY, LLEWELLYN (Cheyenne)
  1913N "My Favorite Sport." Chilocco Annual. Chilocco, OK:
    Chilocco Indian School, 1920, p. 40.

KINGSLEY, NETTIE MARY (Winnebago)
  1914N "Our Campus," Carlisle Arrow, June 4, 1915.
  1915N "Possibilities in Spare Moments," Carlisle Arrow, June 4,
    1915.

KIRKE, CLAYTON (Klamath)
  1916N "Top or Bottom, Which?" Native American, May 30, 1903.

KIRKE, SELDON (Klamath)
  1917N "Honor Waits at Labor's Gates," Native American, May 30,
    1903.

KNOCKSOFFTWO, HENRY (Sioux)
  1918N "Educated Indians Are Successful," Quarterly Journal of
    the Society of American Indians, 2 (January-March, 1914),
    77-78.

KNUDSON, ELIZABETH E. (Klamath)
  1919N "Carlisle Expects Every Indian to Do His Duty," Red Man
    and Helper, February 20-27, 1903.

KOHPAY, HARRY (Osage)
  1920A "Open Doors," Red Man, 10 (June, 1891), 4.

KOLLENBAUM, LILLIAN (Sioux)
  1921N "An Indian Celebration," Indian Leader, April, 1916.

LA FLESCHE, FRANCIS (Omaha)
  1922A [Address to Carlisle Students], Morning Star, 6 (May,
    1886), 3.
  1923N "Death and Funeral Customs Among the Omahas," Journal
    of American Folklore, 2 (October, 1889), 3-11.
  1924N "Omaha Buffalo Medicine-Men, and Two Songs Sung at an
    Operation," Journal of American Folklore, 3 (July, 1890),
    215-221.

1925N Corrections and contributions in James Owen Dorsey, The
Çegiha Language. Washington, DC: Government Printing Office, 1890.

1926N Assistant in Alice C. Fletcher, A Study of Omaha Indian
Music. Cambridge, MA: Peabody Museum of American
Archaeology and Ethnology, 1893.

1927A Address at Carlisle Commencement, Red Man, 14 (April,
1897), 3.

1928M "The Laughing Bird,--The Wren--An Indian Legend,"
Southern Workman, 29 (October, 1900), 554-556.

1929M "The Laughing Bird--The Wren," Indian Leader, November
2, 1900.

1930N "An Indian Allotment," Independent, 52 (November 8, 1900),
2686-2688.

1931N The Middle Five, Indian Boys at School. Boston: Small,
Maynard & Company, 1900. Reprinted in 1901, 1906,
and 1909.

1932F "The Story of a Vision," Southern Workman, 30 (February,
1901), 106-109.

1933N "Who Was the Medicine Man?" Journal of American Folklore, 18 (October, 1905), 269-275.

1934N "The Past Life of the Plains Indians," Southern Workman,
34 (November, 1905), 587-594.

1935A Who Was the Medicine Man? Address by Francis La
Flesche (of the Omaha Tribe). Hampton, VA: Hampton
Institute Press, 1905.

1936N With Alice C. Fletcher. The Omaha Tribe. Twenty-
Seventh Annual Report of the Bureau of American Ethnol-
ogy, 1905-1906. Washington, DC: Government Printing
Office, 1911.

1937N "Osage Marriage Customs," American Anthropologist, 14
(January, 1912), 127-130.

1938N "The Omaha Tribe," Science, n. s. 37 (June 27, 1913),
982-983.

1939N "'One Touch of Nature,'" Southern Workman, 42 (August,
1913), 427-428.

1940M With Alice C. Fletcher. "The Discovery of Maize," Indian
Leader, April, 1915.

1941M With Alice C. Fletcher. "The Peace Pipes--A Ponca Legend," Indian Leader, December, 1915.

1942N "Right and Left in Osage Ceremonies." In Holmes Anniversary Volume; Anthropological Essays Presented to
William Henry Holmes in Honor of His Seventieth Birthday, December 1, 1916, by His Friends and Colaborers.
Washington, DC: J. W. Bryan, 1916.

1943N "The Osage Tribe: Rite of the Chiefs; Sayings of the An-
cient Men." In U.S. Bureau of American Ethnology,
Thirty-Sixth Annual Report, 1914-1915. Washington, DC:
Government Printing Office, 1921, pp. 37-604.

1944N "Symbolic Man of the Osage Tribe," Art and Archaeology,
9 (February, 1920), 68-72.

1945N "Alice C. Fletcher," Science, 58 (August 17, 1923), 115.

1946N Omaha Bow and Arrow-Makers. Rio de Janerio: Imprensa
nacional, 1924.

LA FLESCHE, SUSAN (Omaha)
See PICOTTE, SUSAN LA FLESCHE

LA FLESCHE, SUSETTE (Omaha)
1947L "An Indian Woman's Letter," Southern Workman, 8 (April, 1879), 44.
1948N Nebraska. The Omaha Agency--A Philadelphia Christmas Tree in Nebraska. An Indian Woman's Letter. Omaha Agency, NE, 1879.
1949N "The Indian Question," Christian Union, March 10, 1880.
1950N Introduction in William Justin Harsha, Ploughed Under: The Story of an Indian Chief, Told by Himself. New York: Ford, Howard, and Hulbert, 1881.

LAMERE, OLIVER (Winnebago)
1951N "The Indian Culture of the Future," Quarterly Journal of the Society of American Indians, 1 (October-December, 1913), 361-363.

LAMOUREAUX, CALVIN (Sioux)
1952N "Alcohol," Carlisle Arrow, April 24, 1914.

LAND, VERNOLA (Chickasaw)
1953N With Alexander Hendricks and James Irwin. "A Brief Summary of the Life and Work of Brig. Gen. R. H. Pratt," Indian School Journal, 23 (March, 1924), 215.
1954N "Valedictory," Senior Class Annual. Chilocco, OK: Chilocco Indian School, 1924, p. 24.

LANDRUM, ELIAS M. (Cherokee)
1955N With W. W. Hastings. Sequoyah, the Cherokee Cadmus; The Greatest Genius of All American Indians. [With: The Cherokees, by W. T. Hutchings; History of the Cherokee Nation, and, Hymns]. Tahlequah, I. T.: The Sequoyah Association, [1906?].
1956F "A Cherokee on the Comet," Tahlequah Arrow, May 26, 1910.

LANDRUM, HIRAM TERRELL (Cherokee)
1957N "A Blow at Wire Fencing," Indian Chieftain, June 30, 1892.

LANE, HELEN (Lummi)
1958M "Iroquois Legend of the Three Sisters," Indian Craftsman, 1 (June, 1909), 31.

LANG, HENRY (Skagit)
1959N "Give the Indian Better Academic Training," Quarterly Journal of the Society of American Indians, 3 (January-March, 1915), 39-41.

LARGO, ANTHONY (Mission)
1960A "Storekeeping," Native American, June 16, 1906.

LARIVER, FRANK (Chippewa)
1961N "The Indian's Relation to the Soil," Indian School Journal,
11 (June, 1911), 36-37.

LASSA, NICHOLAS (Flathead)
1962N "The How and Why of Trade Training at Haskell," Indian
Leader, June, 1921.

LA VATTA, EMMA (Bannock)
1963F "The Story of the Deerskin," Red Man, 3 (October, 1910),
78-79.
1964M "Why the Snake's Head Became Flat," Red Man, 3 (January, 1911), 204.

LA VATTA, GEORGE (Shoshoni)
1965N "New York's Interesting Places," Carlisle Arrow, May 2,
1913.

LA VATTA, ISABEL (Shoshoni)
1966F "Babetta's Christmas," Carlisle Arrow, December 27, 1912.

LA VATTA, PHILIP (Shoshoni)
1967N "A Vision of 1893," Red Man, 11 (March-April, 1893), 4.

LAY, THERESA (Seneca)
1968N "The 'Vision' of R. H. Pratt," Carlisle Arrow, June 4,
1915.

LEARY, EVELYN (Iowa)
1969N "Why We Should Answer the Red Cross Christmas Roll
Call," Indian Leader, December, 1918.
1970N "A Story of Modern Knights," Indian Leader, December,
1919.

LEE, LILLY (Cherokee)
1971P "Literary Day Among the Birds," A Wreath of Cherokee
Rose Buds, August 1, 1855.

LEEDS, YAMIE (Pueblo)
1972A "The Pueblo Indians," Red Man, 10 (June, 1891), 1, 4.

LEFLORE, CAMPBELL (Choctaw)
1973N Before the Honorable, the Secretary of the Interior. Appeal of the Choctaw Nation from the Decision of the Commissioner of Indian Affairs Rendered Jan. 23, 1886.
Washington, DC: R. O. Polkinhorn & Son, [1886].
1974N With Edmond McCurtain. Disbursement of Delegate's 20
Per Cent of Net Proceeds Claim. N. p., 1889?

LEICHER, FRED (Stockbridge)
1975N "The City of Carlisle," Carlisle Arrow, April 11, 1911.

LEIDER, CARL (Crow)

1976N "A Memory Sketch of Capt. [James] Eads," Morning Star, 7 (March, 1887), 8.

1977A "Our Flag," Red Man, 10 (April, 1890), 5.

1978N "Montana," Red Man, 10 (May, 1890), 7.

LEVERING, LEVI (Omaha)

1979N "Treat the Indian as a Man," Red Man, 16 (April, 1900), 3.

1980N "The Carlisle Indian School," Red Man, 11 (March-April, 1893), 5. Reprinted from North and West.

1981N "Does It Pay to Christianize the Indian?" Missionary Review of the World, 36 (November, 1913), 857.

LEWIS, ANNIE (Pima)

1982N "Pima Home Life," Native American, February 13, 1909.

LEWIS, JOSE (Papago)

1983M With Pablo Narcho and Jose Antonio. "The Papago Legend of the Formation of the Earth," Indian Leader, October, 1917.

1984M With Pablo Narcho and Jose Antonio. Indian Legends and Superstitions. Lawrence, KS: Haskell Institute, 1917.

LEWIS, ROBERT (Pima)

1985A "Renunciation," Native American, June 3, 1905.

LEWIS, SIMON (Pima)

1986N "The Making of the Native American," Native American, January 16, 1909.

1987N "Flying Machines," Native American, April 16, 1910.

1988N "Cane Sugar," Native American, May 7, 1910.

1989N "Painting," Native American, May 14, 1910.

LOCKE, VICTOR M. (Choctaw)

1990N "The Choctaw Catechism," Indian Sentinel, 2 (January, 1922), 423-424.

LOGAN, HOWARD G. (Winnebago)

1991N "No Footsteps Backward," Red Man, 10 (May, 1890), 3.

1992A "Carlisle's Principles," Red Man, 10 (December, 1890-January, 1891), 6.

LOLORIAS, JOHN (Papago)

1993N "As an Indian Sees It," Southern Workman, 31 (September, 1902), 476-480.

LONDROSH, CECILIA (Winnebago)

1994A "From the Old Land-Marks to the New Mile-Stones," Red Man, 9 (June, 1889), 1.

LONE WOLF, DELOS (Kiowa)

1995A Speech, Red Man, 11 (May-June, 1893), 3.

1996N "Our Development a Necessity," Red Man, 13 (March, 1896), 2.

1997A   "How to Solve the Problem," American Indian Magazine, 4
         (July-September, 1916), 257-259.

LONG, SYLVESTER (Cherokee)
1998M   "The Origin of Names Among the Cherokees," Red Man, 3
         (December, 1910), 173-175.

LONG WOLF, HATTIE (Sioux)
1999N   "The Amusements of the Dakotas," Red Man, 11 (May,
         1892), 3.

LOWREY, GEORGE (Cherokee)
2000N   With John Ross, Major Ridge, and Elijah Hicks. Memorial
         of John Ross, Geo. Lowrey, Major Ridge, and Elijah
         Hicks, Delegates from the Cherokee Nation of Indians.
         April 16, 1824. Washington, DC: Gales & Seaton, 1824.

LOWRY, KATHERINE (Washo)
2001N   "Bread and Bread Making," Native American, May 23,
         1908.

LUGO, FRANCISCO (Mission)
2002A   "Class President's Address," Native American, June 3,
         1905.

LUGO, PATRICIO (Mission)
2003N   "The End Crowns the Work," Native American, May 24,
         1902.
2004N   "Response to Farewell," Native American, May 24, 1902.

LUJAN, MAX (Pueblo)
2005N   "How the Indians Celebrate at Home," Indian Leader, Octo-
         ber 27, 1911.

LYMAN, ANNIE (Sioux)
2006N   "How Some Indians Keep Thanksgiving," Southern Workman,
         12 (January, 1883), 7.

McADAMS, JAMES C. (Shoshoni)
2007N   "The Shoshoni," Quarterly Journal of the Society of Amer-
         ican Indians, 3 (October-December, 1915), 304-307.

McAFEE, JOHNSON (Pima)
2008N   "Agriculture," Native American, June 10, 1916.
2009N   "The Pima Indian Fair," Native American, November 17,
         1917.

McARTHUR, NELLIE (Pima)
2010N   "The First Christmas," Native American, December 25,
         1909.
2011A   "Valedictory," Native American, May 16, 1914.

McCARTY, ADAM (Modoc)
2012N "A Modoc Story," Morning Star, 3 (April, 1883), 4.

McCOMBS, WILLIAM (Creek)
2013A "An Eloquent Oration," Tahlequah Arrow, May 16, 1903.

McCOY, JOHN LOWREY (Cherokee)
2014N With J. M. Bryan and William Wilson. "To the Hon.
    Chairman of the Committee on Territories of the House
    of Representatives," Cherokee Advocate, May 6, 1876.
2015N "Report of John L. McCoy," Indian Journal, December 25,
    1879.
2016L "Letter from John L. McCoy," Indian Chieftain, January
    22, 1885.

McCOY, PAULINE (Sac and Fox)
2017N "Kindergarten Training of the Indian," Indian Leader, July
    4, 1902.

McCURTAIN, BEN F. (Choctaw)
2018N "The Indians of Oklahoma," Sturm's Oklahoma Magazine,
    11 (December, 1910), 19-24.

McCURTAIN, DAVID CORNELIUS (Choctaw)
2019N "The Indian People in the Indian Territory," Indian Citizen,
    December 13, 1894.
2020N Memorial of Choctaw Indians ... In the Indian Territory
    Protesting Against Passage of H. R. 12764. Washington,
    DC: Government Printing Office, 1904.
2021N "Indian Treaties Were Ruthlessly Broken," New-State Tri-
    bune, August 9, 1906.

McCURTAIN, EDMOND (Choctaw)
2022L Letter, Vindicator, May 8, 1875.
2023A "Inaugural Address," Indian Champion, October 25, 1884.
2024A "Governor McCurtain's Retiring Message," Indian Journal,
    October 21, 1886.
2025N With Campbell Leflore. Disbursement of Delegate's 20
    Per Cent of Net Proceeds Claim. N. p., 1889?

McCURTAIN, GREEN (Choctaw)
2026L "The Killing of Squirrel Hoyt," Indian Champion, December
    20, 1884.
2027L "The Choctaw Coal Question," Muskogee Phoenix, April 25,
    1889.
2028A "Green McCurtain's Speech," Muskogee Phoenix, July 5,
    1894.
2029A "Green McCurtain's Speech," Indian Citizen, July 12, 1894.
2030A "Hon. Green McCurtain's Speech at Allotment Convention,"
    Indian Citizen, July 25, 1895.
2031A "McCurtain's Message," Indian Citizen, October 8, 1896.
2032A "Gov. McCurtain's Message," Muskogee Phoenix, October
    15, 1896.

2033A   "Gov. McCurtain's Message," Indian Citizen, October 7, 1897.

2034A   "Special Message," Indian Citizen, November 4, 1897.

2035N   "Proclamation," Indian Citizen, July 21, 1898.

2036A   "Governor's Message," Indian Citizen, October 13, 1898.

2037L   Letter, Indian Citizen, January 5, 1899.

2038L   Letter, Indian Citizen, April 5, 1900.

2039A   "Gov. McCurtain's Message," Indian Citizen, October 11, 1900.

2040A   "Gov. M'Curtain's Message," Indian Citizen, October 16, 1902.

2041A   ["Message of Gov. Green McCurtain, Read Before the Choctaw Legislature,"] Purcell Register, October 24, 1902.

2042A   "Message," Indian Citizen, December 11, 1902.

2043N   "Some Things That I Remember," Twin Territories, 5 (April, 1903), 122-123.

2044L   Letter, Twin Territories, 5 (April, 1903), 132.

2045L   Letter, Shawnee Herald, June 18, 1903.

2046A   "Governor's Message," Indian Citizen, October 8, 1903.

2047A   "Gov. McCurtain's Message," Pauls Valley Enterprise and Valley News, October 5, 1905.

2048A   "Governor's Last Message to the Choctaw Council," Indian Citizen, October 5, 1905.

2049A   "Gov. McCurtain's Message," Purcell Register, October 6, 1905.

2050A   "Gov. Green McCurtain's Message," New-State Tribune, August 16, 1906.

2051A   Annual Message of Governor Green McCurtain to the Choctaw Council, Assembled at Tuskahoma, Okla., Tuesday, Oct. 6, 1908. [Fort Smith, AR: Darby & Bly, 1908.]

2052A   ["Message to the Annual Council"], Oklahoma City Times, October 10, 1909.

McCURTAIN, JACKSON FRAZIER (Choctaw)

2053L   Letter, Cherokee Advocate, July 13, 1881.

2054A   "Governor's Message," Indian Journal, October 13, 1881.

2055A   "Governor McCurtain's Message," Indian Journal, October 19, 1882.

2056A   "Gov. McCurtain's Message," Indian Journal, May 24, 1883.

2057A   "Gov. McCurtain's Message," Indian Journal, October 11, 1883.

2058A   "Gov. J. F. McCurtain's Retiring Address," Indian Champion, October 25, 1884.

McDERMOTT, JESSE J. (Creek)

2059N   "The Creek Indian, as He Is and as He Was," Muskogee Times Democrat, December 1, 1909.

McDONALD, LOUIS (Ponca)

2060N   "What's in a Name," Red Man, 15 (February-March, 1899), 3, 6.

McFARLAND, DAVID (Nez Percé)
2061N "A Dash for Freedom," Red Man, 14 (March, 1898), 6.

McGAA, AGNES (Sioux)
2062M "Legend of an Indian Maiden," Indian School Journal, 9 (March, 1909), 55.

McGILBERRY, CHARLES W. (Choctaw)
2063N "Why the Indian Student Should Receive as Good an Education as Any Other Student in America," Quarterly Journal of the Society of American Indians, 1 (July-September, 1913), 287-288.
2064N "Indian Agriculture," Indian School Journal, 15 (October, 1914), 73-74.
2065N "The Choctaw Indians," Indian School Journal, 16 (September, 1915), 22-23.
2066M "The Deluge as Told by Indians," Indian School Journal, 18 (September, 1917), 260.
2067N "The Indians' Place in History," Indian School Journal, 18 (December, 1917), 151-153.

McGILBRA, SANFORD (Creek)
2068N "The Origin of the Red Man." Bacone Chief. Bacone, OK: Bacone College, 1919, pp. 55-56.
2069N "Legend." Bacone Chief. Bacone, OK: Bacone College, 1920, p. 73.
2070M "Why the Wild Cat is Spotted." Bacone Chief. Bacone, OK: Bacone College, 1920, pp. 84-85.
2071N "Corn Culture." Bacone Chief. Bacone, OK: Bacone College, 1921, pp. 86-87.
2072N "History of Tobacco." Bacone Chief. Bacone, OK: Bacone College, 1921, pp. 73-75.

McINNIS, JOHN (Washo)
2073F "The Sheldrake Duck," Red Man, 3 (January, 1911), 205-206.
2074F "The Sheldrake Duck," Indian's Friend, 23 (June, 1911), 12.

McINTOSH, ALBERT GALLATIN (Creek)
2075N With Joshua Ross. "What Has the Indian to Be Thankful For?" Twin Territories, 4 (November, 1902), 328-329.

McINTOSH, JEANETTA (Creek)
2076N "Our Dining Room." Bacone Chief. Bacone, OK: Bacone College, 1920, pp. 85-86.

McINTOSH, LUKE G. (Creek)
2077N "To Teach Indian Speaking People from English Text Books," Indian Journal, August 25, 1881.
2078N "The Public Schools," Indian Journal, March 1, 1888.
2079L "The Public Schools," Indian Journal, October 3, 1889.
2080L "Allotment," Muskogee Phoenix, September 21, 1893.

McINTOSH, ROBERT (Apache)
 2081A "Address to My White Friends," Southern Workman, 13
   (June, 1884), 62.

McKELLOP, ALBERT PIKE (Creek)
 2082N "The Creek Election," Indian Journal, November 8, 1883.
 2083L "The Position of Noncitizens," Muskogee Phoenix, March
   31, 1892.
 2084L "As to Ownership of Creek Lands," Muskogee Phoenix,
   March 24, 1892.
 2085L "McKellop Comes Back," Muskogee Phoenix, April 28,
   1892.
 2086C Rules of the House of Warriors. Muskogee, I. T.: Phoenix Printing Company, 1892? In English and Creek. He
   was both compiler and translator.
 2087L With Pleasant Porter. "An Open Letter," Muskogee Phoenix, February 16, 1893.
 2088C Constitution and Laws of the Muskogee Nation, as Compiled
   and Codified by A. P. McKellop, Under Act of October
   15, 1892. Muskogee, I. T.: F. C. Hubbard, 1893.
 2089L ["Reply to the Commissioner's Address"], Muskogee Phoenix, February 22, 1894.
 2090L "The Creek Treaty," Muskogee Phoenix, August 12, 1897.
 2091C Acts and Resolutions of the National Council of the Muskogee Nation of 1893 and 1899, Inclusive. Muskogee, I. T.:
   Phoenix Printing Company, 1900.
 2092L "The Anti-Horse Thief Association," Muskogee Democrat,
   October 12, 1904.

McKINNEY, THOMPSON (Choctaw)
 2093A "Address of Thompson McKinney," Muskogee Phoenix,
   October 11, 1888.
 2094A "Gov. McKinney's Message," Indian Journal, October 21,
   1886.

McLAUGHLIN, MARIE L. (Sioux)
 2095M Myths and Legends of the Sioux. Bismarck, ND: Bismarck Tribune Co., 1916.

McLEAN, SAMUEL J. (Sioux)
 2096N "Feathers," Indian's Friend, 21 (May, 1909), 5.

McLEMORE, GUSSIE (Cherokee)
 2097N "An Indian Dance," Indian Leader, November, 1915.

MADDOX, SARAH (Modoc)
 2098N "Class History," Native American, June 15, 1907.

MADRID, SAVANNAH (Pueblo)
 2099M "How Winter Was Vanquished," Indian Leader, May, 1915.

MANUEL, VICTOR (Pima)
 2100A "Address of Class President," Native American, June 16,
   1906.

2101N "The Pimas: Christian Indian Tribe of the Southwest,"
Southern Workman, 39 (March, 1910), 161-162.
2102N "The Pima: Christian Indian Tribe of the Southwest,"
Native American, April 9, 1910.

MAQUIMITIS, MITCHELL (Menominee)
2103N "Menominees," Talks and Thoughts of the Hampton Indian
Students, 2 (April, 1887), 1.

MARISTO, MARTIN (Papago)
2104N "The Papago Indians," Native American, December 25,
1909.
2105N "A Christmas on the Papago Reservation," Native American, December 25, 1909.
2106N "My First Christmas," Native American, December 24,
1910.
2107N "The Home of the Arab," Native American, January 28,
1911.
2108N "Concrete and Its Uses," Native American, May 20, 1911.

MARSDEN, EDWARD (Tsimshian)
2109N "Myself Since 1869," Indian Helper, December 2, 1892.
2110N "An Experience with the Wild West Show," Indian Helper,
January 24, 1896.
2111L "A Journey to Alaska," Indian Helper, May 29, 1896.
2112L "Alaska," Indian Helper, June 12, 1896.
2113L "New Metlakahla, Alaska," Indian Helper, July 31, 1896.
2114N "A Trip to Northern British Columbia," Indian Helper, December 4, 1896.
2115N ["A Trip to Sitka,"] Indian Helper, December 11, 1896.
2116N "On the Steamer 'Maria G. Haaven,'" Indian Helper, January 15, 1897.
2117N "A Speech on Board the Ship," Indian Helper, February 12,
1897.
2118N "Cooking with Only One Kettle," Indian Helper, February
19, 1897.
2119N "Raising and Improving an Alaskan House," Indian Helper,
March 26, 1897.
2120N "Land Surveying," Indian Helper, April 9, 1897.
2121N "The Journey of the Three Alaskans," Indian Helper, April
30, 1897.
2122N "Experiences of an Alaskan Student: On the Wrong Train,"
Indian Helper, July 23, 1897.
2123N "Does the Indian Ever Get Scared?" Indian Helper, September 24, 1897.
2124A Address at Carlisle. Red Man and Helper, May 31, 1902.
2125A "Address," Red Man and Helper, November 13, 1903.

MARTIN, JOE (Pima)
2126N "Building Construction of Anton Nanime," Native American,
June 19, 1915.

MARTIN, JOHN (Cherokee)

2127N   With John Ridge and W. S. Coodey. "Cherokee Memorial,"
         Cherokee Phoenix & Indians' Advocate, March 24, 1832.

MARTIN, JOSEPH LYNCH (Cherokee)
2128L   "Letter from J. L. Martin," Arkansian, July 23, 1859.
2129L   "From the Cherokee Nation," Arkansian, October 22, 1859.
2130L   Letter, Indian Journal, June 5, 1878.
2131L   Letter, Cherokee Advocate, November 12, 1879.
2132L   Letter, Cherokee Advocate, December 10, 1879.
2133L   Letter, Cherokee Advocate, December 17, 1879.
2134L   Letter, Cherokee Advocate, January 21, 1880.
2135L   Letter, Cherokee Advocate, October 13, 1880.
2136L   Letter, Cherokee Advocate, January 26, 1881.
2137P   "A Dream," Cherokee Advocate, February 9, 1881.
2138L   Letter, Cherokee Advocate, March 16, 1881.
2139L   "Council Suggestions," Indian Chieftain, October 17, 1889.
2140L   "Legislation Wanted," Indian Chieftain, November 14, 1889.
2141L   "Safety in the 1866 Treaty," Indian Chieftain, June 12,
         1890.
2142L   "A Characteristic Letter," Indian Chieftain, July 17, 1890.
2143P   "Stanzas by Uncle Joe," Cherokee Advocate, April 1, 1891.
2144L   "Citizenship," Indian Sentinel, October 21, 1891.
2145N   "Passed Away," Indian Sentinel, December 16, 1891.

MASON, MARIE (Digger)
2146N   "A Trip to Philadelphia," Carlisle Arrow, June 4, 1915.

MAYES, JOEL BRYAN (Cherokee)
2147N   "An Indian's Thanksgiving Proclamation," Southern Work-
         man, 18 (January, 1889), 8.
2148A   "Annual Message," Cherokee Advocate, November 6, 1889.
2149A   Third Annual Message of Hon. J. B. Mayes, Principal
         Chief of the Cherokee Nation, Delivered at Tahlequah,
         Cherokee Nation, November 9th, 1889. Tahlequah? I. T.,
         1889?
2150A   First Annual Message of Hon. Joel B. Mayes, Principal
         Chief of the Cherokee Nation. Delivered at Tahlequah,
         I. T., November 4, 1891. Tahlequah? I. T., 1891.

MAYES, SAMUEL HOUSTON (Cherokee)
2151A   Message Concerning Dawes Commission, Indian Citizen,
         November 21, 1895.
2152A   "First Annual Message of Hon. S. H. Mayes, Principal
         Chief of the Cherokee Nation," Muskogee Phoenix, No-
         vember 21, 1895.
2153A   "Chief S. H. Mayes' First Annual Message to Council,"
         Indian Chieftain, November 21, 1895.
2154A   "The Chief's Message," Indian Chieftain, March 26, 1896.
2155A   "The Message," Vinita Leader, August 13, 1896.
2156A   "Chief's Message," Muskogee Phoenix, August 13, 1896.
2157A   "Chief Mayes' Message," Indian Chieftain, November 5,
         1896.
2158A   Second Annual Message of Chief Samuel H. Mayes. De-

         livered at Tahlequah, November 3rd, 1896.   Tahlequah?
         I. T., 1896.

2159L "The Chief Writes Acridly," Indian Chieftain, July 7, 1897.
2160L Letter, Muskogee Phoenix, July 8, 1897.
2161A "The Chief's Message," Indian Chieftain, July 29, 1897.
2162A "Another Message," Indian Sentinel, August 11, 1898.
2163A "A Special Message," Indian Chieftain, August 18, 1898.
2164A "The Annual Message," Indian Sentinel, November 10, 1898.
2165A "The Chief's Message," Daily Chieftain, November 14, 1898.
2166A "The Chief's Message," Indian Chieftain, November 17, 1898.
2167A "The Fourth Annual Message of Principal Chief S. H. Mayes to the Cherokee National Council," Fort Smith Elevator, November 18, 1898.
2168A Fourth Annual Message ... Delivered at Tahlequah, I. T., November 8, 1898. N. p., 1898?

MEANS, HOBART W. (Sioux)
2169N "What Makes a Man Successful in Business?" Indian Leader, June 8-22, 1923.

MEDICINEGRASS, LUCY (Arapaho)
2170N "Care of the Sick," Native American, May 16, 1914.

MELTON, ANNA (Cherokee)
2171M "The Legend of the Black-Snake," Red Man, 4 (November, 1911), 118.

MERRICK, RICHENDA (Cheyenne)
2172N "The Animal Dance," Indian Leader, May, 1915.

MERRILL, GEORGE (Chippewa)
2173N "My First Christmas at Carlisle," Carlisle Arrow, December 18, 1914.

MERRILL, SUSIE (Klamath)
2174N "Class Fun," Native American, May 30, 1903.

METOXEN, ANNA (Oneida)
2175N "New Year's at Home," Indian Leader, December 30, 1910.
2176N "Indian Corn Syrup," Indian Leader, November 10, 1911.
2177N "Indian Corn Soup," Indian's Friend, 24 (December, 1911), 8.

METOXEN, DAISY (Oneida)
2178N "The Duty of Those Who Are Left Behind," Indian Leader, June, 1918.

METOXEN, EVELYN (Oneida)
2179N "Home Economics and the Indian Girl," Indian Leader, June 8-23, 1918.

METOXEN, IVA (Oneida)
    2180F With Cora Elm. "First Book of the Chronicles of the
          Class of 1913," Carlisle Arrow, May 16, 1913.

METOXEN, JOE (Oneida)
    2181N "An Indian Game--La Crosse," Indian Leader, December
          18, 1908.

METOXEN, MALINDA (Oneida)
    2182P "Iceland," Red Man, 13 (January, 1896), 6.

MICHA, LIZZIE (Pima)
    2183N "The Cactus," Native American, December 5, 1908.

MILES, THOMAS J. (Sac and Fox)
    2184N "Printing Office," Southern Workman, 13 (April, 1884), 43.
    2185N "The Other Side of the Sac and Fox Situation," Red Man,
          9 (March, 1889), 2.
    2186L "Teaching in Indian Territory," Southern Workman, 20
          (January, 1891), 142-143.

MILLER, ARTIE E. (Stockbridge)
    2187N "Needs of Our Indian Youth," Red Man, 15 (March, 1900),
          2-3.

MILLER, IVA (Cherokee)
    2188F "Robin Red Breast," Red Man, 4 (January, 1912), 209-210.

MILLER, MARY (Chippewa)
    2189N "Are the Indians Better for the Coming of the White Man?"
          Red Man, 14 (April, 1897), 7.

MILLER, SADIE (Delaware-Cherokee)
    2190M "How Witchcraft Originated," Indian Leader, February,
          1916.
    2191N "For What Are We Fighting?" Indian Leader, April, 1918.

MILLS, INEZ (Pima)
    2192A "Legends," Native American, June 3, 1905.

MINTHORN, AARON (Cayuse)
    2193N "My Home People," Indian Craftsman, 1 (March, 1909), 18.

MITCHELL, CHARLES (Assiniboin)
    2194N "The Caddo Indians," Indian Craftsman, 1 (April, 1909),
          32-34.
    2195N "Totems," Indian Craftsman, 1 (April, 1909), 31-32.
    2196N "Cornstalk, the Great Shawnee," Indian's Friend, 21 (June,
          1909), 2.

MOLLIE, ALMA (Pima)
    2197A "Housekeeping," Native American, June 16, 1906.

MOLLIE, OSSIE (Pima)
2198F "The Man Who Was Changed into an Eagle," Native American, June 15, 1907.

MONTEZUMA, CARLOS (Apache)
2199N "An Apache, to the Students of Carlisle Indian School," Indian Helper, October 14, 1887.
2200L "To the Students of Carlisle," Southern Workman, 16 (November, 1887), 117.
2201N "From an Apache Camp to a Chicago Medical School: The Story of Carlos Montezuma's Life as Told by Himself," Red Man, 8 (July and August, 1888), 3.
2202L "An Apache's Opinion," Red Man, 11 (March-April, 1893), 5. Reprinted from The Review.
2203A "Speech of Dr. Montezuma at the Mohonk Conference," Red Man, 12 (December, 1893), 4.
2204A "The Indian Problem from the Indian's Point of View," Red Man, 14 (February, 1898), 1-2.
2205N ["Indian vs. Cuban,"] Red Man, 15 (December, 1898), 2.
2206A The Indian Problem from an Indian's Standpoint. Chicago: Chicago Indian Association, 1898.
2207N Address at Carlisle Commencement, Red Man, 15 (February-March, 1899), 9.
2208N "Football as an Indian Educator," Red Man, 15 (January, 1900), 8. Reprinted from San Francisco Examiner.
2209N "What Has Christianity Done for the Aboriginal Americans?" Red Man and Helper, December 6, 1901.
2210N "Blockades to Indian Civilization," Red Man and Helper, May 16, 1902.
2211N "Blockades to Indian Civilization," Osage Journal, May 29, 1902.
2212N ["The Indian Dance,"] Red Man and Helper, September 19, 1902.
2213N "Flash Lights on the Indian Question," Red Man and Helper, November 14, 1902.
2214N "How America Has Betrayed the Indian," Red Man and Helper, October 16, 1903. Reprinted from Chicago Sunday Tribune.
2215N "An Undelivered Speech," Tahlequah Arrow, April 15, 1905.
2216N "Two 'White' Indians," Indian School Journal, 5 (September, 1905), 166.
2217N A Review of Commissioner Leupp's Interview, in the New York Daily Tribune, Sunday April 9, 1905, on the Future of Our Indians. Chicago, n. p., 1905.
2218N "A Protest," Indian's Friend, 20 (October, 1907), 10.
2219N Memorial and Papers from the Mohave-Apache Indians of McDowell Reservation, Arizona, in Relation to Their Removal from McDowell Reservation to the Salt River Reservation, Arizona. Committee on Indian Affairs, House of Representatives. Washington, n. p., 1911.
2220A "Light on the Indian Situation," Quarterly Journal of the Society of American Indians, I (April, 1913), 50-55.
2221N "The Indian Reservation System," Quarterly Journal of the

Society of American Indians, 1 (October-December, 1913), 359-360.

2222N   "Reservation System," Odanah Star, January 30, 1914.

2223N   "The Reservation Is Fatal to the Development of Good Citizenship," Quarterly Journal of the Society of American Indians, 2 (January-March, 1914), 69-74.

2224N   "What We Indians Must Do," Odanah Star, October 30, 1914.

2225N   "What Indians Must Do," Quarterly Journal of the Society of American Indians, 2 (October-December, 1914), 294-299.

2226N   Let My People Go. Chicago: Hawthorn Press, 1915. Read before Conference of the Society of American Indians at Lawrence, Kansas, September 30th, 1915.

2227N   "Let My People Go," Tomahawk, January 27, 1916.

2228N   "Let My People Go," Quarterly Journal of the Society of American Indians, 4 (January-March, 1916), 32-33.

2229N   "Let My People Go," Congressional Record, May 12, 1916.

2230-
2330N   "The Repression of the Indian," Tomahawk, May 25, 1916.

2331N   "Arrow Points," Wassaja, 1 (June, 1916), 1-3.

2332N   "Error Dominates the Indian Bureau and Indian Bureau Dominates the Indians," Wassaja, 1 (June, 1916), 1-3.

2333N   "Arrow Points," Wassaja, 1 (July, 1916), 1, 4.

2334N   "The Church and the Indian," Wassaja, 1 (July, 1916), 1-4.

2335A   "Address Before the Sixth Conference," American Indian Magazine, 4 (July-September, 1916), 260-262.

2336N   "Arrow Points," Wassaja, 1 (August, 1916), 1, 4.

2337N   "The Educators and the Indian Schools," Wassaja, 1 (August, 1916), 1-4.

2338N   "Arrow Points," Wassaja, 1 (September, 1916), 1, 3-4.

2339N   "Indians and Indians," Wassaja, 1 (September, 1916), 1-4.

2340N   "Arrow Points," Wassaja, 1 (October, 1916), 1-4.

2341N   "Arrow Points," Wassaja, 1 (November, 1916), 1-3.

2342N   "Ashamed to Know the Indian," Wassaja, 1 (November, 1916), 3.

2343N   "Indian Puzzled," Wassaja, 1 (November, 1916), 3.

2344N   "Let Indians Do Their Own Business," Wassaja, 1 (November, 1916), 3.

2345N   "Logic is Logic," Wassaja, 1 (November, 1916), 1.

2346N   "Buffalo Bill," Wassaja, 1 (January, 1917), 4.

2347N   "Indian Bureau and Government," Wassaja, 1 (January, 1917), 3.

2348N   "Indian Ship," Wassaja, 1 (January, 1917), 3-4.

2349N   "Indian Treaties Are Binding," Wassaja, 1 (January, 1917), 3.

2350N   "Lose and Learn," Wassaja, 1 (January, 1917), 3.

2351N   "The Man Part of an Indian," Wassaja, 1 (January, 1917), 3.

2352N   "'The New Indian Uprising,'" Wassaja, 1 (January, 1917), 3.

2353D   "On the Stage of Indian Affairs," Wassaja, 1 (January, 1917), 1-2.

2354N   "Review of the Winter Number of the American Indian Magazine," Wassaja, 1 (January, 1917), 2.

2355N   "Sledge Hammer Taps," Wassaja, 1 (January, 1917), 2-4.

2356N   "Society of American Indians," Wassaja, 1 (January, 1917), 3.

2357N   "Tattle-Tale," Wassaja, 1 (January, 1917), 4.

2358N   "Thread of 6000 Employees," Wassaja, 1 (January, 1917), 4.

2359N   "Destructive and Not Constructive," Wassaja, 1 (February, 1917), 2.

2360N   "Fear Rules the Indians," Wassaja, 1 (February, 1917), 2.

2361N   "Indian This and Indian That," Wassaja, 1 (February, 1917), 3.

2362N   "Prejudiced," Wassaja, 1 (February, 1917), 1.

2363N   "Sledge Hammer Taps," Wassaja, 1 (February, 1917), 3-4.

2364N   "Wassaja's Appeal," Wassaja, 1 (February, 1917), 1.

2365N   "What Wassaja Believes," Wassaja, 1 (February, 1917), 1.

2366N   "Why Should Indians Work?" Wassaja, 1 (February, 1917), 2.

2367N   "Be Out and Out," Wassaja, 1 (March, 1917), 4.

2368N   "'Facts is Facts,'" Wassaja, 1 (March, 1917), 3.

2369N   "False Notion," Wassaja, 1 (March, 1917), 3-4.

2370N   "Indian Accoutrements," Wassaja, 1 (March, 1917), 3.

2371N   "Sledge Hammer Taps," Wassaja, 1 (March, 1917), 3.

2372N   "To the Newly Formed Indian 'Council,'" Wassaja, 1 (March, 1917), 3.

2373P   "Civilization," Wassaja, 1 (April, 1917), 2-3.

2374N   "How Indians Are Duped Relative to Their Land," Wassaja, 2 (April, 1917), 2.

2375N   "The Next Conference of S. A. I.," Wassaja, 2 (April, 1917), 2.

2376P   "Steady, Indians, Steady," Wassaja, 2 (April, 1917), 3.

2377N   "Wassaja Is One Year Old," Wassaja, 2 (April, 1917), 1.

2378N   "The Curtis Bill," Wassaja, 2 (May, 1917), 2.

2379N   "Exploiting the Indian," Wassaja, 2 (May, 1917), 3.

2380N   "False Alarm: Cato Sells' New Indian Policy," Wassaja, 2 (May, 1917), 1.

2381N   "Freedom for the Indians Goes Unheeded," Wassaja, 2 (May, 1917), 2.

2382N   "Funny People and Strange Ideas," Wassaja, 2 (May, 1917), 3.

2383N   "An Important Hint," Wassaja, 2 (May, 1917), 3.

2384N   "Method and System," Wassaja, 2 (May, 1917), 1.

2385N   "Rights by Laws," Wassaja, 2 (May, 1917), 3.

2386N   "Roosevelt and the Indians," Wassaja, 2 (May, 1917), 2.

2387N   "Strange But True," Wassaja, 2 (May, 1917), 2.

2388N   "Wassaja's Reply to Cato Sells," Wassaja, 2 (May, 1917), 1.

2389N   "What Makes Indians Independent," Wassaja, 2 (May, 1917), 2.

2390N   "Don't Be a Pappoose Forever Mr. Indian, Help Thyself," Wassaja, 2 (June, 1917), 3.

2391N   "Indian Employees in the Indian Service," Wassaja, 2 (June, 1917), 4.

2392N "Indians Are Fighting for Their Freedom, Liberty, and Rights," Wassaja, 2 (June, 1917), 2.

2393N "Responsibility Without Privileges," Wassaja, 2 (June, 1917), 3.

2394N "See for Yourself," Wassaja, 2 (June, 1917), 3.

2395N "Seeds Sown--The Fruits Thereof," Wassaja, 2 (June, 1917), 2-3.

2396N "Sledge Hammer Taps," Wassaja, 2 (June, 1917), 3.

2397N "United States Is Paying to Keep the Indians in Degradation," Wassaja, 2 (June, 1917), 4.

2398N "The Indian Must Do It Himself," Wassaja, 2 (July, 1917), 4.

2399N "What About Our Money?" Wassaja, 2 (July, 1917), 2.

2400N "What Indians Are Good For," Wassaja, 2 (July, 1917), 1-2.

2401N "When Are Indians Competent?" Wassaja, 2 (July, 1917), 2.

2402N "A Noted Indian's Tribute to the Late Publisher," Tomahawk, September 20, 1917.

2403N "Gus Beaulieu," Wassaja, 2 (September, 1917), 4.

2404N "The Indian Is Talking," Wassaja, 2 (September, 1917), 3.

2405N "Indian Office vs. Citizenship," Wassaja, 2 (September, 1917), 2.

2406N "Indians Cry for Deliverance," Wassaja, 2 (September, 1917), 3.

2407N "'Injuns No Savvy,'" Wassaja, 2 (September, 1917), 3.

2408N "The S. A. I. Conference," Wassaja, 2 (September, 1917), 4.

2409N "Wassaja's Simple Substitute Program," Wassaja, 2 (September, 1917), 2-3.

2410N "The Crow Indians," Wassaja, 2 (October, 1917), 4.

2411N "Drafting Indians and Justice," Wassaja, 2 (October, 1917), 3-4.

2412N "Pointed Paragraphs," Wassaja, 2 (October, 1917), 4.

2413N "Pow-wow," Wassaja, 2 (October, 1917), 4.

2414N "Scalping the S. A. I. Again," Wassaja, 2 (October, 1917), 1.

2415N "$12,000,000 Indian Appropriation," Wassaja, 2 (October, 1917), 4.

2416N "Evolution and Not Freedom and Rights for the Indians," Wassaja, 2 (November, 1917), 3.

2417N "Kicking for Liberty," Wassaja, 2 (November, 1917), 4.

2418N "Pow-wow," Wassaja, 2 (November, 1917), 4.

2419N "Red Fox and Tipi Order of America," Wassaja, 2 (November, 1917), 2-3.

2420N "Want a New Trail for the Indians," Wassaja, 2 (November, 1917), 3.

2421N "Wassaja Needs Money," Wassaja, 2 (November, 1917), 2.

2422N "Pointed Paragraphs," Tomahawk, December 6, 1917.

2423N "Want a New Trail for the Indians," Tomahawk, December 13, 1917.

2424N "The Hayden Bill," Wassaja, 2 (December, 1917), 1.

2425N "Indian Wants His Land and Not Land or Silver," Wassaja, 2 (December, 1917), 2.

2426N   "It Does Not Pay to Put Too Much Confidence in the Indian Bureau," Wassaja, 2 (December, 1917), 4.

2427N   "Preliminary to a League for the Extension of Democracy to the American Indians," Wassaja, 2 (December, 1917), 1-2.

2428N   "State Game Laws," Wassaja, 2 (December, 1917), 2.

2429N   "Cato Sells Sees Montezuma's Ghost," Wassaja, 2 (January, 1918), 4.

2430N   "Friends of the Indian," Wassaja, 2 (January, 1918), 2.

2431N   "A Nation 'Misinforming a Race,'" Wassaja, 2 (January, 1918), 1-2.

2432N   "Our Appeal for Financial Aid," Wassaja, 2 (January, 1918), 1.

2433N   "Preliminary to a League for the Extension of Democracy to the American Indian," Wassaja, 2 (January, 1918), 4.

2434N   "Stop Working with the Indian Office," Wassaja, 2 (January, 1918), 3.

2435N   "Take Heed, Indian Office," Wassaja, 2 (January, 1918), 3.

2436N   "Wassaja's Appeal to the Indians," Wassaja, 2 (January, 1918), 1.

2437N   "Carter's Bill," Wassaja, 2 (February, 1918), 1-2.

2438N   "Inconsistent," Wassaja, 2 (February, 1918), 4.

2439N   "Observations," Wassaja, 2 (February, 1918), 3.

2440N   "Pow-wow," Wassaja, 2 (February, 1918), 2-3.

2441N   "Wassaja Is Asked and Answer Requested," Wassaja, 2 (February, 1918), 4.

2442N   "What Think Ye, Indian Employees?" Wassaja, 2 (February, 1918), 3-4.

2443F   "Indian Legend of 1918," Wassaja, 2 (March, 1918), 4.

2444N   "The Truth Is Coming to Light," Wassaja, 2 (March, 1918), 1-2.

2445N   "Arrow Points," Wassaja, 3 (April, 1918), 3.

2446N   "Do Not Blame Us," Wassaja, 3 (April, 1918), 3.

2447N   "A Great Crisis," Wassaja, 3 (April, 1918), 1.

2448N   "Indian Agent or Superintendent," Wassaja, 3 (April, 1918), 4.

2449N   "Pow-wow," Wassaja, 3 (April, 1918), 2.

2450N   "Who Are the First Americans?" Wassaja, 3 (April, 1918), 1.

2451N   "Battle at White Earth," Tomahawk, June 13, 1918.

2452L   ["To the Editor,"] Tomahawk, June 20, 1918.

2453N   "Made to Believe They Are Citizens and Free When They Are Not," Wassaja, 3 (June, 1918), 1.

2454N   "Prejudice," Wassaja, 3 (June, 1918), 1-2.

2455N   "Exception," Wassaja, 3 (July, 1918), 1.

2456N   "Indians Are Not Afraid to Die for Righteousness," Wassaja, 3 (July, 1918), 4.

2457N   "Let Us Have a Pow-wow," Wassaja, 3 (July, 1918), 2.

2458N   "Missions and Civil Service," Wassaja, 3 (July, 1918), 4.

2459N   "Plea of Wassaja," Wassaja, 3 (July, 1918), 4.

2460N   "So Says the Indian Bureau," Wassaja, 3 (July, 1918), 3.

2461N   "What Is an Indian?" Wassaja, 3 (July, 1918), 2-3.

2462N   "Carlisle Indian Industrial School," Wassaja, 3 (August, 1918), 3.

2463N "Democracy and Not Wardship for the Indians," Wassaja, 3 (August, 1918), 1-2.

2464N "Let Carlisle Stand," Wassaja, 3 (August, 1918), 4.

2465N "The Indian Bureau is Autocracy," Wassaja, 3 (September, 1918), 1-3.

2466N "Our Indian Soldiers," Wassaja, 3 (September, 1918), 4.

2467N "Abolish the Indian Bureau," Wassaja, 3 (October, 1918), 4.

2468N "Carlisle Misunderstood," Wassaja, 3 (October, 1918), 3-4.

2469N "Conference of Indians," Wassaja, 3 (October, 1918), 2-3.

2470N "The Indian Is Right," Wassaja, 3 (October, 1918), 1-2.

2471N "Indian Uprising," Wassaja, 3 (October, 1918), 3.

2472N "Indians Do Not Fight Their Friends," Wassaja, 3 (October, 1918), 2.

2473N "Pow-wow," Wassaja, 3 (October, 1918), 4.

2474N "What Is the Society of American Indians Now?" Wassaja, 3 (October, 1918), 3.

2475N "Indians Do Not Fight Their Friends," Tomahawk, November 14, 1918.

2476N "Carlisle U.S. Indian School," Wassaja, 3 (November, 1918), 3.

2477N "Demoralization of the Reservations," Wassaja, 3 (November, 1918), 1-3.

2478N "Four Flushing," Wassaja, 3 (November, 1918), 4.

2479N "The Indian Bureau," Wassaja, 3 (November, 1918), 3.

2480N "It Was a Calamity That the Indian Race Must Suffer," Wassaja, 3 (November, 1918), 4.

2481N "News from the West," Wassaja, 3 (November, 1918), 4.

2482N "Autocracy," Wassaja, 3 (December, 1918), 3-4.

2483N "Hang to Old Ideas About the Indian," Wassaja, 3 (December, 1918), 1-2.

2484N "Indian Bureau Is Going in Wrong Direction with Indians," Wassaja, 3 (December, 1918), 4.

2485N "A Japanese Is Naturalized," Wassaja, 3 (December, 1918), 2.

2486N "Senator Edward S. Johnson of South Dakota, Is Right," Wassaja, 3 (December, 1918), 3.

2487N "Abolish the Indian Bureau," American Indian Magazine, 7 (Spring, 1919), 9-20.

2488N "Demoralization of the Indians," Tomahawk, January 30, 1919.

2489N "Excuses to Abolish the Indian Bureau," Wassaja, 3 (January, 1919), 1-2.

2490N "Fear Not, the Indians Will Not Die," Wassaja, 3 (January, 1919), 3-4.

2491N "Indians, Depend upon Your Own Muscles," Wassaja, 3 (January, 1919), 2-3.

2492N "Indian Bureau Is Going in a Wrong Direction with the Indians," Tomahawk, February 13, 1919.

2493N "The Duty of Every Indian Who Entered the War," Wassaja, 3 (February, 1919), 1-2.

2494N "In Regard to Attorneys for Indians," Wassaja, 3 (February, 1919), 3.

2495N "The Soldier Boy," Wassaja, 3 (February, 1919), 2.

2496N   "Minnestoa Asks Freedom and Citizenship for Her Indians,"
      Wassaja, 3 (February, 1919), 3.
2497N   "Arrow Points," Wassaja, 3 (March, 1919), 2-3.
2498N   "The Bureau Indians," Wassaja, 3 (March, 1919), 1-2.
2499N   "Heap Big Pow-wow," Wassaja, 3 (March, 1919), 3-4.
2500N   "The Indian Bureau," Wassaja, 3 (March, 1919), 2.
2501N   "The Indian Pie Counter," Wassaja, 3 (March, 1919), 2.
2502N   "The Indian Bureau," Tomahawk, June 5, 1919.
2503N   "A Problem for Indian Lawyers," Tomahawk, August 7,
      1919.
2504N   "We Must Stick Together," Tomahawk, December 18, 1919.
2505N   "Golden Rule for the Indians," Wassaja, 4 (February, 1920),
      4.
2506N   "The House Passes a Bill," Wassaja, 4 (February, 1920),
      4.
2507N   "The Indians of To-day," Wassaja, 4 (February, 1920), 3.
2508N   "Rev. Robert Hall Elected Mr. Sloan as President of S.
      A. I.," Wassaja, 4 (February, 1920), 2.
2509N   "Some Very Unwise Logic Put Forth by Some Very Wise
      Heads," Wassaja, 4 (February, 1920), 1-2.
2510N   "Cato Sells the Target," Wassaja, 4 (March, 1920), 3.
2511N   "Indian Meeting at Riverside and Their Supposed Speeches,"
      Wassaja, 4 (March, 1920), 4.
2512N   "The Indian's First Bank," Wassaja, 4 (March, 1920), 1-2.
2513N   "Hon. Cato Sells," Tomahawk, June 17, 1920.
2514N   "The Indian Bureau--A Paradox," Tomahawk, July 8, 1920.
2515N   "Indian Bureau Is Going in a Wrong Direction with the In-
      dians," Tomahawk, July 15, 1920.
2516N   "Cato Sells' Letter to Mrs. Haman, President of the Wom-
      en's Civic Center, San Diego, California," Wassaja, 5
      (July, 1920), 1-2.
2517N   "Junius Says," Wassaja, 5 (July, 1920), 4.
2518N   "Indians Are Breathing, But Are Dead to the Interest of
      Their Race," Wassaja, 5 (July, 1920), 2-4.
2519N   "Great Neglect of the Government Toward the Indians,"
      Tomahawk, August 26, 1920.
2520N   "Commercialize the Indians," Wassaja, 5 (August, 1920),
      4.
2521N   "Indians in Cities and Towns," Wassaja, 5 (August, 1920),
      3-4.
2522N   "Stars and Stripes," Wassaja, 5 (August, 1920), 2.
2523N   "What Is an Indian?" Wassaja, 5 (August, 1920), 1-2.
2524N   "Gen. R. H. Pratt is 80 Years Old," Wassaja, 5 (Novem-
      ber, 1920), 4.
2525N   "The Society of American Indians Conference at St. Louis,"
      Wassaja, 5 (November, 1920), 3-4.
2526N   "Exposure and Injustices on McDowell Agency, Arizona,"
      Wassaja, 6 (May, 1921), 1-4.
2527N   "Indian Bureau Economy," Wassaja, 6 (August, 1921), 3-4
      and 7 (September, 1921), 1-2.
2528N   "It Appears No Hope for the Indians," Wassaja, 6 (August,
      1921), 2.
2529N   "It Is 'The System,'" Wassaja, 6 (August, 1921), 1.

2530N   "Mohave Indians of McDowell Ariz. Need Financial Aid,"
      Wassaja, 6 (August, 1921), 4.

2531N   "The Rape of McDowell Reservation Arizona by the Indian
      Bureau," Wassaja, 6 (August, 1921), 3.

2532N   "Washington, D. C.," Wassaja, 6 (August, 1921), 2.

2533N   "Americanism for the Indians," Wassaja, 7 (September,
      1921), 4.

2534N   "Be on the 'Square' with Indians," Wassaja, 7 (September,
      1921), 3-4.

2535N   "The Bureau and the Indian," Wassaja, 7 (September,
      1921), 2-3.

2536N   "Conference of the Society of American Indians," Wassaja,
      7 (September, 1921), 4.

2537N   "A Plea for the Indians," Tomahawk, January 5, 1922.

2538N   "The American Flag," Indian, March, 1922.

2539N   "Declare Yourself," Wassaja, 8 (September, 1922), 3.

2540N   "The Evils of Indian Bureau System," Indian, September,
      1922.

2541N   "For 'Congress to Respond,'" Wassaja, 8 (September,
      1922), 6-7.

2542N   "How Your Taxes 'Help,'" Wassaja, 8 (September, 1922),
      3-6.

2543N   "Indians--'Get on Your Feet,'" Wassaja, 8 (September,
      1922), 1-2.

2544N   "The Octopus and Want," Wassaja, 8 (September, 1922),
      3-4.

2545N   "A Prayer," Wassaja, 8 (September, 1922), 8.

2546N   "The System--Not Individuals," Wassaja, 8 (September,
      1922), 2-3.

2547N   "Conference of S. A. I. at Kansas City, Mo.," Wassaja,
      8 (October, 1922), 1-2.

2548N   "Be on the 'Square' with Indians," Indian, October, 1922.

2549N   "The Difference Between the Indian Bureau and Other Bu-
      reaus of the Government," Wassaja, 8 (October, 1922),
      3.

2550N   "Dr. Montezuma Is Not Well," Wassaja, 8 (October, 1922),
      3-4.

2551N   "Indian Bureau Philanthropy Is an Economical Farce--Indian
      Money for the Indians? Who Gets It?" Indian, October,
      1922.

2552N   "The Indians," Wassaja, 8 (October, 1922), 4.

2553N   Abolish the Indian Bureau. N. p.

2554N   The Indian of Today, the Indian of Tomorrow. Women's
      Christian Temperance Union, n. d.

MONTIETH, SARA (Nez Percê)
2555N   "My First Thanksgiving," Carlisle Arrow, November 20,
      1914.

MONTION, CARMEN (Pueblo)
2556N   "Occupations of a Pueblo Indian Girl," Southern Workman,
      44 (August, 1915), 445-449.

MOORE, ANNIE T. (Pima)
    2557N "Our Motto," Native American, June 10, 1916.
    2558N "What My People Are Doing for Their Country," Native
        American, June 15, 1918.

MOOSE, JOSEPH (Potawatomi)
    2559L "A Full-blood Indian's Letter," Indian Advocate, 21 (March,
        1909), 125-126.
    2560N "The Kansas Pottawatomies and Their First Fair," Indian
        School Journal, 6 (November, 1905), 22-27.
    2561N "Wanderings of the Pottawatomies," Indian Advocate, 20
        (July, 1908), 232-239.

MORGAN, GIDEON (Cherokee)
    2562L "Changes Are Needed," Indian Chieftain, January 19, 1893.
    2563A "Gideon Morgan on Constitution," New-State Tribune, Au-
        gust 23, 1906.

MORRIN, ALVIS M. (Chippewa)
    2564N "Opportunity," Carlisle Arrow, May 22, 1914.

MORRISETTE, FRED WILLIAM (Chippewa)
    2565N "The Legend of the Old Lighthouse on Minnesota Point,"
        Carlisle Arrow, June 4, 1915.

MORRISON, CARRIE (Chippewa)
    2566N "A Necessary Lesson," Indian Leader, July 4, 1902.

MORRISON, JOE (Chippewa)
    2567A "Remarks of Joe Morrison, Delegate to the General Coun-
        cil, Wednesday, July 10, 1918, in the City Hall, Bemid-
        ji, Minnesota," Tomahawk, August 8, 1918.

MORRISON, JOHN GEORGE, JR. (Chippewa)
    2568N "Amusements," Red Man, 11 (March and April, 1893), 2.
    2569L "Chippewas, Take Notice," Tomahawk, June 12, 1919.

MORTON, ANNIE M. (Pueblo)
    2570N "The Story of an Old Road," Red Man, 14 (March, 1898),
        5.

MOTT, SEWARD (Mohave-Apache)
    2571A "Civilizing the Indian," Native American, June 24, 1905.
    2572N "Indian Medicine Sweat Bath," Native American, December
        23, 1905.

MT. PLEASANT, EDISON (Tuscarora)
    2573M "The Great Spirit and the Monstrous Mosquito," Red Man,
        3 (January, 1911), 203-204.
    2574N "Home Making," Carlisle Arrow, April 11, 1911.
    2575N "Tuscarora and Mohawk Contest," Red Man, 3 (April,
        1911), 341-342.
    2576N "Tuscarora and Mohawk Contest," Indian's Friend, 23
        (July, 1911), 5.

MT. PLEASANT, MAMIE (Tuscarora)
    2577N "My First Thanksgiving," Carlisle Arrow, November 20,
        1914.
    2578N "My First Thanksgiving," Carlisle Arrow, November 19,
        1915.

MOUNTAIN, THIRZA (Arapaho)
    2579N "Russia in Asia," Native American, March 7, 1914.

MUMBLEHEAD, JAMES (Cherokee)
    2580P "Class Poem," Carlisle Arrow, April 21, 1911.
    2581M "A Legend of the Cherokee Rose," Red Man, 4 (September,
        1911), 28.
    2582M "A Legend of the Cherokee Rose," Indian's Friend, 24
        (October, 1911), 10-11.

MURDOCK, WESSON (Assiniboin)
    2583N "Slavery Among the Indians," Red Man, 15 (March, 1900),
        2.

MURIE, JAMES R. (Pawnee)
    2584L "From an Indian," Southern Workman, 9 (March, 1880), 29.
    2585N "From the Indians," Southern Workman, 9 (December,
        1880), 129.
    2586N ["Indians and Work,"] Southern Workman, 10 (January,
        1881), 11-12.
    2587N "From the Indians," Southern Workman, 10 (February,
        1881), 23.
    2588N "From the Indians," Southern Workman, 10 (March, 1881),
        35.
    2589N "Our Visit to Washington," Southern Workman, 10 (May,
        1881), 59.
    2590N "About Our School," Southern Workman, 10 (June, 1881),
        71.
    2591N "Witch Ways Among Them," Southern Workman, 10 (June,
        1881), 71-72.
    2592L "Does It Pay to Educate the Indians?" Southern Workman,
        13 (May, 1884), 55-56.
    2593A "An Indian's View of Indian Education," Southern Workman,
        14 (May, 1885), 55.
    2594L "At Haskell Institute," Southern Workman, 15 (May, 1886),
        56.
    2595N Assistant in Alice C. Fletcher, "The Hako: A Pawnee
        Ceremony." U.S. Bureau of Ethnology, Twenty-Second
        Annual Report, 1900-1901. Washington, DC: Govern-
        ment Printing Office, 1904, pt. 2, pp. 5-372.
    2596N "Pawnee Indian Societies." With introduction and conclu-
        sion by Clark Wissler. Anthropological Papers of the
        American Museum of Natural History. New York: Amer-
        ican Museum of Natural History, 1914, pp. 543-644.
    2597N Pawnee Indian Societies. New York: The Trustees,
        1914.

MUSKRAT, RUTH (Cherokee)

2598A   "Address to President Coolidge," Indian Leader, February
        8, 1924.

NAPAWAT, MARTHA (Kiowa)
  2599N   "Put Yourself in My Place," Red Man, 12 (January-
        February, 1894), 2-3.

NARCHO, PABLO (Papago)
  2600M   "The Papago Legend of the Formation of the Earth," Indi-
        an Leader, September, 1914.
  2601A   "Value of Training for Vocational Efficiency," Indian Lead-
        er, June, 1914.
  2602M   With Jose Lewis and Jose Antonio. "The Papago Legend
        of the Formation of the Earth," Indian Leader, October,
        1917.
  2603M   With Jose Lewis and Jose Antonio. Indian Legends and
        Superstitions. Lawrence, KS: Haskell Institute, 1917.

NARSA, MIDA (Pima)
  2604N   "Pima Basketry," Native American, May 20, 1911.
  2605N   "Basketry of the Pima Tribe," Indian's Friend, 23 (July,
        1911), 2.

NASON, BERTHA (Chippewa)
  2606F   "The Story of Polly's Life," Red Man, 8 (June, 1888), 7.

NATALISH, VINCENT (Apache)
  2607N   "A Plea for Justice and Liberty," Red Man, 15 (February-
        March, 1899), 6-7.
  2608A   Address Before the Brooklyn Indian Association, Red Man
        and Helper, June 20, 1902.

NEAL, DICK (Cherokee)
  2609L   "An Apology," Telephone, January 10, 1889.
  2610L   "Mr. Neal Again," Indian Chieftain, March 7, 1889.
  2611N   "Prison Reform Suggested," Indian Chieftain, October 24,
        1889.
  2612L   "A New Law Needed," Indian Chieftain, November 14, 1889.
  2613N   "Mr. Neal Says a Word," Muskogee Phoenix, June 19,
        1890.
  2614N   "Reason and Treason," Muskogee Phoenix, April 30, 1891.
  2615L   "Mr. Neal Speaks," Muskogee Phoenix, October 27, 1892.
  2616L   "Mr. Neal Speaks," Indian Chieftain, November 3, 1892.
  2617L   "Dick Neal's Characteristic Letter," Indian Chieftain, June
        21, 1894.
  2618N   "Dissertation on Advertising," Muskogee Phoenix, January
        11, 1900.

NEEDHAM, SIMON (Chippewa)
  2619A   "Salutatory," Carlisle Arrow, May 22, 1913.
  2620N   "The Indian's Supernatural Power," Red Lake News, Janu-
        ary 1, 1915. Reprinted from Indian Leader.

NEHOITEWA, ROLAND (Hopi)
2621A "Engineering," Native American, June 16, 1906.

NEWASHE, EMMA M. (Sac and Fox)
2622F "The Merman's Prophecy," Red Man, 5 (December, 1912),
174-175.

NICHOLS, JOSEPHINE (Seneca)
2623N "Health and Happiness," Native American, May 22, 1915.

NICHOLS, ROLAND A. (Potawatomi)
2624P "Pay Your Freight," American Indian Magazine, 5 (July-
September, 1917), 136.

NICOLAR, JOSEPH (Penobscot)
2625N The Life and Traditions of the Red Man, by Joseph Nicolar,
Old Town, Maine. Bangor, ME: C. H. Glass & Co.,
1893.

NILES, HERMAN (Stockbridge)
2626N "Must We Be Dependent?" Red Man and Helper, March 22,
1901.

NORI, SICENI J. (Pueblo)
2627N "My Home," Indian Helper, March 30, 1888.
2628N "The Carlisle Graduate and Returned Student," Red Man,
3 (May, 1911), 400-410.

NOTT, ALICE (Maricopa)
2629N "It Still May Be," Native American, May 30, 1903.

OCCOM, SAMSON (Mohegan)
2630S A Sermon, Preached at the Execution of Moses Paul, an
Indian; Who Was Executed at New-Haven, on the Second
of September, 1772; For the Murder of Mr. Moses Cook,
Late of Waterbury, on the 7th of December, 1771.
Preached at the Desire of Said Paul. By Samson Occom, Minister of the Gospel, and Missionary to the Indians. New Haven, CT: Thomas and Samuel Green,
[1772]. Reprinted in 1772.
2631S A Sermon Preached at the Execution of Moses Paul, an
Indian, Who Was Executed at New-Haven, on the 2d of
September 1772, for the Murder of Mr. Moses Cook,
Late of Waterbury, on the 7th of December 1771.
Preached at the Desire of Said Paul, by Samson Oc-
com, Minister of the Gospel, and Missionary to the In-
dians. 3rd ed. New-London, CT: T. Green, 1772.
2632S A Sermon, Preached at the Execution of Moses Paul, an
Indian, Who Was Executed at New-Haven, on the 2d of
September 1772, for the Murder of Mr. Moses Cook,
Late of Waterbury, on the 7th of December 1771.
Preached at the Desire of Said Paul, by Samson Oc-

com, Minister of the Gospel, and Missionary to the Indians. 4th ed. New-London, CT: T. Green, 1772.

2633S   A Sermon, Preached at the Execution of Moses Paul, an Indian, Who Was Executed at New-Haven, on the 2d of September, 1772, for the Murder of Mr. Moses Cook, Late of Waterbury, on the 7th of December, 1771. Preached at the Desire of Said Paul. By Samson Occom, Minister of the Gospel, and Missionary to the Indians. Boston: J. Boyles, 1773. Reprinted in 1773.

2634S   A Sermon, Preached at the Execution of Moses Paul, an Indian: Who Was Executed at New-Haven, on the 2d of September, 1772, for the Murder of Mr. Moses Cook, Late of Waterbury, on the 7th of December, 1771. Preached at the Desire of Said Paul. By Samson Occom, Minister of the Gospel, and Missionary to the Indians. Boston: Richard Draper and John Boyles, 1773.

2635C   A Choice Collection of Hymns and Spiritual Songs; Intended for the Edification of Sincere Christians, of All Denominations. By Samuel Occom, Minister of the Gospel. New London, CT: Timothy Green, 1774.

2636S   A Sermon Preached at the Execution of Moses Paul, an Indian: Who Was Executed at New-Haven, on the 2d of September, 1772, for the Murder of Mr. Moses Cook, Late of Waterbury, on the 7th of December, 1771. Preached at the Desire of Said Paul. By Samson Occom, Minister of the Gospel, and Missionary to the Indians. 9th ed. Boston, 1774.

2637C   A Choice Collection of Hymns and Spiritual Songs; Intended for the Edification of Sincere Christians, of All Denominations. By Samson Occom, Minister of the Gospel. Norwich, CT: John Trumbull, 1783.

2638C   A Choice Collection of Hymns and Spiritual Songs; Intended for the Edification of Sincere Christians, of All Denominations. By Samson Occom, Minister of the Gospel. 2nd ed. New-London, CT: Timothy Green, 1785.

2639S   A Sermon at the Execution of Moses Paul, an Indian, Who Had Been Guilty of Murder, Preached at New Haven in America. By Samson Occom, a Native Indian, and Missionary to the Indians. To Which Is Added a Short Account of the Late Spread of the Gospel Among the Indians. Also, Observations on the Language of the Muhhekaneew Indians; Communicated to the Connecticut Society of Arts and Sciences, by Jonathan Edwards, D. D. New Haven and London: Buckland, 1788. Reprinted in 1789.

2640S   A Sermon Preached at the Execution of Moses Paul, an Indian, Who Was Executed at New Haven, on the 2d of Sept. 1772 for the Murder of Mr. Moses Cook, on the 7th of Dec. 1771. Preached at the Desire of Said Paul. London, 1789.

2641C   A Choice Collection of Hymns and Spiritual Songs; Intended for the Edification of Sincere Christians, of All Denominations. By Samson Occom, Minister of the Gospel.

3rd ed., with additions. New-London: Timothy Green and Son, 1792.

2642S [A] Sermon, Preached at the Execution of Moses Paul, an Indian, Who Was Executed at New-Haven, on the 2d of September, 1772, for the Murder of Mr. Moses Cook, Late of Waterbury on the 7th of December, 1771. Preached at the Desire of Said Paul. By Sampson Occum, Minister of the Gospel, and Missionary to the Indians. Northampton, MA: n. p. 1801.

2643S A Sermon Preached at the Execution of Moses Paul, an Indian, Who Was Executed at New-Haven, on the 2d of September 1772. For the Murder of Mr. Moses Cook, Late of Waterbury, on the 7th of December 1771. Preached at the Desire of Said Paul. By Samson Occom, Minister of the Gospel, and Missionary to the Indians. Springfield, MA: Henry Brewer, [180?].

2644S A Sermon, Preached at the Execution of Moses Paul, an Indian, Who Was Executed at New-Haven, on the 2d of September 1772, for the Murder of Mr. Moses Cook, Late of Waterbury, on the 7th of December, 1771. Preached at the Desire of Said Paul. By Samson Occom, Minister of the Gospel, and Missionary to the Indians. Exeter, NH: Josiah Richardson, 1819.

2645S A Sermon Preached by Samson Occom, Minister of the Gospel, and Missionary to the Indians, at the Execution of Moses Paul, an Indian: Who Was Executed at New-Haven, September 2, 1772, for the Murder of Moses Cook, Late of Waterbury, on the Seventh of December, 1771; Preached at the Desire of Said Paul. 10th ed. Bennington, VT: William Watson, 181?.

O'DONNELL, STELLA (Chippewa)
2646N "People of the Puckered Moccasin," Southern Workman, 39 (August, 1910), 439-440.

O'FIELD, INA (Cherokee)
2647P "A Sonnet: In the Month of May," Bacone Chief. Bacone, OK: Bacone College, 1923, p. 76.

OHLERKING, WILLIAM (Sioux)
2648N "Indian Customs," Indian Leader, May, 1915.
2649M "How the Snake Lost His Legs," Indian Leader, May, 1916.

OLD COYOTE, BARNEY (Crow)
2650N "An Indian's Appreciation," Indian Sentinel, 2 (April, 1921), 295.

OLD MAN OF THE MOUNTAIN (Cherokee)
See FOREMAN, STEPHEN

OLIVER, JAMES (Chippewa)
2651N "Emancipation Through Work," Indian Leader, July 4, 1902.

O'NEAL, MINNIE ELIZABETH (Shoshoni)
2652A "Salutatory," Carlisle Arrow, June 4, 1915.

OSBORNE, SAMUEL (Pawnee)
2653N "Powhohatawa," Indian Leader, May, 1915.

OSICK, ELOISE (Pima)
2654M "A Pima Legend," Native American, June 4, 1910.
2655N "Hawaii," Native American, July 9-16, 1910.
2656N "An Outing Girl's Summer on the Coast," Native American,
    December 3, 1910.

OSIF, MOLLIE (Pima)
2657N "The Cactus," Native American, December 5, 1908.

OSKISON, JOHN MILTON (Cherokee)
2658N "A Trip to Yosemite Valley," Indian Chieftain, August 8,
    1895.
2659F "I Match You: You Match Me," Indian Chieftain, May 27,
    1897. Reprinted from Stanford Sequoia.
2660F "Tookh Steh's Mistake," Indian Chieftain, July 22, 1897.
2661F "A Schoolmaster's Dissipation," Indian Chieftain, December
    23, 1897.
2662F "Only the Master Shall Praise," Century Magazine, 59
    (January, 1900), 327-335.
2663L "John Oskison Writes of His Visit in Europe," Indian Chief-
    tain, August 9, 1900.
2664F "When the Grass Grew Long," Century Magazine, 62 (June,
    1901), 247-250.
2665N "Biologist's Quest," Overland, n. s. 38 (July, 1901), 52-
    57.
2666N "Cherokee Migration," Tahlequah Arrow, May 31, 1902.
2667N "The President and the Indian: Rich Opportunity for the
    Red Man," Vinita Weekly Chieftain, December 25, 1902.
2668N "The Outlook for the Indian," Southern Workman, 32 (June,
    1903), 270-273.
2669F "To Younger's Bend," Frank Leslie's Monthly, 56 (June,
    1903), 182-188.
2670F "Working for Fame," Frank Leslie's Monthly, 56 (August,
    1903), 372-382.
2671F "The Fall of King Chris," Frank Leslie's Monthly, 56
    (October, 1903), 586-593.
2672F "The Quality of Mercy: A Story of the Indian Territory,"
    Century Magazine, 68 (June, 1904), 178-181.
2673N "Lake Mohonk Conference," Native American, November 4,
    1905.
2674N "Remaining Causes of Indian Discontent," North American
    Review, 184 (March 1, 1907), 486-493.
2675F "The Problem of Old Harjo," Southern Workman, 36 (April,
    1907), 235-241.
2676F "Making an Individual of the Indian," Everybody's Magazine,
    16 (June, 1907), 723-733.
2677F "Young Henry and the Old Man," McClure's, 31 (June,
    1908), 237.

2678N "John Smith Borrows $20," Collier's, 43 (September 4, 1909), 14.

2679N "Exploiters of the Needy," Collier's, 44 (October 2, 1909), 17-18.

2680N "Case of the Western Slope," Collier's, 44 (January 15, 1910), 19.

2681N "Competing with the Sharks," Collier's, 44 (February 5, 1910), 19-20.

2682N "Lung-Mender for the Lord," Collier's, 44 (February 19, 1910), 24.

2683N "Institute and Treatment Frauds," Collier's, 44 (March 5, 1910), 23.

2684F "Koenig's Discovery," Collier's, 45 (May 28, 1910), 20-21.

2685N "Carlisle Commencement," Collier's, 45 (June 4, 1910), 21-22.

2686N "Carlisle Commencement as Seen by Collier's Weekly," Red Man, 3 (September, 1910), 18-22.

2687N "Diverse Tongues: A Sketch," Current Literature, 49 (September, 1910), 343-344.

2688N "Round-up of the Financial Swindlers," Collier's, 46 (December 31, 1910), 19-20.

2689N "Spider and the Fly," Woman's Home Companion, 38 (October, 1911), 9.

2690N "Out of the Night That Covers," Delineator, 78 (August, 1911), 80.

2691N "Cooperative Cost of Living," Collier's, 48 (January 27, 1912), 48.

2692N "The Indian in the Professions," Red Man, 4 (January, 1912), 201-204.

2693A "Address by J. M. Oskison," Red Man, 4 (May, 1912), 397-398.

2694N "Little Mother of the Pueblos," Delineator, 81 (March, 1913), 170.

2695N "An Apache Problem," Quarterly Journal of the Society of American Indians, 1 (April, 1913), 25-29.

2696N "Farming on a Business Basis," System, 23 (April, 1913), 379-384.

2697N "$1,000 on the Farm," Collier's, 51 (April 26, 1913), 24 and 51 (May 3, 1913), 26

2698N "Farm, the Thousand, and the Ifs," Collier's, 51 (May 24, 1913), 24 and 51 (June 7, 1913), 24.

2699F "Walla-Tenaka--Creek," Collier's, 51 (July 12, 1913), 16.

2700N "New Farm Pioneers," Collier's, 51 (August 2, 1913), 27.

2701N "Hired Man's Chance," Collier's, 51 (August 9, 1913), 24-25.

2702N "New Way to Finance the Vacation," Delineator, 83 (August, 1913), 10.

2703F "An Indian Animal Story," Indian School Journal, 14 (January, 1914), 213.

2704N "Acquiring a Standard of Value," Quarterly Journal of the Society of American Indians, 2 (January-March, 1914), 47-50.

2705N "Apples of the Hesprides, Kansas," Forum, 51 (March, 1914), 391-408.

2706N "Arizona and Forty Thousand Indians," Southern Workman, 43 (March, 1914), 148-156.

2707N "Boosting the Thrift Idea," Collier's, 53 (April 4, 1914), 22.

2708N "With Apache Deer Hunters in Arizona," Outing, 64 (April-May, 1914), 65-78, 150-163.

2709N "The Closing Chapter: Passing of the Old Indian," Indian Leader, 17 (May, 1914), 6-9.

2710N "Less Known Edison," World's Work, 28 (June, 1914), 180-185.

2711N "Chemist Who Became King of an Industry," World's Work, 28 (July, 1914), 310-315.

2712N "Road to Betatakin," Outing, 64 (July-August, 1914), 392-409, 606-623.

2713N "American Creator of the Aluminum Age," World's Work, 28 (August, 1914), 438-445.

2714N "What a Modern Sea Fight Is Like," World's Work, 29 (November, 1914), 87-91.

2715N "Why Am I an American?" World's Work, 29 (December, 1914), 209-213.

2716N "How You Can Help Feed and Clothe the Belgians," World's Work, 29 (January, 1915), 275-277.

2717N "Indian Kicking Races," Outing, 65 (January, 1915), 441-447.

2718N "The Record of the Naval Conflicts," World's Work, 29 (January, 1915), 345-350.

2719N "From John Paul Jones to Dewey," World's Work, 29 (February, 1915), 447-469.

2720F "The Man Who Interfered," Southern Workman, 44 (October, 1915), 557-567.

2721N "In Governing the Indian, Use the Indian," American Indian Magazine, 5 (January-March, 1917), 36-41.

2722N "In Governing the Indian, Use the Indian!" Case and Comment, 23 (February, 1917), 722-726.

2723N "The New Indian Leadership," American Indian Magazine, 5 (April-June, 1917), 93-100.

2724N "In Governing the Indian--Use the Indian," Tomahawk, September 20, 1917.

2725N "Back-Firing Against Bolshevism," Outlook, 122 (July 30, 1919), 510-515.

2726N "Herbert Hoover: Engineer--Economist--Organizer," Industrial Management, 61 (January 1, 1921), 2-6.

2727N "Hoover Message to Export Manufacturers," Industrial Management, 65 (March, 1923), 131-135.

2728F "Other Partner," Collier's, 74 (December 6, 1924), 14-15.

OVERTON, BENJAMIN FRANKLIN (Chickasaw)

2729A "Speech of B. F. Overton," Vindicator, August 31, 1872.

2730A "Message of Governor B. F. Overton," Vindicator, September 20, 1876.

2731A "Message of Governor B. F. Overton," Indian Journal, September 21, 1876.

2732A   "Gov. Overton's Message," Atoka Independent, September 14, 1877.

2733A   "Annual Message," Indian Journal, September 15, 1877.

OWEN, NARCISSA (Cherokee)

2734N   Memoirs of Narcissa Owen. Washington, 1907.

2735N   "Claremore," Weekly Chieftain, July 10, 1908.

OWEN, ROBERT LATHAM (Cherokee)

2736L   "Trial of G. W. Whitesides," Indian Journal, March 13, 1884.

2737A   "Speech of Robert L. Owen," Tahlequah Telephone, February 3, 1888.

2738L   "A 'Left Handed' Denial," Indian Chieftain, March 13, 1890.

2739L   "The Intruder Question," Muskogee Phoenix, September 3, 1891.

2740N   "The Cherokee Outlet," Indian Sentinel, October 21, 1891.

2741N   "The Cherokee Outlet," Muskogee Phoenix, October 22, 1891.

2742N   "The Crisis in Indian Territory," Muskogee Phoenix, December 17, 1896.

2743L   "Some Timely Questions," Indian Chieftain, July 14, 1898.

2744L   "Evils of the Curtis Bill," Indian Chieftain, July 28, 1898.

2745L   "Opposition Is Useless," Indian Sentinel, July 29, 1898. Reprinted from Kansas City Times.

2746N   Brief on Behalf of Choctaw Nation. The United States and the Wichita and Affiliated Bands of Indians, Appellants, v. the Choctaw and Chickasaw Nations, Appellees. Washington, DC: Gibson Bros., 1899.

2747N   A Plan for Saving to the Cherokee People Millions of Dollars. Muskogee, I. T.: Phoenix Printing Company, 189?.

2748L   "An Open Letter to Frank J. Boudinot," Twin Territories, 2 (May, 1900), 90.

2749N   "Reply to the Atoka Citizen," Twin Territories, 2 (May, 1900), 90.

2750N   "Fictitious Interview with Col. R. L. Owen," Indian Chieftain, November 1, 1900.

2751N   "Four Million Dollar Claim Cannot Be Sold," Indian Chieftain, November 1, 1900.

2752L   "Col. Owen Explains," Indian Chieftain, March 21, 1901.

2753L   "Answer to Too-qua-stee," Daily Chieftain, March 28, 1901.

2754L   "Answer to Too-qua-stee," Indian Chieftain, March 28, 1901.

2755N   "As the New Year Finds Us," Twin Territories, 4 (January, 1902), 9-13.

2756N   Statehood for Indian Territory and Oklahoma. Remarks of Robert L. Owen Before the Committee on the Territories of the House of Representatives. Washington, DC: Government Printing Office, 1904.

2757N   "The Rights of Women," New-State Tribune, April 12, 1906.

2758L   "Pointed Answer by Robert L. Owen," <u>Muskogee Times Democrat</u>, October 10, 1906.

2759N   "Some Pile Driving Blows at the Tariff," <u>New-State Tribune</u>, October 18, 1906.

2760A   "Restrictions on Sale of Lands Should Be Removed," <u>Muskogee Times Democrat</u>, November 16, 1906.

2761A   "An Address of Robert L. Owen to the Voters of the New State," <u>Daily Oklahoman</u>, March 15, 1907.

2762A   "An Address of Robert L. Owen to Voters of the New State," <u>Shawnee Daily Herald</u>, March 24, 1907.

2763A   "Removal of Restrictions," <u>Tahlequah Arrow</u>, April 13, 1907.

2764N   "Restoration of Popular Rule," <u>Arena</u>, 39 (June, 1908), 642-650.

2765N   <u>Memorial of Initiative and Referendum League of America Relative to a National Initiative and Referendum.</u> Washington, DC: Government Printing Office, 1908.

2766N   <u>Remarks of Senator Owen, at the Request of the National Organization of Women ... Before the Committee on the Judiciary, House of Representatives.</u> Washington, DC: Government Printing Office, 1908.

2767N   "What Removal of Restrictions Means," <u>Sturm's Oklahoma Magazine</u>, 7 (January, 1909), 21-23.

2768N   <u>Amending the Act to Prohibit the Sale of Intoxicating Liquors to Indians ... Report.</u> Washington, DC: Government Printing Office, 1909.

2769N   <u>Balance Due Loyal Creek Indians ... Report.</u> Washington, DC: Government Printing Office, 1909.

2770N   <u>Establishment of the Probation System in United States Courts ... Brief in Support of the Bill (S. 3798) for the Establishment of a Probation System in the United States Courts, Except in the District of Columbia.</u> Washington, DC: Government Printing Office, 1909.

2771N   <u>Extension of Time of Payments on Certain Homestead Entries in Oklahoma ... Report.</u> Washington, DC: Government Printing Office, 1909.

2772N   With George H. Shibley and J. Harry Carnes. <u>Initiative and Referendum a Republican Form of Government. In the Supreme Court of the State of Oregon, January Term, 1909. State of Oregon, Plaintiff and Respondent, vs. Pacific State Telephone and Telegraph Company, a Corporation, Defendant and Appellant. Supplemental Brief for Respondent.</u> Forest Grove, OR: Oregon State Grange, 1909.

2773N   "Discussion of Equal Suffrage for Women," <u>Annals of the American Academy of Political and Social Science</u>, 35 (May, 1910), supp., 6-9.

2774N   "Senator Owen's Plan," <u>Indian Home and Farm</u>, June 25, 1910.

2775N   "True Meaning of Insurgency," <u>Independent</u>, 68 (June 30, 1910), 1420-1423.

2776N   "True Meaning of Insurgency," <u>Sturm's Oklahoma Magazine</u>, 10 (August, 1910), 37-40.

2777N "Popular Government vs. Delegated Government," Every-
       body's Magazine, 23 (November, 1910), 719-720.
2778A An Address by Robert L. Owen, United States Senator
       from Oklahoma, under the Auspices of the Society for
       Ethical Culture, at Carnegie Hall, March 20, 1910, on
       the Initiative and Referendum in Its Relations to the
       Political and Physical Health of the Nation. Washington?
       1910?
2779N The Code of the People's Rule; Compilation of Various
       Statutes, Etc., Relating to the People's Rule System of
       Government and for Terminating the Abuses of Machine
       Politics, viz: An Adequate Registration System: Secret
       Ballot: Direct Primaries: Publicity of Campaign Con-
       tributions: Corrupt Practices Act ... Etc. Washington,
       DC: Government Printing Office, 1910.
2780N National Public Health; Papers, Opinions, Letters, Etc.,
       Relative to the National Public Health, in the Considera-
       tion of Senate Bill (S. 6049) "A Bill Establishing a De-
       partment of Public Health, and for Other Purposes."
       Washington, DC: Government Printing Office, 1910.
2781A Postal Savings Depositories. Speech of Hon. R. L. Owen
       of Oklahoma in the Senate of the United States, February
       25, 1910. Washington, DC: n. p. 1910.
2782N Admission of Territories of New Mexico and Arizona ...
       Report. Washington, DC: Government Printing Office,
       1911.
2783A Election and Recall of Federal Judges. Speech of Hon.
       Robert L. Owen ... In the Senate of the United States,
       Monday, July 31, 1911. Washington: [Government Print-
       ing Office,] 1911.
2784N Lands and Funds of the Osage Indians in Oklahoma ... Re-
       port. Washington, DC: Government Printing Office,
       1911.
2785A On the Right of Election and Recall of Federal Judges.
       Washington, DC: n. p. 1911?
2786N With George H. Shibley and J. Harry Carnes. Pacific
       States Telephone and Telegraph Company, Plaintiff in
       Error, vs. the State of Oregon, Defendant in Error.
       Supplemental Brief for Defendant in Error, and for the
       State of Washington Praying to Be Heard as a Friend of
       the Court. Baltimore: King Bros., 1911.
2787N Post-Office Appropriation Bill [and Increase of Postage
       upon Advertisements in Certain Periodicals.] Views.
       Washington, DC: Government Printing Office, 1911.
2788A Speech in the Senate of the United States, March 4, 1911.
       New Mexico and Arizona. N. p., 1911?
2789C Yellow Fever: A Compilation of Various Publications.
       Results of the Work of Maj. Walter Reed, Medical Corps,
       United States Army, and the Yellow Fever Commission.
       Washington, DC: Government Printing Office, 1911.
2790N "Progressive Democracy," Independent, 72 (April 18, 1912),
       833-835.
2791A "An Address of Robert L. Owen at Webbers Falls," Week-
       ly Chieftain, May 24, 1912.

2792L   Letter to C. N. Haskell, Mangum Weekly Star, July 4, 1912.

2793L   Letter to the People of Oklahoma, Daily Oklahoman, November 2, 1912.

2794L   Letter to the People of Oklahoma, Mangum Weekly Star, November 21, 1912.

2795N   Adjustment of Titles Within the Five Civilized Tribes in Oklahoma ... Report. Washington, DC: Government Printing Office, 1912.

2796N   Indian Coal Lands ... Report. Washington, DC: Government Printing Office, 1912.

2797A   Judicial Recall. Address by Senator Robert L. Owen Before the Bar Association of Muskogee, Okla., and Published in the Daily Oklahoman of Sunday, December 31, 1911, Relative to the Recall of Judges. Washington, DC: Government Printing Office, 1912.

2798N   United States Public Health Service ... Report. Washington, DC: Government Printing Office, 1912.

2799N   "Federal Reserve Bank Bill," Proceedings of the Academy of Political Science, 4 (October, 1913), 1-11.

2800N   "Origin, Purpose, and Plan of the Currency Bill," North American Review, 198 (October, 1913), 556-569.

2801N   "Pending Banking and Currency Bill," Moody's Magazine, 16 (October, 1913), 167-170.

2802N   "Currency Bill and Financial Panics," Independent, 76 (December 25, 1913), 581.

2803L   Banking and Currency. A Letter from the Chairman of the Senate Committee on Banking and Currency to Mr. Joseph T. Talbert, Vice President of the National City Bank of New York, New York City. Washington, DC: Government Printing Office, 1913.

2804N   Banking and Currency ... Report. Washington, DC: Government Printing Office, 1913.

2805N   Banking and Currency. Statement of Hon. Robert L. Owen, Chairman of the Committee on Banking and Currency of the United States Senate, in Regard to Senate Bill 2639, the Currency Bill. Washington, DC: Government Printing Office, 1913.

2806N   Banking and Currency Bill. Comparative Print Showing the Changes Suggested by the Amendment Submitted to the Senate by Mr. Owen, Also the Changes Suggested by the Amendments Intended to be Proposed by Mr. Hitchcock to H. R. 7837, an Act to Provide for the Establishment of Federal Reserve Banks, to Furnish an Elastic Currency, to Afford Means of Rediscounting Commercial Paper, to Establish a More Effective Supervision of Banking in the United States, and for Other Purposes. Washington, DC: Government Printing Office, 1913.

2807L   Banking and Currency Legislation. Letter from the Chairman of the Committee on Banking and Currency, United States Senate, Sixty-Third Congress, First Session, Relative to the Bill S. 2639, a Bill to Provide for the Establishment of Federal Reserve Banks, for Furnishing an

Elastic Currency, Affording Means of Rediscounting Commercial Paper, and to Establish a More Effective Supervision of Banking in the United States, and for Other Purposes. Washington, DC: Government Printing Office, 1913.

2808N Currency Bill. Comparative Print, Showing the Changes Suggested by the Modified Amendment Submitted to the Senate by Mr. Owen, Also the Changes Suggested by the Amendments Intended to be Proposed by Mr. Hitchcock, to H. R. 7837, an Act to Provide for the Establishment of Federal Reserve Banks, to Furnish an Elastic Currency, to Afford Means of Rediscounting Commercial Paper, to Establish a More Effective Supervision of Banking in the United States, and for Other Purposes. Washington, DC: Government Printing Office, 1913.

2809N Legislative Reference Bureau of the Library of Congress ... Report. Washington, DC: Government Printing Office, 1913.

2810N People's Rule Versus Boss Rule ... Remarks ... In the Senate of the United States, March 3, 1913. Washington, DC: Government Printing Office, 1913.

2811N "Why the Panama Tolls Exemption Should Be Repealed," Review of Reviews, 49 (May, 1914), 560-562.

2812N "National Suppression of the Liquor Traffic," Red Man, 6 (March, 1914), 250.

2813N "Tribute to R. L. Williams," Indian Journal, October 30, 1914.

2814A Affairs in Mexico. Speech ... of Robert L. Owen of Oklahoma in the Senate of the United States. Washington, DC: n. p. 1914.

2815N Legislative Reference Bureau. A Statement Setting Forth the Purpose of the Proposed Law, and Giving an Outline of the Plan, by Hon. Robert L. Owen. Washington, DC: Government Printing Office, 1914.

2816N "What Congress Should Do to Develop an American Mercantile Marine," Proceedings of the Academy of Political Science, 6 (October, 1915), 48-60.

2817N "Cloture in the Senate," Harper's Weekly, 61 (November 27, 1915), 508-509.

2818A The Previous Question--Limitation of Debate--Cloture. Speech of Hon. Robert L. Owen, of Oklahoma, in the Senate of the United States, February 18, 1915. Washington, DC: Government Printing Office, 1915.

2819N "Next Election," Harper's Weekly, 62 (March 11, 1916), 243.

2820N "Says Senator Owen," Everybody's, 35 (September, 1916), 292-298.

2821N Amendments to the Federal Reserve Act ... Report. Washington, DC: Government Printing Office, 1916.

2822N Choctaw and Chickasaw Per Capita Payment. Extract from Speech of Hon. Robert L. Owen of Oklahoma in the Senate of the United States, March 27, 1916; Containing Argument of Mr. P. J. Hurley, National Attorney for the Choctaw Nation, Report of Hon. Franklin K. Lane, Secretary of the Interior, and Report of the Subcommittee on Indian Affairs, House of Representatives, Against the Claims of the Mississippi Choctaws and Others for Enrollment as Citizens of the Choctaw and Chickasaw Nations. Washington, DC: Government Printing Office, 1916.

2823A Three Years of Democracy. Shall We Have Peace or War? An Address Delivered Before the Democracy of New Hampshire on the Occasion of Their Annual Banquet Held in the City of Concord, N. H., on March 16, 1916, by Hon. Robert L. Owen. Washington, DC: Government Printing Office, 1916.

2824A The Mobilizing of America: An Address Delivered Before the Park View Community Celebration, at Washington, D. C., on July 4, 1917, by Hon. Robert L. Owen. Washington, DC: Government Printing Office, 1917.

2825A Withdrawing Power from Federal Courts to Declare Acts of Congress Void. An Address Delivered at the Auditorium in Oklahoma City, Okla., January 27, 1917, by Hon. Robert L. Owen. Washington, DC: Government Printing Office, 1917.

2826N "Money [and the United States in the European War]." In National Security League, Inc., Money, Munitions, and Ships. New York: n. p., 1918, pp. 10-16.

2827A Putting the American Dollar Par Abroad. Speech ... In the Senate of the United States, May 1, 1918. Washington, DC: Government Printing Office, 1918.

2828N Remarks of Hon. Robert L. Owen, a Senator from Oklahoma on Senate Bill 3928; to Establish the Federal Reserve Foreign Bank and Thereby Maintain the American Dollar at Gold Par Throughout the World, Furnish American Commerce with Stable Exchange and Credit Facilities in Foreign Countries, and Promote the Foreign Commerce of the United States. In the Senate of the United States, February 25, 1918. Washington, DC: Government Printing Office? 1918.

2829N "Observations on Foreign Exchange," American Economic Review, 9 (March, 1919), supp., 154-155.

2830N "Senator Owen Warns Against Currency Inflation," Bankers Magazine, 98 (May, 1919), 533-534.

2831N "Government by the People Versus Senator Lodge," Public, 22 (November 22, 1919), 1087-1089.

2832N The Covenant of the League of Nations. What It Proposes and What It Does Not Propose. Washington, DC: Government Printing Office, 1919.

2833N The Federal Reserve Act. New York: The Century Co., 1919.

2834N Foreign Exchange. New York: The Century Co., 1919.

2835N National Security and Defense ... Report. Washington, DC: Government Printing Office, 1919.

2836A The Peace Treaty and League of Nations: Speech ... In the Senate of the United States, July 31, 1919. Washington, DC: Government Printing Office? 1919.

2837N   Where Is God in the European War. New York?: For the
        Author, 1919.
2838N   Where Is God in the European War. New York: The Cen-
        tury Co., 1919.
2839A   The Inner Secrets of European Diplomacy Disclosed for the
        First Time to the American Public ... Speech in the
        Senate of the United States, December 18, 1923. Wash-
        ington, DC: Government Printing Office? 1923.

OWENS, JOHN K. (Pima)
2840A   "Address," Native American, May 20, 1905.

OWL, FREL McDONALD (Cherokee)
2841A   "The Cherokee Indians," Southern Workman, 49 (October,
        1920), 453-457.

OWL, GEORGE A. (Cherokee)
2842N   "The American Aboriginal Association," Native American,
        March 31, 1917.

OWL, HENRY M. (Cherokee)
2843N   "Indian Leaders," Native American, April 20, 1918.
2844A   "The Indian in the War," Southern Workman, 47 (July,
        1918), 353-355.
2845A   "Some Successful Indians," Southern Workman, 47 (Novem-
        ber, 1918), 535-540.

OWL, LULA (Cherokee)
2846N   "Life Among the Catawba Indians of South Carolina," South-
        ern Workman, 43 (September, 1914), 484-487.
2847N   "The Catawbas," Indian's Friend, 27 (October, 1914), 8.

OWL, W. DAVID (Cherokee)
2848N   "Community Work Among the Pimas," Southern Workman,
        52 (July, 1923), 331-336.

OWL, WILLIAM (Cherokee)
2849F   "The Beautiful Bird," Red Man, 3 (November, 1910), 131-
        132.
2850N   "Dairying," Carlisle Arrow, April 11, 1911.

PABLO, JOSE XAVIER (Papago)
2851N   "As Seen by a Returned Student," Native American, May
        5, 1906.

PADILLA, POLITA (Pueblo)
2852N   "Christmas at Home," Indian Leader, December 27, 1901.

PAMBAGO, JOHN B. (Potawatomi)
2853N   "Pottawatomie History," Indian School Journal, 9 (April,
        1909), 21-23.

PAMBRUN, FRANCIS (Piegan)
  2854N "Sanitation in Indian Homes," Carlisle Arrow, May 16,
        1913.

PARKER, ANNA (Bannock)
  2855N "The Old and the New," Red Man and Helper, February
        26-March 4, 1904.

PARKER, ARTHUR CASWELL (Seneca)
  2856N Excavation in an Erie Indian Village and Burial Site at Rip-
        ley, Chautauqua County, New York. Albany: New York
        State Education Department, 1907.
  2857N Ed., Myths and Legends of the New York State Iroquois by Har-
        riet Maxwell Converse. Albany: University of the State
        of New York, 1908.
  2858N "Secret Medicine Societies of the Seneca," American An-
        thropologist, 11 (April, 1909), 161-165.
  2859N "Snow-Snake as Played by the Seneca-Iroquois," American
        Anthropologist, 11 (April, 1909), 250-256.
  2860N Snow-Snake, as Played by the Seneca-Iroquois. Lancaster,
        PA: New Era Printing Co., 1909.
  2861N "Origin of Iroquois Silversmithing," American Anthropolo-
        gist, 12 (July, 1910), 349-357.
  2862N "Iroquois Sun Myths," Journal of American Folklore, 23
        (October, 1910), 608-620.
  2863N Iroquois Sun Myths. Boston: n. p., 1910.
  2864N Iroquois Uses of Maize and Other Food Plants. Albany:
        University of the State of New York, 1910.
  2865N "The Influence of the Iroquois on the History and Archaeol-
        ogy of the Wyoming Valley and the Adjacent Region,"
        Proceedings and Collections of the Wyoming Historical
        and Geological Society, 11 (1910), 65-102.
  2866N The Origin of Iroquois Silver-Smithing. Lancaster, PA:
        New Era Printing Co., 1910.
  2867N "Iroquois Silversmithing," American Anthropologist, 13
        (April, 1911), 283-293.
  2868N "The Peace Policy of the Iroquois," Indian School Journal,
        12 (December, 1911), 64-68.
  2869N "The Peace Policy of the Iroquois," Southern Workman, 40
        (December, 1911), 691-699.
  2870N The Influence of the Iroquois on the History and Archeology
        of the Wyoming Valley, Pennsylvania, and the Adjacent
        Regions. Wilkes-Barre, PA: n. p., 1911.
  2871N "The Legal Status of the Indian," Red Man, 4 (June, 1912),
        461-463.
  2872N "A Modern Indian Council," Red Man, 5 (October, 1912),
        51.
  2873N "American Indian Day," Indian Leader, October 25, 1912.
  2874N "American Indian Day," Carlisle Arrow, November 15,
        1912. Reprinted from New York Sun.
  2875N "Progress for the Indian," Southern Workman, 41 (Novem-
        ber, 1921), 628-635.
  2876N "The Third National Conference of Indians and Their
        Friends," Red Man, 6 (November, 1913), 91-104.

2877N   "The Third National Conference of Indians and Their Friends," Indian School Journal, 14 (November, 1913), 93-98.

2878N   Certain Iroquois Tree Myths and Symbols. Lancaster, PA: New Era Printing Co., 1913.

2879N   The Code of Handsome Lake, the Seneca Prophet. Albany: University of the State of New York, 1913.

2880N   "The Red Man Not a Tanned Mongolian," Native American, February 6, 1915.

2881N   "The Quaker City Meeting of the Society of American Indians," Quarterly Journal of the Society of American Indians, 2 (January-March, 1914), 56-59.

2882N   "The Legal Status of the American Indian," Quarterly Journal of the Society of American Indians, 2 (July-September, 1914), 213-218.

2883N   "The Awakened American Indian," Quarterly Journal of the Society of American Indians, 4 (October-December, 1914), 269-274.

2884N   "The Madison Conference of the Society of American Indians," Indian School Journal, 15 (December, 1914), 183-185.

2885N   "The Awakened American Indian," Indian Leader, January, 1915.

2886N   "The Awakened American Indian," Red Man, 7 (January, 1915), 163-168.

2887N   "Certain Important Elements of the Indian Problem," Quarterly Journal of the Society of American Indians, 3 (January-March, 1915), 24-38.

2888N   "Character and Success," Indian Leader, February, 1915.

2889N   "The Red Man Is Not a Tanned Mongolian," Indian Leader, February, 1915.

2890N   "The Awakened American Indian," Indian School Journal, 15 (February, 1915), 287-291.

2891N   "The Red Man Is Not a Tanned Mongolian," Indian School Journal, 15 (March, 1915), 368-369.

2892N   "Industrial and Vocational Foundations in Indian Schools," Quarterly Journal of the Society of American Indians, 3 (April-June, 1915), 86-97.

2893N   "The Status and Progress of Indians as Shown by the Thirteenth Census," Quarterly Journal of the Society of American Indians, 3 (July-September, 1915), 185-208.

2894N   "Sherman Coolidge: A Study in the Complexities of an Indian's Legal Status," Quarterly Journal of the Society of American Indians, 3 (July-September, 1915), 220-223.

2895N   "The Wider Vision," Native American, October 2, 1915.

2896N   With Sherman Coolidge. "Proclamation," Indian Leader, October, 1915.

2897N   "Occupations and Industry of the American Indian," Indian Leader, October, 1915.

2898N   "An Indian Council for Progress," Indian School Journal, 16 (November, 1915), 128-131.

2899N   The Legal Status of the American Indian. Washington, DC: n. p., 1915.

2900N   "The Indian, the Country and the Government: A Plea for an Efficient Indian Service," American Indian Magazine, 4 (January-March, 1916), 38-49.

2901N "The Seneca Indians in the War of 1812," Southern Workman, 45 (February, 1916), 116-122.

2902N "Some of Our Work During the Year," American Indian Magazine, 4 (July-September, 1916), 229-233.

2903N "Social Elements of the Indian Problem," American Journal of Sociology, 22 (September, 1916), 252-267.

2904N "Origin of the Iroquois as Suggested by Their Archaeology," American Anthropologist, 18 (October, 1916), 479-507.

2905N "A Message to Congress," American Indian Magazine, 4 (October-December, 1916), 282-284.

2906N "Problems of Race Assimilation in America," American Indian Magazine, 4 (October-December, 1916), 285-304.

2907N "A Conference on Race Progress," Indian Leader, November, 1916.

2908N "A Conference on Race Progress: The Sixth Annual Conference of the Society of American Indians," Red Man, 9 (November, 1916), 77-84.

2909N The Origin of the Iroquois as Suggested by Their Archeology. Lancaster, PA: American Anthropology Association, 1916.

2910N "The Senecas in the War of 1812," Proceedings of the New York Historical Association, 15 (1916), 78-90.

2911N The Constitution of the Five Nations. Albany: The University of the State of New York, 1916.

2912N The American Indian, the Government and the Country. Philadelphia? 1916? Reprinted from the Quarterly Journal of the Society of American Indians.

2913N "The Perils of the Peyote Poison," American Indian Magazine, 5 (January-March, 1917), 12-13.

2914N "How Flint Arrow Heads Were Made," American Indian Magazine, 5 (July-September, 1917), 160-165.

2915N "The Sioux Outbreak of 1862," American Indian Magazine, 5 (October-December, 1917), 228-229.

2916N "Why the Red Man Fights for Democracy," Carlisle Arrow and Red Man, November 2, 1917. Reprinted from American Indian Y. M. C. A. Bulletin.

2917N "Why the Red Man Fights for Democracy," Native American, December 1, 1917. Reprinted from American Indian Y. M. C. A. Bulletin.

2918N "The Polished Slate Culture in New York." In Warren King Moorehead, Stone Ornaments Used by Indians in the United States and Canada. Andover, MA: n. p., 1917, pp. 170-195.

2919N "Constitution of the Five Nations," American Anthropologist, 20 (January, 1918), 120-124.

2920N Making Democracy Safe for the Indians. Washington, DC: n. p., 1918. Reprinted from American Indian Magazine.

2921N "Making Democracy Safe for the Indians," Southern Workman, 47 (August, 1918), 399. Reprinted from American Indian Magazine.

2922A "The American Indian in the World Crisis," Tomahawk, November 21, 1918.

2923N Notes on the Banner Stone, With Some Inquiries as to Its
      Purpose. Albany: University of the State of New York,
      1918.

2924N A Prehistoric Iroquoian Site on the Reed Farm, Richmond
      Mills, Ontario County, N. Y. Rochester, NY: Morgan
      Chapter, 1918.

2925N American Indian Freemasonry. Albany: Buffalo Consistory,
      1919.

2926N Champlain's Assault on the Fortified Town of the Oneidas
      1615. Albany: University of the State of New York,
      1919.

2927N A Contact Period Seneca Site Situated at Factory Hollow,
      Ontario County, N. Y. Rochester, NY: Researches
      and Transactions of the New York State Archaeological
      Association, 1919.

2928N The Life of General Ely S. Parker, Last Grand Sachem of
      the Iroquois and General Grant's Military Secretary.
      Buffalo, NY: Buffalo Historical Society, 1919.

2929N The New York Complex and How to Solve It. Rochester,
      NY: Lewis H. Morgan Chapter, 1920.

2930N "The New York Indians," Southern Workman, 50 (April,
      1921), 155-160.

2931N The Archeological History of New York. Albany: Univer-
      sity of the State of New York, 1922.

2932N With Alanson Buck Skinner. The Algonkian Occupation of
      New York. Rochester, NY: Researches and Transac-
      tions of the New York State Archaeological Association,
      1923.

2933N Method in Archaeology. Toronto: C. W. James, Printer
      to the King, 1923.

2934N Seneca Myths and Folk-tales. Buffalo, NY: Buffalo His-
      torical Society, 1923.

2935N With G. E. E. Lindquist. The Indians of New York State:
      A Study of Present Day Social, Industrial and Religious
      Conditions and Needs. New York: Home Missions
      Council, 1923?

2936N "The Status of the New York Indians," New York State Mu-
      seum Bulletin, No. 253 (July, 1924), 67-82.

2937N "The Pickering Treaty," Rochester Historical Society Pub-
      lication Fund Series, 3 (1924), 79-91.

2938N "Consider the Arrowhead," Bulletin of the Archaeological
      Society of Delaware, 1 (May, 1933).

2939N "The Amateur's Opportunity," Bulletin of the Archaeological
      Society of Delaware, 1 (March, 1934), 89.

PARKER, ELY SAMUEL (Seneca)

2940L Indian Affairs. Letter from the Secretary of War, Ad-
      dressed to Mr. Schenck, Chairman of the Committee on
      Military Affairs, Transmitting a Report by Colonel Park-
      er on Indian Affairs. Washington, DC: Government
      Printing Office, 1867.

2941N Reports of the Secretaries of War and Interior, in Answer
      to Resolutions of the Senate and House of Representatives
      in Relation of the Massacre at Fort Phil. Kearney, on

December 21, 1866; with the Views of Commissioner
Lewis V. Bogy, in Relation of the Future Policy to Be
Pursued by the Government for the Settlement of the In-
dian Question: Also Reports of Gen. John Pope and Col.
Eli S. Parker, on the Same Subject. Washington, DC:
Government Printing Office, 1867.

2942N   "The Character of Grant." In Military Order of the Loyal
Legion of the United States. New York Commandery.
Personal Recollections (New York, 1891), Ser. 1, 344-
348.

2943N   "Writings of General Parker: Extracts from His Letters
and an Autobiographical Memoir of Historical Interest,"
Publications of the Buffalo Historical Society, 8 (1905),
520-536.

PARKER, ESTHER (Comanche)
2944N   "The United States Indian School," Indian School Journal,
4 (October, 1904), 74.

PARKER, FREDERICK E. (Seneca)
2945N   "The Indian as a Citizen," Quarterly Journal of the Society
of American Indians, 1 (April, 1913), 131-135.
2946A   Commencement Address, Red Man, 5 (May, 1913), 421-3.

PARKER, GABRIEL E. (Choctaw)
2947N   Memorial, Shawnee Daily Herald, January 11, 1907.
2948N   "Kick Against Hitchcock's Order," Muskogee Times Democrat, January 11, 1907.
2949N   "The Indian; Personal vs. Property," Indian School Journal, 14 (December, 1913), 148-152.
2950N   "The Great End: American Citizenship for the Indian,"
Quarterly Journal of the Society of American Indians,
2 (January-March, 1914), 60-63.
2951A   "The Indian--Personal vs. Property," Native American,
February 28, 1914.
2952N   "The American Indian--Changed Conditions," Red Man, 6
(February, 1914), 228-231.
2953N   "Intemperence a National Vice," Red Man, 6 (March, 1914),
268-270.
2954N   "To My Friends the Indian Graduates," Quarterly Journal
of the Society of American Indians, 2 (July-September,
1914), 202.
2955N   "Report of the Superintendent of the Five Civilized Tribes,"
American Indian Magazine, 4 (January-March, 1916), 85-
86.
2956N   "The Indian as the Social Equal of the White Man." In
Irene C. Beaulieu and Kathleen Woodward, comps. Tributes to a Vanishing Race. Chicago: Privately Printed,
1916, pp. 40-42.

PARNELL, ANNIE (Nez Percé)
2957N   "The Story of My People," Red Man and Helper, March
22, 1901.

PARRIS, CAROLINE (Cherokee)
2958N "Going to School," Cherokee Advocate, May 19, 1880.

PASCHAL, LOUIS (Peoria)
2959N "How to Achieve Success," Indian School Journal, 9 (March, 1909), 55-56.
2960N "Abraham Lincoln," Indian School Journal, 9 (July, 1909), 21-24.

PASCHAL, RIDGE (Cherokee)
2961L "Mr. Paschal Contradicts Mr. Adair," Indian Chieftain, August 5, 1886.
2962A "The Concluding Speeches of the Debates on the Lease of the Strip West of 96° Made by Col. E. C. Boudinot, Ridge Paschal and Jesse Cochran, February 1, 1888," Cherokee Advocate, March 7, 1888.
2963L "Answers 'Double Status,'" Tahlequah Arrow, August 5, 1905.

PATTERSON, SPENCER (Seneca)
2964M "Legend of the Bear Star," Red Man, 4 (September, 1911), 24.

PATTON, ALONZO A. (Alaskan Native)
2965M "A Chickasaw Tradition," Indian Craftsman, 1 (June, 1909), 5.
2966N "The Indian Pipe of Peace," Indian Craftsman, 2 (October, 1909), 21-23.

PAUL, GEORGE (Pima)
2967N "Our School," Native American, May 22, 1915.

PAUL, KENDALL (Alaskan Native)
2968N "What Shall Be the Fate of the Alaskan Indians?" Red Man, 15 (February-March, 1899), 2-3.

PAUL, MATILDA K. (Alaskan Native)
2969A "Story of a Native Alaskan," Home Mission Monthly, 16 (July, 1902), 9.

PAUL, WILLIAM L. (Alaskan Native)
2970N "Alaska Native Brotherhood," Southern Workman, 52 (January, 1923), 30-33. Reprinted from Home Mission Monthly.

PAWNEE, WILLIAM (Cheyenne-Arapaho)
2971M "The Morning and Evening Star," Native American, March 6, 1915.

PEAKE, EMILY E. (Chippewa)
2972N "Soliloquy of the Chapel Clock," Red Man, 11 (March-April, 1893), 2-3.

PERRYMAN, JOSEPH M. (Creek)
  2973A "The Inaugural Address," Indian Journal, December 13,
       1883.
  2974A "Chief's Message," Indian Journal, November 6, 1884.
  2975A "Chief Perryman's Message," Indian Journal, October 15,
       1885.

PERRYMAN, LEGUS CHOUTEAU (Creek)
  2976A "Annual Message of Hon. L. C. Perryman, Principal Chief,
       Muskogee Nation," Muskogee Phoenix, October 11, 1888.
  2977A "Chief Perryman's Message," Muskogee Phoenix, October
       3, 1889.
  2978A "Third Annual Message of L. C. Perryman, Principal
       Chief, M. N.," Muskogee Phoenix, October 9, 1890.
  2979C Constitution and Laws of the Muskogee Nation, as Compiled
       by L. C. Perryman, March 1st, 1890. Muskogee, I. T.:
       Phoenix Printing Company, 1890.
  2980A "Fourth Annual Message of L. C. Perryman, Principal
       Chief, M. N.," Muskogee Phoenix, October 8, 1891.
  2981C Constitution and Laws of the Muskogee Nation, as Compiled
       by L. C. Perryman, March 1st, 1890. Muskogee, I. T.:
       F. C. Hubbard, 1893.
  2982A "The Chief's Message," Muskogee Phoenix, April 12, 1894.
  2983A "Chief Perryman's Message," Muskogee Phoenix, October
       6, 1894.
  2984A Message of the Chief of the Muskogees, and Reply of the
       National Council in Extraordinary Session, April 4, 1894,
       to the Dawes Commission. Eufaula, I. T.: Journal,
       1894.
  2985A "The Chief's Message," Indian Citizen, February 7, 1895.

PESHLASKI, FRANK S. (Navajo)
  2986N "Printing," Native American, June 15, 1907.

PETERS, BERT (Pawnee)
  2987P "1924 Class Poem." Bacone Chief. Bacone, OK: Bacone
       College, 1924, p. 106.

PETERS, MYRTLE (Stockbridge)
  2988N "Indian Names in Pennsylvania," Indian Craftsman, 1 (June,
       1909), 18.
  2989N "Indian Names in Pennsylvania," Indian's Friend, 21 (July,
       1909), 2.

PETERS, WILLIAM (Pima)
  2990N "Our Past and Present: What of the Future," Native Amer-
       ican, May 24, 1902.
  2991A "The Medicine Man and the Christian Religion," Native
       American, May 2, 1914.
  2992N "Ditch Work," Native American, June 19, 1915.

PETERSON, EUNICE (Klamath)
  2993N "Is It Worth While?" Native American, May 30, 1903.

PETOSKY, CORNELIUS (Chippewa)
2994N "The Citizen Indians of Michigan," Red Man and Helper,
February 14, 1902.

PHILLIPS, WALTER (Creek)
2995N "A Creek Camp Meeting." Bacone Chief. Bacone, OK:
Bacone College, 1917, pp. 47-49.

PICOTTE, CHARLES F., JR. (Sioux)
2996N "Tin Shop," Southern Workman, 13 (April, 1884), 43.
2997N "Indian Dancers," Southern Workman, 16 (April, 1887), 45.
Reprinted from Talks and Thoughts.

PICOTTE, MARGUERITE LaFLESCHE (Omaha)
2998A "Some Indian Customs," Southern Workman, 16 (August,
1887), 88.
2999L "An Indian Teacher," Southern Workman, 17 (January,
1888), 12.
3000L "Letter," Southern Workman, 17 (April, 1888), 46.
3001L "Rachel," Southern Workman, 18 (December, 1889), 130.

PICOTTE, SUSAN LaFLESCHE (Omaha)
3002L "From an Indian Graduate of Hampton to the Chaplain,"
Southern Workman, 17 (March, 1888), 33.
3003L "The Omahas and Citizenship," Southern Workman, 20
(April, 1891), 177.
3004L "An Indian Mud Lodge a Peculiar Home," Indian Helper,
June 17, 1892. Reprinted from Indian's Friend.
3005N "My Work as Physician among My People," Southern Workman and Hampton School Record, 21 (August, 1892), 133.

PIERCE, DELIA (Seneca)
3006N "Interesting Facts about Indians Near By: The New York
Tribes," Indian Helper, March 13, 1891.

PIERCE, EVELYN (Seneca)
3007M "A Seneca Tradition," Indian Craftsman, 2 (September,
1909), 30-31.
3008M "A Seneca Tradition," Red Man, 3 (September, 1910), 23-
24.
3009M "A Seneca Superstition," Red Man, 3 (January, 1911), 207-
208.
3010N "Citizenship: The Viewpoint of a Haskell Graduate," Indian
Leader, 18 (July, 1914), 13-14.
3011N "The Value of Higher Academic Training for the Indian
Student," Quarterly Journal of the Society of American
Indians, 3 (April-June, 1915), 107-109.

PIERCE, MARIS BRYANT (Seneca)
3012A Address on the Present Condition and Prospects of the
Aboriginal Inhabitants of North America, with Particular
Reference to the Seneca Nation. Buffalo, NY: Steele's
Press, 1838.

3013A Address on the Present Condition and Prospects of the Aboriginal Inhabitants of North America, with Particular Reference to the Seneca Nation. Delivered at Buffalo, New York, by M. B. Pierce, a Chief of the Seneca Nation, and a Member of Dartmouth College. Philadelphia: J. Richards, 1839.

PIERCE, ROGENE A. (Cayuga)
3014A "Iroquois Confederacy," Southern Workman, 46 (July, 1917), 391-394.

PIKE, ELVIRA (Uintah Ute)
3015N "The Right Spirit for the Indian Student and How to Get It," Quarterly Journal of the Society of American Indians, 1 (October-December, 1913), 401-403.
3016N "My People--The Utes," Quarterly Journal of the Society of American Indians, 3 (October-December, 1915), 310-313.

PIKE, MINNIE (Ute)
3017F "In a Snow Drift," Indian Leader, January 26, 1912.

PITCHER, MARY ELVINA (Cherokee)
3018N "Country Life," Children's Play Ground, August 9, 1881.

PITCHLYNN, PETER PERKINS (Choctaw)
3019M ["A Choctaw Tradition,"] Indian Advocate, October, 1849.
3020N Papers Respecting the Rights and Interests of the Choctaw Nation, and Their Relations with the United States, the Chickasaws and Other Indian Tribes. Washington, DC: G. S. Gideon, printer, 1855.
3021A The Inaugural Address of Gov. Pitchlynn. N. p., 1864?
3022N Address by P. P. Pitchlynne, Principal Chief of the Choctaw Nation, and Winchester Colbert, Governor of the Chickasaw Nation, to the Choctaws and Chickasaws: Explanatory of the Circumstances under Which the Treaty with the United States, Concluded April 28, 1866, Was Negotiated, and of the More Important Stipulations Contained Therein, with Suggestions as to the Policy Proper to Be Pursued Hereafter by the Two Nations. Washington, DC: J. L. Pearson, printer, 1866.
3023N Memorial of P. P. Pitchlynn, Choctaw Delegate.... Washington, DC: n. p., 1868.
3024N Statement, Supplemental to Memorial of P. P. Pitchlynn, Choctaw Delegate. Washington, DC: n. p., 1868.
3025N To His Excellency the Principal Chief and General Council of the Choctaw Nation. Washington, DC: McGill and Witherow, 1868.
3026N Reports of P. P. Pitchlynn, Delegate of the Choctaw Nation, to the Principal Chief and General Council of the Said Nation, Respecting the Claims of the Nation Resulting from the Treaties Made with the United States Government During the Years of 1830 to 1866. Washington, DC: n. p., 1868-1873.

3027L Letter of P. P. Pitchlynn, Choctaw Delegate for Himself, and Co-delegates to the Senate's Committee on the Judiciary, Feb. 1870. Washington, DC: n. p., 1870.

3028L To the People of the Choctaw and Chickasaw Nations. Washington, DC: n. p., 1870.

3029N Argument Submitted by P. P. Pitchlynn, Choctaw Delegate, to the Judiciary Committee of the U. S. Senate, upon the Question Whether the People of the Choctaw Nation Have Become Citizens of the United States by Virtue of the Fourteenth Amendment to the Constitution. Washington, DC: Cunningham and McIntosh, 1870.

3030L Letter of P. P. Pitchlynn to the People of the Choctaw and Chickasaw Nations upon the Question of Sectionizing and Dividing Their Lands in Severalty. Washington, DC: n. p., 1870.

3031N Remonstrance, Appeal and Solemn Protest of the Choctaw Nation Addressed to the Congress of the United States. Washington, DC: n. p., 1870.

3032L The Solicitor of the Treasury and the Choctaw Claims. Washington, DC? 1873?

3033N "Address by P. P. Pitchlynn, Principal Chief of the Choctaw Nation, and Winchester Colbert, Governor of the Chickasaw Nation, to the Choctaws and Chickasaws," Vindicator, August 27, 1873.

3034N Report of Peter P. Pitchlynn, to the Principal Chief and General Council of the Choctaw Nation. October, 1873. Washington, DC? 1873.

3035N Reply of Peter P. Pitchlynn, Choctaw Delegate, to a Libellous Pamphlet Published by Douglas H. Cooper. Washington, DC: n. p., 1873.

3036N Claims of the Choctaw Nation. Memorial of the Choctaw Nation, Asking for the Settlement of Their Claims. Washington, DC: Government Printing Office, 1876.

3037L "To the Choctaw People," Indian Journal, July 5, 1877.

3038N Statements to the Secretary of the Interior and the Congress of the United States, Presented by P. P. Pitchlynn, the Delegate of the Choctaw Nation, Respecting the Claims of the Said Nation, Resulting from the Various Treaties Made with the United States Government During the Years of 1830 to 1866. Washington, DC: Government Printing Office? 1877.

3039N Precedents for the Payment of Interest. The Choctaw Nation of Indians Entitled to Interest on the Money Awarded to It by the Senate of the United States, on the Ninth Day of March, 1859, from the Date of Said Award. Washington, DC? 187-?

PLATERO, JOSE KIE (Navajo)
3040N "The Navajoes," Red Man, 13 (February, 1896), 8.

POKAGON, SIMON (Potawatomi)
3041N The Red Man's Greeting. Hartford, MI: n. p., 1893.
3042N The Red Man's Rebuke. Hartford, MI: n. p., 1893.

3043N   "An Indian on the Problems of His Race," Review of Reviews, 12 (December, 1895), 694-695.

3044N   "Future of the Red Man," Forum, 23 (August, 1897), 698-708.

3045N   "The Future of the Red Man," Red Man, 14 (July-August, 1897), 1-2.

3046N   "Simon Pokagon on Naming the Indians," Review of Reviews, 16 (September, 1897), 320-321.

3047N   "Indian Superstitions and Legends," Forum, 25 (July, 1898), 618-629.

3048N   "An Indian's Plea," Red Man, 15 (October-November, 1898), 5, 8.

3049N   "Massacre at Fort Dearborn at Chicago," Harper's, 98 (March, 1899), 649-656.

3050F   O-Gî-Mäw-Kwe Mit-I-Gwä-kî (Queen of the Woods). Hartford, MI: C. H. Engle, 1899. Reprinted in 1901.

3051F   Algonquin Legends of South Haven. Hartford, MI: C. H. Engle, 1900?

3052F   O-Gi-Mäw-Kwe Mit-I-Gwä-ki (Queen of the Woods); also, Brief Sketch of the Algaic Language. By Chief Pokagon. 3rd ed., Hartford, MI: C. H. Engle, 1901.

3053M   Pottawattomie Book of Genesis ... Legend of the Creation of Man. Hartford, MI: C. H. Engle, 1901?

3054N   "The Pottawatomies in the War of 1812," Arena, 26 (July, 1901), 48-55.

3055F   "An Indian Idyll of Love, Sorrow and Death," Indian's Friend, 19 (August, 1907), 2, 12.

PORTER, PETER (Pima)
3056N   "Pima Indians of the Past and Present," Native American, June 19, 1909.

PORTER, PLEASANT (Creek)
3057N   With S. H. Benge and W. P. Ross. "Memorial of the Grand Council of Nations in the Indian Territory," Cherokee Advocate, June 18, 1870.

3058N   With R. M. Wolfe, John F. Brown, and Daniel H. Ross. "Memorial of the Indian Delegations at Washington," Cherokee Advocate, April 28, 1882.

3059N   With Daniel H. Ross, R. M. Wolfe, William L. Byrd, and John F. Brown. "Supplement to Memorial of April 6th, on Railroad Question," Cherokee Advocate, May 5, 1882.

3060N   With R. M. Wolfe and D. H. Ross. "Protest of Cherokee and Creek Delegation Against Passage of S. B. 1573," Cherokee Advocate, May 28, 1882.

3061L   "Gen. Porter's Letter [to Hon. Isparhecher]," Purcell Register, June 26, 1891.

3062L   With A. P. McKellop. "An Open Letter," Muskogee Phoenix, February 16, 1893.

3063L   "A War for Liberty," Muskogee Phoenix, May 12, 1898.

3064A   "Chief Porter's Message," Muskogee Phoenix, December 7, 1899.

3065A   "Chief Porter's Annual Message," Muskogee Phoenix, October 4, 1900.

3066N   "What Is Best for the Indian," Muskogee Phoenix, September 11, 1902.

3067N   "Best for the Indian," Tahlequah Arrow, September 13, 1902.

3068N   "What Is Best for the Indian?" Twin Territories, 4 (October, 1902), 284-286.

3069A   "Chief Porter's Annual Message," Muskogee Democrat, October 3, 1905.

3070A   "Porter's Annual Message," New-State Tribune, October 18, 1906.

3071N   "Chief Pleasant Porter's View of the End," Indian School Journal, 7 (December, 1906), 47.

POSEY, ALEXANDER LAWRENCE (Creek)

3072A   "Sequoyah," Cherokee Advocate, July 22, 1893.

3073A   "Sequoyah," Red Man, 12 (July-August, 1893), 8.

3074N   "Bacone Notes," Indian Journal, February 22, 1894.

3075P   "Spring," Indian Journal, March 29, 1894.

3076P   "The Picnic's Comming," Indian Journal, May 11, 1894.

3077P   "The Whippowill Has Come," Indian Journal, May 25, 1894.

3078P   "The Indian's Past Olympic," Muskogee Phoenix, December 17, 1896.

3079P   "Sea Shells," Muskogee Phoenix, December 23, 1897.

3080P   "To a Humming Bird," Muskogee Phoenix, December 23, 1897.

3081P   "Cuba Libre," Muskogee Phoenix, December 24, 1896.

3082P   "Ode to Sequoyah," Twin Territories, 1 (April, 1899), 102.

3083P   "To a Morning Warbler," Muskogee Phoenix, November 2, 1899.

3084P   "To a Daffodil," Muskogee Phoenix, November 2, 1899.

3085F   "A Creek Fable," Muskogee Phoenix, November 2, 1899.

3086P   "An Outcast," Muskogee Phoenix, November 2, 1899.

3087P   "Nightfall," Muskogee Phoenix, November 2, 1899.

3088P   "Shelter," Muskogee Phoenix, November 2, 1899.

3089P   "Pohalton Lake," Twin Territories, 1 (November, 1899), 246.

3090P   "To a Snowflake," Twin Territories, 1 (December, 1899), 8.

3091P   "Happy Times Fer Me an' Sal," Twin Territories, 1 (December, 1899), 20.

3092F   "Uncle Dick's Sow," Twin Territories, 2 (January, 1900), 32-33.

3093P   "When Love Is Dead," Twin Territories, 2 (January, 1900), 35.

3094P   "My Hermitage," Red Man, 15 (February, 1900), 2.

3095P   "Poem," Twin Territories, 2 (March, 1900), 50.

3096P   "The Sea Shell," Twin Territories, 2 (March, 1900), 50.

3097P   "What Sea-Maid's Longings Dwell," Twin Territories, 2 (March, 1900), 50.

3098P   "The Decree," Red Man, 16 (April, 1900), 3.

3099F   "Jes 'Bout a Mid'lin', Sah," Twin Territories, 2 (April, 1900), 76-77.

3100P   "Song of the Oktahutche," Twin Territories, 2 (May, 1900),
      frontispiece.
3101L   [Letter to Editor], Twin Territories, 2 (May, 1900), 108.
3102P   "To a Robin," Twin Territories, 2 (July, 1900), 139.
3103N   "Note," Twin Territories, 2 (August, 1900), 158.
3104P   "Bob White," Twin Territories, 2 (August, 1900), 172.
3105P   "The Blue Jay," Red Man and Helper, September 7, 1900.
3106N   "Two Famous Prophets," Twin Territories, 2 (September,
      1900), 180-182.
3107F   "A Creek Fable," Twin Territories, 2 (October, 1900),
      213.
3108F   "Mose and Richard," Twin Territories, 2 (November,
      1900), 226-228.
3109P   "The Fall of the Redskin (with Apologies to Edwin Mark-
      ham)," Indian Journal, January 18, 1901.
3110P   "The Man with the Woe (with Apologies to Edwin Mark-
      ham)," Wagoner Record, January 24, 1901.
3111P   "Where the Rivers Meet," Twin Territories, 3 (February,
      1901), 24.
3112F   "Fable of the Foolish Young Bear," Indian Journal, March
      22, 1901.
3113P   "Fus Harjo and Old Billy Hell," Indian Journal, March 22,
      1901.
3114P   "Saturday," Indian Journal, March 22, 1901.
3115P   "Longing," Twin Territories, 3 (March, 1901), 47.
3116P   "To a Winter Songster," Twin Territories, 3 (April, 1901),
      80.
3117P   "Verses Written at the Grave of McIntosh," Twin Terri-
      tories, 3 (June, 1901), 133.
3118N   "The Devil's Parodies," Indian Journal, January 10, 1902.
3119F   Supposed auth. "A Fable," Indian Journal, January 31,
      1902.
3120F   Supposed auth. "A Fable," Indian Journal, February 7,
      1902.
3121F   Supposed auth. "A Fable," Indian Journal, February 14,
      1902.
3122P   "The Evening Star," Twin Territories, 4 (February, 1902).
3123P   "On Hearing a Redbird Sing," Twin Territories, 4 (March,
      1902), 84.
3124P   "An Outcast," Twin Territories, 4 (April, 1902), 134.
3125P   "Nightfall," Twin Territories, 4 (May, 1902), 124.
3126P   Supposed auth. "A Whimsical River," Indian Journal,
      June 13, 1902.
3127N   Supposed auth. "The Cruise of the Good Vrouw from a
      Diary by One of the Crew," Indian Journal, July 25,
      1902.
3128P   "To a Robin," Twin Territories, 4 (September, 1902), 258.
3129F   "From Fus Fixico," Indian Journal, October 24, 1902.
3130F   "Fus Fixico's Letter," Indian Journal, October 31, 1902.
3131P   "To a Robin," Twin Territories, 4 (October, 1902), frontis-
      piece.
3132P   "Bob White!" Twin Territories, 4 (October, 1902), 281.
3133F   "Fus Fixico's Letter," Indian Journal, November 21, 1902.

3134P "An Outcast," Twin Territories, 4 (November, 1902), 330.
3135F "Fus Fixico's Letter," Indian Journal, December 19, 1902.
3136F "Fus Fixico's Letter," Indian Journal, January 2, 1903.
3137F "Fus Fixico's Letter," Indian Journal, January 16, 1903.
3138F "Fus Fixico's Letter," Indian Journal, February 20, 1903.
3139F "Fus Fixico's Letter," Indian Journal, March 6, 1903.
3140F "Fus Fixico's Letter," Indian Journal, March 20, 1903.
3141F "Fus Fixico's Letter," Indian Journal, March 27, 1903.
3142F ["Fus Fixico's Letter,"] Vinita Weekly Chieftain, April 2, 1903.
3143F "Fus Fixico's Letter," Indian Journal, April 3, 1903.
3144F "Fus Fixico's Letter," Indian Journal, April 10, 1903.
3145F "Fus Fixico's Letter," Indian Journal, April 17, 1903.
3146F "Fus Fixico's Letter," Indian Journal, April 24, 1903.
3147F "Fus Fixico's Letter," Indian Journal, May 1, 1903.
3148F "Fus Fixico's Letter," Indian Journal, May 8, 1903.
3149F "Fus Fixico's Letter," Indian Journal, May 15, 1903.
3150F "Fus Fixico's Letter," Indian Journal, May 22, 1903.
3151F "Fus Fixico's Letter," Tahlequah Arrow, May 23, 1903.
3152F "Fus Fixico's Letter," Indian Journal, May 29, 1903.
3153F "Fus Fixico's Letter," Tahlequah Arrow, May 30, 1903.
3154F "Fus Fixico's Letter," Cherokee Advocate, June 4, 1903.
3155F "Fus Fixico's Letter," Claremore Messenger, June 5, 1903.
3156F "Fus Fixico's Letter," Indian Journal, June 5, 1903.
3157F "Fus Fixico's Letter," Tahlequah Arrow, June 6, 1903.
3158F "Fus Fixico's Letter," Vinita Chieftain, June 6, 1903.
3159F "Fus Fixico's Letter," Indian Journal, June 12, 1903.
3160F "Fus Fixico's Letter," Cherokee Advocate, June 13, 1903.
3161F "Fus Fixico's Letter," Tahlequah Arrow, June 13, 1903.
3162F "Fus Fixico's Letter," South McAlester Capital, June 18, 1903.
3163F "Fus Fixico's Funnyisms," Cherokee Advocate, June 20, 1903.
3164F "Fus Fixico's Letter," Indian Journal, June 26, 1903.
3165F "Fus Fixico on Politics," Cherokee Advocate, July 4, 1903.
3166F "Fus Fixico's Letter," South McAlester Capital, July 9, 1903.
3167F "Fus Fixico's Letter," Vinita Weekly Chieftain, July 9, 1903.
3168F "Fus Fixico's Letter," Indian Journal, July 10, 1903.
3169F "Fus Fixico's Letter," Tahlequah Arrow, July 11, 1903.
3170F "Fus Fixico's Letter," Cherokee Advocate, August 15, 1903.
3171F "Fus Fixico's Letter," Vinita Daily Chieftain, August 27, 1903.
3172F "Fus Fixico's Letter," Indian Journal, August 28, 1903.
3173F "Fus Fixico's Letter," Twin Territories, 5 (August, 1903), 309.
3174F "Fus Fixico's Letter," South McAlester Capital, September 17, 1903.
3175F "Fus Fixico's Funnyisms," Cherokee Advocate, November 7, 1903.

3176F   "Fus Fixico's Letter," Vinita Weekly Chieftain, November 12, 1903.

3177F   "Fus Fixico's Letter," Vinita Weekly Chieftain, December 3, 1903.

3178F   "Fus Fixico's Late Letter," Vinita Weekly Chieftain, December 31, 1903.

3179F   "Fixico Knows a Whitewash," Tahlequah Arrow, January 9, 1904.

3180F   "Fixico on Crazy Snake," Tahlequah Arrow, January 16, 1904.

3181F   "Fus Fixico's Letter," Vinita Weekly Chieftain, January 28, 1904. Reprinted from Muskogee Times.

3182F   "Fus Fixico's Letter," Vinita Weekly Chieftain, April 21, 1904.

3183F   "Fus Fixico's Letter," Cherokee Advocate, April 23, 1904.

3184F   "Fus Fixico's Letter," South McAlester Capital, May 5, 1904.

3185F   "Fus Fixico's Letter," Cherokee Advocate, May 7, 1904.

3186F   "Fus Fixico's Letter," Cherokee Advocate, May 28, 1904.

3187F   "Fus Fixico's Letter," South McAlester Capital, June 9, 1904.

3188F   "Fus Fixico's Letter," Vinita Weekly Chieftain, June 23, 1904.

3189F   "Fus Fixico's Letter," Muskogee Democrat, September 20, 1904.

3190F   "Fus Fixico's Letter," Cherokee Advocate, January 14, 1905.

3191F   "Fus Fixico's Letter," Muskogee Phoenix, April 20, 1905.

3192F   "Fus Fixico's Letter," Muskogee Phoenix, August 10, 1905.

3193P   "A Freedman Rhyme," Muskogee Democrat, August 19, 1905.

3194F   "Fus Fixico's Letter," Muskogee Phoenix, August 31, 1905.

3195F   "Fus Fixico's Letter," Muskogee Phoenix, September 7, 1905.

3196F   "Fus Fixico's Letter," Cherokee Advocate, September 9, 1905.

3197P   "Bob White," in "Three Indian Writers of Prominence," Sturm's Statehood Magazine, 1 (October, 1905), 85.

3198P   "Evening Star," in "Three Indian Writers of Prominence," Sturm's Statehood Magazine, 1 (October, 1905), 84.

3199P   "An Outcast," in "Three Indian Writers of Prominence," Sturm's Statehood Magazine, 1 (October, 1905), 84.

3200P   "To a Robin," in "Three Indian Writers of Prominence," Sturm's Statehood Magazine, 1 (October, 1905), 84.

3201F   "Fus Fixico's Letter," Sturm's Statehood Magazine, 1 (October, 1905), 90-91.

3202F   "Fus Fixico's Letter," Muskogee Phoenix, November 2, 1905.

3203P   "Song of the Octahutche," Sturm's Statehood Magazine, 1 (February, 1906), 92.

3204F   "Fus Fixico's Letter," New-State Tribune, March 8, 1906.

3205F   "Fus Fixico's Letter," New-State Tribune, March 15, 1906.

3206F   "Fus Fixico's Letter," Indian Journal, March 16, 1906.

3207F   "Fus Fixico's Letter," New-State Tribune, March 22, 1906.

3208F   "Fus Fixico's Letter," Indian Journal, March 23, 1906.

3209F   "Fus Fixico's Letter," New-State Tribune, March 29, 1906.

3210F   "Fus Fixico's Letter," Indian Journal, March 30, 1906.

3211F   "Fus Fixico's Letter," New-State Tribune, June 28, 1906.

3212P   "The Greek Fullblood (With Apologies to Edwin Markham),"
      Muskogee Times-Democrat, August 9, 1906.

3213N   "Indian Folk Lore," Sturm's Oklahoma Magazine, 3 (Octo-
      ber, 1906), 91-93.

3214F   "Styx," Muskogee Times-Democrat, January 3, 1907.

3215F   "Fus Fixico's Letter," Indian Journal, January 11, 1907.

3216P   "Arkansaw," Muskogee Times-Democrat, June 20, 1907.

3217P   "Arkansaw," Indian Journal, July 5, 1907.

3218P   "The Passing of 'Hot Gun,'" Indian Journal, January 24,
      1908.

3219F   "Fus Fixico's Letter," Indian Journal, April 10, 1908.

3220F   "Fus Fixico's Letter," Indian Journal, April 17, 1908.

3221F   "Fus Fixico's Letter," Indian Journal, April 24, 1908.

3222F   "Fus Fixico's Letter," Indian Journal, May 8, 1908.

3223F   "Fus Fixico's Letter," Shawnee Daily Herald, May 17,
      1908.

3224F   "Fus Fixico's Letter," Indian Journal, May 22, 1908.

3225P   "Hotgun on the Death of Yadeka Harjo," Sturm's Oklahoma
      Magazine, 4 (May, 1908), 43.

3226F   "Fus Fixico's Letter," Sturm's Oklahoma Magazine, 4
      (July, 1908), 16.

3227P   "Sunset," Sturm's Oklahoma Magazine, 4 (July, 1908), 12.

3228P   "Hotgun on the Death of Yadeka Harjo." In O. P. Sturm.
      "The Passing of the Creek Poet," Sturm's Oklahoma
      Magazine, 4 (July, 1908), 13.

3229P   "Nightfall," Sturm's Oklahoma Magazine, 4 (July, 1908),
      17.

3230P   "Shelter." In O. P. Sturm. "The Passing of the Creek
      Poet," Sturm's Oklahoma Magazine, 4 (July, 1908), 14.

3231P   "Song of the Oktahutche," Sturm's Oklahoma Magazine, 4
      (July, 1908), 17.

3232P   "When Love Is Dead," Sturm's Oklahoma Magazine, 4
      (July, 1908), 17.

3233P   "An Outcast," Sturm's Oklahoma Magazine, 4 (July, 1908),
      12.

3234P   "To a Morning Warbler," Sturm's Oklahoma Magazine, 4
      (July, 1908), 12.

3235P   "To a Robin," Sturm's Oklahoma Magazine, 4 (July, 1908),
      12.

3236P   "Daffodil," Sturm's Oklahoma Magazine, 4 (July, 1908), 12.

3237P   "Song of the Oktahutchee," Indian's Friend, 22 (April,
      1910), 7. Reprinted from Kansas City Star.

3238P   "Nightfall," Indian School Journal, 10 (April, 1910), 30.

3239P   "To a Daffodil," Indian School Journal, 10 (April, 1910),
      30.

3240P   "The Mocking Bird," Indian School Journal, 10 (April,
      1910), 30.

3241P   "To the Indian Meadow Lark," Indian School Journal, 10
      (April, 1910), 30.

3242P   "Song of the Oktahutchee," Indian School Journal, 10 (April, 1910), 30.

3243P   "To a Daffodil," Indian's Friend, 22 (June, 1910), 9.

3244P   "Nightfall," Indian's Friend, 23 (September, 1910), 3.

3245P   The Poems of Alexander Lawrence Posey. Comp. Mrs. Minnie H. Posey. Topeka, KS: Crane & Company, 1910.

3246P   "Eyes of Blue and Brown," Indian's Friend, 23 (January, 1911), 7.

3247P   "On the Capture and Imprisonment of Chitto Harjo (Crazy Snake)," Indian's Friend, 23 (January, 1911), 7.

3248P   "Again," Indian's Friend, 24 (June-July, 1912), 12.

3249P   "The Dew and the Bird," Native American, September 14, 1912.

3250P   "Pity," Native American, September 28, 1912.

3251P   "Life's Mystery," Native American, October 5, 1912.

3252P   "Assured," Native American, October 12, 1912.

3253P   "At the Siren's Call," Native American, October 19, 1912.

3254P   "The Open Sky," Native American, October 26, 1912.

3255P   "What I Ask of Life," Indian School Journal, 13 (April, 1913), 362.

3256N   "An Indian Poet's Tale of a River Trip," Kansas City Star, October 3, 1915.

POWLESS, RICHARD S. (Oneida)

3257N   "My Summer Experience," Southern Workman, 17 (January, 1888), 9.

PRATT, JENNIE (Pawnee)

3258F   "Indian Christmas Story," Indian Leader, December 29, 1922.

PROCTOR, EZEKIEL (Cherokee)

3259N   "Objections to the New Code of Laws of the Cherokee Nation," Cherokee Advocate, May 6, 1876.

PRUE, ELLEN M. (Sioux)

3260N   "The U. S. Indian School," Indian School Journal, 4 (October, 1904), 74-75.

QUINNEY, JOHN W. (Stockbridge)

3261N   Memorial of John W. Quinney. To the Honorable the Senate and House of Representatives of the United States, in Congress Assembled. Washington, DC: n. p., 1852.

3262A   "Celebration of the Fourth of July, 1854, at Reidsville, N. Y. Interesting Speech of John W. Quinney, Chief of the Stockbridge Tribe of Indians," in Wisconsin State Historical Society, Report and Collection, 1857-1858, 4 (Madison, 1859), 313-320.

3263N   "Memorial of John W. Quinney. To the Honorable the Senate and House of Representatives of the United States, in Congress Assembled." In Wisconsin State Historical

Society, Report and Collections, 1858-1859, 4 (Madison, 1859), [321]-333.

QUINTANO, SANTIAGO (Pueblo)
3264F "Yoo Pesha Pallaquianna," Morning Star, 4 (November, 1883), 4.

QUOETONE, FRED J. (Kiowa)
3265N "Indian Dance," Indian Leader, April, 1916.

RAICHE, MARY (Chippewa)
3266N "An Imaginary Trip," Carlisle Arrow, June 4, 1915.

RAMONE, JOSEPHINE (Papago)
3267N "The Pimas and Papagoes," Red Man and Helper, February 26-March 4, 1904.

RAMSEY, JOHN (Nez Percé)
3268N "My Home in Idaho," Indian Craftsman, 1 (February, 1909), 28-29.

REDBIRD, SIMON (Ottawa)
3269N "An Indian's View of the Indian Problem," Indian Leader, May 14, 1909.
3270A "Remarks at the Mohonk Conference," Indian School Journal, 9 (May, 1909), 27-29.
3271N "The Spirit the Indian Needs--How It May Be Awakened by Education," Quarterly Journal of the Society of American Indians, 2 (April-June, 1914), 142-145.
3272N "Responsibility of the Indian-School Employee," Indian Leader, October, 1915.
3273N "Responsibility of the Indian School Employee," American Indian Magazine, 4 (January-March, 1916), 28-31.
3274N "My Struggle for Success," American Indian Magazine, 5 (January-March, 1917), 24-28.

RED EAGLE, GRACE (Quapaw)
3275N "The Birch Tree," Red Man, 12 (May, 1895), 4.

RED EAGLE, LEROY (Quapaw)
3276N "The Spring," Carlisle Arrow, April 11, 1911.

REED, ORA V. EDDLEMAN (Cherokee)
3277F "In a Studio," Twin Territories, 1 (February, 1899), 47-48.
3278F "A Returned Prodigal," Twin Territories, 1 (February, 1899), 46-47.
3279F "A Story of Three Little People, Left Alone for a Day," Twin Territories, 1 (February, 1899), 73-75.
3280F "Ellenor," Twin Territories, 1 (April, 1899), 92-94.
3281F "Lizonka, a Creek Girl," Twin Territories, 1 (May, 1899), 113-114, 122-123; 1 (June, 1899), 138-141; 1 (July, 1899),

167-171; 1 (August, 1899), 183-189; 1 (September, 1899), 209-211; 1 (October, 1899), 227-228.

3282N "The Choctaw People," Twin Territories, 1 (June, 1899), 137.

3283F "A Face at the Window," Twin Territories, 1 (July, 1899), 156-159.

3284F "A Pair of Moccasins," Twin Territories, 1 (August, 1899), 176-179; 1 (September, 1899), 200-203; 1 (October, 1899), 230-231; 1 (November, 1899), 251-253; 1 (December, 1899), 16-17, 20.

3285F "Her Thanksgiving Visit," Twin Territories, 1 (November, 1899), 247-250.

3286F "Aunt Mary's Christmas Dinner," Twin Territories, 2 (December, 1899), 9-10.

3287F "Only an Indian Girl," Twin Territories, 2 (February, 1900), 28, 37-38; 2 (March, 1900), 50, 54-55; 2 (April, 1900), 84-85; 2 (May, 1900), 100-102; 2 (June, 1900), 125, 128-129; 2 (July, 1900), 147, 150-151, 154.

3288F "Lucy and I as Missionaries," Twin Territories, 2 (March, 1900), 42, 46; 2 (April, 1900), 79, 83; 2 (May, 1900), 103, 106; 2 (June, 1900), 122-123; 2 (July, 1900), 148-149; 2 (August, 1900), 169-172.

3289F "Her Mother's Daughter," Twin Territories, 2 (July, 1900), 137-139; 2 (August, 1900), 165-167; 2 (September, 1900), 183-185; 2 (October, 1900), 209-211; 2 (November, 1900), 234-236.

3290F "One New Year's Eve," Twin Territories, 3 (January, 1901), 6-7.

3291F "'Rene Pemberton," Twin Territories, 3 (March, 1901), 54-55; 3 (April, 1901), 77-78; 3 (June, 1901), 121-122; 3 (August, 1901), 169-170.

3292N "The Creek Nation and Her People," Sturm's Statehood Magazine, 1 (September, 1905), 82-88.

3293N "The Object of the Indian Department," Sturm's Statehood Magazine, 1 (October, 1905), 83.

3294N "Three Indian Writers of Prominence," Sturm's Statehood Magazine, 1 (October, 1905), 84-85.

3295N Editorial, Sturm's Statehood Magazine, 1 (November, 1905), 82.

3296N "The Choctaws and Chickasaws," Sturm's Statehood Magazine, 1 (November, 1905), 82-88.

3297N "The Story of a War Chief's Medal," Sturm's Statehood Magazine, 1 (December, 1905), 81-84.

3298N "Tradition of the Cherokees," Sturm's Statehood Magazine, 1 (December, 1905), 93-94.

3299N "Cherokee Mythology," Sturm's Statehood Magazine, 1 (December, 1905), 94-96.

3300N "Sa-Go-Ya-Wat-Ha," Sturm's Statehood Magazine, 1 (February, 1906), 81-84.

3301N "Indian Wit and Wisdom," Sturm's Statehood Magazine, 2 (March, 1906), 86.

3302N "Indian Proverbs," Sturm's Statehood Magazine, 2 (March, 1906), 86.

3303N   "Little Sketches of Famous Indians," Sturm's Statehood Magazine, 2 (March, 1906), 81-82.

3304N   "Where the Cowboy Reigned," Sturm's Statehood Magazine, 2 (April, 1906), 12-13.

3305N   "The Averted Catastrophe," Sturm's Statehood Magazine, 2 (April, 1906), 81-89.

3306N   "Red Jacket--Sa-go-ya-wat-ha," Indian School Journal, 6 (April, 1906), 24-29.

3307N   "The Dying of the Council Fires," Sturm's Statehood Magazine, 2 (June, 1906), 81-87.

3308N   "Father of 90,000 Indians," Sturm's Oklahoma Magazine, 2 (July, 1906), 81-83.

3309N   "Great Work of an Indian," Sturm's Oklahoma Magazine, 2 (August, 1906), 7-9.

3310N   "The Passing of the Seminoles," Sturm's Oklahoma Magazine, 3 (September, 1906), 11-12.

3311N   "Indian Tales Between Pipes," Sturm's Oklahoma Magazine, 3 (November, 1906), 86-88.

3312N   "A Noted Creek Indian," Sturm's Oklahoma Magazine, 3 (November, 1906), 89-90.

3313N   "Oklahoma's Skin Tepees," Sturm's Oklahoma Magazine, 3 (November, 1906), 90.

3314N   "Home for Indian Orphans," Sturm's Oklahoma Magazine, 3 (November, 1906), 91-92.

3315N   "Concerning Indians," Sturm's Oklahoma Magazine, 3 (November, 1906), 92.

3316N   "The Indian Orphan," Sturm's Oklahoma Magazine, 5 (January, 1908), 81-84.

3317N   Memorial to Alexander Posey, Sturm's Oklahoma Magazine, 6 (July, 1908), 14-16.

3318F   "Billy Bearclaws, Aid to Cupid," Sturm's Oklahoma Magazine, 9 (September, 1909), 47-53.

3319N   "Daughters of the Confederacy," Sturm's Oklahoma Magazine, 10 (June, 1910), 37-40.

3320N   "Alexander Posey, the Creek Poet," Indian School Journal, 11 (June, 1911), 11-14.

REED, THOMAS B. (Alaskan Native)

3321A   "Alaskan Indians," Southern Workman, 45 (December, 1916), 671-676.

3322N   "Fishing on the Yukon," Southern Workman, 49 (January, 1920), 70-74.

REINKEN, OLGA (Alaskan Native)

3323N   "The Art of Making Pottery," Indian Craftsman, 1 (March, 1909), 15-16.

3324M   "A Chickasaw Tradition," Indian Craftsman, 2 (November, 1909), 4.

RENVILLE, FLORENCE (Sioux)

3325N   "Camp Sells As Seen and Told by a Girl," Carlisle Arrow, October 31, 1913.

RENVILLE, GABRIEL (Sioux)
3326N "A Sioux Narrative of the Outbreak in 1862, and of Sibley's
Expedition in 1863. By Gabriel Renville. With a Bio-
graphical Sketch of the Author by Samuel J. Brown."
In Minnesota Historical Society, Collections, 10, Pt. 2
(St. Paul, 1905), 595-618.

RENVILLE, GERMAINE (Sioux)
3327N "The Pleasures of Camping," Carlisle Arrow, May 22,
1914.

RHODES, MARIANNA (Maricopa)
3328N "Thoughts on Christmas," Native American, December 26,
1914.
3329N "Our Trip to the Desert," Native American, April 3, 1915.
3330N "Our Motto," Native American, May 22, 1915.
3331A ["Returned Students,"] Native American, April 1, 1916.

RICE, SAMUEL (Mission)
3332N "Ice Making," Native American, May 22, 1909.

RICKETTS, HERMAN (Pawnee)
3333N "An Indian Christmas Celebration," Indian Leader, December 29, 1922.

RIDDLE, JEFF C. (Modoc)
3334N The Indian History of the Modoc War and the Causes That
Led to It. San Francisco: Marnell & Co., 1914.

RIDGE, JOHN (Cherokee)
3335L "For the Cherokee Phoenix," Cherokee Phoenix & Indians'
Advocate, June 25 and July 2, 1828.
3336L Letter, Cherokee Phoenix & Indians' Advocate, March 4,
1829.
3337N With William Shorey Coodey and Richard Taylor. "Memorial of the Delegates from the Cherokee Indians," Cherokee Phoenix & Indians' Advocate, March 5, 1831.
3338L Letter, Cherokee Phoenix & Indians' Advocate, March 19,
1831. Reprinted from National Intelligencer.
3339L Letter, Cherokee Phoenix & Indians' Advocate, April 16,
1831. Reprinted from Poulson's American Daily Adver-
tiser.
3340L Letter, Cherokee Phoenix & Indians' Advocate, May 21,
1831.
3341L Letter, Cherokee Phoenix & Indians' Advocate, July 9,
1831.
3342N With William Shorey Coodey and John Martin. "Cherokee
Memorial," Cherokee Phoenix & Indians' Advocate, March
24, 1832.

RIDGE, JOHN ROLLIN (Cherokee)
3343P "To a Mocking Bird," Arkansas Intelligencer, May 29,
1847.

3344F The Life and Adventures of Joaquin Murieta, the Celebrated California Bandit, by Yellow Bird. San Francisco: W. B. Cooke and Company, 1854.

3345P "Poem." In Willard B. Farwell, Oration Delivered Before the Society of California Pioneers, at Their Celebration of the Eighth Anniversary of the Admission of the State of California to the Union. San Francisco: Alta Job Office, 1859.

3346P "Humboldt River," Arkansian, June 1, 1860.

3347P "Humboldt River," Arkansas True Democrat, August 11, 1860. Reprinted from Hesperian, April, 1860.

3348P "Poem," Arkansian, November 9, 1860.

3349P "All Hail the Fairest, Greatest, Best of Days," Daily Alta California, July 7, 1861.

3350P "Maid of the Mountains," Golden Era, August 11, 1861.

3351P "To -- --," Golden Era, September 29, 1861.

3352P "False but Beautiful," Golden Era, November 24, 1861.

3353P "Rosa Dunn," Golden Era, December 22, 1861.

3354P "Poem." In J. D. Whitney, Address Delivered at the Celebration of the Sixth Anniversary of the College of California, 1861. N. p., pp. [51]-54.

3355P "Erinna," Golden Era, March 16, 1862.

3356P "A Scene--The Feather River Sloughs," Pacific Monthly, 11 (April, 1864), 544-546.

3357N Comments on the Objections of Certain Cherokee Delegates to the Propositions of the Government to Separate the Hostile Parties of the Cherokee Nation. Washington, DC: Intelligencer Printing House, 1866.

3358P Poems. San Francisco: H. Payot & Company, 1868.

3359P "On the Laying of the Atlantic Telegraph Cable." In Oscar T. Shuck, comp. The California Scrap-Book: A Repository of Useful Information and Select Reading. San Francisco: H. H. Bancroft & Company, 1869, pp. 483-485.

3360F The Life and Adventures of Joaquin Murieta, the Celebrated California Bandit. 3rd ed. San Francisco: F. MacCrellish & Co., 1871. Reprinted in 1874.

3361P "Indian Cradle Song," Muskogee Phoenix, February 10, 1898.

3362P "Ode to the National Flag," Indian Chieftain, July 5, 1900.

3363P "Mt. Shasta," Twin Territories, 5 (March, 1903), 80-81.

3364P "Mt. Shasta." In Mabel Washbourne Anderson. "The Cherokee Poet and 'Mt. Shasta,'" Sturm's Oklahoma Magazine, 6 (March, 1908), 23-24.

RIGGS, ROLLA LYNN (Cherokee)

3365P "To Vachel Lindsay," University of Oklahoma Magazine, 10 (February, 1922), cover.

3366P "The Patrician," Reviewer, 3 (October, 1922), 622.

3367P "Rhythm of Rain," Poetry, 22 (August, 1923), 252-253.

3368P "I Have Not Looked on Beauty," Contemporary Verse, 16 (December, 1923), 93.

3369P "Beauty Has Gone," University of Oklahoma Magazine, 12 (Fall, 1923), 2.

3370P "Spring Day," Contemporary Verse, 17 (April, 1924), 54.

RILEY, MARY (Cherokee)
3371N "Guess My Subject," Children's Play Ground, August 9, 1881.

ROBERTS, GEORGE (Pawnee)
3372N "Christmas Among the Pawnees," Carlisle Arrow, December 18, 1914.

ROBERTS, VIVIAN (Pawnee)
3373F "Christmas Story," Indian Leader, December 29, 1922.

ROBERTSON, ETTA (Sioux)
3374N "The Pyramids of America," Red Man, 10 (June, 1891), 4.

ROBERTSON, NELLIE (Sioux)
3375N "A Dream of the Future," Red Man, 10 (May, 1890), 5.
3376F "A Trip to the Moon," Indian Helper, June 20, 1890.
3377N "Sensitiveness to Sound in English Poets," Red Man, 13 (May-June, 1896), 2. Reprinted from the West Chester State Normal School Amulet.

ROBINSON, JESSE (Klamath)
3378M "The Origin of the Stars," Indian's Friend, 23 (July, 1911), 2.

RODGERS, THOMAS L. (Cherokee)
3379N Memorial of John Rogers, Principal Chief, and James Carey and Thomas L. Rodgers, Chiefs and Headmen, Being Members of a Committee on Behalf of the Cherokee Old Settlers West of the Mississippi, for Themselves and Their People. April, 1844. Washington, DC: Blair & Rives, 1844.

RODRIGUEZ, FERNANDO (Pueblo)
3380N "History of the Class of 1910," Native American, May 14, 1910.

ROE CLOUD, HENRY
See CLOUD, HENRY ROE

ROGERS, CLEMENT VANN (Cherokee)
3381L "Who Is to Blame?" Cherokee Telephone, August 21, 1890.

ROGERS, EDWARD (Chippewa)
3382A "Import of the Dawes Bill," Red Man, 14 (February, 1897), 4.
3383N "Foot-ball," Red Man, 14 (April, 1897), 7.
3384A "Benefits of Football," Red Man, 14 (January, 1898), 5.

ROGERS, JOHN (Cherokee)
3385N Memorial of John Rogers, Principal Chief, and James Carey and Thomas L. Rodgers, Chiefs and Headmen, Being Members of a Committee on Behalf of the Chero-

kee Old Settlers West of the Mississippi for Themselves and Their People. April, 1844. Washington, DC: Blair & Rives, 1844.

ROGERS, ROBERT (Cherokee)
3386L With William Rogers. "For the Cherokee Phoenix," Cherokee Phoenix & Indians' Advocate, January 21, 1832.

ROGERS, WILL (Cherokee)
3387L "Two Cherokees in South American," Tahlequah Arrow, June 28, 1902. Reprinted from Claremore Progress.
3388N Rogers-isms, the Cowboy Philosopher on the Peace Conference. New York: Harper & Brothers, 1919.
3389N "Batting for Lloyd George," New York Times, December 24, 1922, 7: 2.
3390N "Slipping the Lariat Over," New York Times, December 31, 1922, 8: 3.
3391N "Slipping the Lariat Over," New York Times, January 7, 1923, 8: 3.
3392N "Slipping the Lariat Over," New York Times, January 14, 1923, 8: 2.
3393N "Slipping the Lariat Over," New York Times, January 21, 1923, 8: 2.
3394N "Slipping the Lariat Over," New York Times, January 28, 1923, 8: 2.
3395N "Slipping the Lariat Over," New York Times, February 4, 1923, 8: 2.
3396N "Slipping the Lariat Over," New York Times, February 11, 1923, 8: 2.
3397N "Slipping the Lariat Over," New York Times, February 18, 1923, 8: 2.
3398N "Slipping the Lariat Over," New York Times, February 25, 1923, 8: 2.
3399N "Slipping the Lariat Over," New York Times, March 4, 1923, 8: 2.
3400N "Slipping the Lariat Over," New York Times, March 11, 1923, 9: 2.
3401N "Slipping the Lariat Over," New York Times, March 18, 1923, 8: 2.
3402N "Slipping the Lariat Over," New York Times, March 25, 1923, 9: 2.
3403N "Slipping the Lariat Over," New York Times, April 1, 1923, 8: 2.
3404N "Slipping the Lariat Over," New York Times, April 8, 1923, 9: 2.
3405N "Slipping the Lariat Over," New York Times, April 15, 1923, 8: 2.
3406N "Slipping the Lariat Over," New York Times, April 22, 1923, 8: 2.
3407N "Slipping the Lariat Over," New York Times, April 29, 1923, 8: 2.
3408N "Slipping the Lariat Over," New York Times, May 6, 1923, 8: 3.

3409N "Slipping the Lariat Over," <u>New York Times</u>, May 13, 1923, 9: 2.

3410N "Slipping the Lariat Over," <u>New York Times</u>, May 20, 1923, 8: 2.

3411N "Slipping the Lariat Over," <u>New York Times</u>, May 27, 1923, 8: 2.

3412N "Slipping the Lariat Over," <u>New York Times</u>, June 3, 1923, 8: 2.

3413N "Slipping the Lariat Over," <u>New York Times</u>, June 10, 1923, 8: 2.

3414N "Slipping the Lariat Over," <u>New York Times</u>, June 17, 1923, 8: 2.

3415N "Slipping the Lariat Over," <u>New York Times</u>, June 24, 1923, 8: 2.

3416N "Slipping the Lariat Over," <u>New York Times</u>, July 1, 1923, 7: 2.

3417N "Slipping the Lariat Over," <u>New York Times</u>, July 8, 1923, 7: 2.

3418N "Slipping the Lariat Over," <u>New York Times</u>, July 15, 1923, 7: 2.

3419N "Slipping the Lariat Over," <u>New York Times</u>, July 22, 1923, 7: 2.

3420N "Slipping the Lariat Over," <u>New York Times</u>, July 29, 1923, 7: 2.

3421N "Slipping the Lariat Over," <u>New York Times</u>, August 5, 1923, 7: 2.

3422N "Slipping the Lariat Over," <u>New York Times</u>, August 12, 1923, 7: 2.

3423N "Slipping the Lariat Over," <u>New York Times</u>, August 19, 1923, 7: 2.

3424N "Slipping the Lariat Over," <u>New York Times</u>, August 26, 1923, 7: 2.

3425N "Slipping the Lariat Over," <u>New York Times</u>, September 2, 1923, 7: 2.

3426N "Slipping the Lariat Over," <u>New York Times</u>, September 9, 1923, 8: 2.

3427N "Slipping the Lariat Over," <u>New York Times</u>, September 16, 1923, 8: 2.

3428N "Slipping the Lariat Over," <u>New York Times</u>, September 30, 1923, 3: 2.

3429N "Slipping the Lariat Over," <u>New York Times</u>, October 7, 1923, 10: 2.

3430N "Slipping the Lariat Over," <u>New York Times</u>, October 14, 1923, 9: 2.

3431N "Slipping the Lariat Over," <u>New York Times</u>, October 21, 1923, 9: 2.

3432N "Slipping the Lariat Over," <u>New York Times</u>, October 28, 1923, 9: 2.

3433N "Slipping the Lariat Over," <u>New York Times</u>, November 4, 1923, 9: 2.

3434N "Slipping the Lariat Over," <u>New York Times</u>, November 11, 1923, 9: 2.

3435N "Slipping the Lariat Over," <u>New York Times</u>, November 18, 1923, 9: 2.

3436N "Lassoing a Scotchman in the Dark," New York Times, November 25, 1923, 9: 2.

3437N "Hats Rain into Presidential Ring," New York Times, December 2, 1923, 9: 2.

3438N "The Lasso Captures a Brand New Idea," New York Times, December 9, 1923, 10: 2.

3439N "How to Make Christmas Happy," New York Times, December 16, 1923, 8: 1.

3440N "Casting the Lariat over Week's News," New York Times, December 16, 1923, 10: 2.

3441N "Straw Votes on Coolidge Message," New York Times, December 23, 1923, 8: 4.

3442N "Why a Bonus? Think of Those Knit Sox," New York Times, December 30, 1923, 8: 2.

3443N "Second Issue of the 'Gem of Truth,'" New York Times, January 6, 1924, 8: 2.

3444N "All the Millionaires Are Optimistic," New York Times, January 13, 1924, 8: 2.

3445N "Send Mexico Our Wooden Ships, Too," New York Times, January 20, 1924, 8: 2.

3446N "'Weekly Exposure' Dishes up the News," New York Times, January 27, 1924, 8: 2.

3447N "Putting Beverly Hills on the Map," New York Times, February 3, 1924, 8: 2.

3448N "Wanted: Wet Nurse for Oil Industry," New York Times, February 10, 1924, 8: 2.

3449N "Wilson Could Laugh at Himself," New York Times, February 17, 1924, 8: 2.

3450N "Another Confession in the Oil Scandal," New York Times, February 24, 1924, 8: 2.

3451N "One Lawyer for Each Barrel of Oil," New York Times, March 2, 1924, 9: 2.

3452N "Lassoing a Herd of Wild Rumors," New York Times, March 9, 1924, 9: 2.

3453N "A Comedy Drama--'Boring for Gushers,'" New York Times, March 16, 1924, 9: 2.

3454N "Trying to Find Out Who 'Prunes' Is," New York Times, March 23, 1924, 9: 2.

3455N "Herding Oil Lawyers by Carloads," New York Times, March 30, 1924, 9: 2.

3456N "Another Oklahoman Wants to Testify," New York Times, April 6, 1924, 9: 2.

3457N "Found: One Man in Oil Who Is Pure," New York Times, April 13, 1924, 9: 2.

3458N "Jokesmiths Warned to Spare Prince," New York Times, April 20, 1924, 9: 2.

3459N "Great Season for Questioners," New York Times, April 27, 1924, 9: 2.

3460N "Apple Sauce Test for Diplomats," New York Times, May 4, 1924, 9: 2.

3461N "Six-shooter Quarantining," New York Times, May 11, 1924, 9: 2.

3462N "Formal Opening--New Style," New York Times, May 18, 1924, 8: 2.

3463N   "Back to the Babbitts," New York Times, May 25, 1924, 9: 2.

3464N   "Two Thieves in a Bag," New York Times, June 1, 1924, 8: 2.

3465N   "Congress Funniest When It's Gravest," New York Times, June 8, 1924, 8: 2.

3466N   "Could Have Nominated Coolidge by Postcard," New York Times, June 9, 1924, 1: 5.

3467N   "Cleveland Opens Churches to Give the Delegates Some Excitement," New York Times, June 10, 1924, 1: 6.

3468N   "He's as Ignorant as Before," New York Times, June 11, 1924, 1: 3.

3469N   "Would Substitute Hollywood for Congress," New York Times, June 12, 1924, 1: 3.

3470N   "Will Rogers Breaks Away from Cleveland," New York Times, June 13, 1924, 1: 7.

3471N   "If They'd Hang Some One!" New York Times, June 15, 1924, 8: 2.

3472N   "Radio Fairy Tales of Real Life Behind Scenes," New York Times, June 22, 1924, 8: 2.

3473N   "Will Rogers Fears the Madison Square Show May Rival His in Magnitude of Its Appeal," New York Times, June 23, 1924, 1: 4.

3474N   "Convention a Success So Far, Says Rogers; Would Adjourn Before Nomination Spoils Its," New York Times, June 24, 1924, 1: 4.

3475N   "Rogers Sees Harrison as Rival Monologist; Learns from Hull What Convention Is For," New York Times, June 25, 1924, 1: 5.

3476N   "Will Rogers Comes Out for Vice President; Claims All Qualifications Except Dress Suit," New York Times, June 26, 1924, 1: 5.

3477N   "Will Rogers Doubts Sanity of Delegates; 'The Man I'm About to Name' Agonizes Him," New York Times, June 27, 1924, 1: 7.

3478N   "Will Rogers Drops Vice Presidential Hopes, Wearied by Windy Speeches in the Convention," New York Times, June 28, 1924, 1: 6.

3479N   "Platform Makers' Prayer Impresses Will Rogers, Who Says It's a Bit Late," New York Times, June 29, 1924, 1: 5.

3480N   "Blues That Spotlights Never Show," New York Times, June 29, 1924, 8: 2.

3481N   "Will Rogers Runs into One Delegation That He Admits He Is Unable to Rope," New York Times, June 30, 1924, 1: 6.

3482N   "Convention's Long Stay Looks Like Scheme to Boost City's Census, Says Will Rogers," New York Times, July 1, 1924, 1: 3.

3483N   "Will Rogers Sees Dark Horse Turn White and Describes the 'Scientific Phenomenon,'" New York Times, July 2, 1924, 1: 5.

3484N   "Will Rogers Names the Only Man, He Says, with Whom

the Democrats Can Surely Win," New York Times, July 3, 1924, 1: 5.

3485N "Survivors of Convention Will Get Bonus after Six Years, Says Will Rogers," New York Times, July 4, 1924, 1: 3.

3486N "Convention Met to Celebrate Birthday of President Coolidge, Will Rogers Thinks," New York Times, July 5, 1924, 1: 4.

3487N "Nominating Everybody," New York Times, July 6, 1924, 8: 2.

3488N "He's the Darkest Horse of the Dark Horses Now, Says Will Rogers, Controlling Two Half Votes," New York Times, July 6, 1924, 1: 4.

3489N "Will Rogers Sees M'Adoo and Won't Quit; Trusts Cause to Bryan, Who Sleeps on Job," New York Times, July 7, 1924, 1: 3.

3490N "Will Rogers Pictures Convention in Action; Loathes Its Futility, Holds Leaders to Blame," New York Times, July 8, 1924, 1: 4.

3491N "'Will Rogers Jr.' Reports the Convention for His Father, Worn Out by Long Service," New York Times, July 9, 1924, 1: 3.

3492N "Will Rogers Hails Davis on 'Class of Race'; Thanks Bryan for Effecting Nomination," New York Times, July 10, 1924, 1: 5.

3493N "Calamities (Dem.) of 1924," New York Times, July 13, 1924, 8: 2.

3494N "Mingling with the Bryans," New York Times, July 20, 1924, 8: 2.

3495N "About Candidates' Wives," New York Times, July 27, 1924, 8: 2.

3496N "Random Shots at the News of a Week," New York Times, August 3, 1924, 8: 2.

3497N "Al and Will as a Team," New York Times, August 10, 1924, 8: 2.

3498N "Half a Man, But a Hero," New York Times, August 17, 1924, 8: 2.

3499N "As I Read the Papers," New York Times, August 24, 1924, 8: 2.

3500N "From Nuts to Soup," New York Times, August 31, 1924, 8: 2.

3501N "Thoughts on the Painting of Noses," New York Times, September 7, 1924, 8: 2.

3502N "Hobnobbing with a Regular Prince," New York Times, September 14, 1924, 9: 2.

3503N "Prince Qualifies as a Marathon Dancer," New York Times, September 21, 1924, 8: 2.

3504N "Everybody Is Pulling for Walter," New York Times, September 28, 1924, 8: 2.

3505N The Illiterate Digest. New York: A. & C. Boni, 1924. Reprinted in 1926 and 1935.

ROGERS, WILLIAM (Cherokee)

3506L   With Robert Rogers. "For the Cherokee Phoenix," Chero-
         kee Phoenix & Indians' Advocate, January 21, 1832.

ROGERS, WILLIAM CHARLES (Cherokee)
3507A   "Chief's Message," Tahlequah Arrow, November 12, 1904.
3508A   "Second Annual Message of W. C. Rogers, Principal Chief
         of the Cherokee Nation, Delivered Nov. 9th, 1904,"
         Cherokee Advocate, November 12, 1904.
3509A   "Chief Rogers' Annual Message," Cherokee Advocate, Sep-
         tember 23, 1905.
3510A   "Message of Chief Rogers to the Last Session of the Cher-
         okee Council," Tahlequah Arrow, September 23, 1905.
3511A   "Chief Rogers' Last Message," Vinita Daily Chieftain, Sep-
         tember 27, 1905.
3512A   "Chief's Wise Talk," Tahlequah Arrow, August 1, 1908.

ROMAN NOSE, HENRY C. (Cheyenne)
3513N   "An Indian Boy's Visit to New York," Eadle Keahtah Toh,
         1 (July, 1880), 4.
3514N   "How to Settle the Problem," Quarterly Journal of the So-
         ciety of American Indians, 2 (January-March, 1914), 78.

ROMANOSE, OLIVER (Cheyenne)
3515N   "Home Building," Native American, March 7, 1914.

ROOT, CLARA (Arapaho)
3516N   "What One Indian Girl Thinks of the War," Indian School
         Journal, 18 (April, 1918), 387-389.

ROSS, AMOS D. (Sioux)
3517F   "The Seven Black Stones," Indian Leader, May, 1916.

ROSS, DANIEL H. (Cherokee)
3518L   Letter, Cherokee Advocate, August 31, 1872.
3519C   With W. P. Boudinot and Joseph A. Scales. Constitution
         and Laws of the Cherokee Nation. Published by Authori-
         ty of the National Council. St. Louis: R. & T. A. En-
         nis, 1875.
3520N   With W. P. Adair, John L. Adair, and Rufus O. Ross.
         "To the Congress of the United States," Cherokee Advo-
         cate, June 16, 1876.
3521L   Letter, Cherokee Advocate, June 17, 1876.
3522L   Letter, Cherokee Advocate, July 15, 1876.
3523L   With W. P. Adair. Letter, Cherokee Advocate, January
         12, 1878.
3524N   With W. P. Adair. "Objections of the Cherokee Delegation
         to Bill S. No. 230 and Bill H. R. No. 228, and Similar
         Measures Pending Before the 1st Session, 45th Congress,
         Authorizing the So-called 'Eastern Band' of the Cherokees
         (Citizens of North Carolina,) to Sue the Cherokee Nation,
         &c.," Cherokee Advocate, April 6, 1878.
3525N   With W. P. Adair. "Official Statement of the Cherokee
         Delegation in Regard to the Expenditure of Cherokee Funds

and the Financial Condition of the Cherokee Nation, and in Relation to the Educational Situation of Said Nation," Cherokee Advocate, April 20, 1878.

3526L With W. P. Adair. "To the People of the Cherokee Nation," Cherokee Advocate, July 30, 1879, and August 6 and 13, 1879.

3527N Argument of the Cherokee Delegation as Made by Hon. Dan'l H. Ross, Before the Committee on Indian Affairs of the House of Representatives, June 6, 1879, on the Bill to Authorize the So-Called "North Carolina Cherokees" to Institute Suit in the U. S. Court of Claims for One-Seventh Part of the Funds and Lands and Other Common Property of the Cherokee Nation. Washington, DC: Gibson Brothers, 1879.

3528N With W. P. Ross, W. P. Adair, and Samuel Smith. "Report of the Delegation," Cherokee Advocate, October 13, 1880.

3529N "The Editor to the Cherokee People," Cherokee Advocate, October 13, 1880.

3530L Letter, Cherokee Advocate, January 13, 1882.

3531N "The Sacred Soil--Railroading &c., &c.," Cherokee Advocate, January 27, 1882.

3532L Letter, Cherokee Advocate, February 2, 1882.

3533L Letter, Cherokee Advocate, April 14, 1882.

3534B "A. & P. R. R. Co.," Cherokee Advocate, April 14, 1882.

3535N "Allotment Not Yet," Cherokee Advocate, April 14, 1882.

3536L Letter, Cherokee Advocate, April 28, 1882.

3537N With R. M. Wolfe, Pleasant Porter, and John F. Brown. "Memorial of the Indian Delegations at Washington," Cherokee Advocate, April 28, 1882.

3538N With R. M. Wolfe, Pleasant Porter, William L. Byrd, and John F. Brown. "Supplement to Memorial of April 6th, on Railroad Question," Cherokee Advocate, May 5, 1882.

3539N "The New Secretary," Cherokee Advocate, May 12, 1882.

3540N With R. M. Wolfe and Pleasant Porter. "Protest of Cherokee and Creek Delegation Against Passage of S. B. 1573," Cherokee Advocate, May 28, 1882.

3541N "'A Bad Decision'--A Good Decision," Cherokee Advocate, June 30, 1882.

3542N "Much Play and Little Work," Cherokee Advocate, July 7, 1882.

3543N With R. M. Wolfe. "The 'North Carolina Cherokees,'" Cherokee Advocate, August 4, 1882.

3544N "Home Again," Cherokee Advocate, August 25, 1882.

3545N With R. M. Wolfe. "Report of the Cherokee Delegation," Cherokee Advocate, November 24, 1882.

3546N "Valedictory," Cherokee Advocate, November 11, 1885.

ROSS, DORSIE (Clallam)
3547N "The Four Leaf Clover," Native American, May 30, 1903.

ROSS, JOHN (Cherokee)
3548N With George Lowrey, Major Ridge, and Elijah Hicks. Me-

morial of John Ross, Geo. Lowrey, Major Ridge, and Elijah Hicks, Delegates from the Cherokee Nation of Indians. April 16, 1824. Washington, DC: Gales & Seaton, 1824.

3549A   With William Hicks. "Message of the Principal Chiefs," Cherokee Phoenix & Indians' Advocate, October 22, 1828.

3550N   Memorial of John Ross, and Others, in Behalf of the Cherokee Nation. February 17, 1829. Washington, DC: Gales and Seaton, 1829.

3551N   Memorial of John Ross and Others, Representatives of the Cherokee Nation of Indians. March 3, 1829. Washington, DC: n. p., 1829?

3552A   "Message of the Principal Chief of the Cherokee Nation," Cherokee Phoenix & Indians' Advocate, October 21, 1829.

3553L   Letter, Cherokee Phoenix & Indians' Advocate, February 17, 1830.

3554L   Letter, Cherokee Phoenix & Indians' Advocate, February 12, 1831.

3555A   "Message of the Principal Chief of the Cherokee Nation," Cherokee Phoenix & Indians' Advocate, November 19, 1831.

3556L   Letter, Cherokee Phoenix & Indians' Advocate, May 26, 1832.

3557A   "Message of the Principal Chief," Cherokee Phoenix & Indians' Advocate, November 23, 1833.

3558N   Memorial of John Ross, and Others, Delegates from the Cherokee Indians, Complaining of Injuries Done Them, and Praying for Redress. Washington, DC: n. p., 1834.

3559N   Memorial of John Ross and Others; On Behalf of the Cherokee Nation of Indians, Praying Protection Against Certain Articles of Agreement Between the Agent of the United States and a Certain Part of Said Cherokee Nation of Indians. January 21, 1835. Washington, DC: n. p., 1835.

3560N   Memorial of John Ross and Others, Delegates of the Cherokee Indians, For the Passage of a Law Creating Commissioners to Examine the Validity of Certain Reservations in Tennessee and Alabama; To Ascertain the Value, and Pay the Reserves, &c. February 13, 1835. Washington, DC: n. p., 1835.

3561L   Letter from John Ross, Principal Chief of the Cherokee Nation of Indians, in Answer to Inquiries from a Friend Regarding the Cherokee Affairs with the United States: Followed by a Copy of the Protest of the Cherokee Delegation Laid Before the Senate and House of Representatives at the City of Washington, June 21, 1836. Philadelphia: n. p., 1836.

3562L   Letter from John Ross, Principal Chief of the Cherokee Nation of Indians, in Answer to Inquiries from a Friend Regarding the Cherokee Affairs with the United States. Followed by a Copy of the Protest of the Cherokee Delegation, Laid Before the Senate and House of Representatives at the City of Washington, on the 21st Day of June, Eighteen-hundred and Thirty-six. Washington, DC: n. p., 1836.

3563L Letter from John Ross, the Principal Chief of the Cherokee Nation to a Gentleman of Philadelphia. Philadelphia: n. p., 1837?

3564L Letter from John Ross, the Principal Chief of the Cherokee Nation, to a Gentleman of Philadelphia. Philadelphia: n. p., 1838.

3565A Message of the Principal Chief of the Cherokee Nation, November, 1842. Tahlequah, I. T., 1842?

3566A "Message of the Principal Chief," Cherokee Messenger, 1 (December, 1844), 47.

3567A Message of the Principal Chief, and Correspondence Between the Cherokee Delegation, and the Honorable William Wilkins, Secretary of War. N. p., 1844.

3568A Message of the Principal Chief of the Cherokee Nation. October, 1843. Baptist Mission, I. T.: Baptist Mission Press, 1844.

3569N Memorial of John Ross and Others, Representatives of the Cherokee Nation of Indians, on the Subject of the Existing Difficulties in That Nation, and Their Relations with the United States. Washington, DC: Ritchie and Heiss, 1846.

3570A Annual Message of the Principal Chief of the Cherokee Nation, Delivered Tuesday, October 4th, 1859. Van Buren, AR: Van Buren Press, 1859.

3571A Message of the Principal Chief of the Cherokee Nation. Baptist Mission, I. T.: Cherokee Messenger Office, 1859.

3572A Message of the Principal Chief of the Cherokee Nation, Together with the Declaration of the Cherokee People of the Causes Which Have Led Them to Withdraw Their Connection with the U. States. Tahlequah, I. T., 1861.

3573N Message. In Reply of the Southern Cherokees to the Memorial of Certain Delegates from the Cherokee Nation, Together with the Message of John Ross, Ex-chief of the Cherokees, and Proceedings of the Council of the "Loyal Cherokees," Relative to the Alliance with the So-called Confederate States. To the President, Senate, and House of Representatives. Washington, DC: McGill & Witherow, 1866.

3574L "From the Pen of Cooweescoowee," Twin Territories, 2 (February, 1900), 25-27.

ROSS, JOSEPH C. (Sioux)
3575N "The Indian Missionary," Southern Workman, 31 (November, 1902), 612-614.

ROSS, JOSHUA (Cherokee)
3576N "My Countrymen, the Cherokees," Twin Territories, 1 (November, 1899), 243-244 and 1 (December, 1899), 14-15.

3577N   With Cheesie McIntosh. "What Has the Indian to Be Thankful For?" Twin Territories, 3 (November, 1902), 328-329.

ROSS, MARGUERITE (Clallam)
3578A   "Among the Clouds," Native American, June 11, 1904.

ROSS, RUFUS O. (Cherokee)
3579N   With W. P. Adair, Will P. Ross, and D. W. Bushyhead. "Memorial of Cherokee Delegation Protesting Against Senate Bill No. 505," Cherokee Advocate, March 28, 1874.
3580N   With D. W. Bushyhead, W. P. Ross, and W. P. Adair. "Report of the Cherokee Delegates, 1873-4," Cherokee Advocate, December 26, 1874.
3581N   With D. H. Ross, W. P. Adair, and John L. Adair. "To the Congress of the United States," Cherokee Advocate, June 16, 1876.

ROSS, S. W. (Cherokee)
3582N   "Battle of Claremont Mounds," Indian School Journal, 10 (October, 1910), 35-37.
3583N   "Review of the Life of Dr. Worcester in the Cherokee Country," Weekly Chieftain, June 30, 1911. Reprinted from Oklahoma City Times.
3584N   "The Cherokees," Indian's Friend, 27 (May, 1915), 2, 8.

ROSS, T. D. (Cherokee)
3585F   "Quah Kaw's Dream of Oklahoma," Cherokee Advocate, May 5, 1880.

ROSS, WILLIAM POTTER (Cherokee)
3586N   "Public Education Among the Cherokee Indians," American Journal of Education, 1 (August, 1855), 120-122.
3587N   With S. H. Benge and Pleasant Porter. "Memorial of the Grand Council of Nations of the Indian Territory," Cherokee Advocate, June 18, 1870.
3588N   The Indian Territory. Arguments ... Delivered Before the Committee on Territories of the House of Representatives, in Opposition to Bills Before the Committee to Establish the Territory of Oklahoma on the 1st Day of Feb. and the 5th Day of Mar., 1872. Washington, DC: Chronicle Publishing Company, 1872.
3589N   Indian Territory; Remarks in Opposition to the Bill to Organize the Territory of Oklahoma Before the Committee on Territories of the House of Representatives, February 9th, 1874. Washington, DC: Gibson Bros., 1874.
3590A   "Speech of W. P. Ross, Principal Chief, Cherokee Nation, Before the House Committee on Territories," Cherokee Advocate, February 21, 1874.
3591N   With W. P. Adair, R. O. Ross, and D. W. Bushyhead. "Memorial of Cherokee Delegation Protesting Against Senate Bill No. 505," Cherokee Advocate, March 28, 1874.

3592N With D. W. Bushyhead, Rufus O. Ross, and W. P. Adair. "Report of the Cherokee Delegates, 1873-4," Cherokee Advocate, December 26, 1874.

3593L "Our Washington Letter," Indian Journal, December 21, 1876.

3594A "Cherokee Seminaries," Indian Journal, May 17, 1877.

3595A "Early Creek History," Indian Journal, August 7, 1878.

3596L Letter, Cherokee Advocate, January 4, 1879.

3597N Indian Territory. Remarks of William P. Ross of the Cherokee Delegation, Before the Committee on Territories of the United States Senate. Washington, DC: Gibson Brothers, 1879.

3598N With W. P. Adair, Samuel Smith, and D. H. Ross. "Report of the Delegation," Cherokee Advocate, October 13, 1880.

3599A Early Creek History; Speech at the Tullahassee Manual Labor Boarding School, July 18th, 1878. Muskogee, I. T.: Indian Journal, 1881.

3600L "Those Supreme Court Cases," Indian Chieftain, January 6, 1887.

3601L "Statement of Facts," Cherokee Telephone, January 22, 1891.

3602N The Life and Times of Hon. Wm. P. Ross, of the Cherokee Nation. St. Louis? 189-?

3603N The Life and Times of Hon. William P. Ross of the Cherokee Nation, ed. Mrs. William P. Ross. Fort Smith, AR: Weldon and Williams, 1893.

ROWE, FELIX (Cherokee)
3604N "What the Literary Society Does for Us." Chilocco Annual. Chilocco, OK: Chilocco Indian School, 1920, p. 32.

ROWLAND, EMMA J. (Cheyenne)
3605M "Legend of the Opeche," Red Man, 3 (October, 1910), 79-80.

RULO, LOUIS (Oto)
3606N "A Christmas at Home," Native American, December 24, 1910.

3607N "Selection of Seed Corn," Native American, April 29, 1911.

RULO, ZALLIE (Sioux)
3608L "A Student's Vacation," Southern Workman, 14 (January, 1885), 8.

3609A "The Indian Woman," Southern Workman, 14 (June, 1885), 62.

3610L "A Letter to the 'Lend-a-Hand Club,'" Southern Workman, 15 (April, 1886), 44.

RUNNELS, LOUIS H. (Sanpoil)
3611N "Toloman Mountain," Red Man, 3 (September, 1910), 22.

3612M "The Struggle Against Darkness," Red Man, 4 (September, 1911), 26.

RUSSELL, INA (Hupa)
3613N "The Making of a Dress," Native American, May 22, 1909.

RUSSELL, SENNAN (Yuma)
3614N "Advancement of the Yuma Indians," Native American, May 14, 1910.

SAHENTI, MARY (Yuma)
3615M "A Yuma Legend," Native American, June 15, 1907.

ST. CYR, JULIA (Winnebago)
3616L "From an Indian Graduate," Southern Workman, 15 (September, 1886), 98.

SANBORN, JOHN (Gros Ventre)
3617A Farewell Address at His County School, Red Man, 11 (May-June, 1893), 3.

SANDERSON, HOWARD (Pima)
3618A Address, Native American, May 27, 1905.

SARCOXIE, HENRY B. (Delaware)
3619N "Westward, Ho!" Twin Territories, 2 (August, 1900), 158-159, and 2 (September, 1900), 191-192.
3620P "Rhymes Written at Las Vagas[sic]," Twin Territories, 2 (September, 1900), 193.

SAUNOOKE, NAN (Cherokee)
3621N "The Story of the Corn," Red Man, 3 (December, 1910), 175.
3622N "How Medicine Originated Among the Cherokees," Red Man, 3 (January, 1911), 210-211.
3623M "Why the Turkey Is Bald," Red Man, 3 (February, 1911), 255-256.
3624N "Home Making," Carlisle Arrow, April 11, 1911.

SCALES, JOSEPH ABSALOM (Cherokee)
3625C With W. P. Boudinot and Daniel H. Ross. Constitution and Laws of the Cherokee Nation. Published by Authority of the National Council. St. Louis: R. & T. A. Ennis, 1875.
3626L "An Open Letter," Indian Chieftain, March 10, 1887.
3627L "Judge Scales' Letter," Indian Chieftain, March 20, 1890.
3628L "An Emphatic Letter," Indian Chieftain, April 17, 1890.

SCHANANDORE, EDWIN (Oneida)
3629N "Civilization or Barbarism," Red Man, 9 (June, 1887), 3.
3630N "The Reservation," Red Man and Helper, March 28, 1902.

SCHOLDER, FRITZ (Mission)
3631A "Service," Indian Leader, June 13-20, 1924.

SCHREIBER, MIGNON (Cherokee)
See REED, ORA V. EDDLEMAN

SCRAPER, ETTA (Cherokee)
3632N "Desks," Children's Play Ground, August 9, 1881.

SELKIRK, CHARLES (Chippewa)
3633N "Complaints Made of Indian Office," Tomahawk, April 11,
1918. Reprinted from Minneapolis Journal.
3634N "'Warning' to the White Race," Tomahawk, August 16,
1923.

SELKIRK, GEORGE B. (Chippewa)
3635N "Landscape at the Fair," Indian School Journal, 4 (October,
1904), 73-74.
3636N "The Warrior's Farewell," Tomahawk, December 27, 1923.

SETIMA, MACK Q. (Hopi)
3637N "The American Indian--The Indian of the Past," Indian
School Journal, 10 (June, 1910), 52-53.

SHAW, NELLIE (Paiute)
3638A "The Teacher's Opportunity," Indian Leader, June 13-20,
1924.

SHAW, ROSS (Pima)
3639N "Training an Indian Boy," Native American, June 10, 1916.

SHELTON, WILLIAM (Tulalip)
3640M "Indian Totem Legends of the Northwest Coast Country,"
Indian School Journal, 15 (November, 1914), 127-134.
3641M "Indian Totem Legends of the Northwest Coast Country,"
Indian School Journal, 15 (December, 1914), 189-196.

SHERRILL, WILLIAM (Cherokee)
3642A "Indian Citizenship--Its Import," Red Man, 14 (February,
1897), 5.

SHIELDS, LIZZIE (Pima)
3643N "The Superstition Mountain," Native American, June 27,
1908.
3644N "Some Beliefs of the Pima," Native American, April 17,
1909.
3645M "A Tradition of the Flood," Indian's Friend, 22 (December,
1909), 8.

SICKLES, MARTHA L. (Oneida)
3646N "Benefits of the Outing System to the Indian Girls," Red
Man, 14 (March, 1898), 4.

SILAS, ROGER (Oneida)
3647N "Base Ball Playing," Red Man, 11 (June-July, 1892), 3.

SIMON, ELMER (Chippewa)
3648A [Speech in the Fifth Street M. E. Church, Harrisburg, December 4, 1894], Red Man, 12 (December, 1894-January, 1895), 7-8.
3649N "The Indian--A Man," Red Man, 13 (March, 1896), 2-3.
3650A [Address at Carlisle Commencement], Red Man, 15 (February-March, 1899), 11.

SIMPSON, PETER (Alaskan Native)
3651N "The Native Viewpoint on Citizenship," Indian's Friend, 23 (July, 1911), 9-10. Reprinted from Home Mission Monthly, June, 1911.

SIOW, BESSIE (Pueblo)
3652N "Art Among the Indians," Native American, May 23, 1914.
3653N "Art Among the Indians," Indian's Friend, 26 (September, 1914), 7-8.

SITTINGBULL, JENNIE (Arapaho)
3654A "Salutatory," Senior Class Annual. Chilocco, OK: Chilocco Indian School, 1923, pp. 212, 222.

SIXKILLER, SAMUEL (Cherokee)
3655L "From Carlisle School," Muskogee Phoenix, November 17, 1892.
3656N "Columbus," Red Man, 11 (November-December, 1892), 5.
3657P "To Class '95," Red Man, 12 (February, 1895), 6.
3658P "Sixkiller," Indian Helper, January 10, 1896.

SKENADORE, IDA (Oneida)
3659N "Indian Customs," Indian Leader, April 30, 1909.

SKIUHUSHU (Blackfoot)
3660N "The Pilgram [sic] Tercentenary," Tomahawk, December 22, 1921.
3661N "How to Give the Indian Equal Opportunity," American Indian Advocate, 4 (Winter, 1922), 12.
3662P "My Creed," American Indian Advocate, 4 (Winter, 1922), 3.
3663N "A Short Sermon," American Indian Advocate, 4 (Winter, 1922), 8.
3664N "Why Nation Should Honor 'Original Landlords' American Indian Day," American Indian Advocate, 4 (Winter, 1922), 2-3.

SKYE, HAZEL N. (Seneca)
3665N "Conduct Becoming a Lady," Carlisle Arrow, May 23, 1914.
3666N "An Indian Conception of 'A Lady,'" Indian's Friend, 26 (September, 1914), 6-7.
3667M "Legend of the White Canoe," Carlisle Arrow, November 20, 1914.

SKYE, MAZIE L. (Seneca)

3668N "The Medicine Dance," Red Man, 3 (March, 1911), 299.

3669M "The Green Corn Legend," Red Man, 3 (April, 1911), 343-344.

3670M "Origin of the Green Corn," Red Man, 4 (September, 1911), 28-29.

SLEEPINGBEAR, PAUL (Gros Ventre)
3671N "Should the Indian Have a High Education?" Quarterly Journal of the Society of American Indians, 1 (July-September, 1913), 289-291.

SLINKER, THOMAS DEWEY (Choctaw)
3672P "Help a Fellow Forward," Carlisle Arrow, October 27, 1916.

3673P "Our Side of It," Carlisle Arrow and Red Man, March 22, 1918.

SLOAN, THOMAS (Omaha)
3674A "Valedictory Address of Thomas Sloan," Southern Workman, 18 (August, 1889), 91.

SMALL, MARY T. (Sioux)
3675N "Indian Christmas Night," Indian Leader, December 29, 1922.

SMALLWOOD, BENJAMIN FRANKLIN (Choctaw)
3676A "Inaugural Address of B. F. Smallwood," Muskogee Phoenix, October 18, 1888.

3677A ["Message,"] Muskogee Phoenix, October 24, 1889.

SMART, LETA V. MYERS (Omaha)
3678N "Be Cautious, Be Careful," Tomahawk, January 20, 1921.

3679N "What Our First Step Should Be," Tomahawk, January 27, 1921.

3680P "On a Nickel," Tomahawk, March 10, 1921.

3681P "A Picture," Tomahawk, March 17, 1921.

3682N "The Man and His Barn That Came to Harm," Tomahawk, May 25, 1922.

3683N "How the Indian Office Was Started and What Has Happened Ever Since," Tomahawk, July 6, 1922.

3684N "Indians Take Heed," Tomahawk, July 27, 1922.

3685N "The Blue Indians and the Red Indians," Tomahawk, August 10, 1922.

3686N "A Little More on the Indian and His Problem," Tomahawk, August 31, 1922.

3687P "A Young Man's Adventure with Opportunity," Tomahawk, September 28, 1922.

SMITH, CALINA (Yokaia)
3688A "Class President's Address, 1902," Native American, May 24, 1902.

3689N "Extend Thy Horizon," Native American, May 24, 1902.

SMITH, CLARENCE (Arapaho)
  3690M "Legend of the Big Dipper," Indian Craftsman, 1 (March, 1909), 16-17.

SMITH, DAVID (Pima)
  3691N "What Schools and Churches Have Done for the Pima," Native American, June 11, 1910.
  3692N "What Schools and Churches Have Done for the Pima," Indian's Friend, 22 (August, 1910), 2.

SMITH, ELIJAH B. (Oneida)
  3693A "The Man and His Job," Indian Leader, June 13-20, 1924.

SMITH, FANNIE (Cherokee)
  3694M "An Indian Legend." Bacone Chief. Bacone, OK: Bacone College, 1924, p. 83.

SMITH, HARRISON B. (Oneida)
  3695N "Law-Ghood, the Indian Friend," Carlisle Arrow, June 6, 1913.

SMITH, HENRY E. (Little Lake, or Mitomkai Pomo)
  3696A "Opportunities," Native American, June 11, 1904.

SMITH, HOKE (Apache)
  3697A "Growth," Native American, June 3, 1905.
  3698N "Can the Apache Children in Arizona Receive Higher Education Without the Consent of Uneducated Parents?" Quarterly Journal of the Society of American Indians, 2 (July-September, 1914), 210-212.

SMITH, JAMES (Warm Springs)
  3699N "Education and Progress for the Indian," Quarterly Journal of the Society of American Indians, 1 (July-September, 1913), 292-294.
  3700N "Higher Academic Training for the Indian," Quarterly Journal of the Society of American Indians, 3 (January-March, 1915), 42-45.

SMITH, JEFFERSON B. (Gros Ventre)
  3701N "Separation of Crows and Gros Ventre," Red Man, 3 (November, 1910), 132.

SMITH, JENNIE (Cherokee)
  3702M "An Indian Legend." Bacone Chief. Bacone, OK: Bacone College, 1924, p. 83.

SMITH, LENA (Klamath)
  3703N "Memories," Native American, May 30, 1903.

SMITH, MARTHA (Oneida)
  3704F "Indian Story," Indian Leader, November 10, 1911.

SMITH, SAMUEL (Cherokee)
    3705L With W. P. Adair, C. N. Vann, George W. Scraper, and
            Lewis Downing. "Letter from the Cherokee Delegation,"
            Cherokee Advocate, April 1, 1871.
    3706N With W. P. Ross, W. P. Adair, and D. H. Ross. "Re-
            port of the Delegation," Cherokee Advocate, October 13,
            1880.
    3707L "A Refutation," Indian Chieftain, January 27, 1887.

SNAKE, JOHN E. (Shawnee)
    3708N "Our Duty," Indian Scout, 2 (June, 1916), 10.

SNEED, JOSEPH (Pima)
    3709N "Advantages of Allotments to Gila Crossing Indians," Na-
            tive American, May 24, 1913.

SNOW, OLIVER LEO (Cherokee-Seneca)
    3710N "Au Revoir--But Not Good Bye to Chilocco." Senior Class
            Annual. Chilocco, OK: Chilocco Indian School, 1924,
            p. 216.

SNOW, ROSE THELMA (Seneca)
    3711M "An Old Legend," Carlisle Arrow, June 4, 1915.
    3712N "A Shakespearian Evening," Carlisle Arrow, June 4, 1915.

SNYDER, CORA (Seneca)
    3713P "The Frequent Showers of April," Red Man, 12 (May,
            1895), 5.

SOUCEA, HUGH (Pueblo)
    3714A Address at Carlisle Commencement, Red Man and Helper,
            February 20-27, 1903.
    3715N "'Man Alive,' with Greetings," Red Man, 12 (January-
            February, 1894), 1-2.

SPEARS, JOHN ALBION (Cherokee)
    3716L "Mr. Spears on Mr. Bunch," Indian Chieftain, April 1,
            1886.

SPLITLOG, CARRIE B. (Seneca)
    3717N "Our Vocational Course and What It Provides for Girls,"
            Indian Leader, 20 (June, 1917), 15-18.

SPRINGSTON, JOHN LEAF (Cherokee)
    3718N "As Indians View the Situation," Cherokee Advocate, July
            9, 1904.
    3719L "From Vian," Cherokee Advocate, May 20, 1905.

STANDING BEAR, HENRY (Sioux)
    3720A "Dakota and the Dakotas," Red Man: His Present and Fu-
            ture, 10 (June, 1891), 5.

STARR, ELLIS (Cherokee)

3721L   "Ellis Starr's Defense," Cherokee Telephone, May 12, 1892.

STARR, EMMET (Cherokee)
3722N   "Sketch of Judge Russell--Dawes Commission," Indian Chieftain, August 2, 1900.
3723N   "Sequoyah," Vinita Daily Chieftain, September 12, 1905.
3724N   "Fort Gibson," Muskogee Phoenix, September 14, 1905.
3725N   "Sequoyah," Tahlequah Arrow, September 23, 1905.
3726N   Cherokees "West," 1794-1839. By Cephas Washburn. Claremore, OK: n. p., 1910.
3727N   Encyclopedia of Oklahoma, vol. I. Oklahoma City: n. p., 1912.
3728N   A Series of Absolutely Correct Calendars, from September 14, 1752, to December 31, 2200. Claremore, OK: n. p., 1916?
3729N   Early History of the Cherokees Embracing Aboriginal Customs, Religion, Laws, Folk Lore and Civilization. Claremore, OK: n. p., 1917?
3730N   History of the Cherokee Indians and Their Legends and Folk Lore. Oklahoma City: The Warden Company, 1921.

STARR, EZEKIEL EUGENE (Cherokee)
3731N   With C. J. Harris and J. T. Cunningham. "Report of the Late Delegation to Washington, to Negotiate a Loan on the Strip Debt," Cherokee Advocate, June 17, 1893.

STARR, HENRY (Cherokee)
3732L   "Henry Starr's Letter," Indian Chieftain, October 28, 1897.

STARR, IDA (Cherokee)
3733N   "The Pygmies," Indian School Journal, September 12, 1904.
3734N   "Ireland on the Pike," Indian School Journal, October 15, 1904.

STARR, JOHN CALEB (Cherokee)
3735N   "Commission Work," Indian Chieftain, August 9, 1900.
3736N   "History of Tom Starr," Muskogee Daily Phoenix, October 21, 1901.
3737N   "Ratified Treaty," Tahlequah Arrow, August 16, 1902.
3738L   "Would Sell Surplus Land," Vinita Weekly Chieftain, November 19, 1903.
3739L   "Still Wants to Sell," Vinita Weekly Chieftain, November 19, 1903.

STEEPS, GEORGE (Sioux)
3740N   "An Indian's Plea for Justice," Tomahawk, May 1, 1924. Reprinted from Minneapolis Journal.

STEPHENS, SPENCER SEAGO (Cherokee)
3741L   Letter to Editor, Cherokee Advocate, June 18, 1870.

3742L   Letter, Cherokee Advocate, March 18, 1871.
3743L   Letter, Cherokee Advocate, June 6, 1874.
3744N   "Selection of Teachers," Cherokee Advocate, June 27, 1874.
3745N   "Instruction in Arithmetic," Cherokee Advocate, July 11, 1874.
3746L   "Schools in the Cherokee Nation," Cherokee Advocate, April 22, 1876.
3747A   "Our Illustrious Dead," Cherokee Advocate, December 3, 1879.
3748L   "A Nation's Generosity to Its Orphans," Indian Journal, November 29, 1883.
3749L   "Begin Anew," Indian Chieftain, December 17, 1885.
3750L   "The Indian's Future," Indian Chieftain, January 14, 1886.
3751L   "The Indian's Future," Indian Chieftain, February 4, 1886.
3752N   "United States Courts," Indian Chieftain, February 11, 1886.
3753L   "Indian Civilization," Indian Chieftain, April 8, 1886.
3754L   "The Cherokee Lands," Indian Chieftain, August 26, 1886.
3755L   "A Boom for Fort Gibson," Indian Chieftain, September 16, 1886.
3756L   Letter, Indian Chieftain, October 28, 1886.
3757N   "Statehood," Muskogee Phoenix, February 19, 1891.
3758N   "Indian Statehood Continued," Muskogee Phoenix, March 5, 1891.
3759N   "Statehood Continued," Muskogee Phoenix, March 19, 1891.
3760N   "How to Solve the Intruder Question," Muskogee Phoenix, February 6, 1896.
3761N   "Big Cherokee Claim," Cherokee Advocate, June 2, 1900. Reprinted from Wagoner Sayings.
3762N   "Observations of a Cherokee," Wagoner Record, March 7, 1901.
3763N   "Observations of a Cherokee," Wagoner Record, March 21, 1901.
3764N   "Statehood's Value," Daily Chieftain, December 7, 1901.
3765N   "B. I. T.," Tahlequah Leader, August 5, 1904.
3766N   "Territorial Beauty and Richness," Tahlequah Leader, August 5, 1904.
3767N   "Stephens on Schools," Tahlequah Leader, September 30, 1904.
3768N   "Alluwee," Tahlequah Leader, September 30, 1904.
3769N   "Removal of Restrictions," Wagoner Record, October 19, 1905.
3770N   "What Statehood Means," Wagoner Record, October 26, 1905.

STEVENS, AMELIA (Nez Percé)
3771F   "The Fox and the Bear," Indian Leader, May 7, 1909.

STIDHAM, GEORGE WASHINGTON (Creek)
3772L   "What G. W. Stidham Thinks of Vest's Oklahoma Bill," Indian Journal, January 29, 1880.
3773L   ["Congress,"] Indian Journal, February 10, 1881.
3774L   "The Truth Remains," Muskogee Phoenix, October 3, 1889.

STIDHAM, GEORGE WASHINGTON, JR. (Creek)
3775A "Do Not Procrastinate," Indian Journal, June 7, 1877.

STINSON, LIZZIE M. (Cherokee)
3776N "If We Would Mind Our Own Business," Children's Play
       Ground, August 9, 1881.

STRONG, NATHANIEL T. (Seneca)
3777N Appeal to the Christian Community on the Condition and
       Prospects of the New-York Indians, in Answer to a
       Book, Entitled The Case of the New-York Indians, and
       Other Publications, of the Society of Friends. New
       York: E. B. Clayton, 1841.
3778N Appeal to the Christian Community on the Condition and
       Prospects of the New York Indians, in Answer to a
       Book, Entitled The Case of the New York Indians, and
       Other Publications, of the Society of Friends. 2nd ed.
       New York: n. p., 1841.
3779N Appeal to the Christian Community on the Condition and
       Prospects of the New-York Indians, in Answer to a
       Book Entitled The Case of the New-York Indians, and
       Other Publications of the Society of Friends. Buffalo,
       NY: Press of Thomas & Co., 1841.

STRONG WOLF (Chippewa)
3780N "American Indian Club," American Indian Advocate, 4
       (Winter, 1922), 5.
3781N "A Message," American Indian Advocate, 4 (Winter, 1922),
       19.
3782N "Editorial," Indian Tepee, 6 (Summer, 1924), 4.

STUART, MARIE (Cherokee)
3783N "Beauty," Wreath of Cherokee Rose Buds, August 2, 1854.

SUIS, GEORGE (Crow)
3784N "Has Civilization Increased Human Happiness?" Red Man,
       12 (February, 1895), 4-5.

SULLIVAN, NAPOLEON BONAPARTE (Creek)
3785N "Muskokes, Arouse!" Indian Journal, August 19, 1880.

SUNCHIEF, STARRY (Pawnee)
3786A "Honor Is Burdened with Responsibilities," Native Ameri-
       can, June 11, 1904.

SUTTON, HENRY P. (Seneca)
3787N "An Imaginary Christmas," Carlisle Arrow, December 18,
       1914.
3788N "Our Trip to Washington--Flag Day," Carlisle Arrow, July
       21, 1916.

SWAMP, JOEL (Oneida)
3789N "Farm Dairying Among the Oneida Indians," Indian Leader,
       July 8, 1910.

TABISCHADDIE, IRENE (Apache)
    3790N "Practical Education for the Indians," Native American,
           May 30, 1903.

TAHAMONT, ROBERT J. (Abnaki)
    3791N "How the Term 'Fire Water' Originated," Indian's Friend,
           23 (November, 1910), 10.
    3792N "How the Term 'Fire Water' Originated," Red Man, 3 (No-
           vember, 1910), 113.
    3793M "The Grasshopper War," Red Man, 4 (September, 1911),
           29.
    3794N "Chief Teedyuscung," Red Man, 3 (January, 1911), 212.

TALAVENKA, CLARA M. (Hopi)
    3795N "Some Hopi Customs," Native American, December 12,
           1908.
    3796M "Saquavicha, the Fox Girl," Native American, May 29,
           1909.
    3797M "Saquavicha, the Fox-Girl," Indian's Friend, 21 (July,
           1909), 2.

TATIYOPA, HENRY (Sioux)
    3798N "Barriers to the Progress of the Sioux," Red Man and
           Helper, February 20-27, 1903.

TAYLOR, JOHN M., JR. (Cherokee)
    3799L "Hon. Rabbit Bunch," Indian Chieftain, November 25, 1886.
    3800L "Taylor and His Rabbit," Indian Chieftain, January 6, 1887.
    3801L "A Reply to Fullblood," Indian Chieftain, January 27, 1887.
    3802L "An Answer to 'Indian,'" Indian Arrow, January 10, 1889.
    3803L "Tackled by Taylor," Indian Chieftain, March 28, 1889.
    3804L "Claremore Mound," Tahlequah Leader, August 5, 1904.
    3805N "An Old Indian Battle Ground," Tahlequah Arrow, August
           6, 1904.

TAYLOR, RICHARD (Cherokee)
    3806N With John Ridge and W. S. Coodey. "Memorial of the
           Delegates from the Cherokee Indians," Cherokee Phoenix
           & Indians' Advocate, March 5, 1831.

TEHEE, HOUSTON BENGE (Cherokee)
    3807N "Memoir of Mrs. Tenny Mary Fuller," Twin Territories,
           3 (June, 1901), 100-101.
    3808N "Cherokee Fight Growing Critical," Muskogee Democrat,
           November 14, 1905.
    3809N "Senate Sustains the Charge Against Rogers," Muskogee
           Democrat, November 20, 1905.
    3810L "To the Democratic Voters of Cherokee County," Tahlequah
           Herald, July 19, 1912.

TEMPLE, JACKSON (Klamath)
    3811A "Mascots," Native American, June 3, 1905.

TENLJIETH, SILAS (Apache)

3812N "A Reservation Christmas," <u>Native American</u>, December 26, 1914.

TEQUAWA, BERT (Apache)
3813N "My First Trip Out of Arizona," <u>Native American</u>, September 17, 1913.

THAYER, WILLIAM JOSEPH (Chippewa)
3814N "My Autobiography," <u>Carlisle Arrow</u>, June 4, 1915.

THOMAS, ALBERT L. (Pima)
3815N "Christmas on the Reservation," <u>Native American</u>, December 25, 1909.
3816M "A Legend of the Pima," <u>Native American</u>, April 16, 1910.
3817N "Painting," <u>Native American</u>, May 14, 1910.

THOMAS, DANIEL (Pima)
3818N "Yesterday and Today with the Pimas," <u>Southern Workman</u>, 45 (September, 1916), 503-507.
3819N "Customs and Superstitions of the Pimas," <u>Southern Workman</u>, 46 (April, 1917), 227-229.

THOMAS, FANNIE (Cherokee)
3820N "Dogs," <u>Children's Play Ground</u>, August 9, 1881.

THOMAS, MYRTLE (Chippewa)
3821N With Fred Broker. "Class History," <u>Carlisle Arrow</u>, May 22, 1914.

THOMPSON, JOSEPH FRANKLIN (Cherokee)
3822L "The Training School," <u>Cherokee Advocate</u>, April 18, 1874.
3823L Letter, <u>Cherokee Advocate</u>, March 21, 1894.
3824N "In Memoriam," <u>Tahlequah Arrow</u>, September 7, 1899.

THOMPSON, MARTHA (Tuscarora)
3825P "The Red Cross Christmas Roll Call," <u>Indian Leader</u>, 22 (December, 1918), 15.

THOMPSON, WALTER A. (Cherokee)
3826N "Some Thoughts," <u>Indian Sentinel</u>, April 15, 1898.

THREE STARS, CLARENCE (Sioux)
3827A Address at Carlisle Commencement, <u>Red Man</u>, 15 (February-March, 1899), 8.
3828L "The Wyoming Pale-Face Uprising," <u>Red Man and Helper</u>, December 11, 1903.

TIAOKASIN, JOHN (Sioux)
3829L "An Indian Boy's Thoughts About Land in Severalty," <u>Southern Workman</u>, 17 (February, 1888), 22.

TIBBETTS, JESSE (Chippewa)
3830M "The Origin of Thunder," <u>Indian Leader</u>, March 29, 1912.

TIBBETTS, LUZENIA E. (Chippewa)
   3831N "One Year with the Minnesota Chippewas," Red Man and
         Helper, March 22, 1901.

TIBBLES, SUSETTE (Omaha)
   3832N "Perils and Promises of Indian Citizenship," Our Day, 5
         (June, 1890), 460-471.
   See also LaFLESCHE, SUSETTE

TIGER, EUNAH J. (Creek)
   3833F "The Magic Mirror." Bacone Chief. Bacone, OK: Bacone
         College, 1924, pp. 35-36.

TIGER, HELEN MAY (Creek)
   3834N "Books." Bacone Chief. Bacone, OK: Bacone College,
         1919, pp. 47-49.

TIGER, IDA R. (Creek)
   3835N "The Ideal Young Woman." Bacone Chief. Bacone, OK:
         Bacone College, 1915, pp. 33-34.
   3836N "Indian Superstitions." Bacone Chief. Bacone, OK: Ba-
         cone College, 1917, pp. 44-45.

TIGER, MARY J. (Creek)
   3837N "Music." Bacone Chief. Bacone, OK: Bacone College,
         1919, p. 43.
   3838N "Music Department." Bacone Chief. Bacone, OK: Bacone
         College, 1921, pp. 90-91.

TIGER, MOTY (Creek)
   3839N "Benediction," Muskogee Times Democrat, September 19,
         1907. In Creek and English.
   3840N Muskogee Indian Allotments. Memorial by Chief Tiger on
         Behalf of Certain Citizens of the Muskogee (Creek) Na-
         tion of Indians for the Equalization of the Value of Their
         Allotments. Washington, DC: Government Printing Of-
         fice, 1910.
   3841A Message of Moty Tiger, Principal Chief of the Creek Na-
         tion, to the Extra-Ordinary Session of the National Coun-
         cil of Said Nation Called by Authority of an Act of Con-
         gress, Which Convened at Okmulgee on September 1st,
         1914, and the Actions and Proceedings Thereof in the
         Creek and English Languages. Rendered into Creek by
         G. W. Grayson. Eufaula, OK: Indian Journal, 1914?

TOO-QUA-STEE
   See DUNCAN, DeWITT CLINTON

TOWNSEND, HARVEY (Pueblo)
   3842N "Postage Stamps," Red Man, 8 (November, 1888), 8.

TOWNSEND, SAMUEL (Pawnee)
   3843N "The School News," Cheyenne Transporter, August 25, 1880.

3844N "What Is Expected of Us?" Morning Star, 7 (July, 1887), 7.

3845N "A Trip to Wilmington, Delaware," Indian Helper, March 23, 1888.

TRACY, CALVIN BRADLEY (Chickasaw)
3846N "Native American Artisans, Artists, and Authors," Indian Leader, June 8-22, 1923.

TRIPP, DORA (Klamath)
3847N "Ways of the Klamath Indians," Native American, January 10, 1903.

TROTT, WILLIAM LaFAYETTE (Cherokee)
3848L "Letter from Mr. Trott," Indian Chieftain, March 26, 1885.

3849L "Not Yet," Indian Chieftain, August 28, 1890.

3850L "The Cause and the Cure," Indian Chieftain, March 12, 1891.

TSATOKE, MONROE (Kiowa)
3851F With James Ahgoon. "An Indian Fairy Tale." Bacone Chief. Bacone, OK: Bacone College, 1921, p. 69.

TUTTLE, T. W. (Sioux)
3852A "Can the Indian Be Civilized?" Southern Workman, 13 (February, 1884), 19.

TWISS, FRANK W. (Sioux)
3853N "Go Forward," Morning Star, 3 (June, 1883), 4.

TWOGUNS, EVELYN R. (Seneca)
3854N "The Indian Fondness for Music," Quarterly Journal of the Society of American Indians, 3 (April-June, 1915), 135-136.

TWOGUNS, SELINA (Seneca)
3855N "Iroquois Burial Customs," Red Man, 2 (March, 1910), 28-29.

UPSHAW, ALEXANDER (Crow)
3856N "What the Indians Owe to the United States Government," Red Man, 14 (April, 1897), 8.

VALENZUELA, JUANA (Pima)
3857N "Indians from the Time of Columbus to the Present Day," Native American, May 23, 1914.

VALENZUELA, KATHERINE (Pima)

3858A "Are We Equal to It?" Native American, June 11, 1904.

VALENZUELA, MYRA (Pima)
3859N "The Plants of the Desert," Native American, November 28, 1908.
3860N "Milk and Its Uses," Native American, May 22, 1909.

VALENZUELA, THOMAS (Pima)
3861M "The Legend of the Coyote," Native American, October 31, 1908.
3862M "The Legend of the Coyote," Indian's Friend, 21 (March, 1909), 10.
3863N "Carpentry," Native American, May 22, 1909.

VANN, CLEMENT NEELY (Cherokee)
3864L With W. P. Adair, Samuel Smith, George W. Scraper, and Lewis Downing. "Letter from the Cherokee Delegation," Cherokee Advocate, April 1, 1871.
3865C With W. P. Adair. History of the Claim of the Texas Cherokees. New York, 1873.

VANN, DANIEL WEBSTER (Cherokee)
3866L "Regarding That $6,250," Indian Chieftain, December 27, 1888.
3867L "'Twas the Senate's Fault," Indian Chieftain, January 30, 1890.
3868L "An Able Argument," Indian Sentinel, January 26, 1899.
3869L "A Cherokee's Reply," New-State Tribune, October 4, 1906.

VANN, DAVID (Cherokee)
3870L Letter, Cherokee Phoenix & Indians' Advocate, June 11, 1831.

VAUGHN, GERALD (Yuma)
3871N "Boilers," Native American, June 12, 1909.

VENNE, ALFRED (Chippewa)
3872N "Bond or Free?" Red Man and Helper, February 26-March 4, 1904.

VENNE, ERNESTINE (Chippewa)
3873M "Facts About the Chippewas," Red Man, 4 (March, 1912), 295.

VERIGAN, FRANCIS L. (Tlinget)
3874P "Be a Carlisle Student," Carlisle Arrow and Red Man, November 2, 1917.
3875P "Stick: After General Pratt's Address," Carlisle Arrow and Red Man, November 9, 1917.
3876P "To Our Service Men," Carlisle Arrow and Red Man, December 21, 1917.

3877P   "To the 'Mysterious Stranger,'" <u>Carlisle Arrow and Red Man</u>, January 25, 1918.

3878F   "The Spud Patch of Wapato Dan," <u>Carlisle Arrow and Red Man</u>, February 8, 1918.

3879P   "The Martyrdom of Funny Face," <u>Carlisle Arrow and Red Man</u>, March 22, 1918.

3880N   "Indian Fishermen of the North," <u>Southern Workman</u>, 49 (November, 1920), 509-511.

WAITE, AGNES V. (Serrano)

3881M   "The Legend of Tacquish," <u>Indian's Friend</u>, 24 (January, 1912), 10.

3882M   "The Legend of the Tacquish," <u>Red Man</u>, 4 (April, 1912), 340.

3883N   "The Pueblo of De Taos," <u>Red Man</u>, 5 (September, 1912), 25.

WALKER, BERTRAND N. O. (Wyandot)

3884P   "A Mojave Lullaby," <u>Twin Territories</u>, 5 (May, 1903), 165.

3885P   "Sunset in the Colorado Desert," <u>Sturm's Statehood Magazine</u>, 1 (January, 1906), 94.

3886P   "Pontiac," <u>Indian School Journal</u>, 6 (April, 1906), 49-50.

3887P   "The Song of the Navajo Weaver," <u>Indian School Journal</u>, 6 (July, 1906), 9.

3888N   "Sketches of the Wyandots," <u>Indian School Journal</u>, 6 (September, 1906), 21-25.

3889P   "A Mojave Lullaby," <u>Indian School Journal</u>, 7 (January, 1907), 31.

3890F   "Indian Stories Told in the Lodges of the North-east Long Ago," <u>Indian School Journal</u>, 7 (January, 1907), 33-45.

3891P   "A Desert Memory," <u>Indian School Journal</u>, 7 (February, 1907), 64.

3892F   "Tah-seh-tih's Sacrifice," <u>Indian School Journal</u>, 7 (March, 1907), 33-39.

3893P   "Sunset in Mojave Land," <u>Indian School Journal</u>, 7 (May, 1907), 24.

3894N   "Some Wyandot History," <u>Indian School Journal</u>, 8 (November, 1907), 25-29.

3895N   "Noted Indian Passes Away," <u>Indian School Journal</u>, 9 (June, 1908), 19.

3896P   "The Song of a Navajo Weaver," <u>Indian Leader</u>, April 30, 1909.

3897P   "A Wyandot Cradle Song," <u>Red Man</u>, 2 (March, 1910), 25.

3898M   "A Wyandotte Myth--Why the Toad Was Called Grandmother," <u>Indian Leader</u>, November 24, 1911.

3899N   "Wyandot Research," <u>Indian School Journal</u>, 12 (December, 1911), 63-64.

3900P   "Arrow-heads," <u>Indian School Journal</u>, 15 (February, 1915), 291.

3901P   "A Strand of Wampum," <u>Indian School Journal</u>, 15 (April, 1915), 112.

3902P "The Warriors' Plume," Indian School Journal, 15 (May, 1915), 474.

3903P "A Strand of Wampum," Indian's Friend, 27 (July, 1915), 8.

3904P "A Wyandot Lullaby." In Tributes to a Vanishing Race. Comp. Irene C. Beaulieu and Kathleen Woodward. Chicago: Privately Printed, 1916, p. 45.

3905P "Arrow-Heads." In Tributes to a Vanishing Race. Comp. Irene C. Beaulieu and Kathleen Woodward. Chicago: Privately Printed, 1916, p. 29.

3906P "The Calumet or Peace-Pipe," Southern Workman, 48 (January, 1919), 30.

3907F Tales of the Bark Lodges, by Hen-Toh, Wyandot. Oklahoma City: Harlow Publishing Company, 1919.

3908F Tales of the Bark Lodges, by Hen-Toh, Wyandot. 2nd ed. Oklahoma City: Harlow Publishing Company, 1920.

3909P Yon-doo-shah-we-ah (Nubbins) by Hen-Toh (Wyandot). Oklahoma City: Harlow Publishing Company, 1924.

WALKER, GEORGE (Creek)
3910N "Manual Training Department." Bacone Chief. Bacone, OK: Bacone College, 1921, p. 93.

3911M "Why the Mole Lives Under Ground." Bacone Chief. Bacone, OK: Bacone College, 1923, p. 81.

WALKER, JOHN G. (Navajo)
3912A "My People, the Navajoes," Southern Workman, 27 (March, 1898), 52-53.

3913N "The Mission of the Educated Indian," Southern Workman, 27 (August, 1898), 160.

3914N "Handicraft of the Southwestern Indians," Southern Workman, 28 (March, 1899), 111-112.

3915N "Navajo Thrift," Southern Workman, 29 (July, 1900), 413-416.

WALKER, LILLIAN (Ottawa)
3916N "My Summer at Carlisle," Carlisle Arrow, June 4, 1915.

WALKER, WISEY (Creek)
3917M "Why the Turtle Has Red Eyes," Indian Leader, May, 1915.

WALKINGSTICK, SIMON RALPH (Cherokee)
3918F "The Story of the School Desk." Bacone Chief. Bacone, OK: Bacone College, 1911, p. 31.

3919N "The Boy Then and Now." Bacone Chief. Bacone, OK: Bacone College, 1913, pp. 23-24.

3920N "The Indian's Outlook To-Day," American Indian Advocate, 4 (Winter, 1922), 10-11.

WALLACE, RICHARD (Crow)
3921N "The American Indians," Red Man, 8 (June, 1888), 8.

WANNEH, GAWASA (Seneca)

3922N   "The League of Peace," Quarterly Journal of the Society
      of American Indians, 2 (July-September, 1914), 191-195.
3923N   "Situwaka, Chief of the Chilcats," Quarterly Journal of the
      Society of American Indians, 2 (October-December, 1914),
      280-283.
3924N   "Situwaka, Chief of the Chilcats," Indian Leader, April,
      1915.
3925N   "Sophia C. Pitchlynn: A Choctaw Lady Who Believes in
      Raising Better Chickens," Quarterly Journal of the So-
      ciety of American Indians, 3 (April-June, 1915), 104-106.
3926N   "The American Indian as a Warrior," American Indian
      Magazine, 4 (January-March, 1916), 25-27.
3927P   "Faith," American Indian Magazine, 4 (October-December,
      1916), 317.
3928N   "The Red Man's Love of Mother Earth," American Indian
      Magazine, 5 (January-March, 1917), 14-16.

WARD, J. L. (Cherokee)
3929L   "Not at All Uneasy," Indian Chieftain, April 18, 1889.
3930L   "Judge Ward's Position," Indian Chieftain, January 19,
      1893.

WARD, ROBERT J. (Choctaw)
3931L   "From Scullyville," Vindicator, March 29, 1876.

WARDEN, ROBERT (Arapaho)
3932M   "The Red Pipe." Chilocco Annual. Chilocco, OK: Chiloc-
      co Indian School, 1920, p. 20.

WARREN, WILLIAM WHIPPLE (Chippewa)
3933N   History of the Ojibways, Based upon Traditions and Oral
      Statements in Minnesota Historical Society Collections,
      5 (St. Paul: Minnesota Historical Society, 1885), 21-394.

WATERMAN, CHARLES E. (Seneca)
3934N   "A Smoke Talk," Carlisle Arrow and Red Man, November
      2, 1917.
3935F   "The Century Clock: The Story of a Forty-Niner," Car-
      lisle Arrow and Red Man, December 7, 1917.

WATERMAN, LEILA (Seneca)
3936M   "An Iroquois Legend," Carlisle Arrow, September 20, 1912.
3937P   "Farewell to Carlisle," Carlisle Arrow, May 16, 1913.
3938N   "My Trip to Columbus," Carlisle Arrow, May 16, 1913.
3939N   "My Vacation," Carlisle Arrow, May 16, 1913.

WATSON, D. C. (Creek)
3940C   Acts and Resolutions of the Creek National Council of the
      Extra Session of April, 1894, and the Regular Session of
      October, 1894. Muskogee, I. T.: E. H. Hubbard &
      Co., 1894. In Creek and English. Watson compiled and
      translated these and 3941C and 3942C.
3941C   Acts and Resolutions of the Creek National Council of the

Extra Session of January, 1895. Muskogee, I. T.: E.
H. Hubbard & Co., 1895. In Creek and English.
3942C Acts and Resolutions of the Creek National Council of the
Called Session of August, and the Regular Session of
October, 1896. Muskogee, I. T.: The Phoenix Print-
ing Company, 1896. In Creek and English.

WATTA, VENTURA (Mission)
3943A "The Purpose and Influence of Schools," Native American,
June 3, 1905.

WEBB, EMMA (Pima)
3944M "The Great Doctor," Native American, April 17, 1909.
3945N "Pima Life," Native American, September 11, 1909.

WEBBER, DOTTIE (Pima)
3946N "Agriculture Among the Pima," Native American, May 16,
1914.

WEBSTER, CYNTHIA (Oneida)
3947N "Indian Girls as Teachers," Red Man, 13 (March, 1896), 2.

WELCH, JAMES (Chippewa)
3948N "Thanksgiving," Carlisle Arrow, November 20, 1914.

WELCH, WILSON H. (Cherokee)
3949N "A People Who Would Not Be Driven," Red Man, 14
(March, 1898), 5-6.

WELLINGTON, JOSEPH E. (Pima)
3950N "Be of Some Use to Your People," Native American, January 23, 1909.

WEST, BESSIE (Creek)
3951N "The Carlisle School," Morning Star, 5 (August, 1884), 4.

WEST, LUCY (Pawnee)
3952N "My Trip to Eagles Mere," Carlisle Arrow, September 4,
1914.

WHEELOCK, DENNISON (Oneida)
3953N "The Dawes Severalty Act," Red Man, 10 (May, 1890), 6-7.
3954N "The Oneidas," Red Man, 11 (September, 1891), 4.
3955A "Methodism Among the Oneidas," Red Man, 13 (July, 1895),
5-6.
3956N "Is It Right for the Government to Stop the Teaching of Indian Languages in Reservation Schools?" Indian Helper,
November 18, 1887.
3957A "Should Football Be Abolished?" Red Man, 14 (January,
1898), 5.
3958N "Not an Indian Problem, but a Problem of Race Separation," Quarterly Journal of the Society of American Indians, 1 (October-December, 1913), 366-372.

3959N "Present Situation of the Indian," Quarterly Journal of the Society of American Indians, 1 (April, 1913), 188-193.

3960N "Citizen Indians," Tomahawk, July 25, 1918. Reprinted from American Indian Magazine.

WHEELOCK, JAMES (Oneida)
3961P ["The Long Dreary Winter Weather,"] Red Man, 12 (May, 1895), 5.

WHEELOCK, JEMIMA (Oneida)
3962N "A Woman's Work in the World," Red Man, 10 (May, 1890), 7.

WHEELOCK, LIDA O. (Oneida)
3963N "The Arapahoes' Belief in Mescal," Red Man, 5 (January, 1913), 207-208.

3964N "Interesting Features of Lancaster County," Carlisle Arrow, May 16, 1913.

3965N "Sewing," Carlisle Arrow, May 16, 1913.

WHEELOCK, MARTIN F. (Oneida)
3966N "The Indian as an Athlete," Red Man and Helper, February 14, 1902.

WHIPPER, DALLAS (Sioux)
3967N "My People, Their Needs, and How Haskell Helps to Meet These Needs," Indian Leader, June, 1921.

WHIPPER, ROSE (Sioux)
3968P "Pride of Our Nation," Carlisle Arrow, May 22, 1913.

WHITE, JOHN (Mohawk)
3969N "Picture Writing and Sign Language," Indian Craftsman, 1 (April, 1909), 29-31.

3970M "Beginning of the Osage Tribe," Indian Craftsman, 2 (November, 1909), 30.

WHITE, MINNIE (Mohawk)
3971M "A Mohawk Legend," Red Man, 3 (November, 1910), 126.

WHITE, RENA S. (Chippewa)
3972N "Chippewa Indians," Indian Leader, December 29, 1922.

WHITEBULL, JAMES (Sioux)
3973N "Christmas for the Indian Youth," Indian Leader, December, 1915.

WHITEWOLF, HOWARD (Comanche)
3974N "A Short Story of My Life," American Indian Magazine, 5 (January-March, 1917), 29-31.

WHITMAN, ATALOYA (Pima)
3975A "Indian Music," Native American, June 3, 1905.

WILDCAT, THOMAS (Absentee Shawnee)
See ALFORD, THOMAS WILDCAT

WILKIE, MICHAEL (Chippewa)
3976F   With Ovilla Azure. "The Boys of Carlisle '15 Twenty-five
        Years Hence," Carlisle Arrow, June 4, 1915.

WILLIAMS, ELEAZER (Mohawk)
3977N   Good News to the Iroquois Nation. A Tract, on Man's
        Primitive Rectitude, His Fall, and His Recovery Through
        Jesus Christ. By Eleazer Williams. Burlington, VT:
        Samuel Mills, 1813.
3978N   The Salvation of Sinners Through the Riches of Divine
        Grace. Two Homilies, Pronounced at Oneida Castle, in
        the Audience of the Oneida Indians at Their Eighth Tri-
        ennial Anniversary, Since the Conversion of Six Hundred
        Pagans of That Tribe to the Christian Faith: On the 8th
        of August, 1841. By Eleazer Williams. Green Bay,
        WI: Printed at the Republican Office, 1842.
3979N   Life of Te-ho-ra-gwa-ne-gen, alias Thomas Williams, a
        Chief of the Caughnawaga Tribe of Indians in Canada.
        By the Rev. Eleazer Williams. Albany, NY: J. Mun-
        sell, 1859.

WILLIAMS, EMMA LOWREY (Cherokee)
3980P   "Life." In Emmet Starr. History of the Cherokee Indians
        and Their Legends and Folk Lore. Oklahoma City: The
        Warden Company, 1921, p. 234.

WILLIAMS, GEORGE (Pueblo)
3981N   "The American Indian--The Indian of the Future," Indian
        School Journal, 10 (June, 1910), 53-54.

WILLIAMS, JAMES P. (Ponca)
3982N   "The Ponca People," Indian Leader, May 9, 1902.

WILLIAMS, JOHNSON (Puyallup)
3983N   "School and Indian Village Life," Indian School Journal, 11
        (September, 1911), 33-37.

WILLIAMS, JULIA (Chippewa)
3984N   "A Century's Growth Among the Chippewas," Red Man, 14
        (April, 1897), 8.

WILLIAMS, LEWIS (Nez Percé)
3985N   "I Wonder Why," Red Man, 12 (February, 1895), 3-4.

WILLIAMS, S. F. (Seneca)
3986N   "Progress of the Indian," Indian Craftsman, 1 (June, 1909),
        33.
3987N   "The Indian and White of To-day," Indian's Friend, 21 (Au-
        gust, 1909), 5.

WILLIS, JAMES (Choctaw)
3988N "A Crying," Indian Leader, May, 1915.

WILLIS, LILLIE (Choctaw)
3989M "The Indian Cry," Indian Leader, June 14, 1912.
3990N "Movements to Better Health Conditions," Indian Leader, June, 1915.

WILMETT, ANTOINE (Potawatomi)
3991N "Why Take a Commercial Course?" Indian Leader, June, 1921.

WILSEY, FREDERICK (Concow, or Konkau)
3992N "Horseshoeing," Native American, May 23, 1908.

WILSON, MARIE (Delaware)
3993N "From the Window of the Senior Class Room." Chilocco Annual. Chilocco, OK: Chilocco Indian School, 1920, p. 25.

WILSON, PETER (Cayuga)
3994A Speech of Wa-o-was-was-na-onk Addressed to the Committee of Baltimore Yearly Meeting of Friends on Indian Concerns, 10 mo. 29, 1848. Baltimore? 1848.

WILSON, WILLIAM (Cherokee)
3995N With J. M. Bryan and John L. McCoy. "To the Hon. Chairman of the Committee on Territories of the House of Representatives," Cherokee Advocate, May 6, 1876.
3996L With J. M. Bryan and William Hendricks. "What the Old Settlers Say," Cherokee Advocate, May 2, 1877.
3997L "To the Old Settler Cherokees," Cherokee Advocate, April 11, 1884.

WINNEMUCCA, SARAH (Paiute)
3998N Life Among the Paiutes, Their Wrongs and Claims. Mrs. Horace Mann, ed. Boston: Cupples, Upham, 1883.

WISTAR, MARY (Ottawa)
3999N "Citizenship," Indian Leader, September, 1914.

WOLF, JONAS (Chickasaw)
4000A "Gov. Wolf's Message," Indian Champion, November 8, 1884.
4001A "The Governor's Message to the Chickasaw Legislature," Chickasaw Enterprise, January 25, 1894, supplement.
4002A "Governor Wolf's Message," Indian Citizen, February 1, 1894.

WOLFCHIEF, JOHN (Arapaho)
4003A "The Duty of an American," Native American, June 9, 1906.

WOLFE, JOE (Papago)
4004N "Beet Sugar," Native American, July 9-16, 1910.

WOLFE, KATHRINE E. (Cherokee)
4005N "The Chinookan Family," Red Man, 2 (March, 1910), 35.
4006N "A Cherokee Ball Game," Indian's Friend, 22 (June, 1910), 2.
4007N "A Cherokee Ball Game," Red Man, 3 (October, 1910), 76-77.

WOLFE, LIZZIE (Papago)
4008N "Housekeeping," Native American, May 20, 1911.

WOLFE, MICHAEL (Chippewa)
4009N "The Plea for the Young Indian," Quarterly Journal of the Society of American Indians, 1 (April, 1913), 186-188.
4010A "Address of Mr. Michael Wolf [sic]," Red Man, 5 (May, 1913), 431-433.

WOLFE, REUBEN (Omaha)
4011N "The American Flag," Red Man, 11 (May, 1892), 2-3.

WOLFE, RICHARD MURRELL (Cherokee)
4012N With Pleasant Porter, John F. Brown, and Daniel H. Ross. "Memorial of the Indian Delegations at Washington," Cherokee Advocate, April 28, 1882.
4013N With Daniel H. Ross, Pleasant Porter, William L. Byrd, and John F. Brown. "Supplement to Memorial of April 6th, on Railroad Question," Cherokee Advocate, May 5, 1882.
4014N With D. H. Ross and Pleasant Porter. "Protest of Cherokee and Creek Delegation Against Passage of S. B. 1573," Cherokee Advocate, May 28, 1882.
4015N "The North Carolina Cherokees," Cherokee Advocate, August 4, 1882.
4016N With D. H. Ross. "Report of the Cherokee Delegation," Cherokee Advocate, November 24, 1882.
4017N With Robert B. Ross. "Protest of the Cherokee Delegation Against the Claim of the North Carolina Cherokees Against the Cherokee Nation, as Set Forth in Executive Document N. 79, 47 Congress 2nd Session," Cherokee Advocate, March 9, 1883.

WOODWARD, KATHLEEN (Osage)
4018N "The War Bonnet." In Tributes to a Vanishing Race. Comp. Irene Beaulieu and Kathleen Woodward. Chicago: Privately Printed, 1916, pp. 68-69.
4019N "Nature's Children." In Tributes to a Vanishing Race. Comp. Irene C. Beaulieu and Kathleen Woodward. Chicago: Privately Printed, 1916, pp. 79-80.
4020C With Irene Campbell Beaulieu. Tributes to a Vanishing Race. Chicago: Privately Printed, 1916.

WOOLWORTH, ROSE (Arapaho)
    4021N "My Favorite Composer." Chilocco Annual. Chilocco, OK:
          Chilocco Indian School, 1920, p. 39.

WRIGHT, ALLEN (Choctaw)
    4022L "The Intercourse Law," Vindicator, June 12, 1875.
    4023L "Whither Are We Drifting?" Vindicator, April 5, 1876.
    4024A "National Liberty," Atoka Independent, July 12, 1878.
    4025A "Speech of Gov. Wright at the Fort Scott Celebration on
          July the 4th," Atoka Independent, July 12, 1878.
    4026N Chahta Leksikon. A Choctaw in English Definition. For
          the Choctaw Academies and Schools. St. Louis: Pres-
          byterian Publishing Company, 1880.
    4027L "New Hope Seminary Examinations," Indian Journal, July
          14, 1881.
    4028N Chahta Leksikon. A Choctaw in English Definition. For
          the Choctaw Academies and Schools. 2nd ed. Rev. by
          T. L. Mellen. Nashville, TN: M. E. Church South,
          1904.

WRIGHT, ALLEN, JR. (Choctaw)
    4029N "Why the Indian Should Not Be a Republican," Indian Citi-
          zen, September 13, 1906.
    4030N "Wheelock Seminary," Chronicles of Oklahoma, 1 (October,
          1921), 117-120.

WRIGHT, MURIEL HAZEL (Choctaw)
    4031N The Story of Oklahoma. Ed. Joseph B. Thoburn. Okla-
          homa City: Webb Publishing Co., 1924.

YANDELL, MINNIE (Bannock)
    4032N "Reflections," Red Man, 12 (January-February, 1894), 2.

YELLOWBIRD, FRANCIS (Sioux)
    4033N "My Country," Southern Workman, 10 (June, 1881), 67.

YELLOWROBE, CHAUNCEY (Sioux)
    4034N ["Moody's Summer School,"] Red Man, 11 (September-
          October, 1892), 7.
    4035A Address Before the Congress of Nations at Chicago, Red
          Man, 11 (May-June, 1893), 2-3.
    4036N "The World's Fair Seen by an Aborigine," Red Man, 12
          (February, 1895), 14.
    4037N "The Indian and the Wild West Show," Quarterly Journal
          of the Society of American Indians, 2 (January-March,
          1914), 39-40.
    4038N "The Menace of the Wild West Show," Quarterly Journal
          of the Society of American Indians, 2 (July-September,
          1914), 224-225.
    4039N "My Boyhood Days," American Indian Magazine, 4 (January-
          March, 1916), 50-53.

4040A "Indian Patriotism," American Indian Magazine, 6 (July-September, 1917), 129-130.

4041N "The Fighting Sioux," American Indian Magazine, 5 (October-December, 1917), 226-227.

YELLOWTAIL, ROBERT (Crow)

4042N "The Indian and His Problems," Red Man, 5 (May, 1913), 412-416.

4043N "Why the Crow Indian Reservation Should Not Be Opened," Red Man, 8 (April, 1916), 265-270.

YOUNGBULL, TYLER (Arapaho)

4044N "If Our American Indian Can Fight for His Country, Why Not Let Him Vote?" Bacone Chief. Bacone, OK: Bacone College, 1919, pp. 49-51.

4045N "The Qualities of a Gentleman." Bacone Chief. Bacone, OK: Bacone College, 1920, p. 79.

4046P "Just Imagine!" Bacone Chief. Bacone, OK: Bacone College, 1921, p. 110.

4047N "A Glimpse into the Future." Bacone Chief. Bacone, OK: Bacone College, 1921, p. 70-71.

4048M "An Indian Legend." Bacone Chief. Bacone, OK: Bacone College, 1923, pp. 77-78.

YUCKKU, LEMUEL (Hopi)

4049N "History of the Hopi," Native American, June 10, 1916.

YUPE, SUSIE (Shoshoni)

4050N "Which Doorway Shall We Enter?" Red Man, 15 (March, 1900), 2.

ZITKALA-SA
See BONNIN, GERTRUDE SIMMONS

PART II

A BIBLIOGRAPHY OF NATIVE AMERICAN WRITERS
KNOWN ONLY BY PEN NAMES

"A" (Cherokee)
- 4051L "Washington Letter," Cherokee Advocate, June 16, 1880.
- 4052N "Deaf and Blind," Cherokee Advocate, September 1, 1880.
- 4053P "The Two Ships," Cherokee Advocate, February 9, 1881.
- 4054L "Our School Law," Cherokee Advocate, August 17, 1881.
- 4055N "Pic-Nic and Anniversary of the Opening of the Male and Female Seminaries," Cherokee Advocate, May 12, 1882.
- 4056N "Chief Justice E. M. Adair," Cherokee Advocate, May 19, 1882.
- 4057N "Citizenship," Cherokee Advocate, June 16, 23, and 30 and July 7, 1882.
- 4058N "Citizenship--'The High Jinx,'" Cherokee Advocate, July 21 and 28 and August 4, 1882.
- 4059N "Wire Fencing East of Ninety-Six," Cherokee Advocate, November 17, 1882.

A (Cherokee)
- 4060L "The Court Defended," Indian Chieftain, January 27, 1887.
- 4061L "'A' Still in the Arena," Indian Chieftain, March 10, 1887.

ACHILLAHCULLAGHEE (Cherokee)
- 4062L "For the Cherokee Phoenix," Cherokee Phoenix and Indians' Advocate, July 8, 1829.

ADA (Cherokee)
- 4063N "The First Sabbath," Wreath of Cherokee Rose Buds, August 1, 1855.

ADA MAY (Cherokee)
- 4064N "Thoughts in Study Hour," Wreath of Cherokee Rose Buds, August 2, 1854.

AH-STO-LA-TA (Cherokee)
- 4065L "Ahstolata's Letter," Cherokee Telephone, June 4, 1891.

ALICE (Cherokee)
- 4066N "The Rose," Wreath of Cherokee Rose Buds, August 2, 1854.

ARNA-WAKY (Creek)
- 4067L "Arnawaky's Letter," Wagoner Record, December 7, 1899.

ATHOME (Cherokee)
    4068L "Don't Like the Way Things Look," Cherokee Advocate, October 1, 1904.
    4069L "Athome Writes Again," Cherokee Advocate, October 8, 1904.

"AUNT SUSAN" (Cherokee)
    4070L Letter, Cherokee Advocate, December 8, 1882.

B. W. A. (Cherokee)
    4071N "Statehood," Cherokee Advocate, July 29, 1893.

"BALLOA" (Cherokee)
    4072L "Cooweescowee District," Cherokee Advocate, January 21, 1880.

BELLE (Cherokee)
    4073N "The Wind," Wreath of Cherokee Rose Buds, August 2, 1854.

BESSIE (Cherokee)
    4074N "Tardiness," Wreath of Cherokee Rose Buds, August 2, 1854.

BIG CREEK SCRIBE (Cherokee)
    4075F "A Sermon Reported by Our Big Creek Scribe," Indian Chieftain, July 31, 1890.

BIG INDIAN (Cherokee)
    4076N "'Big Indian' Speaks," Indian Chieftain, February 23, 1899.

"BIG INJIN" (Cherokee)
    4077L Letter, Cherokee Advocate, September 2, 1876.

BILL (Cherokee)
    4078L Letter, Cherokee Advocate, April 21, 1882.

BLACK FOX (Cherokee)
    4079L "From the Cherokee Nation," Arkansian, October 22, 1859.

BLACKBURN, CYRUS LEONIDUS (Cherokee)
    4080L "The Jubilee in Sight," Indian Chieftain, January 26, 1888.

"BOOD GUY" (Cherokee)
    4081L "High Schools," Cherokee Advocate, August 31, 1881.
    4082L Letter, Cherokee Advocate, September 14, 1881.

BROKEN WING BIRD (Chippewa)
    4083F "When His Father Died," Tomahawk, October 27, 1921.
    4084N "On the Next Conference," Tomahawk, October 30, 1921.
    4085N "Isn't This True?" Tomahawk, November 3, 1921.
    4086P "Come Back, Indians of Yesterday," Tomahawk, November 17, 1921.

4087N "Broken Wing Bird Offers Some Advice for Indians," Tomahawk, January 12, 1922.
4088N "What's in an Indian Name?" Tomahawk, January 19, 1922.
4089N "The Greatest Reason Why Indians Have Never Been Able
to Get Anywhere--They Can't," Tomahawk, May 11, 1922.

"CANADIAN" (Cherokee)
4090L Letter to Editor, Cherokee Advocate, June 18, 1870.

"CAPTAIN JACK" (Cherokee)
4091L "From Cooweeskoowee," Cherokee Advocate, August 17,
1878.

CAWLAHNAH OONAKAH (Cherokee)
4092L "For the Cherokee Phoenix," Cherokee Phoenix, December
29, 1828.

CHA-LAH-GEE (Cherokee)
4093N "The Grave of Goingsnake," Tahlequah Arrow, August 25,
1906. Reprinted from Westville American.

CHA-WAH-YOO-KAH (Cherokee)
4094N "A Rainy Night," Wreath of Cherokee Rose Buds, August
2, 1854.

CHEROKEE (Cherokee)
4095N "The Rights of the Cherokees," Cherokee Phoenix & Indians' Advocate, August 11, 1832.

"CHEROKEE" (Cherokee)
4096N "Dissipation," Wreath of Cherokee Rose Buds, August 2,
1854.

CHEROKEE (Cherokee)
4097N "Duties of Cherokee Youth," Arkansian, May 21, 1859.

"CHEROKEE" (Cherokee)
4098P "Faster and Fiercer Rolls the Tide," Cherokee Advocate,
July 8, 1871.

"CHEROKEE" (Cherokee)
4099L Letter, Cherokee Advocate, December 9, 1881.
4100L Letter, Cherokee Advocate, April 14, 1882.

CHEROKEE (Cherokee)
4101L "Nuts to Crack," Telephone, July 26, 1889.
4102L "Allotment Ideas," Indian Chieftain, August 13, 1891.
4103L "A Scrap of Cherokee History," Indian Chieftain, January
17, 1895.

CHEROKEE (Cherokee)
4104N "Object Lesson," Cherokee Advocate, March 15, 1902.

A CHEROKEE (Cherokee)
    4105L "Money and Principles," Cherokee Phoenix, March 20, 1828.
    4106L "For the Cherokee Phoenix," Cherokee Phoenix, April 10, 1828.
    4107L "For the Cherokee Phoenix," Cherokee Phoenix, June 4, 1828.
    4108L Letter, Cherokee Phoenix & Indians' Advocate, February 11, 1832.
    4109N "Historical," Cherokee Phoenix & Indians' Advocate, April 14, 1832.
    4110L "For the Cherokee Phoenix," Cherokee Phoenix & Indians' Advocate, May 19, 1832.
    4111L "For the Cherokee Phoenix," Cherokee Phoenix & Indians' Advocate, May 26, 1832.
    4112L "For the Cherokee Phoenix," Cherokee Phoenix & Indians' Advocate, July 7, 1832.

A CHEROKEE (Cherokee)
    4113L "Will Chief Mayes Explain?" Indian Arrow, February 24, 1888.
    4114L "This Tells the Tale!" Cherokee Telephone, July 14, 1892.
    4115L Letter, Cherokee Advocate, August 5, 1893.

CHEROKEE BY BLOOD (Cherokee)
    4116L "Allotment," Indian Chieftain, March 25, 1886.
    4117L "That Citizenship Association," Indian Chieftain, May 20, 1886.

A CHEROKEE FARMER (Cherokee)
    4118L "For the Cherokee Phoenix," Cherokee Phoenix, and Indians' Advocate, March 18, 1829.

A CHEROKEE INDIAN (Cherokee)
    4119N "What Shall We Do to Be Saved?" Indian Chieftain, October 29, 1891.

"CHICAMAUGA" (Cherokee)
    4120L "From the Old Nation," Cherokee Advocate, September 7, 1878.

CHICKASAW (Chickasaw)
    4121L "The Star," Vindicator, September 6, 1876.

CHOCTAW (Choctaw)
    4122L "Washington Letter," Atoka Independent, May 3, 1878.
    4123L Letter, Indian Journal, August 25, 1881.

CHOON-NOO-LUS-KY (Cherokee)
    4124L "Choon-noo-lus-ky," Cherokee Telephone, July 17, 1890.
    4125L "Chunulusky Is Happy Over the 'Capita,'" Cherokee Telephone, December 18, 1890.
    4126L "Chunulunsky's Letter," Cherokee Telephone, March 5, 1891.

4127L   "Choo-Noo-Lusky Heard From," Cherokee Telephone, May 18, 1893.

CHOON-STOO-TEE (Cherokee)
4128N   "Nation vs. People," Cherokee Advocate, February 24, 1882.
4129N   "Nation vs. People," Cherokee Advocate, April 14, 1882.
4130L   "Cherokee Cattle in the Creek Country," Cherokee Advocate, March 30, 1883.
4131L   ["From Choon-stoo-stee,"] Telephone, February 22, 1888.
4132L   "Choon-stoo-stee's Letter," Telephone, May 16, 1888.
4133L   "Choon-stoo-stee Talks," Telephone, April 5, 1889.
4134L   "Quaint Sayings of a Crude Philosopher," Arrow, May 24, 1895.
4135L   "Choon-stoo-stee," Arrow, May 31, 1895.
4136L   "He Complains of How the Local Preacher Is Treated," Arrow, June 14, 1895.
4137L   "Choon-stoo-tee," Arrow, July 5, 1895.
4138L   "Choonstootie," Arrow, August 2, 1895.
4139L   "Choon-stoo-tee," Arrow, October 5, 1895.
4140L   "Choonstootee," Tahlequah Arrow, May 7, 1898.

A CITIZEN (Cherokee)
4141L   Letter, Cherokee Advocate, January 17, 1894.

A CITIZEN (Cherokee)
4142N   "The Present Necessity," Cherokee Advocate, May 30, 1903.

CLOD HOPPER [or DICK CLOD HOPPER] (Cherokee)
4143L   Letter, Cherokee Advocate, June 17, 1893.
4144L   Letter, Cherokee Advocate, July 15, 1893.

"CORNSILK" (Cherokee)
4145N   "The Fourth Principle of Man," Cherokee Advocate, February 7, 1894.
4146N   "For Lands in Severalty, and Statehood," Cherokee Advocate, April 18, 1894.
4147N   "Measure for Measure," Cherokee Advocate, July 11, 1894.
4148N   "Another Band of Robbers in the Indian Territory," Cherokee Advocate, January 9, 1895.
4149N   "Cornsilk Again," Arrow, May 31, 1895.
4150N   "Is It Only a Myth," Arrow, July 5, 1895.
4151N   "Red Man's Origin," Indian Chieftain, January 2, 1896. Reprinted from Capital.
4152N   "The Holy State of Samadhi," Indian Sentinel, April 1, 1898.
4153N   "The Mystic Craft or Free Masonry," Indian Sentinel, May 6, 1898.
4154N   "The Mystic Craft, or Free Masonry," Cherokee Advocate, May 7, 1898.
4155N   "The Doctrine of Karma or The Law of Retribution," Indian Sentinel, May 13, 1898.

CORRINNE (Cherokee)
    4156P "The Wreath of Rose Buds," Wreath of Cherokee Rose
         Buds, August 2, 1854.

COYOTE (Cherokee)
    4157L "And Still They Come," Indian Chieftain, April 28, 1887.

DAH-LO-NE (Cherokee)
    4158L "The Law of the Case," Indian Chieftain, February 23,
         1888.

DICK CLOD HOPPER See CLOD HOPPER

DORA (Cherokee)
    4159F "Queer Matty," Wreath of Cherokee Rose Buds, August 2,
         1854.

ECHO-HUTKA (Creek)
    4160L "State of Columbia," Muskogee Phoenix, April 22, 1891.

EDITH (Cherokee)
    4161N "A View from Our Seminary," Wreath of Cherokee Rose-
         buds, August 2, 1854.

EMARTHLA (Creek)
    4162L Letter, Indian Journal, February 5, 1880.

ESTE MASKOKE (Creek)
    4163N "Negroes as Law Makers," Muskogee Phoenix, October 31,
         1889.
    4164N "The Allotment of Our Land Question," Muskogee Phoenix,
         November 7, 1889.
    4165N "The Allotment of Our Lands," Muskogee Phoenix, Novem-
         ber 28, 1889.

FANNY (Cherokee)
    4166N "Two Scenes in Cherokee Land, Scene II," Wreath of Cher-
         okee Rose Buds, August 1, 1855.

FIX-E-CO (Creek)
    4167L "Correspondence," Arkansas Intelligencer, June 21, 1845.

FULL BLOOD (Cherokee)
    4168L "Indian Civilization and Its Retarding Influences," Indian
         Journal, August 18, 1877.
    4169L "Indian Civilization and Its Retarding Influences," Indian
         Journal, September 1, 1877.

FULLBLOOD (Cherokee)
    4170L "Reply from Fullblood," Indian Chieftain, February 24,
         1887.

4171L   "Fullblood Heard From," Indian Chieftain, January 20, 1887.
4172L   Letter, Cherokee Advocate, October 26, 1892.

FULL BLOOD (Chickasaw)
4173L   "Our Chickasaw Letter," Vindicator, March 22, 1876.
4174L   "Letter from Full-Blood," Vindicator, May 17, 1876.

FULL BLOOD (Choctaw)
4175L   "The Reviewer Reviewed," Vindicator, November 15, 1876.

GA-YU-GA (Cherokee)
4176N   "Stars," Wreath of Cherokee Rose Buds, August 1, 1855.

GITCHIE MANITOU (Chickasaw)
4177L   Letter, Indian Journal, March 3, 1881.

GOING SNAKE (Cherokee)
4178L   Letter, Cherokee Advocate, May 16, 1874.

GRACE (Cherokee)
4179N   "Intemperance," Wreath of Cherokee Rose Buds, August 1, 1855.

"GU-LA-TSI" (Cherokee)
4180L   "Pour Passer Le Temps," Cherokee Advocate, July 6, 1883.

HAIDE (Cherokee)
4181N   "Spring," Wreath of Cherokee Rose Buds, August 1, 1855.

HATTAK SIPOKINI (Choctaw)
4182L   "Oklahoma," Vindicator, March 15, 1876.
4183L   "Province of Oklahoma," Vindicator, April 26, 1876.
4184L   "Province of Oklahoma," Vindicator, May 3, 1876.

HATTIE (Cherokee)
4185N   "The Power of Kindness," Wreath of Cherokee Rose Buds, August 2, 1854.

HOPISAHUBBEE (Choctaw)
4186L   ["The Star,"] Vindicator, August 30, 1876.

HORS DE COMBAT (Cherokee)
4187P   "This Ends the Poetry," Indian Chieftain, April 14, 1887.

ICY (Cherokee)
4188F   "The Two Companions," Wreath of Cherokee Rose Buds, August 1, 1855.

IDA (Cherokee)
4189F   "The Curious Garden," Wreath of Cherokee Rose Buds, August 1, 1855.

"INDIAN" (Cherokee)
    4190L "The Contented Indian," Cherokee Advocate, January 21,
        1880.

INDIAN (Cherokee)
    4191L [Letter], Cherokee Advocate, January 9, 1895.

AN INDIAN (Creek)
    4192L "Two Vital Questions," Muskogee Phoenix, October 6, 1892.
    4193L "Taxation and Allotment," Muskogee Phoenix, October 20,
        1892.

INEZ (Cherokee)
    4194N "A Peep into the Future," Wreath of Cherokee Rose Buds,
        August 2, 1854.

INJUN (Cherokee)
    4195N "'Injun' Has Spoken," Indian Chieftain, January 13, 1898.

I-NO-LI (Cherokee)
    4196L Letter, Cherokee Advocate, April 18, 1884. Signed in
        Cherokee script.
    4197L Letter, Cherokee Advocate, May 9, 1884. Signed in Cher-
        okee script.

IONIA (Cherokee)
    4198N "Noble Names," Wreath of Cherokee Rose Buds, August 1,
        1855.

ISABELLA (Cherokee)
    4199N "A Day's Experience," Wreath of Cherokee Rose Buds,
        August 1, 1855.

ISTECHULE (Creek)
    4200N "The White Man and the Red Man," Twin Territories, 4
        (October, 1902), 286-8.

JONES, ABRAHAM LINKUM (Cherokee)
    4201N "The Sage of Gooseneck Bend," Indian Chieftain, May 28,
        1885.

JUSTICE (Cherokee)
    4202N "Cherokee Difficulties," Indian Journal, September 23,
        1880.

JUSTICE (Cherokee)
    4203L "The Voice of 'Justice,'" Indian Chieftain, February 19,
        1885.
    4204L "In Answer to 'Fair Play,'" Indian Chieftain, March 3,
        1887.
    4205L "The Indian Question," Indian Chieftain, July 18, 1895.

KA-YA-KUN-STAH (Cherokee)

4206N "An Osage Wedding," Wreath of Cherokee Rose Buds, August 2, 1854.

KAH-TOO (Cherokee)
4207L Letter, Cherokee Advocate, March 31, 1882.

"KATE" (Cherokee)
4208N "Music," Wreath of Cherokee Rose Buds, August 2, 1854.

KAW-LA-NAH (Cherokee)
4209L "Bread, and Not 'Bread Money,'" Cherokee Advocate, March 10, 1882.

KENAH TETLAH (Cherokee)
4210N "The First Sunday School," Indian Chieftain, December 20, 1900.
4211L "Kenah Tetlah Dissents," Indian Chieftain, July 11, 1901.

KEPLER (Cherokee)
4212N "Hints on Penmanship," Cherokee Advocate, November 18, 1891.

KINGFISHER (Cherokee)
4213P "After the Curtis Bill Passes," Tahlequah Arrow, April 9, 1898.

KITTY (Cherokee)
4214N "Se-Quah-Yah," Wreath of Cherokee Rose Buds, August 1, 1855.

KULLY CHAHA (Choctaw)
4215L "Choctaw Enterprise," Indian Journal, April 14, 1881.
4216L "A Visit to the Creek Nation," Indian Journal, May 5, 1881.

LELIA (Cherokee)
4217N "Critics and Criticism," Wreath of Cherokee Rose Buds, August 1, 1855.

"LEN-OH-PEH" (Cherokee)
4218L "Cooweescoowee District," Cherokee Advocate, May 14, 1879.

LEONORA (Cherokee)
4219N "The Mouse's Will," Wreath of Cherokee Rose Buds, August 1, 1855.

LETILLA (Cherokee)
4220N "The Gardening Season--A Great Time Among All Matrons," Wreath of Cherokee Rose Buds, August 2, 1854.

"LONE TREE" (Cherokee)
4221L Letter, Cherokee Advocate, April 28, 1880.

LUSETTE (Cherokee)
    4222F "Kate M---'s Composition," Wreath of Cherokee Rose Buds,
          August 1, 1854.

MAHIA (Creek)
    4223L ["The Seminoles,"] Indian Journal, May 6, 1880.

MOHARJO (Creek)
    4224N "The New York Observer Again," Indian Journal, August
          17, 1876.

MURREL (Cherokee)
    4225L "Cherokee Land Patent," Cherokee Advocate, January 27,
          1882.
    4226L Two Letters, Cherokee Advocate, March 3, 1882.

NA-LI (Cherokee)
    4227N "An Address to the Females of the Cherokee Nation,"
          Wreath of Cherokee Rose Buds, August 2, 1854.
    4228F "The Algebra Sum Soliloquy," Wreath of Cherokee Rose
          Buds, August 2, 1854.
    4229N "The Seed," Wreath of Cherokee Rose Buds, August 1,
          1855.
    4230N "Two Scenes in Cherokee Land, Scene I," Wreath of Cher-
          okee Rose Buds, August 1, 1855.

NATIVE (Cherokee)
    4231L Letter, Cherokee Advocate, June 6, 1874.

NATIVE (Cherokee)
    4232N "Smart Alecks," Cherokee Advocate, August 14, 1885.

NE-WO-TA-KA (Cherokee)
    4233L Letter, Cherokee Advocate, January 17, 1874.

OAKFUSKIE (Cherokee)
    4234L "For the Cherokee Phoenix," Cherokee Phoenix & Indians'
          Advocate, April 3, 1828.

OBSERVER (Cherokee)
    4235L "Humanity and Wisdom," Cherokee Advocate, January 19,
          1878.
    4236L "What the Council Did," Cherokee Advocate, January 19,
          1878.
    4237L Letter, Cherokee Advocate, April 2, 1879.
    4238L "Sequoyah School House," Cherokee Advocate, December
          10, 1879.
    4239L Letter, Cherokee Advocate, December 17, 1879.

"OC" (Cherokee)
    4240N "Our School Law," Cherokee Advocate, August 31, 1881.
    4241N "Our School Law," Cherokee Advocate, September 14,
          1881.

"OCEOLA" (Cherokee)
    4242L Letter, Cherokee Advocate, May 18, 1878. Reprinted from
            Atoka Independent.

OCONESTOTA (Cherokee)
    4243L "Signs of the Times," Cherokee Phoenix & Indians' Advo-
            cate, February 23, 1834.
    4244L "Signs of the Times," Cherokee Phoenix & Indians' Advo-
            cate, March 2, 1834.
    4245L "Signs of the Times--Union, State Rights and Nullification,"
            Cherokee Phoenix & Indians' Advocate, March 15, 1834.
    4246L "Signs of the Times: The Emigration," Cherokee Phoenix
            & Indians' Advocate, March 29, 1834.

OLD INJIN (Cherokee)
    4247L Letter, Cherokee Advocate, September 28, 1887.

OLD TIMER (Choctaw)
    4248L "An Old Timer's Opinion," Indian Champion, February 14,
            1885.

OO-DA-SA-TIH (Cherokee)
    4249L Letter to A. S., Cherokee Advocate, August 14, 1848.

OO-NA-KAH-TUH (Cherokee)
    4250L "The Permit Law," Cherokee Advocate, June 11, 1879.
    4251N "How to Save Our Lands," Indian Chieftain, July 10, 1890.

OOGALAH (Cherokee)
    4252N "The Cherokee People," Cherokee Advocate, December 9,
            1905.
    4253N "Oolagah [sic] on Statehood," Cherokee Advocate, Decem-
            ber 23, 1905.
    4254N "Oogalah Advises the Fullbloods," Cherokee Advocate, Jan-
            uary 13, 1906.

OOH-LA-NEE-TER (Cherokee)
    4255L "A Fullblood's View," Indian Chieftain, October 18, 1900.

OOLAGAH (Cherokee)
    4256N "Legends of the Creeks," Tahlequah Arrow, January 20,
            1906. Reprinted from Fort Smith Elevator.

"OR-GUN-STAU-TAH" (Cherokee)
    4257L Letter, Cherokee Advocate, June 24, 1876.

PEDAGOGUE (Cherokee)
    4258L Letter, Cherokee Advocate, March 17, 1882.
    4259L Letter, Cherokee Advocate, April 21, 1882.

PEWTER DICK (Cherokee)
    4260L "Pewter Dick at Council," Indian Chieftain, December 31,
            1885.

POO INJUN (Cherokee)
    4261L "The Poo' Injun Kicks," Cherokee Advocate, September 24,
        1904.

POOR LO (Creek)
    4262N "The Old and the New," New-State Tribune, April 5, 1906.

QUA-TSY (Cherokee)
    4263N "Female Influence," Wreath of Cherokee Rose Buds, August
        1, 1855.

QUALE-U-QUAH (Cherokee)
    4264N "A Small River or Creek," Wreath of Cherokee Rose Buds,
        August 2, 1854.

RAVEN (Cherokee)
    4265L Letter, Cherokee Advocate, March 7, 1874.
    4266N "The Great Question," Indian Chieftain, July 2, 1885.
    4267N "'I' Did It with My Hatchet," Indian Chieftain, July 10,
        1890.
    4268L "The Reasons Why," Arrow, August 16, 1895.

REDBIRD (Cherokee)
    4269L "Our Western Lands," Indian Chieftain, May 7, 1885.
    4270L "Land Selling," Indian Chieftain, May 21, 1885.
    4271L "Our Western Lands," Indian Chieftain, July 9, 1885.
    4272N "That $300,000," Indian Chieftain, July 30, 1885.

SAH-LE-GU-GE (Cherokee)
    4273L "Agrees with Uncle Joe," Indian Chieftain, October 24,
        1889.

SALINE (Cherokee)
    4274N "Bread-Stuff," Cherokee Advocate, April 14, 1882.

"SA-LOO" (Cherokee)
    4275N "Ah-dah-lv Kah-too," Cherokee Advocate, March 17, 1882.

SAPSUCKER (Cherokee)
    4276N "Cherokee Lands West," Indian Chieftain, July 16, 1885.

SKA-QUAH (Cherokee)
    4277N "Going-Snake District Temperance Society," Cherokee Mes-
        senger, 1 (August, 1844), 15-16.

SKIATOOK (Cherokee)
    4278L "An Essay on Hosses: Second Letter," Indian Arrow, June
        13, 1889.
    4279L "An Essay on Hosses: Third Letter," Indian Arrow, July
        11, 1889.

SLEEPING RABBIT (Cherokee)
    4280N "No. 1 of 'Solutions to the Indian Question,'" Indian Chief-
        tain, September 10, 1885.

4281L "From the Old Home," Indian Chieftain, August 19, 1886.

SLIMKINS JONER (Cherokee)
4282L "Brother Joner Talks to the Natives and Inquires How They Intend to Vote," Indian Chieftain, April 21, 1887.

SOPE STIX (Choctaw)
4283L "'Honest Jonny-Thin,' Etc.," Vindicator, March 29, 1876.

SPECTATOR (Cherokee)
4284N "Visitors Find Tahlequah a Dull Town," Cherokee Advocate, September 28, 1887.

TECUMSEH (Cherokee)
4285L ["Railroads,"] Vindicator, January 19, 1876.
4286L ["Allotment,"] Vindicator, February 16, 1876.
4287L "'Tecumseh' Talks," Indian Chieftain, February 4, 1886.
4288L "'Tecumseh' Talks Politics," Indian Chieftain, March 11, 1886.

TICKANOOLY (Cherokee)
4289L "The Osage Nation," Cherokee Advocate, August 24, 1878.

TOO STOO (Cherokee)
4290L "Too Stoo's Budget," Indian Chieftain, January 31, 1889.
4291L "Political Matters," Indian Chieftain, February 21, 1889.

TOY-AH-NEE-TAH (Cherokee)
4292L "Correspondence," Arkansas Intelligencer, June 21, 1845.

TREE-TEE (Cherokee)
4293N "Citizenship--Again," Cherokee Advocate, September 12, 1884.
4294N "Citizenship--Again," Cherokee Advocate, September 19, 1884.

TURTLE (Cherokee)
4295L [Letter to Editor], Cherokee Advocate, June 1, 1872.

TUSKAHOMMA (Choctaw)
4296L Letter, Vindicator, June 5, 1875.
4297L "Our Minerals," Vindicator, June 12, 1875.
4298L ["Coal,"] Vindicator, June 19, 1875.
4299L ["Choctaw Rights,"] Vindicator, July 10, 1875.
4300L ["Education,"] Vindicator, July 24, 1875.
4301L Letter, Vindicator, August 28, 1875.

TUSTENUCK EMARTHLA (Creek)
4302N "Forty Miles West," Indian Journal, June 15, 1876.
4303N "Muskogee Institute," Indian Journal, June 29, 1876.
4304N "Indian Ball Play," Indian Journal, August 10, 1876.

"U-NA-KUH" (Cherokee)

4305L Letter, Cherokee Advocate, November 2, 1878.
4306L Letter, Cherokee Advocate, January 11, 1879.
4307L "The Duty of School Directors," Cherokee Advocate, February 19, 1879.
4308L "Work for the Council," Cherokee Advocate, October 29, 1879.
4309F "Unakuh Writeth and Poureth Out His Woes," Cherokee Advocate, December 17, 1879.
4310F "U Na Kuh Enjoyeth a New Years Holiday, He Relished It Muchly," Cherokee Advocate, January 21, 1880.
4311F "Unakuh Dialogueth with Miranda Emeline. They Argueth the 'Indian Question,'" Cherokee Advocate, January 28, 1880.
4312F "The 'Indian Question,'" Cherokee Advocate, February 11, 1880.
4313F "The 'Indian Question,'" Cherokee Advocate, February 18, 1880.
4314F "The 'Indian Question,'" Cherokee Advocate, March 24, 1880.
4315F "U-Na-Kuh's Dream of Oklahoma," Cherokee Advocate, March 31, 1880.
4316N "Chapter First," Cherokee Advocate, June 2, 1880.
4317L "The Pay of Public School Teachers," Cherokee Advocate, June 23, 1880.
4318F "Unakuh as a Poet," Cherokee Advocate, October 13, 1880.
4319P "School Episode," Cherokee Advocate, October 13, 1880.
4320N "The Story of 'Aunt Nancy'--Reminiscences of the Removal," Cherokee Advocate, December 1, 1880.
4321N Letter, Cherokee Advocate, March 30, 1881.
4322L Letter, Cherokee Advocate, March 28, 1884.
4323L Letter, Cherokee Advocate, April 11, 1884.
4324F "How Unakah Got Even; or Unakah's Troubles, No. 3," Cherokee Advocate, September 12, 1884.
4325F "'Unakah' Heard From--He and 'Miranda Emmeline' Still Surviveth the Sod," Cherokee Advocate, February 26, 1886.

UTALETAH (Cherokee)
4326L "To the People of the Cherokee Nation," Cherokee Phoenix, May 6, 1828.

"V" (Cherokee)
4327N "The Cherokee Nation West of the 103 Meridian," Cherokee Advocate, May 16, 1884.

VALLEY OF MOUNTAINS (Klamath)
4328P "Indian Memory," American Indian Advocate, 3 (Grass Moon, 1922), 1.

VERITAS (Cherokee)
4329L Letter, Cherokee Advocate, March 2, 1892.

VIDOCO (Cherokee)
4330L Letter, Cherokee Advocate, January 23, 1889.

VOTER (Cherokee)
    4331L "Prohibition," Cherokee Advocate, September 21, 1883.
    4332L "Prohibition," Cherokee Advocate, October 5, 1883.
    4333L "Prohibition," Cherokee Advocate, October 12, 1883.
    4334N "Among White Folks," Cherokee Advocate, March 28, 1884.

WAH-LE-AH (Cherokee)
    4335N "A Journal of a Day at School," Wreath of Cherokee Rose
        Buds, August 2, 1854.

WAH-LIE (Cherokee)
    4336N "Childhood," Wreath of Cherokee Rose Buds, August 2,
        1854.

WAR-TOO-HEE (Cherokee)
    4337L "'Quilike' Manipulates Again," Indian Chieftain, December
        26, 1889.

WASHAKSHIHOMA (Choctaw)
    4338N "The Grave of Pushmataha," Indian Sentinel (1903-1904),
        11.
    4339N "The Grave of Pushmataha," Indian Advocate, 17 (April,
        1905), 111.

WEEWAH (Cherokee)
    4340N "How the Negro Hung 'Hisself,'" Arkansian, February 10,
        1860.

WENONAH (Cherokee)
    4341P "Thanksgiving," Indian Chieftain, November 25, 1886.

WHITE ARROW (Cherokee)
    4342L "White Arrow's Shot," Indian Chieftain, February 3, 1887.
    4343L "'White Arrow' Pierces 'Fair Play,'" Indian Chieftain,
        March 10, 1887.

WHITE HORSE (Cherokee)
    4344N "Old Times," Cherokee Advocate, December 2, 1876.
    4345N "Old Times," Cherokee Advocate, December 9, 1876.
    4346N "Old Times," Cherokee Advocate, December 16, 1876.
    4347N "Old Times," Cherokee Advocate, January 6, 1877.
    4348N "Old Times," Cherokee Advocate, January 13, 1877.
    4349N "Old Times," Cherokee Advocate, January 20, 1877.
    4350N "Old Times," Cherokee Advocate, January 27, 1877.
    4351N "Long Ago," Cherokee Advocate, February 10, 1877.
    4352N "Long Ago," Cherokee Advocate, February 28, 1877.
    4353N "Old Times," Cherokee Advocate, March 7, 1877.
    4354N "Long Ago," Cherokee Advocate, March 21, 1877.
    4355L Letter, Cherokee Advocate, May 26, 1880.
    4356L "The Young Men of the Cherokee Nation," Cherokee Advo-
        cate, December 1, 1880.
    4357N "Letter from a Youngster," Cherokee Advocate, December
        8, 1880.

4358N "The Last Annual Council of the Old Nation," Cherokee Advocate, January 5, 1881.
4359N ["Tahlequah,"] Cherokee Advocate, January 12, 1881.
4360L Letter, Cherokee Advocate, June 8, 1881.
4361L Letter, Cherokee Advocate, July 20, 1881.
4362N "Old Times with Cherokees," Wagoner Record, July 26, 1900.

WOOCHEE OCHEE (Cherokee)
4363L ["To Editor Sallisaw Star,"] Sallisaw Star, July 17, 1903.
4364L "A Letter by Woochee Ochee," Tahlequah Arrow, July 25, 1903.

THE WOODPECKER (Cherokee)
4365N "Our Western Lands," Indian Chieftain, June 25, 1885.
4366N "Western Lands," Indian Chieftain, July 16, 1885.

YELLOW HAMMER (Cherokee)
4367L Letter, Cherokee Advocate, January 13, 1877.
4368L "Cooweescoowee Politics," Cherokee Advocate, August 8, 1877.
4369N "Our Lands," Indian Chieftain, June 26, 1890.

YOUNG BEAVER (Cherokee)
4370F "A Revery," Cherokee Phoenix, July 9, 1828.
4371L "Indian Emigration," Cherokee Phoenix, September 17, 1828.

PART III

BIOGRAPHICAL NOTES

ADAIR, B. K. (Cherokee)
B. K. Adair lived at Chelsea, Cherokee Nation.

ADAIR, HUGH MONTGOMERY (Cherokee)
Hugh Montgomery Adair was born in Flint District, Cherokee Nation, on January 30, 1840, the son of Walter Scott and Nancy Harris Adair. He attended Cherokee public schools, the Cherokee Male Seminary, and Cane Hill College in Arkansas. He taught school before the Civil War, during which he fought in Watie's Confederate Regiment. After the war, he resumed teaching and farmed. In 1891 and 1892 he edited the Cherokee Advocate. He was married to Elizabeth Jane Hurst, Martha Johnson, and Mrs. Phoebe Morris.

ADAIR, J. W. (Cherokee)
J. W. Adair was from the Indian Territory. In 1870 he was a delegate to the International Council at Okmulgee.

ADAIR, JOHN LYNCH (Cherokee)
John Lynch Adair was born in the eastern Cherokee Nation on April 12, 1828, the son of Thomas Benjamin Adair, a white man, and Rachel Lynch Adair, a Cherokee. Orphaned at a young age, Adair was reared by relatives. After removal of the Cherokees to the West, he was sent to a Moravian mission school and then put under the tutelage of the Reverend Cephas Washburn at Bentonville, Arkansas. There he found Classical languages a favorite study. Struck by gold fever in 1849, he went to California, returning to the Cherokee Nation in 1853. He fought for the Confederacy during the Civil War, moving his family to Bellview, Texas. After the war, he settled at Tahlequah, the Cherokee capital, and served as national auditor, clerk of the Cherokee Senate, and executive councilor under Chief Lewis Downing (q. v.), and held a number of other significant offices such as delegate to Washington. He was, as well, editor of three newspapers: Cherokee Advocate, published at Tahlequah, and the Indian Chieftain and the World, published at Vinita. Adair died in October, 1896.

ADAIR, LENA HARNAGE (Cherokee)
Lena Harnage Adair was born in the Cherokee Nation in 1869, the daughter of John Griffith and Emily Walker Mayfield Harnage. She married Thomas James Adair.

ADAIR, WALTER (Cherokee)

Walter Adair was born on December 11, 1783, in the eastern Cherokee Nation, the son of John and Gehoga Adair. He removed to the West in 1837 and settled near present-day Salina, Oklahoma. He married Rachel Thompson. Adair died on January 12, 1845.

ADAIR, WALTER THOMPSON (Cherokee)
Walter Thompson Adair was born in the eastern Cherokee Nation in Georgia in December, 1837, the son of George Washington and Martha Martin Adair. He graduated from the Cherokee Male Seminary and then studied medicine with Dr. J. L. Thompson, the first Cherokee medical graduate. In 1858 Adair graduated from St. Louis Medical College and during the Civil War served as surgeon for Watie's Confederate Regiment. From 1866 to 1876 he conducted a private practice in the Cherokee Nation. From 1876 to 1881 he served as medical superintendent of the Cherokee seminaries and of the Cherokee Insane Asylum. Adair was married to Mary Buffington Adair, Ruth Markham, and Fanny Gray. He died near present-day Salina, Oklahoma, on August 14, 1899.

ADAIR, WASHINGTON (Cherokee)
Washington Adair was from the Indian Territory.

ADAIR, WILLIAM PENN (Cherokee)
William Penn Adair was born in the Cherokee Nation in Georgia on April 15, 1830, the son of George Washington and Martha Martin Adair. He was educated in the Cherokee National schools and studied law. He was a Mason, and during the Civil War he served in the Confederate army. He was twice married, to Sarah Ann Adair and to Susannah McIntosh Drew, and made his home on Grand River, east of present-day Adair, Oklahoma. A prominent public figure, he served in various capacities in the Cherokee Nation: senator, justice of the Supreme Court, delegate to Washington, and assistant principal chief. He died on October 23, 1880.

ADAMS, ALEX (Pawnee)
Alex Adams, from Pawnee, Oklahoma, graduated from Chilocco Indian School in 1920.

ADAMS, RICHARD CALMIT (Delaware)
Richard Calmit Adams was from the Cherokee Nation. Born in 1864, he lived in Bartlesville and represented his tribe in Washington for a number of years. He died at Washington on October 4, 1921.

AGOSA, ROBERT D. (Chippewa)
Robert D. Agosa was from Traverse Bay, Michigan.

AITSAN, LUCIUS BEN (Kiowa)
Lucius Ben Aitsan was born about 1864 and attended school on Cache Creek, Indian Territory. In 1878 he entered the school at Fort Sill and then spent three years at Carlisle. He and his wife Mabel lived at Saddle Mountain in the Kiowa Reservation.

ALBERTY, ELIAS CORNELIUS (Cherokee)
Elias Cornelius Alberty was born in the Cherokee Nation on
July 20, 1860, the son of James and Martha Wright Alberty.   He
attended Cherokee public schools, the Cherokee Male Seminary, and
Kimball Union Academy.   He briefly attended Dartmouth Law School.
In 1885 he became a teacher at the Male Seminary, and except for
four years that he served as prosecuting attorney for Cooweescoowee
District, he taught and farmed.   He served a number of years as
principal of the Cherokee Orphan Asylum and was appointed superintendent shortly before it burned in 1903.   In 1905 he served as a
delegate to the Sequoyah constitutional convention.   He married Sue
Mary Eaton.

ALBERTY, JOHN WRIGHT (Cherokee)
John Wright (Jack) Alberty was born in the Cherokee Nation
on July 26, 1834, the son of John and Mary Wright Alberty.   He was
married to Clara Buffington West and Maria Hildebrand.   During the
Civil War he served in Captain George H. Starr's Company of the
Confederate Cherokee Mounted Rifles.   Alberty served as chief jus-
tice of the Cherokee Supreme Court from 1883 to 1885.   He died on
August 29, 1905.

ALEXANDER, JACOB (Creek)
Jacob Alexander was born at Wetumka, Creek Nation, in 1900,
the son of John L. and Hettie Alexander.   He graduated from Bacone
College in 1924.

ALEXANDER, JOHN C. (Choctaw)
John C. Alexander was born about 1895 in the Choctaw Nation,
the son of Isaac and Sillin Harris Alexander.   He graduated from
Bacone College in 1922.

ALFORD, THOMAS WILDCAT (Absentee Shawnee)
Thomas Wildcat Alford, born about 1860 near present-day Sa-
sakwa, Oklahoma, was the son of George Wildcat Alford and Way-lah-
skse.   He attended school at the Shawnee Mission school near the
Sac and Fox agency and entered Hampton Institute in 1879, graduating
in 1882.   He returned to the Indian Territory and taught among the
Potawatomies and Shawnees.   He later gave up teaching and worked
as a government surveyor and alloting agent.   In 1904 he passed the
civil service test and became a clerk at the Shawnee School.   Alford
married Mary Grinnell.   He retired from public life and wrote a
traditional history of his people, published under the title of Civilization.

ALIS, HERMAN (Mission)
Herman Alis, from California, was born about 1890.   He attended the Phoenix Indian school, graduating in 1909.   He worked as
a temporary teacher at the Indian school at Gila Crossing, Arizona.
He married Mollie Osif (q. v.), who served as housekeeper at the
school for several years.

ALLEN, JOSIAH (Pima)

Josiah Allen was born about 1885. He graduated from the Phoenix Indian School in 1905.

ANDERSON, ALICE (Choctaw)
Alice Anderson was born about 1900. She attended Haskell Institute.

ANDERSON, ARTHUR (Yuki)
Arthur Anderson, from California, graduated from the Phoenix Indian School in 1909.

ANDERSON, HELEN REBECCA (Cherokee)
Helen Rebecca Anderson was born at Vinita, Cherokee Nation, the daughter of John Carlton and Mabel Washbourne Anderson (q. v.).

ANDERSON, MABEL WASHBOURNE (Cherokee)
Mabel Washbourne Anderson was the daughter of Josiah Woodward and Catherine Ridge Washbourne. She was the granddaughter of John Ridge (q. v.) and Cephas Washbourne, a well known missionary to the Cherokees. She was an 1883 graduate of the Cherokee Female Seminary. For a number of years she taught in the Cherokee schools in Vinita, where she lived before moving to Pryor, Oklahoma. She married John Carlton Anderson.

ANDERSON, PASQUALA (Mission)
Pasquala Anderson, from California, graduated from Carlisle in 1900. After graduation, she worked at the government school at Oraibi Pueblo in Arizona and at the Keams Canyon School as well as at the Toreva day school near Oraibi. She married Arnijo and was living at Oraibi in 1916.

ANDERSON, PHENIA (Concow, or Konkau)
Phenia Anderson, from California, was born about 1893 and attended Carlisle. She later lived at Covela, California.

ANTON, FLORENCE (Pima)
Florence Anton was born in the Salt River valley in Arizona in July, 1889. She lived a traditional life with her grandmother until the age of seven, when she was sent to the Phoenix Indian School. She graduated in 1907.

ANTON, WALLACE (Pima)
Wallace Anton attended the Phoenix Indian School.

ANTONE, LOLA (Pima)
Lola Antone was born on her father's farm near Blackwater, Arizona, about 1890. She had a traditional upbringing until she was sent to the kindergarten class at the Phoenix Indian School, where she remained until she graduated in 1908.

ANTONIO, HAL (Pima)
Hal Antonio attended the Phoenix Indian School during the first decade of the twentieth century.

ANTONIO, JOSE (Papago)
Jose Antonio attended Haskell Institute.

APACHE, ANTONIO (Apache)
Antonio Apache was the son of Juan, a brother of Cochise. In the mid-1890's he lived in Chicago and in 1896 entered Phillips Academy at Exeter, New Hampshire.

APES, WILLIAM (Pequot)
William Apes was born near Colrain, Massachusetts, on January 31, 1798, of Pequot parents. Because of harsh treatment by his parents, he was taken and reared by whites. He ran away at an early age and joined the army. After his military experience, he became a Methodist preacher. He became a missionary to and leader of the Cape Cod Indians, whose tribe he joined. He was their active spokesman for a number of years.

ARCASA, ALEXANDER (Colville)
Alexander Arcasa was born on the Colville Reservation in Washington about 1890. He attended Carlisle, from which he graduated in 1912. After graduation he went to work in the boiler shops at Altoona, Pennsylvania.

ARCHAMBEAU, LORENA (Sioux)
Lorena Archambeau was a Yankton from Wagner, South Dakota. She studied nursing at Haskell Institute, from which she graduated in 1924.

ARCHIQUETTE, MARTIN D. (Oneida)
Martin D. Archiquette, from Wisconsin, was born about 1870. He graduated as valedictorian of his class at Carlisle in 1891. He entered government service at Ponemah, Minnesota, and later returned to Tomah, Wisconsin, where he farmed. He then reentered government service, and for twenty years served as a teacher, disciplinarian, clerk, and assistant supervisor of employment at various places, including Fort Semco, Washington, and the agency in Anadarko, Oklahoma. He finally became superintendent of the Indian school at Grand Portage, Minnesota.

ARROW, ARTHUR (Sioux)
Arthur Arrow was a graduate of Haskell Institute. He later worked in the Indian service. He was agency clerk at Lower Brule, South Dakota, and in 1923 he was transferred to Pipestone, Minnesota.

ARTESHAW, MARIE (Chippewa)
Marie Arteshaw attended Carlisle.

ASHMUN, H. C. (Chippewa)
H. C. Ashmun, from the Bad River Reservation, was editor and proprietor of the Odanah Star at Odanah, Wisconsin.

AVALOS, CIPRIANA (Pueblo)
Cipriana Avalos attended the Phoenix Indian School.

AVALOS, JUAN B. (Pueblo)
Juan B. Avalos graduated from the Phoenix Indian School in 1901. After graduation he worked at an Indian school for two years and then entered Park College in Missouri. He died about 1907.

AVELINE, FRANK D. (Miami)
Frank D. Aveline, from the Indian Territory, was born about 1865. He worked for a number of years at Newark, New Jersey.

AXTELL, OBED (Nez Percé)
Obed Axtell, from Idaho, was born about 1893. He went to Carlisle in 1912 and returned to Idaho in 1915, suffering from tuberculosis. He died at Tola, Idaho, on November 15, 1916.

AZURE, OVILLA (Chippewa)
Ovilla Azure was from Belcourt on the Turtle Mountain Reservation, North Dakota. He was born about 1888 and graduated from Carlisle in 1915, after which he returned to North Dakota. There he followed his trade as a carpenter, first in the construction of a new sanitorium at Belcourt, then with a construction company at Devils Lake, North Dakota, and then at the Wahpeton Indian school.

BAGNELL, AMY (Rogue River, or Tututni)
Amy Bagnell, from Oregon, attended the Chemawa Indian School and then spent a year in Oklahoma. She graduated from the Phoenix Indian School in 1902 and then attended Hampton Institute.

BAKER, LILLIE (Navajo)
Lillie Baker was from Gallup, New Mexico. She graduated from Chilocco Indian School in 1920.

BALDWIN, MARIE L. BOTTINEAU (Chippewa)
Marie L. Bottineau Baldwin was born about 1864, the daughter of John B. Bottineau, a Chippewa lawyer who fought for Chippewa rights. Mrs. Baldwin graduated from the Washington School of Law in 1914. She worked in the Education Division of the Indian Office while she was in school and continued there after graduation. In 1915 she was in charge of the railroad transportation department of the Indian Office and that year toured the Indian schools and reservations.

BALENTI, MICHAEL R. (Cheyenne)
Michael R. Balenti was born at Darlington Agency, Indian Territory. He was the son of Mike Balenti and Cheyenne Belle. Balenti, a soldier at Fort Reno, became a tailor at the Indian school. Belle was the daughter of Charlie Rath, the founder of Dodge City, and Roadmaker, a Cheyenne woman, and served as interpreter for General Sheridan during the Stone Calf uprising of 1885. Michael Balenti graduated from Carlisle in 1909. He distinguished himself in sports, and after graduation played shortstop for the St. Louis Browns. At the close of the American League season in 1913, Balenti became assistant football coach at St. Louis University. Balenti also briefly attended Texas Agricultural and Mechanical College.

BALENTI, WILLIAM M. (Cheyenne)
William M. Balenti was born at Darlington Agency, Indian Territory, in 1880. He was the son of Mike Balenti and Cheyenne Belle. (For material on their lives, see biographical sketch of Michael R. Balenti.) William Balenti attended school in Halsted, Kansas, and then returned to Oklahoma and became a farmer and stockman in Canadian County. He died at Bethany in 1948.

BALL, JOSEPH (Klamath)
Joseph Ball was born at Fort Klamath, Oregon, in 1885. At the age of eight, he was sent to the reservation school and then attended the public schools for three or four years. After attending Carlisle for a year, Ball entered the Phoenix Indian School from which he graduated in 1903. He became a prosperous livestock grower.

BALLARD, WILLIAM HOUSTON (Cherokee)
William Houston Ballard was born near Grove, Cherokee Nation, on May 29, 1884, the son of William and Charlotte Mayes Ballard.

BAPTISTE, JOHN (Winnebago)
John Baptiste, from the Winnebago Reservation, Nebraska, was an 1893 graduate of Carlisle. He returned to the West and made his home at Winnebago, Nebraska. He held a number of positions in the Indian service. In 1911 he was interpreter for the Dutch Reformed minister at Winnebago. He also assisted the Bureau of American Ethnology in gathering data on the Winnebago tribe.

BARADA, MITCHELL (Omaha)
Mitchell Barada, from Nebraska, graduated from Carlisle in 1898. In 1902 he lived at Bancroft, Nebraska, and later moved to Plainview, South Dakota.

BARNABY, JOSEPHINE (Omaha)
Josephine Barnaby was born in Nebraska about 1863, the daughter of William Barnaby. She entered Hampton Institute in 1884 and graduated in 1887. In 1890 she was in charge of the Standing Rock Hospital. She married John Van Felden.

BARSE, ALCESTA (Sioux)
Alcesta Barse, from South Dakota, was a student at Haskell Institute in 1916.

BASKIN, SAMUEL (Sioux)
Samuel Baskin was a Santee Sioux from Santee, Nebraska. He attended Hampton Institute in the mid-1890's.

BASTIAN, JOHN (Puyallup)
John Bastian, from Washington, graduated from Carlisle in 1910, after which he followed his trade as a carpenter at Tacoma.

BATTICE, CORA MELBOURNE (Sac and Fox)

Cora Melbourne Battice was the daughter of Walter Battice (q. v.) of Shawnee, Oklahoma. She attended Carlisle from which she graduated in 1915. She married Jesse M. Ellis of Oklahoma City.

BATTICE, WALTER (Sac and Fox)
Walter Battice (Paminathuskuk) was born about 1863 near Topeka, Kansas. He attended the Sac and Fox school in Indian Territory before entering Hampton Institute in 1882. While he was at Hampton, he edited the student monthly Talks and Thoughts. After graduation in 1887, he attended normal school in Bridgewater, Massachusetts, graduating in 1889. He returned to the Indian Territory and taught at the Sac and Fox school. After a year, he entered a partnership in a store at Econtuchka. In 1896 he took business courses at Haskell Institute. He served as secretary of the Sac and Fox tribe for a time. Battice married the daughter of principal chief Mahkoshtoe.

BEALE, GRACE HENRIETTA (Navajo)
Grace Henrietta Beale, from New Mexico, graduated from the normal department of Haskell Institute in 1923.

BEAN, J. S. (Cherokee)
J. S. Bean lived in the Indian Territory.

BEAR, JOHN (Winnebago)
John Bear, from Nebraska, was born about 1866, the son of Little Bear. He attended Hampton Institute from 1885 to 1888. He married Cora Frenchman.

BEAR, JOHNSON (Cherokee)
Johnson Bear was from Stillwell, Oklahoma, and graduated from Chilocco Indian School in 1920.

BEAR, JOSEPH L. (Sioux)
Joseph L. Bear attended Carlisle.

BEAR, STELLA V. (Arickara)
Stella V. Bear, from the Fort Berthold Reservation in North Dakota, was born about 1883. She was a 1910 graduate of Carlisle. She became field matron at the Cheyenne and Arapaho agency at Cantonment, Oklahoma. In 1913 she was boys' matron at the Standing Rock school in North Dakota, and in 1916 she was seamstress in a boarding school at Elbowoods, North Dakota.

BEARFACE, ROSA (Sioux)
Rosa Bearface (or Topala), a Hunkpapa from the Standing Rock Reservation, was born about 1863, the daughter of Bear Face. She attended the Benedictine School on the reservation and attended Hampton Institute from 1881 to 1884 and from 1885 to 1888. She died on February 13, 1891.

BEARSKIN, CORA (Seneca)

Cora Bearskin, from Oklahoma, was a student at Haskell Institute in 1915.

BEAULIEU, C. H. (Chippewa)
C. H. Beaulieu, from the White Earth Reservation in Minnesota, was the son of Clement H. Beaulieu, a fur trader and founder of Crow Wing, Minnesota. C. H. Beaulieu was elected in 1916 as part of a delegation to Washington to discuss Chippewa affairs. In 1917 he assumed the editorship of the White Earth Tomahawk upon the death of his brother Gustave (q. v.). He later lived at LeSueur, Minnesota, where he was a minister of the gospel.

BEAULIEU, CLARENCE R. (Chippewa)
Clarence R. Beaulieu, from the White Earth Reservation, was the son of Theodore H. and Julia Beaulieu. He studied law in Minneapolis.

BEAULIEU, GUSTAVE H. (Chippewa)
Gustave H. Beaulieu, of the White Earth Reservation, was born at Crow Wing, Minnesota, on June 12, 1852, the son of Clement H. Beaulieu, who founded Crow Wing. He moved to White Earth in 1869. Gustave Beaulieu was founder and editor of the White Earth Tomahawk, which he edited until his death at Barrows, Minnesota, on August 8, 1917. He married Ella Holmes.

BEAULIEU, IRENE CAMPBELL (Sioux)
Mrs. Irene Campbell Beaulieu was born in 1888 on the Santee Reservation. In 1916 she lived at Pawhuska, Oklahoma, and wrote under the name of Wenonah.

BEAULIEU, THEODORE H. (Chippewa)
Theodore H. Beaulieu was born near Kaukauna, Wisconsin, on September 4, 1850, the son of Bazil and Mary (Saulliard) Beaulieu. He was twelve years a printer and then entered the International Marine Service between Philadelphia and Liverpool. In 1879 he entered the U. S. service in various capacities among the Chippewas and as U. S. land examiner, having charge of the land department on the White Earth Reservation, of which he was a member. In 1887 he established the first aboriginal newspaper in the Chippewa country, forming the nucleus for the Tomahawk, published at White Earth in the early years of this century. For fifteen years before his death, he was in the real estate business. He was always involved in Chippewa affairs, served on the Chippewa council, and wrote in their behalf, publishing in various newspapers. Beaulieu died on May 13, 1923.

BEAUREGARD, MARGARET (Chippewa)
Margaret Beauregard attended Chilocco Indian School.

BEBEAU, GENEVIEVE (Chippewa)
Genevieve Bebeau, born about 1891, attended Carlisle.

BECK, JOHN H. (Cherokee)

John H. Beck was a promising young lawyer in the Cherokee Nation, but in 1894 he was accused of forging certificates of Cherokee citizenship during the per capita payment that year. He was convicted in federal court of illegal use of the mails. He died on June 3, 1895, shortly after arriving at the federal prison at Albany, New York.

BECK, STACEY (Cherokee)
Stacey Beck was a 1910 graduate of Carlisle and after graduation held jobs at the Oto Indian Training School in Oklahoma and in the Indian school at Albuquerque. She married Alfred Hardy.

BELL, LUCIEN BURR (Cherokee)
Lucien Burr (Hooley) Bell was born on February 13, 1838, in the eastern Cherokee Nation, the son of John A. and Jane Martin Bell. He attended Ozark Institute and Cane Hill College in Arkansas. He joined the Confederate army during the Civil War and remained in Texas after the war, returning to the Cherokee Nation in 1867. Bell farmed and served in various governmental capacities, including clerk for the Senate, member of the national board of education, national treasurer, senator, and delegate to Washington.

BELL, MATTIE (Cherokee)
Mattie Bell lived in the Cherokee Nation and attended the Cherokee Female Seminary.

BELL, OREGONIA (Cherokee)
Oregonia Bell was the daughter of Dr. Moses Bell, a white man, and his Cherokee wife. She attended the Cherokee Female Seminary and married Spratt Scott.

BELL, WILLIAM WATIE (Cherokee)
William Watie Bell, from the Indian Territory, was the son of James Madison and Caroline Lynch Bell.

BELLANGER, ALICE (Chippewa)
Alice Bellanger, from Minnesota, graduated from the domestic arts department of Haskell Institute in 1915.

BELLECOURTE, CHARLES JAMES (Chippewa)
Charles James Bellecourte was from the White Earth Reservation. In 1923 he was elected secretary of the White Earth Local Council.

BENDER, CHARLES ALBERT (Chippewa)
Charles Albert Bender was born at Brainerd, Minnesota, on May 5, 1883, a member of the Bad River band of Chippewas. He graduated from Carlisle in 1902. He became a professional baseball player with the Philadelphia Athletics, with whom he played from 1903 to 1914. He was a star pitcher, and led the league in pitching in 1911. After he retired from baseball in 1914, he coached at the U. S. Naval Academy and for the Chicago White Sox and the Athletics. He was admitted to the Baseball Hall of Fame in 1953. Bender died at Brainerd on May 22, 1954.

BENDER, FRED (Chippewa)
Fred Bender, a member of the Bad River band, attended Hampton Institute.

BENGE, SAMUEL HOUSTON (Cherokee)
Samuel Houston Benge was born in the Eastern Cherokee Nation on January 28, 1832, the son of Martin and Eliza Lowry Benge. During the Civil War he served in the Union army. He held public office for thirty-five years, during which time he held every national office except Supreme Judge and Principal Chief. Benge was married to Lucy Blaire and Nancy Brewster.

BISHOP, ALBERT (Seneca)
Albert Bishop, from New York, was an 1892 graduate of Carlisle.

BISHOP, B. FRANKLIN (Seneca)
B. Franklin Bishop, from New York, attended Hampton Institute.

BISHOP, WILLIAM C. (Cayuga)
William C. Bishop was born about 1893; he attended Carlisle.

BLACKBEAR, JOSEPH (Cheyenne)
Joseph Blackbear, from the Indian Territory, was an 1899 graduate of Carlisle. He resided at Hammon, Oklahoma, where he worked for a mercantile establishment. He married Cora Blindman.

BLACKBEAR, THOMAS (Sioux)
Thomas Blackbear, an Oglala from the Pine Ridge Reservation in South Dakota, graduated from Carlisle in 1894. After graduation he returned to South Dakota and became a farmer and stock raiser at Porcupine.

BLACKBIRD, ANDREW J. (Ottawa)
Andrew J. Blackbird, or Mac-ke-te-pe-nas-sy, was born about 1810 and was the hereditary chief at l'Arbre Croche in Michigan.

BLACKWOOD, MARGARET O. (Chippewa)
Margaret O. Blackwood attended Carlisle.

BLUESKY, BERTRAM (Seneca)
Bertram Bluesky was from New York.

BLUESKY, LOUISE (Chippewa)
Louise Bluesky was born about 1892. She was a 1914 graduate of Carlisle. After graduation she attended a preparatory school in Massillon, Ohio, and in 1915 entered Wooster College, Wooster, Ohio.

BOND, T. J. (Choctaw)
T. J. Bond was born in the Choctaw Nation in Mississippi on June 16, 1829. Because he lost his father at an early age, he attended Choctaw boarding schools and attended medical school in Ken-

tucky at Choctaw expense. In 1854 he returned to his nation to practice medicine, one of the first of his tribe to do so. During the
Civil War he served as surgeon for the First Regiment of Choctaw
and Chickasaw Confederate Volunteers. After the war he was twice
national treasurer, twice national superintendent of schools, and once
senator from Atoka County. He married the daughter of Israel Folsom (q. v.). Bond died on March 31, 1878, at Atoka.

BONNIN, GERTRUDE SIMMONS (Sioux)

Gertrude Simmons Bonnin, or Zitkala-Sa (Red Bird), was a
Yankton, born on February 22, 1875, on the Pine Ridge Reservation
in South Dakota, the daughter of John Haysting and Ellen Taté Iyohi-
win Simmons. She received her early education on the reservation
and then was sent to the Quaker missionary school at Wabash, Indiana. After three years there, she returned to the reservation, where
she remained four years before returning to school. She graduated
from Earlham College at Richmond, Indiana, and became a teacher
at Carlisle. While there, she became an accomplished musician,
studied at the Boston Conservatory, and played with the Carlisle band
at the 1900 Paris Exposition. She also began writing for magazines
such as Harper's and Atlantic Monthly. She then accepted a clerkship
at the Standing Rock Reservation, where she met and married Raymond
T. Bonnin. The Bonnins then worked on the Ute reservation in Utah
where they became affiliated with the Society of American Indians.
Zitkala-Sa was elected secretary of the Society in 1916, and she and
her husband moved to Washington, D. C., where she worked with the
Society and edited the American Indian Magazine. In 1926 she founded the National Council of American Indians. During the next several
years, she lectured and worked for reform in Indian affairs. She
died in Washington on January 25, 1938, and was buried in Arlington
National Cemetery.

BONSER, HARRY (Sioux)

Harry Bonser was born about 1890. He graduated from Carlisle in 1914, and he was married to Cecelia Ducharme.

BOUDINOT, ELIAS (Cherokee)

Elias Boudinot was born in the eastern Cherokee Nation about
1802, the son of Oo-watie. He studied at Cornwall, Connecticut, under the sponsorship of the Philadelphia philanthropist whose name he
took. He married Harriet Gold, a Cornwall native. Upon his return
to the Cherokee Nation, Boudinot became editor of the Cherokee Phoenix. After his first wife's death, he married Delight Sargeant, who
cared for his children after he was assassinated on June 22, 1839,
for having signed the Cherokee removal treaty at New Echota in 1835.

BOUDINOT, ELIAS CORNELIUS (Cherokee)

Elias Cornelius Boudinot was born at New Echota in the eastern
Cherokee Nation in 1835, the son of Elias (q. v.) and Harriet Gold
Boudinot. When his father was assassinated in 1839 for having signed
the removal treaty, his stepmother, Delight Sargeant Boudinot, took
Elias and his brothers to New England. He was educated at Manchest-
er, Vermont, and at the age of seventeen began working for an Ohio

railway company. He then went to Fayetteville, Arkansas, where he studied law in the office of A. M. Wilson, earning admission to the Arkansas bar in 1856. He was also admitted to the bar of the U. S. Court for the Western District of Arkansas. He edited the Fayetteville weekly Arkansian and, before the Civil War, the Little Rock True Democrat. In 1860 he was chairman of the Arkansas Democratic State Central Committee, and in 1861 he was secretary of the state's secession convention. During the war he served in the regiment of Cherokee volunteers under the command of his uncle Stand Watie and reached the rank of major in the Confederate army. In 1863 he was chosen as the Cherokee delegate to the Confederate Congress in Richmond. After the war he strongly advocated the dissolution of the tribal governments and allotment of lands. Because of his stand on those issues, he was not generally well liked in the Cherokee Nation. Although he maintained his Cherokee citizenship, he made his home in Fort Smith, Arkansas, where he died on September 27, 1890.

BOUDINOT, ELIAS CORNELIUS, JR. (Cherokee)
Elias Cornelius Boudinot, Jr., was born in the Cherokee Nation on January 2, 1854, the son of William Penn and Caroline Fields Boudinot. He was a lawyer, editor of the Cherokee Advocate, chairman of the Cherokee commissioners who negotiated the sale of the Cherokee Outlet, attorney for the Old Settler Cherokees, and special delegate to Washington to protect Cherokee rights against freedman claims. He was serving in the latter capacity when he died in February, 1896. Boudinot married Addeline Foreman.

BOUDINOT, FRANKLIN JOSIAH (Cherokee)
Franklin Josiah (Frank) Boudinot was born on August 20, 1866, the son of William Penn (q. v.) and Caroline Fields Boudinot. He graduated from the Indian Baptist University, then from high school in Flint, Michigan. He returned to the Cherokee Nation where he was executive secretary to the principal chief, was placed in charge of the Cherokee Advocate, which was edited by his father, and served as clerk of the senate. In 1894 he entered the law school of Michigan State University and was later admitted to the bar. In 1896 he served as attorney for the Cherokee Nation and later for the Keetoowah Society. Boudinot made his home at Fort Gibson. He married Anna S. Meigs.

BOUDINOT, WILLIAM PENN (Cherokee)
William Penn Boudinot was born in the eastern Cherokee Nation in 1830, the son of Elias (q. v.) and Harriet Gold Boudinot. When his father was assassinated in 1839 for having signed the removal treaty, his stepmother, Delight Sargeant Boudinot, took William and his brothers to New England. Boudinot was educated in Vermont and Connecticut. Then he learned the trade of ornamental jewelry engraving in Philadelphia. During the Civil War, he served in the Confederate forces under the command of his uncle Stand Watie. Following the Civil War, Boudinot was a leader of the National Party, he was twice editor of the Cherokee Advocate, and he served as executive secretary to Chief Dennis Wolfe Bushyhead (q. v.) and as Cherokee delegate to Washington.

BOURASSA, ROSA (Chippewa)
Rosa Bourassa, from Michigan, was an 1890 graduate of Carlisle. She also attended Metzger College. From 1891 through 1893 she worked as a helper in the girls' quarters at Carlisle and later worked at the Phoenix Indian School and at the school in Rapid City, South Dakota. She was appointed stenographer and typist in the Indian Building of the St. Louis World's Fair. She later worked in the Indian Office at Washington and in 1915 was transferred to Chilocco Indian School in Oklahoma. She was twice married, to James A. Brown, a Wyandot, and Francis La Flesche (q. v.), an Omaha.

BOUTWELL, LEON (Chippewa)
Leon Boutwell, from White Earth, Minnesota, was born about 1892. He was a student at Carlisle from 1910 to 1914. During World War I he served in the army and played in the field band.

BOW, CLAUDE (Sioux)
Claude Bow (Istazipa), from the Standing Rock Reservation, was born about 1863, the son of Pretty Bear. He attended Hampton Institute from 1886 to 1889.

BOWKER, MABEL (Sioux)
Mabel Bowker graduated from Haskell Institute. Her married name was Mitchell, and in 1923 she and her husband lived at Mt. Pleasant, Michigan.

BRACKLIN, EDWARD (Chippewa)
Edward Bracklin of Stone Lake, Wisconsin, was from the Lac Court Oreilles Reservation. He was born about 1887 and attended Carlisle. Bracklin married Minnie B. Hawk.

BRADLEY, ESTELLE (Chippewa)
Estelle Bradley was from Rosebush, Michigan, on the Isabella Reservation. She was born about 1887 and graduated from Carlisle in 1913, after which she entered the Indian service, working for a time at the school at Sisseton, South Dakota.

BRAVE, BENJAMIN (Sioux)
Benjamin Brave (Ohitika), from the Lower Brule Reservation, was born about 1865, the son of Long Feather. He was taken in by the Rev. Luke C. Walker, a missionary. In 1881 he was sent to Hampton Institute. He returned to the Lower Brule as a teacher and lay reader. Then he worked at the Rosebud and other agencies. He was associated with several missionaries and traveled, giving lectures. In 1897 he went on an extended lecture tour of the North. In 1918, he was head of the tribal council and in 1920 was postmaster at the Lower Brule agency.

BRAZZANOVICH, FLORENCE (Paiute)
Florence Brazzanovich, from California, graduated from the home economics department of Haskell Institute in 1921.

BRECKINRIDGE, JOHN C. (Pima)

John C. Breckinridge graduated from the Phoenix Indian School in 1912. He married Alice Morris.

BRECKINRIDGE, MARY (Pima)
Mary Breckinridge graduated from the Phoenix Indian School in 1912.

BRESETTE, FRANCIS (Chippewa)
Francis Bresette, a Bad River Chippewa, was born about 1894, the son of Alex H. and Madaline Bresette. He lived at Odanah, Wisconsin.

BREWER, ELLA L. (Puyallup)
Ella L. Brewer graduated from the Chemawa Indian School in Oregon.

BROKER, FREDERICK (Chippewa)
Frederick Broker, from the White Earth Reservation in Minnesota, was a 1914 graduate of Carlisle. After graduation he worked for the Ford Motor Company in Detroit. During World War I, he was in the army and served abroad.

BROKER, JOSEPH HENRY (Chippewa)
Joseph Henry Broker, from the White Earth Reservation, was a 1913 graduate of Carlisle. After graduation, he worked for the Ford Motor Company in Detroit, and he served in the army during World War I.

BROWN, DAVID J. (Cherokee)
David J. (Cookee) Brown was born in the Cherokee Nation, the son of John Lowrey and Ann E. Schrimsher Brown of Fort Gibson. He attended the Cherokee Male Seminary from which he graduated in 1878. Described as "one of the most promising young men of the country," Brown was shot down in the streets of Muskogee, Creek Nation, in February, 1879.

BROWN, HARRY (Sioux)
Harry Brown (Wakicunla), from the Cheyenne River Reservation, was born about 1863, the son of White Horse. He attended Hampton Institute from 1878 to 1881 and from 1883 to 1885. Between his terms at Hampton, he served as assistant teacher at the government school on the reservation. He died in March, 1885.

BROWN, IRENE M. (Sioux)
Irene M. Brown was a 1909 graduate of Carlisle. She was a teacher at Pine Point, Minnesota, and later a general merchant at the Sisseton agency.

BROWN, JOHN F. (Seminole)
John F. Brown was born in 1843 in the Cherokee Nation, the son of Dr. John F. Brown, a white man, and Lucy Redbird Brown, a full-blood Seminole. He attended Cherokee schools. In 1867 he moved to Wewoka, Seminole Nation, and entered the merchandizing

and cotton ginning business. He was a delegate to the Okmulgee
Council in 1870. He became principal chief of the Seminoles in 1885
and served in that capacity for many years.

BROWN, MARGARET JEANE (Alaskan Native)
Margaret Jeane Brown graduated from Carlisle in 1915 and
then attended West Chester Normal School in West Chester, Pennsylvania.

BRUCE, LOUIS (Mohawk)
Louis Bruce was from New York, and he attended Carlisle.

BRUNETT, JOSEPH M. (Menominee)
Joseph M. Brunett was from Wisconsin.

BRUNETTE, CECILIA (Menonimee)
Cecilia Brunette was born in 1897 on the Menominee Reservation in Wisconsin, the daughter of Mrs. Mary Ann Brunette. She
attended Haskell Institute, graduating from the business department in
1919. She worked in government service as assistant clerk at the
Indian schools at Chemawa, Oregon, and White River, Arizona. At
the latter place in 1922, she married Arthur K. Knoop.

BRUNETTE, WILLIAM A. (Chippewa)
William A. Brunette, from the White Earth Reservation, lived
at Mahnomen, Minnesota. Brunette was the founder of the United
Chippewa Council.

BRYANT, CHARLIE (Cherokee)
Charlie Bryant lived in the Indian Territory.

BUCK, GEORGE (Sioux)
George Buck, from the Fort Peck Reservation in Montana,
graduated from Carlisle in 1895.

BUCK, MABEL (Sioux)
Mabel Buck, from the Fort Peck Reservation, graduated from
Carlisle in 1897. She then went to Pittsburgh, Pennsylvania, to live
with the Rev. and Mrs. S. E. Snyder, with whom she had lived on
the reservation. She married Robert Black and lived at Watonga and
Pawhuska, Oklahoma.

BUFFINGTON, EZEKIEL (Cherokee)
Ezekiel Buffington was from the Cherokee Nation, Indian Territory.

BUFFINGTON, THOMAS MITCHELL (Cherokee)
Thomas Mitchell Buffington was born in Going Snake District,
Cherokee Nation, on October 19, 1855. He attended tribal schools
and began farming, settling in 1887 in Delaware District. In 1889
he became judge of the district and in 1891 its senator. As president of the Senate, he served briefly as principal chief when Joel
Bryan Mayes (q. v.) died in office in 1891. Buffington also served

as mayor of Vinita and was elected principal chief of the Cherokees in 1899.

BURKE, JOSEPH (Pima)
   Joseph Burke attended the Phoenix Indian School during the first decade of the twentieth century.

BURKE, ROBERT (Pima)
   Robert Burke graduated from the Phoenix Indian School in 1914 and became a ranch hand near Glendale, Arizona.

BURNEY, BENJAMIN CROOKS (Chickasaw)
   Benjamin Crooks Burney was born at Shreveport, Louisiana, during his parents' journey from Mississippi to the western Chickasaw country.   They settled near present-day Burneyville, Love County, Oklahoma, but died when Burney was quite young.   Thus he was educated at the Chickasaw Orphans School at Tishomingo.   During the Civil War he served as a private in Shocoe's Chickasaw Battalion of Mounted Volunteers (Confederate), and after the war settled down to farming and stock raising in present-day Marshall County, Oklahoma. He served one term as national treasurer and one as governor, elected in 1878.   After his governorship, he went back to farming.   He died on November 25, 1892.

BUSCH, ELMER (Pomo)
   Elmer Busch, from California, was born about 1889.   He graduated from Carlisle in 1913.

BUSH OTTER, GEORGE (Sioux)
   George Bush Otter, born about 1864, was from the Yankton Reservation.   He entered Hampton Institute in 1878 and attended the Theological Seminary at Alexandria, Virginia.   He became a teacher at the government school on the Lower Brule Reservation.

BUSHYHEAD, DENNIS WOLFE (Cherokee)
   Dennis Wolfe Bushyhead was born near present-day Cleveland, Tennessee, on March 18, 1826, son of the Reverend Jesse and Elizabeth Wilkinson Bushyhead.   He attended mission schools in the eastern and western Cherokee Nations.   From 1841 through 1844 he attended school at Lawrenceville, New Jersey, and was enrolled briefly at Princeton before returning to the Indian Territory, where he was a clerk in a mercantile establishment.   In 1847 he became clerk of the Cherokee National Committee.   In 1849 he went to the gold fields of California and did not return to the Cherokee Nation until 1868. In 1871, he became national treasurer, and from 1879 through 1887 he served as principal chief.   Bushyhead was married to Elizabeth Alabama Schrimscher Adair.   He died on February 4, 1898.

BUSSELL, CLARA (Klamath)
   Clara Bussell was born in northern California in 1888.   She attended Willow Creek public school and in 1905 entered the Phoenix Indian School, from which she graduated in 1907.

BUTLER, GEORGE OLIVER (Cherokee)
George Oliver Butler was born about 1862 the son of Joseph
L. and Frances Butler. He married Catherine E. Ross.

BUTTERFIELD, ANGELINE (Chippewa)
Angeline Butterfield, of the Bad River Band, lived at Bayfield,
Wisconsin.

BYRD, WILLIAM LEANDER (Chickasaw)
William Leander Byrd was born on August 1, 1844, son of
John and Mary Moore Byrd, the latter of Chickasaw descent. The
family lived at Doaksville, Choctaw Nation, but Byrd attended the
Chickasaw Academy at Tishomingo. In 1864 he entered the Confed-
erate service as a private in the First Choctaw-Chickasaw Brigade.
During the 1880's Byrd served as superintendent of schools for the
Chickasaw Nation and delegate to Washington and helped codify the
national laws. He was elected governor of the nation in 1888 and
reelected in 1890. After his term in office he ran a business at
Stonewall until 1898, farmed until 1902, and then retired in Ada.
Byrd was a Mason and an Odd Fellow. His wife was Susan Kemp.
He died on April 21, 1915.

CAIN, ARCHIBALD (Creek)
Archibald Cain graduated from Bacone College in 1925.

CAJUNE, FRANK (Chippewa)
Frank Cajune was from the White Earth Reservation. He attended Carlisle and then worked as a day laborer and lived at Mahnomen, Minnesota. In 1907 he was elected justice of the peace and for
several years after 1908 he was a deputy sheriff. He was defeated
in the election for sheriff in 1910. Cajune also served as clerk of
the local school board and as a delegate to the general council of
Minnesota Chippewas. In 1922 he became subagent for the White
Earth Chippewas at Bena.

CALAC, CLAUDINA (Mission)
Claudina Calac, from southern California, attended boarding
school from 1893 to 1896. She was then assistant matron at the
Fort Mohave school for two years. In 1898 she entered the Phoenix
Indian School, from which she graduated in 1903. After graduation
she went to Pasadena, California, to work in a private home and remained in that position for sixteen years.

CALAC, GEORGIA E. (Mission)
Georgia E. Calac, from California, was a student at Haskell
Institute in 1915.

CALLAHAN, SOPHIA ALICE (Creek)
Sophia Alice Callahan was born on January 1, 1868, the daughter of Samuel Benton and Sarah Elizabeth Thornberg Callahan. Her
father was of Creek descent. He was a businessman and in 1887 became editor of the Indian Journal at Muskogee. Miss Callahan was
well educated and taught in the Creek Nation at Wealaka Mission

School and at Harrell Institute. Her single work Wynema was a novel which has its setting in the Creek Nation. Miss Callahan died on January 7, 1894.

CAMPBELL, JOSEPH (Wichita)
Joseph Campbell, from Oklahoma, was a student at Haskell Institute in 1915.

CAREY, JAMES (Cherokee)
In 1840, James Carey was a member of the Old Settler Cherokee delegation who went to Washington to press Old Settler claims.

CARLIN, WALTER (Sioux)
Walter Carlin attended Haskell Institute.

CARR, ROBERT L. (Creek)
Robert L. Carr, from Oklahoma, was a student at Haskell Institute in 1916.

CARTER, CALEB (Nez Percé)
Caleb Carter was born about 1887. He attended Haskell Institute before going to Carlisle, from which he graduated in 1911. After graduation he worked briefly at the Kickapoo agency at Horton, Kansas, returning to his home in Kamiah, Idaho, in early 1913. He married Mary Amera.

CARTER, CHARLES D. (Chickasaw)
Charles D. Carter was born in August, 1869, at Boggy Depot, Choctaw Nation, the son of B. W. Carter, a Cherokee, and Serena Guy Carter, a Chickasaw. He attended the Chickasaw national schools, Harley Institute at Tishomingo, and Austin College at Sherman, Texas. Carter worked as a cowboy and a store clerk until 1892, when he became auditor of the Chickasaw Nation. In 1894 he was appointed superintendent of schools for the nation and in 1897 was elected to the legislature and, while serving, was director of the City National Bank of Ardmore. After Oklahoma statehood, Carter was elected the state's first congressman from the third district. He had a long career in the House of Representatives, part of which time he served as chairman of the House Committee on Indian Affairs. Carter died at Ardmore in April, 1929.

CARTER, MINOT (Sioux)
Minot Carter, from Los Molinos, California, was born in 1878.

CASH, A. WARREN (Sioux)
A. Warren Cash, or Spotted Elk, was an officer in the American Indian Association.

CASWELL, BENJAMIN (Chippewa)
Benjamin Caswell, from Minnesota, entered Carlisle in 1889 and graduated valedictorian of his class in 1892. He was sent into the Indian service as a teacher at Fort Belknap, Montana. In 1902 he was superintendent of the Cass Lake Indian School, at which post

he remained for a number of years. In 1916 he sought but failed to be appointed superintendent of one of the Minnesota reservations under an amendment to an appropriations bill giving Indians preference in such jobs. In 1919 he was a leader of a group who opposed the duly elected officials of the Minnesota Chippewas and tried to establish a separate council. Caswell married Leila Cornelius, an Oneida.

CETAN SAPA (Sioux)

Publishers identified Cetan Sapa as a Sioux. This may have been Cetan Sapa from the Fort Berthold Reservation. He attended Hampton Institute during the 1880's and could read and write in Dakota.

CHAPMAN, ARTHUR (Chippewa)

Arthur Chapman was from the White Earth Reservation.

CHASE, HIRAM (Omaha)

Hiram Chase, from Nebraska, was a lawyer. He served as county attorney of Thurston County, Nebraska, and as lawyer for the Omahas. In the 1920's he was a leader in the Native American Church.

CHASE, HIRAM, JR. (Omaha)

Hiram Chase, Jr., was from Pender, Nebraska. He graduated from Carlisle in 1915.

CHECOTE, SAMUEL (Creek)

Samuel Checote was born on the Chattahooche River in Alabama in 1819, a full-blood Creek of the McIntosh faction. At the age of nine he entered Asbury Manual Labor School near Fort Mitchell, Alabama. After removal to the West, Checote was a Methodist preacher, often persecuted by the traditional Creeks for his religious work. During the Civil War he reached the rank of lieutenant in the Confederate army. In 1867 he was elected principal chief and was reelected in 1871. He was elected to a third term in 1879. Checote died on September 3, 1884.

CHEERLESS, LUCIANA (Pima)

Luciana Cheerless attended the Phoenix Indian School.

CHICKENEY, CHARLES W. (Menominee)

Charles W. Chickeney was from Wisconsin.

CHIEFCHILD, DELIA (Crow)

Delia Chiefchild was a student at Haskell Institute in 1908.

CHILDERS, ELLIS BUFFINGTON (Creek)

Ellis Buffington Childers was born on January 10, 1866, in the Creek Nation, the son of Napoleon B. and Sophia Melford Childers. His father was half Cherokee, and his mother was Creek. Childers was educated at Tullahassee Mission and at Carlisle, which he left in 1884. He returned to the Creek Nation and became a rancher and farmer. He served two terms in the Creek House of Warriors and one term as national treasurer. He also practiced law in the firm of Childers and Mingo. He married Fannie Davis.

CHILDERS, ROBERT C. (Creek)
Robert C. Childers was born in the Indian Territory about 1869.

CHOATE, ROBERT M. (Cherokee)
Robert M. Choate, from Bunch, Oklahoma, graduated from Haskell Institute in 1915. He married Jane Taylor and lived at Bunch.

CHOORO, EMMA (Hopi)
Emma Chooro graduated from the Phoenix Indian School in 1909. Her married name was Poncho, and in 1921 she lived at Winslow, Arizona.

CHOOROMI, JOHN (Hopi)
John Chooromi attended the Phoenix Indian School and then went to Hampton Institute.

CHOTEAU, LUZENA (Wyandot)
Luzena Choteau was an 1892 graduate of Carlisle. She attended business college in Chicago and worked for the Chicago Inter-Ocean. In 1902 she worked as a stenographer and clerk in San Francisco. She later moved to Washington where she worked for the Treasury Department. She married Joseph Stanley Roscamp.

CHOUTEAU, EDMOND (Cherokee)
Edmond Chouteau was born in the Cherokee Nation about 1867, the son of William and Mary Chouteau.

CLARK, EMMA P. (Pima)
Emma P. Clark was born about 1897. She attended the Phoenix Indian School.

CLARKE, FRANCIS (Walapai)
Francis Clarke was born in northwestern Arizona. He led a traditional life until 1890 when he entered the government school at Fort Mohave. In 1896 he served as assistant disciplinarian at the school and then entered the Phoenix school, from which he graduated in 1903. He worked at times as disciplinarian and in other capacities at the Valentine school in Arizona. In 1921 he lived at Kingman.

CLARKE, MALCOLM (Piegan)
Malcolm Clarke was from the Blackfoot Reservation in Montana. After graduation from Carlisle in 1893, he graduated from the normal school at Valparaiso, Indiana. He worked for a number of years as a clerk in the Indian service but gave up the service and made his home at Midvale, Montana, where he ranched and took a leading part in the councils of his people.

CLARKE, PETER DOOYENTATE (Wyandot)
No information is available.

CLEMENTS, LUTHER (Michopdo)
     Luther Clements, from California, was a student at Haskell Institute in 1915.

CLINTON, MARY L. (Modoc)
     Mary L. Clinton was born at Whiskey Creek, Oregon. She first attended school at Yainax and entered the Phoenix school in 1902. She graduated in 1907.

CLOUD, BENEDICT D. (Sioux)
     Benedict D. Cloud graduated from Carlisle in 1912. After graduation, he lived for a number of years at Bismarck, North Dakota, where he continued his education. In 1917 he was a sergeant-major in the North Dakota State Militia.

CLOUD, ELIZABETH BENDER (Chippewa)
     Elizabeth Bender Cloud was a member of the Bad River Band in Minnesota. She graduated from Hampton Institute in 1907 and did post-graduate work for a year before becoming a teacher among the Blackfeet. In 1914 she returned to Hampton to do some special work in practice teaching and then became a teacher at Carlisle, where she remained until her marriage to Henry Roe Cloud (q. v.) in 1916.

CLOUD, HENRY ROE (Winnebago)
     Henry Cloud was born in Thurston County, Nebraska, on December 28, 1884, of Winnebago parents, Nah´ilayhunkay and Hard-to-see. He attended the Genoa Indian School, the Santee Mission School, and Dwight Moody's Academy at Mount Hermon, Massachusetts. He was befriended by the Rev. and Mrs. Walter C. Roe, long-time missionaries to the Indians, who urged him to attend Yale, from which he graduated in 1910, the first Indian to earn a bachelor of arts degree from the institution. He later studied at Oberlin and Auburn and earned a master of arts degree from Yale. Because of his gratitude to the Roes, he added their name to his. A Presbyterian clergyman, Cloud founded the American Indian Institute at Wichita, Kansas, where he remained for a number of years. He held several advisory posts in the government, and he became superintendent at Haskell Institute and made a reputation as a reform administrator. In 1936 he became supervisor of Indian education and in the 1940's supervisor of the Umatilla agency. He married Elizabeth A. Bender (q. v.), a Chippewa. Cloud died on February 9, 1950.

COACHMAN, WARD (Creek)
     Ward Coachman (Co-cha-my) was born at Wetumpka, Alabama, in the Creek lands in 1823. His parents died when he was young, and he was reared by his uncle Lachlan Durant of Macon County, Georgia, where he received a limited education in the neighborhood schools. He removed to the West almost a decade after the tribe, returning to Alabama in 1848 to guide to the West a group of Creeks that had been held in slavery by the whites. Coachman was an interpreter and a farmer. During the Civil War he fought with the Confederate regiment of Chilly McIntosh. He held several public offices: clerk of Deep Fork District, member and speaker of the House of

Warriors, clerk of Wewoka District, member and president of the
House of Kings, delegate to Washington, and principal chief (1876).
He was married to Lizzie Carr and Lizzie Yohler. He died on
March 13, 1900.

COCHRAN, JESSE (Cherokee)
 Jesse Cochran was born in Delaware District, Cherokee Nation, on November 27, 1847, the son of Jesse Cochran. Cochran
was a farmer and public official, serving two terms as district
sheriff, two terms as district attorney, three years as supreme
judge, and one term as delegate to Washington. Cochran married
Susan Ross. He died in November, 1905.

COFFEY, ROBERT (Comanche)
 Robert Coffey, from Oklahoma, graduated from Bacone College in 1923.

COLBERT, BEN H. (Choctaw)
 Ben H. Colbert lived in the Choctaw Nation, Indian Territory.

COLBERT, DAUGHERTY (Chickasaw)
 Daugherty (Winchester) Colbert was born of uncertain parentage
near Cotton Gin Port, Monroe County, Mississippi, in 1810. He was
reared by Levi Colbert, whose surname he took, and he gave himself
the name Winchester. He attended Presbyterian mission school near
Cotton Gin Port. In 1826-27 he stayed at the Washington, D. C.,
home of Thomas L. McKenney, the Commissioner of Indian Affairs,
and there received training in surveying. After removal to the West
he settled at Oil Springs, northwest of Tishomingo, where he farmed.
He was instrumental in drafting the treaty that separated the Choctaw
and Chickasaw Nations in 1856. In 1858, 1862, and 1864 he was
elected Governor of the Chickasaw Nation. During the Civil War, he
was pro-Southern and sought refuge in Texas, and after the war,
headed the delegation that negotiated the Treaty of 1866. In his later
years he farmed, served in the Chickasaw senate, and often traveled
to Washington on tribal business. Colbert's wife was Annica Kemp.
He died in 1880.

COLBERT, HUMPHREY (Chickasaw)
 Humphrey Colbert was born in the Choctaw Nation in 1842,
the son of Daugherty (Winchester) Colbert (q. v.), a well-known
Chickasaw leader. During the Civil War he served in the Chickasaw
Confederate battalion under Colonel Lem Reynolds. After the war
he served terms as sheriff and judge of Pontotoc County, three terms
as a member of the Chickasaw House of Representatives, interpreter
in the House, and county and district clerk. Colbert was married to
Elmira Parker and Selina Hamilton. He made his home near Frisco,
Oklahoma.

COLE, COLEMAN (Choctaw)
 Coleman Cole was born about 1800 in present-day Yalobusha
County, Mississippi, the son of Robert Cole, a half-blood Chickasaw,
and Sallie, a Choctaw. He was sent to school in Georgetown, Ken-

tucky. In 1845, Cole removed to the West, settling in the Kiamichi Mountains in the Choctaw Nation. He was elected to the Choctaw National Council from Cedar County in 1850, 1855, 1871, and 1873. He was elected principal chief in 1874 and 1876. Cole made his living by raising livestock. He died in 1886.

COLEMAN, CHARLES F. (Mission)
Charles F. Coleman, from California, graduated from Carlisle in 1902. In 1916 he lived at Gallup, New Mexico.

COLT, LEWIS (Pima)
Lewis Colt attended the Phoenix Indian School.

COMINGDEER, JOHN (Cherokee)
John Comingdeer was from the Indian Territory.

COMPLAINVILLE, LILLIAN T. (Nez Percé)
Lillian T. Complainville was from Idaho. An 1898 graduate of Carlisle, she entered the Indian service as a teacher at the Indian school at Grand Junction, Colorado. She later made her home at Troy, Idaho. Her married name was Keller.

CONGER, LUCILLE (Sioux)
Lucille Conger, a Yankton Sioux from Greenwood, South Dakota, graduated from Hampton Institute in 1897 and taught at the Yankton and Sisseton schools. In 1902 she entered the post-graduate department at Hampton. She married A. O. Bonnin and lived at Lake Andes, South Dakota.

CONLAN, CZARINA M. COLBERT (Choctaw)
Czarina M. Colbert was born in 1875 in the Choctaw Nation, the daughter of James Allen and Athenius Folsom Colbert and granddaughter of Israel Folsom (q. v.). She was educated in the neighborhood schools of the Chickasaw Nation, at a convent in Denison, Texas, and at Mary Baldwin College. In 1894 she married Michael Conlan and made her home in Atoka, Choctaw Nation. She was active in numerous civic organizations and served for many years as Curator of the Oklahoma Historical Society.

CONROY, HARRY (Sioux)
Harry Conroy, born about 1893 on the Pine Ridge Reservation, attended Carlisle.

COOCHASNEMA, JESSIE (Hopi)
Jessie Coochasnema graduated from the Phoenix Indian School in 1906. In 1907 she worked at the Sunlight Mission on First Mesa and then briefly took a job with a trader's wife. She then became housekeeper at the school at Toreva on Second Mesa, a position she still held in 1921.

COODEY, WILLIAM SHOREY (Cherokee)
William Shorey Coodey was born near Chattanooga in the eastern Cherokee Nation, the son of Joseph and Jane Ross Coodey. In

1830 he became a Cherokee delegate to Washington, in which capacity he served for a number of years. In 1834 he removed to the West, where he operated a salt works on Lee's Creek. He made his home at Bayou Menard. Coodey was the principal author of the Cherokee Constitution of 1839 and served as president of the National Committee. He was married to Susan Henley and to Elizabeth Fields. Coodey died on April 16, 1849.

COOK, CHARLES SMITH (Sioux)
    Charles Smith Cook, an Oglala, was an 1881 graduate of Trinity College. He studied theology at Seabury Divinity School, was ordained, and worked as a minister and teacher on the Pine Ridge Reservation in the 1880's. He died at the Pine Ridge agency on April 15, 1892, and was buried at Greenwood, South Dakota.

COOK, WILLIAM TUTTLE (Cherokee)
    William Tuttle Cook was born near Fort Gibson, Cherokee Nation, on December 18, 1873, the son of James Cook. As a youth, Cook worked as a wrangler. He became one of the most infamous outlaws in the Indian Territory as head of a gang known as the Cook Gang. He was convicted of robbery in Judge Isaac Parker's court and died in federal prison at Albany, New York, on February 7, 1900.

COOKE, CLIFFORD (Ottawa)
    Clifford Cooke, from Missouri, was a student at Haskell Institute in 1915.

COOKSON, EDLEY LEVI (Cherokee)
    Edley Levi Cookson was born in the Cherokee Nation in 1853, the son of John Hildebrand and Elizabeth Adair Cookson. He married Agnes Petit and made his home at Cookson, Cherokee Nation. He served as a delegate to Washington and as a Cherokee delegate to meet with the Dawes Commission. He ran unsuccessfully for principal chief in 1903. Cookson died on June 30, 1921.

COOLIDGE, SHERMAN (Arapaho)
    Sherman Coolidge was born at Goose Creek, Wyoming, in 1863, the son of Arapaho parents, Banasda and Ba-ah-noce. When he was seven or eight years old, he was taken in following a battle by General Coolidge and his wife. He received his education at Shattuck Military School in Faribault, Minnesota, Seabury Divinity School, and Hobart College. An episcopal priest, Coolidge was a missionary to the Arapahoes and Shoshonis of Wyoming and to the tribes in western Oklahoma. He was well known as a lecturer on Indian affairs and served on national committees dealing with Indian matters. He married Grace D. Wetherbee. Coolidge died in January, 1932.

COOPER, ELECTA (Oneida)
    Electa Cooper was born about 1894 on the Oneida Reservation in Wisconsin, the daughter of Filmore Cooper. She graduated from Haskell Institute in 1915.

COOPER, STELLA (Potawatomi)
    Stella Cooper graduated from Chilocco Indian School in 1911.

COPWAY, GEORGE (Chippewa)
George Copway (Kah-ge-ga-gah-bowh) was born in Ontario in 1818. An hereditary chief of the Ojibwa, he was educated traditionally but was later converted to Christianity. In 1838-39 he attended Ebenezer Academy in Illinois. He served as an assistant to a Methodist missionary and then became a missionary himself, serving in Illinois, Iowa, Michigan, Minnesota, and Wisconsin. He traveled to Europe in 1850 and wrote extensively. He married Elizabeth Howell. Copway died in Michigan in 1863.

CORNELIUS, BRIGMAN (Oneida)
Brigman Cornelius (also known as Buchanan) was born in Wisconsin about 1878. After graduating from Carlisle in 1897, Cornelius returned to Wisconsin where he farmed and interpreted for the Episcopal Church.

CORNELIUS, CHESTER POE (Oneida)
Chester Poe Cornelius was from Wisconsin. Though qualified to be a chief of the Turtle Clan, he left Wisconsin and practiced law in Oklahoma. He settled at Gore, where he conducted his legal business and was an officer in a bank. In the early 1920's he was legal advisor for the Redbird Smith faction of Nighthawk Keetoowah Cherokees.

CORNELIUS, E. L. (Oneida)
E. L. Cornelius was from Wisconsin.

CORNELIUS, ELECTA (Oneida)
Electa Cornelius, from Wisconsin, was a student at Haskell Institute in 1906.

CORNELIUS, LILLY (Oneida)
Lilly Cornelius, from Wisconsin, was an 1889 graduate of Carlisle.

CORNELIUS, NANCY O. (Oneida)
Nancy O. Cornelius, from Wisconsin, attended Carlisle and the Hartford School of Nursing, from which she graduated in 1891, the first Indian woman to be trained as a professional nurse. She ran the Oneida Hospital in Wisconsin. She died about 1909.

CORNPLANTER, EDWARD (Seneca)
Edward Cornplanter was from New York.

COSAR, GALVOS (Creek)
Galvos Cosar was born at Sapulpa, Creek Nation, in 1902, the son of Tom and Jennie Cosar. He attended Bacone College.

COSTO, MARTIN (Mission)
Martin Costo was from California. He graduated from Carlisle in 1903.

COSTO, NATTIE (Mission)

Nattie Costo, from California, was a student at Haskell Institute in 1908.

CRABTREE, MARY (Little Lake, or Mitomkai Pomo)
Mary Crabtree was born in Mendocino County, California, on November 8, 1888. She began school at six and in 1906 entered the Phoenix Indian School, from which she graduated in 1908.

CROTZER, GRACE (Wyandot)
Grace Crotzer was born in the Indian Territory about 1893, the daughter of Mrs. Catharine Crotzer. She attended Haskell Institute, graduating from the domestic arts and sciences department in 1911.

CROWE, JANIE (Seneca)
Janie Crow was a student at Haskell Institute in 1915.

CRUTCHFIELD, JOSEPH VANN (Cherokee)
Joseph Vann Crutchfield was born in the Cherokee Nation on October 16, 1841, the son of John and Mary E. Ladd Crutchfield. He married Mary Maria Landrum. Crutchfield ran a store and in 1880 became postmaster at Poulas, Cherokee Nation. He died on November 5, 1884.

CUNNINGHAM, JETER THOMPSON (Cherokee)
Jeter Thompson Cunningham was born December 1, 1843, near Tahlequah, Cherokee Nation, the son of Andrew and Maria Lynch Cunningham. He attended neighborhood schools. During the Civil War he served in Watie's Cherokee Regiment. After the war he farmed, ran a drug store in Vinita, and worked as a drug clerk in Tahlequah. He was later elected clerk of Delaware District and served in the National Council, as associate justice and chief justice of the Cherokee Supreme Court, and as executive secretary under Chief Joel B. Mayes (q. v.).

CURTIS, CHARLES (Kansa)
Charles Curtis was born on his grandmother's allotment (now North Topeka, Kansas) on January 25, 1860, the son of Orren Arms and Hélène Papan Curtis, the latter of whom was part Kansa. His mother died in 1863, and for two years he lived with his father's family. He returned to his mother's people in 1865 and attended Indian mission school in Morris County. By the time he was twenty-one, he had been admitted to the bar. In 1884 he was elected attorney for Shawnee County and was reelected in 1886. In 1892 he was elected to the U. S. House of Representatives in which he served seven terms. In 1906 he was elected to the Senate and served there for twenty years. From 1928 to 1933 he was Vice President of the United States. His wife was Anna Elizabeth Baird. He died on February 8, 1936. Although he had a small quantum of Indian blood, Curtis was considered an Indian by his contemporaries, perhaps because of campaign publicity; however, one of the most destructive pieces of Indian legislation of the nineteenth century--the Curtis Act--bears his name.

CUSHING, GEORGE (Alaskan Native)
George Cushing was a student at Carlisle in 1917.

CUSICK, DAVID (Tuscarora)
David Cusick, from New York, died about 1840.

DAGENETT, CHARLES EDWIN (Peoria)
Charles Edwin Dagenett was born in the Miami-Peoria Reservation in Indian Territory. He graduated from Carlisle in 1891 and became editor of the Miami Chieftain in Indian Territory until 1894. That year he and his wife Esther Miller Dagenett entered the Indian service at Fort Thompson, South Dakota, as teachers. He later taught among the Apaches in Arizona and at Chilocco Indian School. In 1899-1900 he worked at Carlisle and in the latter year became head clerk at the Quapaw agency in Indian Territory. In 1902 he was issue clerk at Fort Apache, Arizona. In 1903 he taught in New Mexico, and in 1905 he was supervisor of Indian employment at Albuquerque and held the same post later at Denver. In 1907-08 he was special agent to the Utes and in 1910-11 to the Seminoles in Florida. Dagenett retired in 1927.

DALE, WILLIAM (Caddo)
William Dale, from Oklahoma, attended Carlisle.

DAMON, NELLIE (Navajo)
Nellie Damon was a student at Haskell Institute in 1908.

DAVIDSON, HAL O. (Mohave)
Hal O. Davidson was born on October 7, 1888, near Mellen, Arizona. At seven he entered the Fort Mohave school, and in 1905 he entered the Phoenix Indian School, from which he graduated in 1907.

DAVIS, GILBERT (Apache)
Gilbert Davis attended the Phoenix Indian School.

DAVIS, OSCAR DE FOREST (Chippewa)
Oscar De Forest Davis was from the White Earth Reservation. He graduated from Carlisle in 1903, after which he worked as a printer for the White Earth Tomahawk. In late 1903 he moved to Lisbon, North Dakota, and in 1906 he entered the dental school of the University of Minnesota, graduating in 1909. He practiced in Minneapolis and served as an officer in the local dental society.

DAVIS, RICHARD (Cheyenne)
Richard Davis lived the life of a plains Cheyenne until 1879 when he went to Carlisle. In 1881 he entered the outing program and learned farming at Danboro, Pennsylvania, and in 1882 learned fruit culture. He also studied printing and worked on the school's paper, The Morning Star, and later worked as a coachman in Philadelphia. In 1888 he married Nannie Aspenall, a Pawnee, and he and his wife took farm jobs at West Grove, Pennsylvania. He was induced finally to return to the reservation with his family. He took a job at the

agency but soon lost it to other office seekers. He was a good farmer and dairyman. In 1904 he lived at Seger's Colony, Oklahoma.

DAVIS, SAMUEL G. (Haida)
Samuel G. Davis was from southern Alaska.

DAWSON, ANNA (Arickara)
Anna Dawson, from the Fort Berthold Reservation, graduated
from Hampton Institute in 1895. She then became a field matron on
the Fort Berthold Reservation. Her married name was Wilde.

DE CORA, ANGEL (Winnebago)
Angel De Cora was born on the Winnebago Reservation in Nebraska on May 3, 1871, the daughter of David De Cora. She was
educated for four years at the reservation school and then entered
Hampton Institute, from which she graduated in 1891. She attended
Miss Burnham's school at Northampton, Massachusetts, and then
studied art at Smith College, Drexel Institute, and the Boston Museum of Fine Arts. She maintained a studio in New York where she
illustrated books. In 1906 she went to Carlisle as an art teacher
and stayed there until 1915. She then worked for the New York State
Museum at Albany and in 1918 returned to New York where she again
worked as an illustrator. She married William Deitz (q. v.), a
Sioux, who illustrated the covers of the Carlisle Red Man. She died
on February 6, 1919.

DEDRICK, EDITH (Klamath)
Edith Dedrick was a student at the Phoenix Indian School in
1905.

DE FOND, SAMUEL C. (Sioux)
Samuel De Fond (or Cingekerdan), from the Yankton Reserva-
tion, was born about 1870, the son of Battice De Fond. He attended
Hampton Institute from 1885 to 1888. In 1890 he taught at St. Paul's
School on the Yankton Reservation.

DE GRASSE, ALFRED (Mashpee)
Alfred De Grasse, born about 1889, was from New Bedford,
Massachusetts. He was the grandson of Watson F. Hampton, a Cape
Cod Indian elected to the Massachusetts State Legislature in 1885.

DEITZ, WILLIAM (Sioux)
William Deitz (Lone Star) was the son of a German civil engineer and his wife, a member of Red Cloud's band of Sioux. His
father returned to the East and when Deitz was eight, took him there
and put him in school. He graduated from high school ten years
later and then worked as an artist for various newspapers. In 1904
he supervised the interior and mural work for the Indian exhibit at
the Louisiana Purchase Exposition in St. Louis. In 1908 he became
an instructor of art at Carlisle. He married Angel De Cora (q. v.).

DELORIA, ELLA CARA (Sioux)
Ella Cara Deloria, a Yankton, was born at Wakpala, South

Dakota, on January 3, 1888, the daughter of Philip Deloria. After attending local schools, she went to Oberlin and Columbia, where she received a bachelor's degree in 1915. She then taught and worked in Indian health for a number of years. In 1929 she returned to Columbia and worked with Franz Boaz on Siouan languages. In the years that followed she wrote extensively on Siouan linguistics; she also lectured during that time. From 1955 to 1958 she was principal of St. Elizabeth's School at Wakpala. Miss Deloria died on February 12, 1971.

DE MARRIAS, FRANCES (Sioux)
Frances De Marrias, from South Dakota, graduated from the domestic arts department of Haskell Institute in 1915.

DENETSOUENBEGA, MANUELITO (Navajo)
Manuelito Denetsouenbega was from Shiprock, New Mexico. He attended Haskell Institute.

DENOMIE, ANTOINE (Chippewa)
Antoine Denomie, a Bad River Chippewa, was a businessman at Odanah, Wisconsin. He had homesteaded in Alaska and in 1914 began spending his winters in California because of his health.

DENOMIE, S. F. (Chippewa)
S. F. Denomie, a Bad River Chippewa, was a leader in 1915 of a group that sought to establish a cooperative store on the reservation.

DENOMIE, WILLIAM (Chippewa)
William Denomie, from the Lac Court Oreilles Reservation in Wisconsin, was born about 1878. He graduated from Carlisle in 1894 and taught at the day school at Reserve, Wisconsin.

DE PELTQUESTANGUE, ESTAIENE M. (Kickapoo)
Estaiene M. De Peltquestangue, a graduate of Carlisle, was superintendent of the Lakeside Hospital at Cleveland, Ohio, from 1905 to 1910. She worked for a number of years in the World War I period as a private nurse in Massillon, Ohio.

DICK, COFFEE (Cherokee)
Coffee Dick was from the Indian Territory.

DICK, JOHN HENRY (Cherokee)
John Henry Dick was born in Flint District, Cherokee Nation, on January 1, 1869, the son of Charles and Margaret Tickaneskie Dick. He graduated from the Indian University in 1888 at which time he became assistant interpreter for the lower house of the National Council. In 1890 he taught school and the following year translated for the Cherokee Advocate until he was elected district attorney for Tahlequah District. Shortly after the turn of the century, Dick was involved in schemes of the Cherokee fullbloods to emigrate to Mexico.

DODSON, JOHN (Shoshoni)

John Dodson graduated from the Phoenix Indian School in 1904 and later from Hampton Institute. He returned to Phoenix and worked as assistant carpenter at the school, leaving there in 1914 to take a similar post at the Fort Apache School, Whiteriver, Arizona. He married Myra Valenzuela (q. v.). In 1921 he was farming at Lehi, Arizona, Mrs. Dodson's home.

DOHERTY, JOHN J. (Chippewa)
    John J. Doherty, of the Bad River band, was from Ashland, Wisconsin. He was an inventor of novelties.

DOOLITTLE, OTTOWELL (Little Lake, or Mitomkai Pomo)
    Ottowell Doolittle, from California, attended the Phoenix Indian School.

DORCHESTER, DANIEL (Yuma)
    Daniel Dorchester graduated from the Phoenix Indian School in 1904 and that fall entered Hampton Institute, where he died of typhoid fever on October 22.

DOWNING, LEWIS (Cherokee)
    Lewis Downing (Lewie-za-wau-na-skie) was born in the Cherokee Nation in eastern Tennessee in 1823, the son of Samuel and Susan Daugherty Downing. After removal, the family settled in Going Snake District, where Downing attended Baptist mission schools. He became an ordained Baptist minister and was named pastor of the Flint Baptist Church in 1844. He moved to Saline District from which he was elected to the Cherokee Senate in 1851 and in 1859. He also served as delegate to Washington in 1851. During the Civil War, he was chaplain for a pro-Union Cherokee regiment and in 1866, finished out the term of Chief John Ross (q. v.), who died in office. He was elected principal chief in 1867 and 1871. He was married three times, to Lydia Price, Lucinda Griffin, and Mary Eyre. He died on November 9, 1872.

DOXON, CHARLES (Onondaga)
    Charles Doxon, from New York, was orphaned at age six. He spoke no English until he was eighteen, when a missionary obtained a job for him on a farm. During the three years that he worked as a laborer, the farm family helped him with his English. Doxon then made his way to Hampton, which he had heard about, but upon arrival there he was disappointed to learn that the federal government would not support Indians from New York. Nevertheless, Doxon remained at Hampton from 1883 to 1886, working during the day and going to school at night. From Hampton, he went to Syracuse, New York, where he worked in a railroad shop for fifteen years. He was admitted to the union, which barred blacks, and was active in the labor movement around the turn of the century. After he was injured on the job, he returned to Hampton for a time and then returned to Syracuse where he worked as an "automobile expert" for the Thomas Manufacturing Company. Doxon served as president of the Six Nations Temperance League and as a member of the Executive Council of the Society of American Indians. He died on February 3, 1917.

DOXTATOR, MARGARET (Oneida)
Margaret Doxtator, from Wisconsin, graduated from the domestic arts department of Haskell Institute in 1914.

DOYETO, MORRIS (Kiowa)
Morris Doyeto, from Oklahoma, graduated from Bacone College in 1924.

DRAPEAU, AGNES (Sioux)
Agnes Drapeau was a student at Haskell in 1915.

DREW, HARVEY (Klamath)
Harvey Drew graduated from the Phoenix Indian School in 1905.

DU BRAY, JOSEPH (Sioux)
Joseph Du Bray (or Cankaksa), from the Yankton Reservation, was born about 1872, the son of Peter Du Bray. He entered Hampton Institute in 1890.

DUCKWORTH, M. ZOE (Delaware)
M. Zoe Duckworth, a Delaware, was born in the Cherokee Nation, the daughter of John Bullette, a well known Delaware leader. In 1905 she and her husband Frank lived in Claremore, Cherokee Nation, but later moved to Siloam Springs, Arkansas.

DUNCAN, DE WITT CLINTON (Cherokee)
De Witt Clinton Duncan was born in 1829 at Dahlonega in the Cherokee Nation in Georgia, the son of half-blood John Duncan and Elizabeth Abercrombie Duncan. Duncan was educated in mission and Cherokee national schools before he went to Dartmouth College, from which he graduated with honors in 1861, a member of Phi Beta Kappa. Because of the Civil War, Duncan did not return to the Indian Territory but taught school in New Hampshire, Wisconsin, and Illinois, finally settling in 1866 at Charles City, Iowa, where he practiced law, served as mayor for a year, and taught school. By 1880 Duncan was again in the Cherokee Nation, where, during the next several years, he served the Cherokees in various capacities: legal counsel, teacher and principal of the Cherokee Male Seminary, and political writer and poet. He studied Cherokee history and linguistics, and writing under his English name and under Too-qua-stee, he contributed widely to Cherokee and U. S. publications. He died at Vinita, Oklahoma, in November, 1909.

DUNCAN, EMMA (Cherokee)
Emma Duncan was born in the Cherokee Nation, the daughter of Walter Adair Duncan (q. v.).

DUNCAN, J. C. (Cherokee)
J. C. Duncan was born in the Cherokee Nation about 1860, the son of John Tommason and Elizabeth Sanders Duncan. He lived in Sequoyah District.

DUNCAN, JAMES W. (Cherokee)

James W. Duncan was born at Knobnoster, Missouri, in 1861, the son of Morgan H. and Penelope C. Craig Duncan. Because of the civil strife that followed removal, his family had moved to Missouri. In 1869 they were readmitted to the Cherokee rolls. The family settled in Delaware District, where Duncan attended Cherokee neighborhood schools. He graduated from the Male Seminary in 1885. After teaching for a short time he entered Emory College, receiving his bachelor's degree in 1890. He returned to the Cherokee Nation where he became a professor at the Male Seminary and often spoke out in behalf of education. He served as the U. S. government surveyor and as alloting agent in the Cherokee Outlet.

DUNCAN, JENNIE (Cherokee)

Jennie Duncan was born in the Cherokee Nation, the daughter of Walter Adair Duncan (q. v.).

DUNCAN, WALTER ADAIR (Cherokee)

Walter Adair Duncan was born in the eastern Cherokee Nation in March, 1823, the son of John and Elizabeth Abercrombie Duncan. His family removed to the West in 1828 and settled in Flint District. He attended school near Evansville, Arkansas. In 1847 he was licensed to preach and became a circuit rider. In the early 1850's he was private secretary to Chief John Ross (q. v.) and later served as a member of the National Council. From 1872 to 1884, he was superintendent of the Cherokee Orphan Asylum, and in his later years he lived at Park Hill. Duncan married Martha Bell, Martha Wilson, and Catherine A. L. Caleb. He died on October 17, 1907.

DURANT, WILLIAM A. (Choctaw)

William A. (Will) Durant was born in the Choctaw Nation on March 16, 1866, the son of Sylvester and Martha Robinson Durant. He was educated in the Choctaw neighborhood schools and at Arkansas College at Batesville, from which he graduated in 1886. He taught in the Choctaw schools, worked in the cattle business, and studied law. He practiced law in the Choctaw and Chickasaw courts and later in the federal courts. Durant served in the Choctaw legislature and was Speaker of the House. After Oklahoma statehood, he was a member of the Oklahoma legislature for eleven years. In 1937 he was appointed principal chief of the Choctaws by President Franklin D. Roosevelt.

DYE, BERTHA E. (Seneca)

Bertha E. Dye, from New York, was an 1899 graduate of Carlisle. She married Jacob Jamison (q. v.) and lived at Gowanda, New York.

EASCHIEF, ANNIE (Pima)

Annie Easchief attended the Phoenix Indian School.

EASCHIEF, MANUEL (Pima)

Manuel Easchief was born at Gila Crossing, Arizona. He attended reservation day school before entering the Phoenix Indian School, from which he graduated in 1907. Easchief married Ida Temple.

EASCHIEF, OLDHAM (Pima)

Oldham Easchief was a student at the Phoenix Indian School in 1895. In 1915 he was farming at Gila Crossing, Arizona.

EASTMAN, CHARLES ALEXANDER (Sioux)

Charles Alexander Eastman (Ohiyesa) was born at Redwood Falls, Minnesota, in 1858, the son of Jacob Eastman (Many Lightnings), a Santee, and Nancy Eastman, a half-blood Sioux. His father and uncle saw to his early education, instilling in him a knowledge of the traditions of the tribe. He later attended mission schools near his home and at the Santee agency. In 1876 he was sent for further study at Beloit College in Wisconsin, where he remained three years before entering Knox College in Illinois. He returned to Dakota and taught school before receiving a scholarship to Dartmouth, where he pursued a premedical course from 1883 to 1887. After graduation he attended Boston University, from which he received an M. D. degree. He served as the physician at the Pine Ridge agency from 1890 to 1893. He married Elaine Goodale, a reservation teacher who later became a well-known writer. In his later life, Eastman wrote extensively, lectured, and held national posts in the Y. M. C. A. and Boy Scouts of America. During the Coolidge administration he served as U. S. Indian Inspector. Eastman died in 1939.

EASTMAN, PETER (Sioux)

Peter Eastman, a Sisseton from Peever, South Dakota, graduated from Carlisle in 1913.

EATON, RACHEL CAROLINE (Cherokee)

Rachel Caroline Eaton was born west of Mayesville, Arkansas, in the Cherokee Nation on July 7, 1869, the daughter of George Washington and Nancy Ward Eaton. Her mother descended from Nancy Ward, the last Beloved Woman of the Cherokees. In 1874 the family moved to Claremore Mound. After attending Cherokee public schools and graduating from the Cherokee Female Seminary, she entered Drury College at Springfield, Missouri, in 1887. Graduating with honors in 1895, she then attended the University of Chicago, where she earned an M. A. and Ph. D., writing her dissertation on John Ross of the Cherokees. Miss Eaton then taught in the Cherokee Female Seminary; the Industrial Training School for Girls at Columbus, Mississippi; Lake Erie College at Painesville, Ohio; and Trinity University at Waxahatchie, Texas. She returned to her home town and in 1920 was elected to the first of two terms as superintendent of schools for Rogers County, Oklahoma. She died at Claremore on September 20, 1938.

EDMONDSON, BULA BENTON (Cherokee)

Bula Benton Edmondson was born in the Cherokee Nation in 1884, the daughter of Michael L. and Florence Williams Edmondson. She graduated from the Cherokee Female Seminary and then became a teacher. She studied voice and expression in Paris and at the Boston School of Expression, later opening her own studio in Muskogee, Oklahoma. She married Richard Coker.

ELLIS, ESTELLA W. (Sac and Fox)
Estella W. Ellis, from Oklahoma, attended Carlisle.

ELM, CORA (Oneida)
Cora Elm, from Wisconsin, was born about 1890, the daughter of Nicholas and Jane Elm. She graduated from Carlisle in 1913 and then took nurse's training at the Episcopal Hospital in Philadelphia.

EMERSON, CALVIN (Pima)
Calvin Emerson attended the Phoenix Indian School.

ENAS, LASALLE (Pima)
Lasalle Enas graduated from the Phoenix Indian School in 1911.

ENMEGAHBOWH (Chippewa)
Enmegahbowh (John Johnson) was born about 1808 in Canada. He moved first to La Pointe, Wisconsin, and then to Rabbit Lake as minister to the Chippewas. He worked in lumber camps to support himself. He then took over the Gull Lake mission near Brainerd, Minnesota, where he stayed until the outbreak of 1862. He then moved to Crow Wing, twelve miles away, where he lived until 1868 when he moved to White Earth where he remained for the rest of his life. He died on June 14, 1902.

ENOS, JOHNSON (Pima)
Johnson Enos, also known as John E. Johnson, was born about 1886 and attended Carlisle, from which he graduated in 1910. He made his home at Blackwater, Arizona.

ESTES, JOSEPH FOLSOM (Sioux)
Joseph Folsom Estes (or Standing Crane), from the Standing Rock Reservation, was born about 1868, the son of Benjamin Estes. He attended Hampton Institute from 1881 to 1884. He married Harriet Benoist. He died at Orlando, Florida, in March, 1918.

ETHELBA, KAY (Apache)
Kay Ethelba was first sent to school at Fort Lewis, Colorado, and then entered the Phoenix Indian School in 1898.

ETTAWAGESHIK, J. WILLIAM (Ottawa)
J. William Ettawageshik was born about 1889 and graduated from Carlisle in 1911. In 1913 he was assistant editor of the Onaway, Michigan, Outlook, and in 1914 he settled at St. Ignace, Michigan, where he worked as a job printer for the St. Ignace Enterprise.

EUBANKS, WILLIAM (Cherokee)
William Eubanks was born in the Cherokee Nation in 1841, the son of William and Nancy Eubanks. He was a teacher and for many years served as an interpreter for the Cherokee government. He studied the Cherokee language and reduced Sequoyah's syllabary from eighty-six to eighty-five characters. Eubanks married Eliza C. Thompson.

FERRIS, GEORGE (Klamath)
George Ferris, from northern California, graduated from Carlisle in 1901. He returned to California and lived at Hoopa on the Hoopa Valley Reservation.

FIELDS, ARTHUR (Pawnee)
Arthur Fields, from Pawnee, Oklahoma, graduated from Bacone College in 1925.

FIELDS, RICHARD (Cherokee)
Richard Fields was born in Alabama, the son of Richard Fields. In 1834 he was a member of the Cherokee National Council and in 1835 was named editor of the Cherokee Phoenix, but the Georgians seized the press before he could take control. In 1838, he was a member of the Cherokee delegation to Florida to negotiate with the Seminoles. In the West, he was a lawyer and merchant at Menard Bayou. In 1866 he was one of the Southern Cherokee delegates to Washington.

FIELDS, RICHARD H. (Cherokee)
Richard H. Fields was a full-blood Cherokee who spoke flawless English. He served as national auditor and chancellor from Saline District. For many years he was in the mercantile business in Tahlequah until he was seriously injured by an attempt on his life. He retired from business and wrote prolifically for local newspapers. He never married. Fields died on March 22, 1900.

FINLEY, MINNIE (Caddo)
Minnie Finley, from Indian Territory, graduated from Carlisle in 1899. After graduation she went to work at the Great Nemaha agency in Kansas. The following year she went to Chilocco, where in 1902 she was a matron.

FIRE THUNDER, ELLA (Sioux)
Ella Fire Thunder (or Ziyawin), the daughter of Charging Hawk, was from the Lower Brule Reservation. She was born about 1878 and entered Hampton Institute in 1890, graduating in 1896. She then went to the Osage agency to teach. The following year she returned to Hampton.

FISH, CHARLES L. (Sioux)
Charles L. Fish, from Lower Brule, North Dakota, was born about 1886. He graduated from Carlisle in 1911. He worked as school farmer at White Earth, Minnesota, after which he returned to Lower Brule, where he farmed and followed his trade as a painter.

FISHER, HENRY CLAY (Creek)
Henry Clay Fisher was born at Fishertown, Creek Nation, on March 16, 1862, the son of William (q. v.) and Sarah P. Lampkin Fisher. He attended public schools in the Creek Nation, and at the age of fourteen he was sent to Franklin High School in Clinton, Missouri, from which he graduated in 1881. Upon his return to the Creek Nation he worked with his father in the mercentile trade until

1892 and served as postmaster at Fishertown. From 1890 through 1894, he was coal weigher for the Creek Nation and in 1895 was elected to the House of Warriors in the Creek Council. He married Lucy B. Willison and after 1892 made his home at Checotah.

FISHER, WILLIAM (Creek)
William Fisher was born in the eastern Creek Nation in Alabama, the son of Samuel Fisher. In 1847 he was sent to school at Shawnee Mission, Kansas, where he remained for two years. He returned to the Creek Nation, married Sarah P. Lampkin, and entered the mercantile business at Fishertown. He fought in Chilly McIntosh's Confederate regiment during the Civil War. After the war he reestablished his business and operated as well a cotton gin and saw mill. Fisher served in the Creek National Council for eight years and was a Supreme Court judge. In 1892 he moved his store from Fishertown to Checotah, where he died in 1902.

FLAME, SYLVESTER (Yuma)
Sylvester Flame, from the Yuma Reservation in California, graduated from the Phoenix Indian School in 1905.

FLOOD, HENRY J. (Sioux)
Henry J. Flood, from Martin, South Dakota, graduated from the business department of Haskell Institute in 1914 and became assistant disciplinarian at the school. He was later appointed financial clerk at Rosebud, South Dakota, but then returned to Haskell. In 1924 he resigned at Haskell and became the coach at Dakota Wesleyan College at Mitchell, South Dakota.

FOLSOM, DON D. (Choctaw)
Don D. Folsom lived at Atoka, Choctaw Nation.

FOLSOM, ISRAEL (Choctaw)
The Reverend Israel Folsom was born in the Choctaw Nation in Mississippi on May 1, 1802, the son of Nathaniel Folsom, a white trader, and his Choctaw wife. He assisted in moving the Choctaws to their lands west of the Mississippi and settled near old Fort Washita in the western Choctaw Nation. He died at Perryville, Choctaw Nation, on April 24, 1870.

FOLSOM, JOSEPH P. (Choctaw)
Joseph P. Folsom was born in the Choctaw Nation in Mississippi in 1823. He received his early education at the Choctaw Academy in Kentucky. He entered Moor's Indian Charity School in 1844 and Dartmouth in 1850, graduating in 1854 with training in Latin and Greek. He served as a member of the Choctaw National Council and as a member of the Okmulgee International Council in 1870. In 1875 he was one of the organizers of the International Printing Company, which issued the Indian Journal at Muskogee. He also compiled a digest of the laws of the Choctaw Nation before 1869.

FONTENELLE, EUGENE (Omaha)
Eugene Fontenelle, from Nebraska, was born about 1860, the

son of Henry Fontenelle. He attended Hampton Institute from 1885 to 1888.

FOREMAN, HARRISON (Cherokee)
Harrison Foreman lived in the Cherokee Nation, Indian Territory.

FOREMAN, STEPHEN (Cherokee)
Stephen Foreman was born in the eastern Cherokee Nation on October 22, 1807, the son of Anthony Foreman, a Scot, and his Cherokee wife Elizabeth Gurdaygee. He studied at Brainerd Mission school under the Reverend Samuel Austin Worcester and then went on to the College of Richmond and Princeton Theological Seminary. Licensed to preach by the Presbyterians, he preached at Brainerd in the 1830's and helped Worcester translate the New Testament. In the West, in addition to his work as a clergyman, Foreman organized the Cherokee national public school system and was its first superintendent. He also served as a supreme court judge in 1844 and in the Executive Council from 1847 to 1855. After the Civil War he established Park Hill Mission near his home at Park Hill where he died on November 20, 1881. Foreman was married to Sarah Watkins Riley and Ruth Riley Candy. Besides his work as a translator, Foreman wrote under the pen name of Old Man of the Mountain.

FOSTER, WIMMIE (Paiute)
Wimmie Foster was born at Yainax, Oregon. He attended school there and in 1903 enrolled in the Phoenix Indian School where he distinguished himself in art, oratory, choir, and baseball. He graduated in 1907.

FRECHETTE, JULIA (Chippewa)
Julia Frechette graduated from Carlisle in 1915.

FREEMAN, ALBERT B. (Sioux)
Albert B. Freeman (or Gaiwahgowa) was born in Boston and was a student at De Pauw University in 1917.

FREEMAN, THEODORE R. (Creek)
Theodore R. Freeman was born at Henryetta, Creek Nation, in 1903, the son of John W. and Lena Freeman. He graduated from Chilocco Indian School in 1924.

FREEMONT, HENRIETTA R. (Omaha)
Henrietta R. Freemont (Nedawe) was born about 1870 on the Omaha Reservation in Nebraska, the daughter of Wajaepa. She had several years of education at the mission school on the reservation and at Elizabeth, New Jersey, before entering Hampton Institute in 1884. She left the school because of illness in 1887, studied at home for two years, and then entered Carlisle from which she graduated in 1895. She then took courses in stenography and typing at Banks' Business College in Philadelphia and briefly attended Swarthmore. She entered government service and worked for a time at Pierre and Crow Creek, South Dakota. She returned to Nebraska and lived at Walthill.

FRENCH, WILLIAM (Cherokee)
William French, from the Indian Territory, was a student at the Cherokee Orphan Asylum in 1881.

FRIDAY, MOSES (Arapaho)
Moses Friday was born about 1888 and graduated from Carlisle in 1911.

FROST, ALICE (Crow)
Alice Frost was from Stillwell, Oklahoma, and graduated from Bacone College in 1924.

FULLER, ELSIE (Omaha)
Elsie Fuller was born in Nebraska about 1870, the daughter of Stephen Fuller. She attended Hampton Institute from 1885 to 1888. She married Alfred Bruce.

FULWILDER, PENROSE (Little Lake, or Mitomkai Pomo)
Penrose Fulwilder, from California, was a student at the Phoenix Indian School in 1909.

GABRIEL, CHRISTIANA (Serrano)
Christiana Gabriel, from California, was born about 1887. She attended Carlisle.

GADDY, VIRGINIA (Delaware)
Virginia Gaddy, from the Indian Territory, was born about 1886. She attended Carlisle.

GANSWORTH, HOWARD EDWARD (Tuscarora)
Howard Edward Gansworth, from Lewiston, New York, was an 1894 graduate of Carlisle. After graduation, he took courses at Dickinson College, at Carlisle, Pennsylvania, preparatory to entering Princeton in 1897. At Princeton, he was appointed Junior Orator in 1900; he graduated in 1901. After graduation he returned to Carlisle as assistant disciplinarian and was placed in charge of the outing program. Gansworth then lived in Buffalo, New York, where he was a department manager of the General Specialty Company. He served on the advisory committee of the Society of American Indians and was a contributing editor of the Quarterly Journal.

GANSWORTH, LEANDER NEWTON (Tuscarora)
Leander Newton Gansworth, from Lewiston, New York, was an 1896 graduate of Carlisle. From the time he graduated until 1903 he lived at Booneville, New York, where he worked at the Booneville Herald as a linotype operator and assistant foreman. In 1903, he moved to Davenport, Iowa, as a linotype operator for the Davenport Times. He married Louise Harding of Davenport and became active in the community. He was a member of the Masons and the Odd Fellows and was active in the Mt. Ida Presbyterian Church. In 1912 he was secretary-treasurer of the Tri-City Allied Printing Trades Council, and in 1914 was the director of a local labor paper and a delegate to the A. F. of L. convention in Philadelphia.

GARDNER, LUCIE (Sioux)
Lucie Gardner was a student at Haskell Institute in 1902.

GAREN, MARY (Iroquois)
Mary Garen, from Pawhuska, Oklahoma, graduated from Chilocco Indian school in 1920.

GARLOW, WILLIAM (Tuscarora)
William Garlow, from Lewiston, New York, was born about 1887 and was a 1913 graduate of Carlisle.

GARVIE, JAMES WILLIAM (Sioux)
James William Garvie, from the Santee Reservation in Nebraska, graduated from Carlisle in 1915.

GARVIN, ISAAC L. (Choctaw)
Isaac L. Garvin was born in the Choctaw Nation in Mississippi, the son of Henry Garvin, a white man, and his Choctaw wife. In the western Choctaw Nation, he resided near the present-day town of Garvin, Oklahoma, where he served as judge of Red River County and was for several years judge of the Choctaw Supreme Court. Garvin was elected principal chief of the nation in 1878 and died in office in February, 1880. He married Melvina Miashambi.

GASHOIENIM, NORA (Hopi)
Nora Gashoienim was born at Oraibi. She attended Oraibi day school and the Keams Canyon boarding school before entering the Phoenix Indian School in 1899. She graduated in 1907.

GEORGE, DAHNEY E. (Cherokee)
Dahney E. George, from North Carolina, graduated from Carlisle in 1899 and then entered West Chester Normal School at Carlisle, Pennsylvania.

GEORGE, LEWIS (Klamath)
Lewis George graduated from Carlisle in 1910 and worked for a time in the town of Carlisle.

GIBBS, ADIN C. (Delaware)
Adin C. Gibbs, from Pennsylvania, was born about 1797. He was part white and spoke English well when he began school at Cornwall, Connecticut, in 1818. He remained at Cornwall until 1822. During that time he preached and conducted such meetings that they were remembered fifty years later by residents of Cornwall. Gibbs taught and did missionary work among the Choctaws, with whom he lived for many years.

GIBSON, CHARLES (Creek)
Charles Gibson was born near Eufaula, Creek Nation, on March 20, 1846, the son of John C. Gibson, who emigrated from Alabama in 1832. The family first settled on Grand River near Fort Gibson and farmed. Charles Gibson, who was self-taught, obtained what little formal education he had in the common schools of the Creek

Nation and at Asbury Mission. He ran a store in the western part of the nation for a short time and then worked twenty years as head clerk and buyer in the Grayson Brothers store at North Fork Town. In 1896 he established his own store in Eufaula. At age 55 he married Mrs. Modeania Aultman, by whom he had one child. After 1900, he wrote extensively for Indian Territory newspapers and journals. Gibson died in 1923.

GILMORE, GUS (Apache)
Gus Gilmore, from San Carlos Reservation, entered the San Carlos school in 1891, after which he attended the Grand Junction, Colorado, school for seven years. He worked as a shoemaker at the Yuma school for three years and then became disciplinarian at the Phoenix Indian School.

GIVEN, JOSHUA H. (Kiowa)
Joshua H. Given was the son of the Kiowa leader Satank but took the name of a government physician. He attended reservation school before being sent to Carlisle. In 1887 he attended Lincoln University in Chester, Pennsylvania. The following year he acted as interpreter for the Presbyterian mission near Lawton, Indian Territory. In 1892 he was the official interpreter for the Jerome commissioners at Fort Sill. He contracted tuberculosis, as did many Indians who returned from the East, and died in March, 1893.

GOODY, IDA (Apache)
Ida Goody (or Gooday) graduated from the Phoenix Indian School in 1923.

GORDON, JANE ZANE (Wyandot)
Jane Zane Gordon, from Oklahoma, lived in Los Angeles.

GORDON, PHILIP B. (Chippewa)
Philip B. Gordon (Ti-bish-ko-gi-jik) was born at Gordon, Wisconsin, in 1887, the son of William D. Gordon and A-ta-ge-kew, his Chippewa wife. He attended public schools in Douglas County, St. Mary's Indian School at Odanah, St. Thomas College and Seminary in St. Paul, Propaganda University at Rome, Insbruck University at Lyrol, Austria, and St. John's Abbey at St. Paul. He was fluent in Chippewa, German, French, and Italian. On December 8, 1913, Gordon was ordained as the first Indian priest in the United States and the second in the world. He became a missionary to the Chippewas at Reserve, Wisconsin, and in 1916 he edited The War-Whoop and in 1918 founded and edited A-ni-shi-na-bwe E-na-mi-ad in behalf of Chippewa Catholic missions. In 1924 he became pastor at St. Patrick's Church, Centuria, Wisconsin. He died on October 1, 1948.

GOUGE, JOSEPH J. (Chippewa)
Joseph J. Gouge, a Fond du Lac Chippewa, was born about 1878. He graduated from Carlisle in 1899. He joined the American Army and served in the Philippines.

GOULETTE, EMMA D. JOHNSON (Potawatomi)

Emma D. Johnson Goulette lived at Shawnee, Oklahoma, in the early part of the century. She taught at Haskell Institute and served as a vice president of the Society of American Indians. In later years she lived at Tucson, Arizona. Her husband was J. D. Goulette, a Sioux.

GOURD, LOUIS B. R. (Cherokee)

Louis B. R. Gourd (or Louis B. Rattlingourd), from the Indian Territory, was born in 1894, the son of Daniel and Lulu R. Gourd. He was a 1918 graduate of the business department of Haskell Institute.

GOYITNEY, ANNIE (Pueblo)

Annie Goyitney, from New Mexico, graduated from Carlisle in 1901 and then attended Bloomsbury Normal School. Her married name was Canfield, and in 1909 she and her husband were teaching at Zuni. In 1913 and for several years thereafter, she worked at the Paraje Day School at Casa Blanca on the Laguna Reservation.

GRAY, STAND WATIE (Cherokee)

Stand Watie Gray, from the Indian Territory, served as a delegate to Washington. He married Electa Victoria Bertholf and made his home in Canadian District, Cherokee Nation. He died in December, 1896.

GRAYSON, GEORGE WASHINGTON (Creek)

George Washington Grayson was born near Eufaula, Creek Nation, in 1843, the son of James and Jennie Wynn Grayson. He attended Creek public schools, Asbury Manual Labor School, and Arkansas College at Fayetteville. He served as national treasurer for eight years and delegate to Washington several times. He was also a member of the House of Warriors and a delegate to the International Council at Okmulgee. In 1877 he edited the "Creek Department" of the Indian Journal, of which he was associate editor in 1889. Grayson married Georgiana Stidham. In 1917 he was named Creek chief by the President. He served as chief until his death on December 2, 1920, at which time he was writing a history of his tribe.

GRAYSON, GEORGE WASHINGTON (Creek)

George Washington Grayson was a student at Bacone College in 1922.

GREEN, FLORA (Cherokee)

Flora Green, from the Indian Territory, was a student at the Cherokee Female Seminary in 1854.

GREEN, TZULKO (Navajo)

Tzulko Green was born about 1897. She knew no English when she entered the Phoenix Indian School at the age of seven.

GREENBRIER, ADELINE (Menominee)

Adeline Greenbrier, from Wisconsin, was born about 1891 and graduated from Carlisle in 1910. Her married name was Shawandosa and in 1915 she was living in Cleveland, Ohio.

GREENBRIER, CARLYSLE (Menominee)
Carlysle Greenbrier, born about 1889, was from Wisconsin. She attended Carlisle.

GREENSKY, NAOMI EVELYN (Chippewa)
Naomi Evelyn Greensky, from Micada, Michigan, was born about 1891 and graduated from Carlisle in 1915. After graduating, she worked for a family in Bay City, Michigan, and attended high school.

GREENWAY, MINNIE (Cherokee)
Minnie Greenway, from the Indian Territory, was the daughter of Andrew Jackson and Lucy Riley Greenway. She was a student at the Indian University in 1882.

GREGG, CLARK (Assiniboin)
Gregg Clark, from the Fort Peck Reservation in Montana, graduated from Carlisle in 1895.

GREGORY, JAMES ROANE (Yuchi)
James Roane Gregory was born near Coweta, Creek Nation, on January 11, 1842, the son of Edward W. and Eliza Roane Gregory. He was educated in the mission schools of the nation, served in the Union Army during the Civil War, farmed, ran a ferry, and finally settled near Inola in 1883. He served as a member of the Creek National Council, an interpreter, judge of Coweta District, and superintendent of schools for the Creek Nation. He married Anna Johns and was an active Mason.

GRITTS, DANIEL (Cherokee)
Daniel Gritts was born in 1851 in the Cherokee Nation, the son of Blackhawk and Alie. He died in 1906.

GRUMBOISE, EMMA (Chippewa)
Emma Grumboise, born about 1891, attended Carlisle.

GUY, JAMES HARRIS (Chickasaw)
James Harris Guy, from the Indian Territory, was the son of William Guy. He was a deputy U. S. marshal and a member of the Indian police force in the Chickasaw Nation. He was killed in a gun battle with outlaws on May 1, 1885. He supposedly wrote a great deal of poetry, but apparently little of it has survived.

HALFBREED, RICHARD (Cherokee)
Richard Halfbreed, a Cherokee from the Indian Territory, was the son of Jesse and Jennie Fields Halfbreed.

HAMILTON, JOSEPH H. (Piegan)
Joseph H. Hamilton, a Piegan, was a Carlisle graduate of 1892.

HAMILTON, ROBERT J. (Piegan)
Robert J. Hamilton, from the Blackfoot Reservation in Montana, attended Carlisle. He made his home near Browning. For a

while, he was a clerk in a trading house and then ranched. He was active in tribal affairs, urging his people to attend nonreservation schools. In 1925, he was elected to the Business Council of the Blackfoot tribe from the Browning District.

HAMLIN, GEORGE (Chippewa)
George Hamlin, from Mahnomen on the White Earth Reservation in Minnesota, graduated from Hampton in 1903. He died in 1905.

HAMMONDS, JAMES P. (Yuma)
James P. Hammonds graduated from the Phoenix Indian School in 1904 and then went to work in Los Angeles.

HARDY, JAMES ORA (Seneca)
James Ora Hardy of Tiff City, Missouri, was born about 1896 in the Indian Territory. The son of Mrs. Susan Whitecrow Hardy, he graduated from Chilocco in 1923.

HARDY, PERCY (Seneca)
Percy Hardy of Tiff City, Missouri, was born in the Indian Territory on January 22, 1900. The son of Mrs. Susan Whitecrow Hardy, he graduated from Chilocco in 1920.

HARE, DE WITT (Sioux)
De Witt Hare was a newspaper editor in North Dakota, and in 1918 he lived in Minneapolis. He served as the Y. M. C. A. general secretary for Indians.

HARKINS, GEORGE W. (Chickasaw)
George W. Harkins was the son of Willis J. Harkins, a Choctaw, but lived in the Chickasaw Nation most of his life. He served as Superintendent of the Chickasaw board of education and as delegate to Washington. He was an effective speaker, and his speeches before the U. S. Congress earned him the title of "Rawhide Orator." Harkins died in August, 1890.

HARRIS, ARTHUR T. (Mohave-Apache)
Arthur Harris, of Hayden, Arizona, graduated from the Phoenix Indian School in 1910. He then entered Hampton, from which he graduated in 1916. He returned to the West and went to work for the Jerome Copper Company at Clarksdale.

HARRIS, COLONEL JOHNSON (Cherokee)
Colonel Johnson Harris was born in Georgia on April 19, 1856, the son of William Harris and Susan Collins, the latter of Cherokee descent. After his father died, his mother moved to the Cherokee Nation in the early 1870's. Harris was educated in the common schools of Canadian District and at the Male Seminary. He was married three times--to Nannie E. Fields, daughter of Richard F. Fields; Mary E. Adair, the daughter of William Penn Adair (q. v.); and Mrs. Caroline A. (Hall) Collins. He was elected to the Cherokee Senate in 1881, 1883, 1885, and 1899, serving as its president from 1883 to 1885. He was a delegate to Washington in 1886 and 1895, and in 1891 he was elected principal chief of the nation.

HARRIS, CYRUS (Chickasaw)
Cyrus Harris was born in the Chickasaw Nation in Mississippi, where he received a limited education at Monroe Presbyterian Mission before being sent to an Indian school in Giles County, Tennessee. He served as delegate to Washington in 1854 and in 1856 was elected the first governor of the western Chickasaw Nation, to which post he was reelected four times between 1860 and 1872. He married Kizzia Kemp, Tenesey, and Hettie Frazier. Harris died on January 6, 1888.

HARRIS, DAVID A. (Catawba)
David A. Harris served as chief of the Catawbas. In 1905 he lived at Rodney, South Carolina.

HARRIS, FRANCES (Sac and Fox)
Frances (Fannie) Harris, from Oklahoma, graduated from Carlisle in 1900. She taught at the Ponca School at White Eagle, Oklahoma. In 1903 she moved to St. Louis where her husband was in business. Her married name was Bannister.

HARRIS, GEORGE (Cherokee)
George Harris was born in the Cherokee Nation in 1895, the son of Parker C. Harris. He graduated from Bacone College in 1919.

HARRIS, ROBERT MAXWELL (Chickasaw)
Robert Maxwell Harris was born near Tishomingo, Chickasaw Nation, on April 1, 1850, the son of Joseph D. and Catharine Nail Harris. He attended tribal schools and a private school in Paris, Texas. He farmed, raised stock, and conducted a mercantile business and telephone company. As a public official, he served as a county judge, a sheriff, a member of the legislature, and governor, to which office he was elected in 1896. Under his administration, a new orphan school and a new capitol were built and Bloomfield Academy, which had burned, was rebuilt. He married Incy McCoy and Virginia Wyatt. Harris died on November 11, 1927.

HARRIS, WILLIAM (Creek)
William Harris, a Creek from Oklahoma, graduated from the engineering department of Haskell Institute in 1918.

HART, HOMER (Cheyenne)
Homer Hart was a student at Haskell in 1915.

HASTINGS, WILLIAM WIRT (Cherokee)
William Wirt Hastings was born in Arkansas on December 31, 1866, the son of William Archibald Yell and Louisa J. (Stover) Lynch Hastings, the latter a member of the Cherokee tribe. He was reared at Beatties Prairie, Cherokee Nation and attended Cherokee common schools and the Cherokee Male Seminary, from which he graduated in 1884. After teaching in Cherokee schools for one year, Hastings entered Vanderbilt, receiving a law degree in 1889. He formed a partnership with E. C. Boudinot (q. v.) and served as attorney for the Cherokee Nation. After Oklahoma statehood, he represented the state in Congress for eighteen years. He married Lulu Starr. Hastings died on April 8, 1938.

HAUSER, ANNA (Cheyenne)
Anna Hauser, born about 1891, was a 1913 graduate of Carlisle, after which she attended Metzger College.

HAWKINS, EDNA (Cheyenne)
Edna Hawkins was from Geary, Oklahoma, and graduated from the Chilocco Indian School in 1920.

HAWKINS, KISH (Cheyenne)
Kish Hawkins, a Cheyenne from the Indian Territory, was among the first students to go to Carlisle, from which he graduated in 1889. He then briefly attended Marietta College in Ohio. He made his home at Darlington, Oklahoma, for a number of years. In 1902 he was a clerk in the government store there. In 1916 and 1917, he was the farmer at the Shawnee Indian School at Shawnee, Oklahoma. He later worked at Fort Defiance, Arizona, among the Navajoes.

HAWLEY, ALVIN (Sioux)
Alvin Hawley, from the Fort Peck Reservation in Montana, graduated from Haskell Institute in 1916.

HAYES, HENRY HORACE (Creek)
Henry Horace Hayes, from Sapulpa, Oklahoma, graduated from Carlisle in 1915.

HAYES, JOSEPH WILLIAM (Chickasaw)
Joseph William Hayes was born in the Chickasaw Nation in 1901. He lived at Ada and graduated from Chilocco Indian School in 1923.

HAYES, NOAH (Nez Percé)
Noah Hayes was from Kamiah, Idaho, and graduated from the Chilocco Indian School in 1920.

HAZEN, BESSIE (Chippewa)
Bessie Hazen, a Chippewa, was born in Nevada. She graduated from Haskell Institute in 1916.

HAZLETT, MALCOLM (Caddo)
Malcolm Hazlett, from Fort Cobb, Oklahoma, graduated from Chilocco Indian School in 1920.

HENDERSON, KATE (Sioux)
Kate Henderson, from the Fort Peck Reservation in Montana, was born about 1868, the daughter of One Soldier. She attended Hampton Institute from 1888 to 1891. Her married name was Calvert, and in 1914 she resided in Seattle.

HENDERSON, WILLIAM PENN (Cherokee)
William Penn Henderson was born in the Cherokee Nation, the son of William Henderson and Sabra England. He married Susie Ballard and Eliza Condon Marshall.

HENDRICKS, GEORGE (Cherokee)
George Hendricks, from Bartlesville, Oklahoma, was born in
1901, the son of Alexander Hendricks. He graduated from Chilocco
Indian School in 1925.

HENDRICKS, WILLIAM H. (Cherokee)
William H. Hendricks was born in the eastern Cherokee Nation
on February 28, 1831, the son of William and Susanna Hendricks.
After removal to the West, he attended Park Hill Missionary School
until age twelve, the only formal education he had. During the Civil
War, he served in the Confederate Army. After the war, he farmed
and held political office. He served in both houses of the National
Council, as superintendent of the Insane Asylum, and as an Old Settler Cherokee commissioner. In 1883 he became postmaster at Menard, where he also ran a store and farmed. He was married twice,
to Narcissa Crittenden and Ann Eliza (Linder) Benge.

HERROD, MARY LEWIS (Creek)
Mary Herrod was born in the western Creek Nation in the early
1840's, the daughter of John and Louisa Kernels Lewis. She attended
Tullahassee Mission near present-day Muskogee, Oklahoma, and later
taught there, at Wewogufkee Town, among the Euchees, and at the
Old Agency School. She married Goliath Herrod and settled at North
Fork Town. After his death, Mrs. Herrod returned to teaching and
had a long and distinguished career in the Creek public schools. She
died at Wagoner, Oklahoma, in 1917.

HEWITT, JOHN NAPOLEON BRINTON (Tuscarora)
John Napoleon Brinton Hewitt was born at Lewiston, New York,
on December 16, 1859, the son of David Hewitt and Harriet Brinton
Hewitt, the latter of whom was of Tuscarora descent. He attended
schools in Niagara Falls, Lockport, and Lewiston. He had plans for
a medical career but in 1880 began working for Ermine A. Smith,
whom he helped collect Iroquois myths during the next four years.
When Smith died in 1886, Hewitt was called on by the Bureau of
American Ethnology to help complete Smith's work. Hewitt was associated with the Bureau for a half century, during which time he
wrote extensively on the Six Nations. He was one of the founders of
the American Anthropological Association. He was fluent in Tuscarora, Onondaga, and Mohawk. Hewitt died on October 14, 1937.

HEYL, RICHARD D. (Apache)
Richard D. Heyl was captured in Arizona about 1872 by the
U. S. Army. The child was reared by Colonel Heyl and his family
in the East. Heyl lived in Camden, New Jersey, where he worked
in the office of the assistant engineer of the Amboy Division of the
Pennsylvania Railroad. He married Louise Eaton Odenheimer.

HICKS, CLARA (Cherokee)
Clara Hicks, from the Indian Territory, married Nicholas Mc-
Nair Thornton.

HICKS, ELIJAH (Cherokee)

Elijah Hicks was born in the eastern Cherokee Nation on June 20, 1796, the son of Charles Renatus Hicks, who was principal chief in 1827. In 1822, he served as clerk of the National Council; in 1826-1827, he was president of that body. In 1832, John Ross (q. v.), whose sister Margaret he married, appointed him editor of the Cherokee Phoenix. In 1839, Hicks settled near present-day Claremore, Oklahoma. He was one of the framers of the 1839 constitution and was several times a delegate to Washington. Hicks died on August 6, 1856.

HICKS, WILLIAM (Cherokee)
William Hicks was born in the eastern Cherokee Nation, the son of Nathan Hicks, a Scots trader, and Nancy, the daughter of Broom. Hicks was the second chief of the Cherokees to serve under the Constitution of 1827, having finished the term of his brother, who died in office.

HIGHEAGLE, ROBERT P. (Sioux)
Robert P. Higheagle was an 1895 graduate of Hampton Institute. He became a teacher at Lower Brule and later became assistant clerk at Standing Rock. He reentered the teaching field at Bull Head, South Dakota, on the Standing Rock Reservation and remained there for about two decades. During this time, he also assisted in the work of the Bureau of American Ethnology on the music of the Teton Sioux. Higheagle married Mary Louisa Ribble.

HILL, JESSE (Seneca)
Jesse Hill, a native of New York, attended Hampton Institute.

HILLMAN, LEVI (Oneida)
Levi Hillman was from Wisconsin and attended Carlisle.

HODGE, DAVID McKILLOP (Creek)
David McKillop Hodge was born in the Creek Nation, the son of Nathaniel and Nancy McKillop Hodge. He assisted Mrs. A. E. W. Robertson of Tulluhassee Mission in translating many works into Creek. In 1905, he was a delegate to the Sequoyah Constitutional Convention.

HODJKISS, WILLIAM D. (Sioux)
William D. Hodjkiss, from the Cheyenne River Reservation, served as clerk at Cheyenne, Arapaho, and Quapaw agencies.

HOLMES, FRANK (Chippewa)
Frank Holmes, from the Bad River Reservation in Wisconsin, was born about 1890. He graduated from Carlisle in 1913. He then went to the normal school at Valparaiso, Indiana, and in the fall of 1915 entered Haskell Institute.

HOWARD, BARNEY (Pima)
Barney Howard was born at Sacaton on the Gila River Reservation in Arizona. He attended the Sacaton Indian School.

HOXIE, SARA (Noamlaki)
Sara Hoxie was born at Covelo, California. She attended the Round Valley school and then entered the Phoenix Indian School from which she graduated in 1907.

HOXIE, WILLIAM (Mission)
William Hoxie taught at the Sac and Fox school at Stroud, Oklahoma.

HUDSON, FRANK (Pueblo)
Frank Hudson of Laguna Pueblo graduated from Carlisle in 1896. While at Carlisle, he received great public notice as a drop kicker in football. After graduation, he moved to Pittsburgh, Pennsylvania, returned to Carlisle in 1901 as an assistant coach of the football team, and then returned to Pittsburgh once more, where in 1903 he was assistant bookkeeper at the City Deposit Bank.

HUGHES, EULA A. (Chickasaw)
Eula Hughes was born about 1898, the daughter of Mrs. Mamie Hughes, from Tishomingo; she graduated from Chilocco Indian School in 1920.

HUGHES, MARTHA (Pima)
Martha Hughes graduated from the Phoenix Indian School in 1914.

HUNT, EVELYN (Pueblo)
Evelyn Hunt was a student at Haskell Institute in 1915.

HUNTER, LUCY E. (Winnebago)
Lucy E. Hunter graduated from Hampton in 1915 and entered the Training School for Christian Workers in New York.

IGNATIUS, JOE MACK (Potawatomi)
Joe Mack Ignatius was Chief of the Prairie Band of Potawatomies in Kansas.

INGALLS, SADIE M. (Sac and Fox)
Sadie M. Ingalls, born in the Indian Territory about 1889, was a 1913 graduate of Carlisle, after which she attended Metzger College for a short time before returning to her home at Cushing, Oklahoma.

ISHAM, IRA O. (Chippewa)
Ira Isham, a Lac Court Oreilles Chippewa, was born about 1857, the son of Ira Isham. He was a tribal interpreter at Reserve, Wisconsin, on the Lac Court Orielles Reservation and a fighter for his tribe's rights.

ISRAEL, ELLA (Cherokee)
Ella Israel, a Cherokee, was the daughter of William M. and Sallie Israel. She graduated from Carlisle in 1915 and went on to high school in Narberth, Pennsylvania.

IVEY, AUGUSTUS E. (Cherokee)
Augustus E. Ivey was born in the Cherokee Nation in 1855, the son of James W. and Charlotte Ivey. His father was white and his mother was of Cherokee descent. He married Julia A. Sixkiller. He was by profession a newspaper man. In the 1890's, he edited the Tahlequah Telephone. In 1910 he published the Indian Home and Farm Journal at Muskogee in English, Cherokee, Creek, and Choctaw.

JACKSON, ALFRED (Pima)
Alfred Jackson, born about 1896, was from Sacaton, Arizona, and graduated from the printing department of the Phoenix Indian School.

JACKSON, BERNARD S. (Yuma)
Bernard S. Jackson was born on the Yuma Reservation in California in 1886. He had a traditional upbringing until 1895 when he was sent to school. He entered the Phoenix Indian School in 1904 and graduated in 1908 from the engineering department. He went to work for the Yuma Water and Light Company. In 1921, he was working for the Southern Pacific Railroad.

JACKSON, CHARLES (Chippewa)
Charles Jackson lived near Cloquet, Minnesota.

JACKSON, EMMA (Klamath)
Emma Jackson graduated from the Phoenix Indian School in 1904 and then attended Hampton Institute until 1907. Her married name was Wilson.

JACKSON, HELEN (Pima)
Helen Jackson graduated from the Phoenix Indian School in 1905. She married Louis Nelson and lived at Vahki, Arizona.

JACKSON, ROBERT (Chehalis)
Robert Jackson graduated from Carlisle in 1896 and became a teacher at Lower Brule. In 1902, he was a teacher at the Santa Fe Indian School.

JACKSON, THOMAS FRED (Pima)
Thomas Fred Jackson graduated from the Phoenix Indian School in 1923.

JAEGER, AGNES R. (Yuma)
Agnes Jaeger graduated from the Phoenix Indian School in 1905. She died that same year.

JAMES, ALICE (Choctaw)
Alice James was from the Choctaw Nation, Indian Territory.

JAMES, FREMONT (Digger)
Fremont James was a student at the Phoenix Indian School in 1909.

JAMES, JULIA (Oneida)
Julia James attended Carlisle.

JAMES, OTWIN (Potawatomi-Kansa)
No information is available.

JAMISON, JACOB M. (Seneca)
Jacob M. Jamison, from the Cattaraugus Reservation in New York, graduated from Carlisle in 1898. He later lived at Gowanda, New York, where he farmed. Jamison married Bertha E. Dye (q. v.).

JEROME, ELMIRA (Chippewa)
Elmira Jerome attended Carlisle. After graduation, she became assistant seamstress at the government school at Fort Totten, North Dakota.

JEROME, MARCELLE (Chippewa)
Marcelle Jerome graduated from the business department of Haskell Institute in 1911.

JOCKS, JOSEPH M. (Mohawk)
Joseph Jocks, from the St. Regis Reservation in New York, was born about 1892 and graduated from Carlisle in 1914. In October of that year, he was killed in a fall from a thirteen-story building where he was working in Toronto.

JOHNS, DELLA MAY (Seneca)
Della May Johns, born about 1887, graduated from Carlisle in 1915.

JOHNS, LILLIAN (Maricopa)
Lillian Johns, from the Gila River Reservation, graduated from the Phoenix Indian School in 1905. She married Lawrence Donahue.

JOHNSON, A. ELLA (Seneca)
A. Ella Johnson, born in New York about 1887, graduated from Carlisle in 1912. She lived in Batavia, New York.

JOHNSON, ELIAS (Tuscarora)
Elias Johnson, of New York, was a chief of the Tuscaroras.

JOHNSON, ELIZA (Pima)
Eliza Johnson, from Blackwater, Arizona, graduated from the Phoenix Indian School in 1914.

JOHNSON, RUTH ADELIA (Seneca)
Ruth Adelia Johnson was from Wyandotte, Oklahoma, and graduated from the Chilocco Indian School in 1920.

JOHNSON, S. ARTHUR (Wyandot)
S. Arthur Johnson, born in the Indian Territory about 1871,

graduated from Carlisle in 1893. In 1895, he worked at the government school at Wyandotte, Indian Territory. In 1902, he was the agency farmer at the Oto Agency, Oklahoma.

JOHNSON, VICTOR H. (Dalles)
Victor H. Johnson, from Washington, graduated from Carlisle in 1904.

JOHNSTON, DOUGLAS HENRY (Chickasaw)
Douglas Henry Johnston was born on October 13, 1856, at Scullyville, Choctaw Nation; he attended school at Tishomingo and Bloomfield Academy. In 1884, he was placed in charge of the Academy. Johnston was married to Nellie Bynum and Bettie Harper.

JONES, FLORA E. (Munsee)
Flora E. Jones, born about 1891, was a student at Carlisle, graduating in 1908.

JONES, FRANK (Sac and Fox)
Frank Jones was born in the Indian Territory, the son of Henry Clay and Sarah E. Penny Jones. He was an 1897 graduate of Carlisle and an 1898 graduate of the normal department of Haskell Institute. He then taught for two years. In 1902, he worked in the First National Bank of Okmulgee, Creek Nation, and later moved to Wellington, Kansas, where he became involved in the milling industry. He specialized in sales promotions and for over two decades developed sales organizations for milling companies throughout the country.

JONES, JOHN (Creek)
John Jones, from Oklahoma, graduated from the Shawnee Indian School at Shawnee, Oklahoma. In 1914, he became clerk at the school, often acting as superintendent in the absence of that official. In 1917, he was transferred as field clerk in the office of Gabe Parker (q. v.), Superintendent for the Five Civilized Tribes. In 1918, he became chief clerk at Pine Ridge. Jones married Maud Pecore, a Chippewa.

JONES, STEPHEN (Sioux)
Stephen Jones was from the Santee Reservation and attended Haskell Institute. He resided at Santee, Nebraska, where he worked as a financial clerk.

JONES, WILLIAM (Sac and Fox)
William Jones was born near present-day Stroud, Oklahoma, in the Sac and Fox reservation on March 28, 1871, the son of Henry Clay and Sarah E. Penny Jones, from whom he inherited a mixture of Fox, English, and Welsh blood. Sarah Jones died when Jones was quite small, and for his first nine years he was raised by his grandmother, Kitiqua, the daughter of the Fox Chief Wa-shi-ho-wa, who taught Jones the traditions, language, and customs of his Fox ancestors. At ten, Jones was sent to Indian school at Newton, Kansas, and later spent three years at the Friends' boarding school in Wabash, Indiana. In 1889, he entered Hampton Institute and later enrolled in

Philips Academy at Andover, Massachusetts. In 1896, he entered
Harvard, where he received his A. B. degree in 1900. He received
his A. M. degree in 1901 and went on to earn a Ph. D. In 1906,
he accepted an assignment from the Field Columbian Museum in Chicago to study the native tribes of the Philippines. He remained there
for three years, living among the native peoples of Luzon. On March
28, 1909, he was speared to death by members of the Ilongot tribe,
whom he was studying.

JORDAN, JOHN W. (Cherokee)
        John W. Jordan was born in the Cherokee Nation in 1861, the
son of Levi and Malinda Jordan. Jordan farmed for a number of
years in Canadian District and then moved to the Cherokee Strip in
the early 1880's and began ranching. When the Cherokee Strip was
opened to settlement in 1893, Jordan and his family received allotments near the town site of Kildare. Jordan married Sallie Bean
Thompson, Martha Rowland, and Tennessee Riley.

JORDAN, PETER JOSEPH (Chippewa)
        Peter Joseph Jordan, born about 1885 in Wisconsin, was a
1914 graduate of Carlisle, after which he attended Keewaton Academy
at Prairie du Chien, where he also coached football.

JOSE, MAGELA (Papago)
        Magela Jose, from Arizona, graduated from the Phoenix Indian
School in 1910, after which she returned to the Papago Reservation.

JUAN, JOSE (Pima)
        Jose Juan, from the Salt River Reservation, attended the Phoe-
nix Indian School.

KAH O SED, E. C. (Chippewa)
        E. C. Kah O Sed, a Chippewa from the White Earth Reserva-
tion in Minnesota, came there from Walpole Island, Ontario. During
the 1920's, he was pastor at St. Columba's Episcopal Mission at
White Earth.

KAKAQUE, MARY (Potawatomi)
        Mary Kakaque, from Oklahoma, was a student at Haskell Insti-
tute in 1915.

KALAMA, FRANCIS (Puyallup)
        Francis Kalama, from Oregon, graduated from Haskell Institute
in 1915.

KALKA, JOSE (Pima)
        Jose Kalka was a student at the Phoenix Indian School in 1905.

KANARD, BETTIE (Creek)
        Bettie Kanard was born in 1899 at Schulter, Creek Nation, the
daughter of Washington and Fannie Watson Kanard. She graduated
from Bacone College in 1920.

KATE, CLARA M. (Hopi)
Clara M. Kate attended the Phoenix Indian School.

KEALEAR, CHARLES H. (Sioux)
Charles H. Kealear, a Yankton from South Dakota, received several years of education at the Episcopal mission at the Yankton agency and at Jubilee, Illinois, before entering Carlisle. In 1888, he attended Moody's School at Northfield, Massachusetts, and graduated from Hampton Institute the following year. After graduation, he assisted in the mission on the Standing Rock Reservation, worked as an industrial teacher at the government school there, taught at St. Paul's School, and then went to Genoa, Nebraska, where he was an employee and a student. In 1892, he moved to Wyoming where he later served as postmaster at Arapaho and worked for the Chicago and Northwestern Railroad. He died in November, 1922.

KELLOGG, LAURA MINNIE CORNELIUS (Oneida)
Laura Minnie Cornelius Kellogg, from Wisconsin, was a graduate of Carlisle.

KELTON, HOMER (Mohave)
Homer Kelton was a student at the Fort Mojave School in 1901.

KENDALL, HENRY J. (Pueblo)
Henry J. Kendall of Isleta Pueblo was born in 1868. He was named for Dr. Henry Kendall, a Presbyterian missionary. He entered Carlisle in 1880 and remained there three years.

KENNAWA, HERB (Mohave)
Herb Kennawa was a student at the Fort Mojave School in 1897.

KENNEDY, ALVIN W. (Seneca)
Alvin W. Kennedy, from Salamanca, New York, was born in 1892. A graduate of Carlisle in 1911, he joined the U. S. Navy and was stationed on the U. S. S. Jenkins and later in the Canal Zone as a wireless operator. He later worked as a telegrapher for the Chicago and Northwestern Railroad at Shawano, Wisconsin. Kennedy married Mary A. Bailey.

KENNEY, LOUISE (Klamath)
Louise Kenney attended Carlisle.

KEOKUK, FANNIE (Sac and Fox)
Fannie Keokuk, born about 1890 in the Indian Territory, attended Carlisle.

KERSHAW, WILLIAM J. (Menominee)
William J. Kershaw, from Wisconsin, was a prominent attorney at Milwaukee. He served as the first vice president of the Society of American Indians. In 1916, he ran for Congress from the Third Congressional District of Wisconsin.

KESHENA, ELIZABETH (Menominee)

Elizabeth Keshena, from Wisconsin, was a 1911 graduate of Carlisle. In 1914, she was working as a clerk at Pipestone, Minnesota.

KEWAYGESHIK, MARY WONITA (Ottawa)
Mary Wonita Kewaygeshik, from Goodheart, Michigan, was a 1915 graduate of Carlisle.

KE-WA-ZE-ZHIG (Chippewa)
No information is available.

KING, BIRDIE (Oneida)
Birdie King, from Wisconsin, was a student at Haskell in 1915.

KING, INEZ M. (Stockbridge)
Inez M. King, from Wisconsin, was a 1902 graduate of Carlisle. After graduation, she became a teacher at the Lutheran Mission School at Stockbridge.

KING, JOHN (Absentee Shawnee)
John King was from the Indian Territory. He attended Hampton Institute from 1879 to 1884.

KING, KENNETH (Sioux)
Kenneth King was born about 1893 at Wolf Point on the Fort Peck Reservation in Montana, the son of Richard King, a Sioux from South Dakota. His mother was white. At age seven, King was sent to mission school in northern Wisconsin. In 1906, he was sent to Park College in Parkville, Missouri, and in 1910, he entered Carlisle, from which he graduated in 1915. After graduation, he attended Haskell Institute.

KING, LEWIS (Chippewa)
Louis King attended Haskell Institute and Bacone College, graduating from the latter in 1919.

KING, MARIE (Oneida)
Marie King, from Wisconsin, graduated from Haskell in 1916.

KINGSLEY, LLEWELLYN (Cheyenne)
Llewellyn Kingsley was from Cantonment, Oklahoma, and graduated from Chilocco Indian School in 1920.

KINGSLEY, NETTIE MARY (Winnebago)
Nettie Mary Kingsley, born about 1889 in Nebraska, was a 1915 graduate of Carlisle. After graduation, she attended West Chester Normal School.

KIRKE, CLAYTON (Klamath)
Clayton Kirke was born at Yainax, Oregon, in 1883. From 1892 to 1898, he attended the Klamath Agency boarding school. He then worked for a party surveying the Klamath Reservation. In 1900, he attended Carlisle for a short time and then entered the Phoenix Indian School, from which he graduated in 1903.

KIRKE, SELDON (Klamath)
Seldon Kirke was born in 1885. At age six, he began his primary education at home. In 1893, he entered the Klamath boarding school where he remained until 1900 when he went to Carlisle for a short time. Kirke then entered the Phoenix Indian School, graduating in 1903.

KNOCKSOFFTWO, HENRY (Sioux)
Henry Knocksofftwo, from the Rosebud Reservation, attended Carlisle and returned to the West where he farmed on his allotment.

KNUDSON, ELIZABETH E. (Klamath)
Elizabeth E. Knudson, from California, was a 1903 graduate of Carlisle. She married Charles Wilson.

KOHPAY, HARRY (Osage)
Harry Kohpay, from Indian Territory, was an 1891 graduate of Carlisle. He then graduated from Eastman Business College at Poughkeepsie, New York. He made his home at Pawhuska in the Osage Reservation and worked for many years as an interpreter for the Osages. He also served as assistant clerk at the Osage agency at Pawhuska.

KOLLENBAUM, LILLIAN (Sioux)
Lillian Kollenbaum, from the Fort Peck Reservation in Montana, was a student at Haskell in 1916.

LA FLESCHE, FRANCIS (Omaha)
Francis La Flesche was born about 1860 on the Omaha Reservation in Nebraska, the son of Joseph La Flesche, a former head chief of the tribe, and Tianne. His early years were spent in the relative freedom of the Indian camp, where he was carefully taught in the ways and about the subjects that Omaha boys had been taught traditionally. He was then sent to the Presbyterian mission school at Bellevue, Nebraska, and he later went to Washington, D. C., where he worked as a clerk in the Bureau of Indian Affairs from 1881 to 1910. In 1881, he interpreted for Alice C. Fletcher, who undertook a study of the Omaha tribe and with whom he collaborated for years. He also studied law at the National University Law School in Washington, receiving his LL. B. in 1892 and his LL. M. in 1893. In 1910, La Flesche became an ethnologist for the Bureau of American Ethnology, in which capacity he served until his death on September 5, 1932. He was married to Alice Mitchell and Rosa Bourassa (q. v.).

LA FLESCHE, SUSAN see PICOTTE, SUSAN LA FLESCHE

LA FLESCHE, SUSETTE (Omaha)
Susette La Flesche (Bright Eyes) was born on the Omaha Reservation in Nebraska in 1854, the daughter of Joseph La Flesche (Iron Eyes) and Mary Gale La Flesche. She attended mission school and the Elizabeth Institute for Young Ladies in New Jersey. She taught school on the reservation and toured the East, lecturing for

reform in Indian policy, particularly regarding the Poncas. With her husband, Thomas H. Tibbles, she toured Scotland in 1881. During the 1890's, she lived in Washington, D. C. Her last years were spent in Lincoln, Nebraska. She died in May, 1903.

LAMERE, OLIVER (Winnebago)
No information is available.

LAMOUREAUX, CALVIN (Sioux)
Calvin Lamoureaux was a student at Carlisle in 1914.

LAND, VERNOLA (Chickasaw)
Vernola Land, from Roff, Oklahoma, was a 1924 graduate of Bacone College.

LANDRUM, ELIAS M. (Cherokee)
Elias M. Landrum, from the Indian Territory, was born about 1866. He served as judge of Delaware District, and, in 1932, he was elected treasurer of Delaware County, Oklahoma. In 1934, he was elected the county's judge.

LANDRUM, HIRAM TERRELL (Cherokee)
Hiram Terrell Landrum was born in the Cherokee Nation, the son of Hiram Terrell and Mary Muskrat Landrum.

LANE, HELEN (Lummi)
Helen Lane attended Carlisle.

LANG, HENRY (Skagit)
Henry Lang attended Cushman Trade School, Tacoma Washington.

LARGO, ANTHONY (Mission)
Anthony Largo, from California, graduated from the Phoenix Indian School in 1906 and then from Hampton Institute. He returned to the West in 1909 and worked at Phoenix. He married Sarah Valenzuela.

LARIVER, FRANK (Chippewa)
Frank Lariver graduated from Chilocco Indian School in 1911.

LASSA, NICHOLAS (Flathead)
Nicholas Lassa, from the Flathead Reservation in Montana, graduated from the masonry department of Haskell Institute in 1921.

LA VATTA, EMMA (Bannock)
Emma La Vatta, born about 1890 on the Fort Hall Reservation, Idaho, was a 1911 graduate of Carlisle. After graduation, she settled at Pocatello and married Alphonso Hutch of Fort Hall.

LA VATTA, GEORGE (Shoshoni)
George La Vatta, born about 1894, attended Carlisle.

LA VATTA, ISABEL (Shoshoni)
Isabel La Vatta attended Carlisle.

LA VATTA, PHILIP (Shoshoni)
Philip La Vatta, from the Fort Hall Reservation in Idaho, attended Carlisle. He lived at Pocatello in 1896 and worked in the office of the Idaho Herald.

LAY, THERESA (Seneca)
Theresa Lay, from Irving, New York, was a 1915 graduate of Carlisle. After graduation, she returned to New York, where she became a music teacher at Buffalo.

LEARY, EVELYN (Iowa)
Evelyn Leary, from Kansas, was a 1920 graduate of the home economics department of Haskell Institute.

LEE, LILLY (Cherokee)
Lilly Lee, from the Indian Territory, was a student at the Cherokee Female Seminary in 1855.

LEEDS, YAMIE (Pueblo)
Yamie Leeds, from Laguna Pueblo, was an 1891 graduate of Carlisle. After graduation, he returned to the Laguna Reservation where he farmed and raised stock at Cubero, New Mexico.

LEFLORE, CAMPBELL (Choctaw)
Campbell Leflore was born in the Choctaw country in Mississippi in 1830, the son of Ben Leflore. In 1852, he was one of the Choctaw commissioners sent to persuade his remaining tribesmen in Mississippi to emigrate to the West. In his early years in the West, he lived at Skullyville, Choctaw Nation, but in the 1870's he moved to Fort Smith, Arkansas. He was a delegate to the Okmulgee Convention in 1870. Leflore was a lawyer, often representing the Choctaw Nation, and was a delegate to Washington for sixteen years. He was married to Josephine V. Wilder and Louisa Tebbets. He died in 1896.

LEICHER, FRED (Stockbridge)
Fred Leicher, born about 1893, attended Carlisle.

LEIDER, CARL (Crow)
Carl Leider, from Montana, was an 1890 graduate of Carlisle. He ranched and worked as an interpreter and a surveyor. In 1902, he was employed at the Crow agency.

LEVERING, LEVI (Omaha)
Levi Levering, from Nebraska, was an 1890 graduate of Carlisle. He then attended Bellevue College in Nebraska. Levering entered the Indian service as a teacher and taught for a number of years on the Fort Hall Reservation in Montana. In 1912, he was appointed superintendent at the Nuyaka Boarding School at Beggs, Oklahoma. By 1915, he had returned to Nebraska and settled at Macy.

LEWIS, ANNIE (Pima)
Annie Lewis was a student at the Phoenix Indian School in 1909.

LEWIS, JOSE (Papago)
Jose Lewis attended Haskell Institute.

LEWIS, ROBERT (Pima)
Robert Lewis, from Blackwater, Arizona, graduated from the Phoenix Indian School in 1905. In 1908, he was in charge of the printing of The Native American, published at the school. And in 1914, he and his wife worked at the Cheyenne and Arapaho boarding school at Darlington, Oklahoma, and in 1921 he lived at Pawnee, Oklahoma. He served as band leader and disciplinarian.

LEWIS, SIMON (Pima)
Simon Lewis graduated from the Phoenix Indian School in 1910. He then took a literary and printing course at Hampton Institute, from which he graduated in 1914.

LOCKE, VICTOR MURAT, JR. (Choctaw)
Victor Murat Locke, Jr., was born at Fort Towson, Choctaw Nation, on March 23, 1876, the son of Victor Murat and Susan Pricilla McKinney Locke. He attended local schools, Austin College at Sherman, Texas, and Drury College at Springfield, Missouri. He was a veteran of the Spanish American War and World War I, in which he reached the rank of major. From 1911 to 1918, he was principal chief of the Choctaws. He later served as superintendent for the Five Civilized Tribes. Locke made his home at Antlers, Oklahoma.

LOGAN, HOWARD G. (Winnebago)
Howard G. Logan, from Nebraska, was an 1890 graduate of Carlisle. After graduation, he returned to Nebraska, where he worked as County Surveyor in Thurston County. He died at his home in Winnebago on May 19, 1892, at the age of twenty-one.

LOLORIAS, JOHN (Papago)
John Lolorias attended Hampton Institute.

LONDROSH, CECILIA (Winnebago)
Cecelia Londrosh, from Nebraska, was an 1889 graduate of Carlisle. She married Louis Maurice Herman, and she and her husband made their home in Sioux City, Iowa.

LONE WOLF, DELOS (Kiowa)
Delos Lone Wolf, from the Indian Territory, was an 1896 graduate of Carlisle. After graduation, he returned to the Indian Territory where he farmed and worked as an interpreter for Chief Lone Wolf and instituted a number of lawsuits in behalf of the Kiowas to protect their rights during allotment and dissolution of the Kiowa Reservation. He married Ida Wasee, and they lived near Rainy Mountain School.

LONG, SYLVESTER (Cherokee)
Sylvester Long, from North Carolina, attended Carlisle.

LONG WOLF, HATTIE (Sioux)
Hattie Long Wolf, an Oglala from the Pine Ridge Reservation, was the daughter of Long Wolf, who died in England in 1892 while on tour with a Wild West show. Hattie Long Wolf graduated from Carlisle in 1892. She married Pretty Weasel and lived on the Cheyenne River Reservation, South Dakota.

LOWREY, GEORGE (Cherokee)
George Lowrey was born in the eastern Cherokee Nation about 1770, the son of George and Nannie Lowrey. He was one of the early members of the Presbyterian Church at Willstown. He was a veteran of the War of 1812. Lowrey translated parts of the Book of Isaiah into Cherokee, and he and his son-in-law David Brown were working on a Cherokee spelling book in English characters when Sequoyah announced his syllabary. After removal, Lowrey lived at Park Hill and was actively involved in Cherokee affairs. Lowrey served as assistant principal chief from 1843 to 1851. He married Lucy Benge. Lowrey died on October 20, 1852.

LOWRY, KATHERINE C. (Washo)
Katherine C. Lowry was born in the Shasta Mountains in California on July 26, 1889. She attended local schools until she was sent to the Greenville, California, Indian school, where she remained for three years. In 1904, she entered the Phoenix Indian School from which she graduated in 1908.

LUGO, FRANCISCO (Mission)
Francisco Lugo, from California, graduated from the Phoenix Indian School in 1905.

LUGO, PATRICIO (Mission)
Patricio Lugo, from California, attended St. Boniface School at Banning, California. In 1899, he entered the Phoenix Indian School from which he graduated in 1902. He died that same year.

LUJAN, MAX (Pueblo)
Max Lujan attended Haskell Institute.

LYMAN, ANNIE (Sioux)
Annie Lyman, from the Yankton Reservation, was born about 1863, the daughter of W. P. Lyman. She attended Hampton Institute from 1879 to 1881. She married Thomas Arrow.

McADAMS, JAMES C. (Shoshoni)
James McAdams was from the Wind River Reservation in Wyoming.

McAFEE, JOHNSON (Pima)
Johnson McAfee graduated from the Phoenix Indian School in 1916 and attended Phoenix Union High School.

McARTHUR, NELLIE (Pima)
Nellie McArthur graduated from the Phoenix Indian School in 1914.

McCARTY, ADAM (Modoc)
Adam McCarty attended Carlisle.

McCOMBS, WILLIAM (Creek)
William McCombs was born on July 22, 1844, the son of Samuel and Susan Stinson McCombs, the latter a mixed Cherokee and Creek. He attended public schools in the Creek Nation until the outbreak of the Civil War, at which time he joined the Confederate regiment of D. N. McIntosh. After the war, McCombs served four years in the House of Warriors, six years as Superintendent of Public Instruction, and for years as a Supreme Court judge. McCombs also served as Superintendent of Eufaula High School and as interpreter for Chief Pleasant Porter. He was instrumental in the founding of Bacone College at Muskogee. McCombs was an ordained Baptist minister, preaching in Creek at Tuskegee Church west of Eufaula. He married Sallie Jacobs. McCombs died on December 28, 1929.

McCOY, JOHN LOWREY (Cherokee)
John Lowrey McCoy was born on December 21, 1812, in the eastern Cherokee Nation, the son of No-na. He had a limited formal education but was self-educated. He removed to the West in 1835 and was one of the first delegates to Washington for the Old Settler Cherokees. As a delegate, he spent a number of years in Washington and was one of the signers of the Cherokee Treaty of 1846. He married Charlotte Ratliff, Emma Bennett, and Lucy Jane Adair. McCoy died on February 3, 1892.

McCOY, PAULINE (Sac and Fox)
Pauline McCoy was from the Indian Territory. She graduated from Haskell Institute in 1902 and became a kindergarten teacher.

McCURTAIN, BEN F. (Choctaw)
Ben F. McCurtain was born in the Choctaw Nation in 1876, the son of Green McCurtain.

McCURTAIN, DAVID CORNELIUS (Choctaw)
David Cornelius McCurtain was born at Skullyville, Choctaw Nation, on January 29, 1873, the son of Green and Martha Ainsworth McCurtain. He was educated in the Choctaw common schools, Roanoke College, Kemper Military School, University of Missouri Law School, and Columbian University in Washington, D. C. He served as clerk of the district court from Moshulatubbee District, two terms as District Attorney, delegate to Washington, and, from 1907 to 1912, Choctaw attorney. In 1911, he was appointed by the President to fill the vacancy left by his father as Chief of the Choctaws. After Oklahoma statehood, he practiced law in Poteau and was County Attorney and County Judge of Leflore County. From 1925 to 1935, he was Judge of the Fifth Judicial District of Oklahoma. He was married to Kate N. Mitchell and Mrs. Kate H. Partridge.

McCURTAIN, EDMUND (Choctaw)
Edmund McCurtain was born near Fort Coffee, Choctaw Nation, on June 4, 1842, the son of Cornelius and Mahayia McCurtain. During the Civil War, he served in the First Regiment of Choctaw and Chickasaw Mounted Rifles (Confederate). After the war, he made his home at San Bois. He served in various capacities such as County Judge, trustee of the schools, representative to the National Council, Senator, and Superintendent of Education. In 1884, he replaced his brother Jackson (q. v.) as Principal Chief and served two terms. McCurtain died November 9, 1890. He was married to Harriet Austin and Clarissa LeFlore.

McCURTAIN, GREEN (Choctaw)
Green McCurtain was born at Skullyville, Choctaw Nation, on November 28, 1848, the son of Cornelius and Mahayia McCurtain. He attended the common schools of the Nation. McCurtain served as sheriff of Skullyville County, three terms as a representative to the National Council, trustee of schools for his district, District Attorney, two terms as Treasurer, and one as a Senator. He served two terms as Principal Chief beginning in 1896 and was reelected in 1902, that time serving until his death on December 27, 1910. McCurtain was married to Martha A. Ainsworth and Kate Spring.

McCURTAIN, JACKSON FRAZIER (Choctaw)
Jackson Frazier McCurtain was born in the Choctaw Nation, Mississippi, on March 4, 1830, the son of Cornelius and Mahayia McCurtain. He attended Spencer Academy in the western Choctaw Nation. During the Civil War, he served in the First Regiment of Choctaw and Chickasaw Mounted Rifles (Confederate), reaching the rank of lieutenant colonel. After the war, he lived at his home "The Narrows" near Red Oak. He had served as a representative to the National Council from Sugar Loaf County in 1859, and he served as a Senator from there from 1866 to 1880. He served out the term of Chief Garvin, who died, and, in 1882, was elected to a full term. In 1884, he went back to the Senate from Wade County and that year became one of the incorporators of the Choctaw Oil and Refining Company. McCurtain died on November 14, 1885. He was married to Marie Riley and Jane Frances Austin.

McDERMOTT, JESSE J. (Creek)
Jesse J. McDermott was born near Eufaula, Creek Nation, about 1880, the son of Daniel Thompson. Orphaned when he was an infant, he was reared by an uncle, Paddy McDermott. He attended Creek public schools and the Indian High School at Eufaula and then attended business college in Fort Smith, Arkansas, where he became a stenographer. In 1905, he became an interpreter for the Dawes Commission and later worked as interpreter in the Chief's office. A member of the old Hickory Town clan, he was much interested in the history of his people. McDermott was an admirer of the works of Alexander Posey (q. v.).

McDONALD, LOUIS (Ponca)
Louis McDonald attended Carlisle from 1896 to 1901. After graduation, he returned to Oklahoma and lived at Ponca City.

McFARLAND, DAVID (Nez Percé)
David McFarland, from Idaho, graduated from Carlisle in 1898. After graduation, he made his home at Fort Lapwai, where he farmed and raised livestock.

McGAA, AGNES (Sioux)
Agnes McGaa was a student at Chilocco Indian School in 1909.

McGILBERRY, CHARLES W. (Choctaw)
Charles W. McGilberry was born in the Choctaw Nation in 1891, the son of Abel McGilberry. He graduated from Chilocco Indian School in 1914 and from Mercerburg in 1917. He entered Princeton that fall as a Wanamaker scholar but was drafted into the army.

McGILBRA, SANFORD (Creek)
Sanford McGilbra was born at Eufaula, Creek Nation, in 1901, the son of Lewis and Leah Green McGilbra. He was a 1924 graduate of Bacone College.

McINNIS, JOHN (Washo)
John McInnis, born about 1888, attended Carlisle.

McINTOSH, ALBERT GALLATIN (Creek)
Albert Gallatin (Cheesie) McIntosh was born in the Creek Nation on January 27, 1848, the son of Daniel N. and Jane Ward McIntosh. In 1862, he was sent to Texas to school. He returned to the Creek Nation but, in 1874, moved to Texas and then to Smith County, Tennessee, where he took the name of James Gentry Brown, practiced law at Carthage, and served for eight years as County Superintendent of Schools. While there, he married Mollie B. Boulton. About 1901, he moved his family to the Creek Nation, reassumed his name, and enrolled himself and his children in the tribe. He served as Superintendent of Schools for the Creek Nation and was a delegate to the Sequoyah Convention in 1905. From 1907 to 1911, he was Superintendent of Schools for McIntosh County, Oklahoma. He also practiced law. McIntosh died at Checotah on August 8, 1915.

McINTOSH, JEANETTA (Creek)
Jeanetta McIntosh was born in 1899 at Eufaula, Creek Nation, the daughter of Bunnie and Leah McIntosh. She graduated from Bacone College in 1922.

McINTOSH, LUKE G. (Creek)
Luke G. McIntosh was born in the Creek Nation, the son of Chillie and Leah McIntosh. In 1881, he was appointed postmaster at Hillabee. He married P. H. Raiford and later made his home at Eufaula. McIntosh died in November, 1912.

McINTOSH, ROBERT (Apache)
Robert McIntosh (Naki, or Firy Bob), from the San Carlos Reservation, was born about 1860. He attended Hampton Institute from 1881 to 1884. He served as a U. S. Scout. McIntosh died at San Carlos on May 31, 1914.

McKELLOP, ALBERT PIKE (Creek)
    Albert Pike McKellop was born at Choska, Creek Nation, on
September 25, 1858, the son of James McKellop. He was educated
at Tullahassee Mission and Wooster University at Wooster, Ohio,
which he attended from 1876 to 1881. In 1881, he became Clerk of
the House of Warriors, in which capacity he served for over a decade.
In 1882, he was National Tax Collector and, in 1889, a member of
the Board of Examiners for Indian teachers. He served as well as
Attorney General of the Creek Nation. In 1905, he was a Creek delegate to the Sequoyah Constitutional Convention and, in 1906, he was
one of the organizers of the Alamo Savings Bank of Muskogee.

McKINNEY, THOMPSON (Choctaw)
    Thompson McKinney (Red Pine) served as the Choctaw delegate
to Washington for several years and as Principal Chief of the Choctaws from 1886 through 1888.

McLAUGHLIN, MARIE L. (Sioux)
    Marie L. McLaughlin was born at Wabasha, Minnesota, on
December 8, 1842, the daughter of Joseph and Mary Graham Buisson,
the latter of the Medakawakanton Band of the Sioux. At age fourteen,
she was sent to school at Prairie du Chien, Wisconsin. She married
Major James McLaughlin, an Indian agent who served at Devil's Lake,
North Dakota, and then at the Standing Rock agency. In later years,
Mrs. McLaughlin lived at McLaughlin, South Dakota.

McLEAN, SAMUEL J. (Sioux)
    Samuel J. McLean graduated from Carlisle in 1909. After
graduation, he worked as a blacksmith before taking a position in
1913 as art and penmanship teacher at St. Mary's Mission near Omak,
Washington.

McLEMORE, GUSSIE (Cherokee)
    Gussie McLemore, from Oklahoma, was a student at Haskell
Institute in 1915.

MADDOX, SARAH (Modoc)
    Sarah Maddox was born at Somes Bar, California, on Novem-
ber 26, 1889. She first attended the Hoopa Valley Indian School and,
in 1901, entered the Phoenix Indian School, from which she graduated
in 1907. She then took a preparatory course and entered Phoenix High
School. She died that same year.

MADRID, SAVANNAH (Pueblo)
    Savannah Madrid was a student at Haskell Institute in 1915.

MANUEL, VICTOR (Pima)
    Victor Manuel graduated from the Phoenix Indian School in
1906 and then attended Hampton Institute until 1911. In 1911-1912,
he attended Eastman College, where he studied commercial law, book-
keeping, shorthand, and typing. In 1912, he became the manager of
the eastern agency of the Francis E. Lister Company at Lake Mohonk,
New York. He returned to the Salt River Reservation in 1914 and

became a printer for the Watkins Printing Company at Phoenix, a position he held for some years. He married Tomasa Holmes.

MAQUIMITIS, MITCHELL (Menominee)
Mitchell Maquimities (or Marquemitis, and also called Michael Maquimetas) was born about 1861 on the Menominee Reservation in Wisconsin, the son of Makimitis. He attended Hampton Institute from 1879 to 1883, when he was sent home for an infraction of the rules. He later returned and graduated in 1887. Maquimitis returned to the Menominee Reservation and followed his trade as a wheelwright and worked as a logger.

MARISTO, MARTIN (Papago)
Martin Maristo was a student at the Phoenix Indian School from 1909 to 1911.

MARSDEN, EDWARD (Tsimshian)
Edward Marsden was born on May 19, 1869, in northern British Columbia, the son of a native evangelist. He entered day school at New Metlakatlah in 1880. His family moved to Alaska, and, in 1888, Marsden went to Sitka to resume his studies. He came to the United States in 1891. He graduated from Marietta College in Ohio in 1891 and later studied medicine and law. He returned to Alaska in 1898 as a Presbyterian missionary at Saxman.

MARTIN, JOE (Pima)
Joe Martin was a farmer and an adobe builder from Gila Crossing, Arizona. In 1915, he assisted in the construction of the dining hall and dormitory at the St. John School at Gila Crossing.

MARTIN, JOHN (Cherokee)
John Martin was born on October 20, 1781, in the eastern Cherokee Nation, the son of Joseph and Susannah Emory Martin. He was a wealthy and influential man before removal. He was a member of the Cherokee Constitutional Convention of 1827 and served as the Nation's Treasurer and first Chief Justice. He married Nellie McDaniel and Lucy McDaniel. Martin died at Fort Gibson on October 17, 1840.

MARTIN, JOSEPH LYNCH (Cherokee)
Joseph L. Martin was born at the Cherokee town of Narcoochi, in present-day Habersham County, Georgia, in 1817, the son of John and Nellie McDaniel Martin. He was educated in mission schools and at St. Louis. In the West, he made his home at Green Brier on Grand River. During the Civil War, he commanded a company of cavalry in Bryan's Confederate Regiment. Martin was married to Julia Lombard, Sallie Childers, Lucy Brown Rogers, Caroline Garrett, and Jennie Harlin. Known in later life as "Greenbrier Joe," Martin died on November 6, 1891.

MASON, MARIE (Digger)
Marie Mason was a 1915 graduate of Carlisle.

MAYES, JOEL BRYAN (Cherokee)
Joel Bryan Mayes was born in the Cherokee Nation in Georgia on October 2, 1833, the son of Samuel and Nancy Mayes. He attended Cherokee common schools and the Cherokee Male Seminary, from which he graduated in 1855. He taught school for two years and then began ranching in Cooweescoowee District. During the Civil War, he reached the rank of major in the Confederate Army. Following the war, after a brief stay in the Choctaw Nation, he returned to the Cherokee Nation and took up ranching once more. He served as clerk of Cooweescoowee District, Circuit Judge, and Justice of the Supreme Court. In 1887, he was elected Principal Chief and was reelected in 1891. He died shortly after his reelection on December 14, 1891.

MAYES, SAMUEL HOUSTON (Cherokee)
Samuel Houston Mayes was born in the Cherokee Nation near present-day Stilwell, Oklahoma, on May 11, 1845. He was the son of Samuel and Nancy Mayes. He attended tribal schools and, though a youth, joined the Confederate Army. After the Civil War, he remained in Texas, attending school in Rusk County. In 1867, he returned to the Cherokee Nation and began ranching. In 1880, he was elected Sheriff of Cooweescoowee District, and from 1885 through 1891, served as Senator from the district. Like his brother Joel Bryan Mayes (q. v.), he served as Principal Chief, being elected in 1895. He died on December 12, 1927.

MEANS, HOBART W. (Sioux)
Hobart W. Means, from North Dakota, graduated from the commercial department of Haskell Institute in 1923.

MEDICINEGRASS, LUCY (Arapaho)
Lucy Medicinegrass graduated from the Phoenix Indian School in 1914.

MELTON, ANNA (Cherokee)
Anna Melton was born in the Cherokee Nation in 1892, the daughter of William T. and Louisa G. Melton. She was a 1912 graduate of Carlisle. She then attended St. Mary's Academy at Sacred Heart, Oklahoma, and, in 1914, began teaching in a rural school near Grove, Oklahoma.

MERRICK, RICHENDA (Cheyenne)
Richenda Merrick was a student at Haskell in 1915.

MERRILL, GEORGE (Chippewa)
George Merrill, born about 1890, was a student at Carlisle from 1910 to 1914.

MERRILL, SUSIE (Klamath)
Susie Merrill was born in 1884 in northern California. She attended public school for two years and then went to the Hoopa Valley Indian School. In 1898, she entered the Phoenix Indian School, from which she graduated in 1903. She died that same year.

METOXEN, ANNA (Oneida)

Anna Metoxen, from Wisconsin, was born about 1893, the daughter of Simon W. and Lavinia Metoxen. She attended Haskell Institute.

METOXEN, DAISY (Oneida)

Daisy Metoxen was born in 1896 on the Oneida lands in Wisconsin, the daughter of Adam and Sophia Metoxen. She graduated from the Home Economics department of Haskell Institute in 1918.

METOXEN, EVELYN (Oneida)

Evelyn (or Evaline) Metoxen was born on the Oneida lands in Wisconsin on June 6, 1901, the daughter of Nelson and Louisa Metoxen. She graduated from the Home Economics department of Haskell Institute in 1923.

METOXEN, IVA (Oneida)

Iva Metoxen, from Wisconsin, was born in 1890. She graduated from Carlisle in 1913.

METOXEN, JOE (Oneida)

Joe Metoxen, from Wisconsin, was born about 1888, the son of Simon W. and Lavinia Metoxen. He attended Haskell Institute.

METOXEN, MALINDA (Oneida)

Malinda Metoxen, from Wisconsin, was a 1902 graduate of Carlisle. After graduation, she returned to Wisconsin, where she worked as a seamstress at the Oneida school.

MICHA, LIZZIE (Pima)

Lizzie Micha attended the Phoenix Indian School.

MILES, THOMAS J. (Sac and Fox)

Thomas J. Miles (Muckutuwishek), a member of the Sac and Fox tribe of the Indian Territory, was born about 1862, the son of John Miles. He attended public schools in Kansas before entering Hampton Institute in 1882. After graduating in 1885, he attended preparatory school at Meridan, New Hampshire, and then entered the medical department at the University of Pennsylvania, but after two years dropped out because of ill health. He went home and taught at the Sac and Fox school, returned to the East, attempted to finish school, but dropped out once more. He taught at the Sac and Fox school from 1889 to 1891 and then moved to Philadelphia, the home of his wife.

MILLER, ARTIE E. (Stockbridge)

Artie E. Miller, from Wisconsin, was a 1900 graduate of Carlisle.

MILLER, IVA (Cherokee)

Iva Miller was a graduate of Carlisle. In 1912, she entered the Indian Service as boys' matron at the Oto Boarding School.

MILLER, MARY (Chippewa)
Mary Miller was an 1897 graduate of Carlisle. Her married name was Dodge, and, in 1902, she was a teacher at the Indian school in Harlem, Montana.

MILLER, SADIE (Delaware-Cherokee)
Sadie Miller, from Oklahoma, graduated from the business department at Haskell Institute in 1920.

MILLS, INEZ (Pima)
Inez Mills graduated from the Phoenix Indian School in 1905.

MINTHORN, AARON (Cayuse)
Aaron Minthron, born about 1890, attended Carlisle and Jenkins Institute, Spokane, Washington.

MITCHELL, CHARLES (Assiniboin)
Charles Mitchell was a 1909 graduate of Carlisle. He returned to Montana, where he worked as a store clerk at Wolfe Point in 1913.

MOLLIE, ALMA (Pima)
Alma Mollie graduated from the Phoenix school in 1906. She married Jackson Thomas and lived in Phoenix.

MOLLIE, OSSIE (Pima)
Ossie Mollie was born on July 15, 1888, at Sacaton on the Gila River Reservation, Arizona. She attended school at Sacaton and then entered the Phoenix Indian School in 1896, graduating in 1907.

MONTEZUMA, CARLOS (Apache)
Carlos Montezuma was born in Arizona in 1867, the son of Co-lu-ye-vah of the Pinal Apaches. As a young child, Montezuma, whose name was Wassaja, was captured by the Pimas, who later sold him to a photographer, C. Gentile, who took him to Chicago in 1872. He was educated in the public schools in Chicago, in Galesburg, Illinois, and in Brooklyn, New York. He received a B. S. degree from the University of Illinois in 1884 and an M. D. from Chicago Medical College in 1889. From 1889 until 1896, he was a physician in the U. S. Indian Service. He conducted a private practice and taught medicine in Chicago. He traveled widely, lectured, and founded and edited Wassaja, a magazine devoted to Indian affairs. His wife was Mary Keller. Montezuma died on January 31, 1923.

MONTIETH, SARA (Nez Percé)
Sara Montieth attended Carlisle.

MONTION, CARMEN (Pueblo)
Carmen Montion, from El Paso, Texas, attended Hampton Institute.

MOORE, ANNIE T. (Pima)
Annie T. Moore graduated from the Phoenix Indian School in 1918 and from Phoenix Union High School in 1920.

MOOSE, JOSEPH (Potawatomi)
Joseph Moose lived at Mayetta, Kansas, in 1909.

MORGAN, GIDEON (Cherokee)
Gideon Morgan was born on April 3, 1851, the son of William and Martha Mayo Morgan, the latter of Cherokee descent. He was educated by private tutors. In 1871, Morgan moved to Fort Gibson, Cherokee Nation. He was a farmer and rancher and owner of the Capital Hotel in Tahlequah and Morgan's Inn Resort north of Salina, Oklahoma. He died in March, 1937. His wife was Mary Llewallan Payne.

MORRIN, ALVIS M. (Chippewa)
Alvis M. Morrin, a Red Cliff Chippewa from Bayfield, Wisconsin, was born about 1896, the son of Michael Morrin. He was a 1914 graduate of Carlisle. After Carlisle, he entered Haskell Institute, where he took commercial studies courses, graduating in 1915. In 1917, he became assistant clerk at the Indian school at Flandreau, South Dakota. He was later placed at the Keshena Agency, from which he was transferred in 1924 to the Menominee Mills at Neopit, Wisconsin.

MORRISETTE, FRED WILLIAM (Chippewa)
Fred William Morrisette, from Superior, Wisconsin, was a 1915 graduate of Carlisle.

MORRISON, CARRIE (Chippewa)
Carrie Morrison was a normal student at Haskell in 1902.

MORRISON, JOE (Chippewa)
Joe Morrison was from the White Earth Reservation in Minnesota.

MORRISON, JOHN GEORGE, JR. (Chippewa)
John G. Morrison, from the White Earth Reservation in Minnesota, was an 1893 graduate of Carlisle. He was born at Crow Wing in 1875, the son of John George and Margaret Fairbanks Morrison. He taught school at the Crow Agency Boarding School and other places for a number of years and in 1904 was Superintendent of the Cross Lake School. Morrison went to Red Lake where in 1908 he became proprietor of the Chippewa Trading Post. In 1914, he was elected County Commissioner for Beltrami County. He was active in tribal affairs, serving as a representative from White Earth to the General Council of Minnesota Chippewas for a number of years and as President of the Council.

MORTON, ANNIE M. (Pueblo)
Annie M. Morton, from Laguna Pueblo in New Mexico, was an 1898 graduate of Carlisle. Her married name was Lubo and, in 1916, she lived in Riverside, California.

MOTT, SEWARD (Mohave-Apache)
Seward Mott was born on the San Carlos Reservation in Ari-

zona. His only schooling was at the San Carlos Agency School. In 1905, he was the agency farmer.

MT. PLEASANT, EDISON (Tuscarora)
Edison Mt. Pleasant, born about 1890, was from New York and graduated from Carlisle in 1911.

MT. PLEASANT, MAMIE (Tuscarora)
Mamie Mt. Pleasant, born about 1893, was from Lewiston, New York, and was a 1915 graduate of Carlisle.

MOUNTAIN, THIRZA (Arapaho)
Thirza Mountain graduated from the Phoenix Indian School in 1914.

MUMBLEHEAD, JAMES W. (Cherokee)
James Mumblehead, born about 1882, graduated from Carlisle in 1911. In 1914, he was a bandmaster and printer and was managing the Oglala Light at Pine Ridge, South Dakota.

MURDOCK, WESSON (Assiniboin)
Wesson Murdock, from the Fort Peck Reservation, was a 1900 graduate of Carlisle. He returned to Montana and lived at Wolf Point.

MURIE, JAMES (Pawnee)
James Murie (Young Eagle), from the Indian Territory, was born at Grand Island, Nebraska about 1863, the son of James Murie. He received eight years of education in eastern schools and at the Pawnee Agency at Genoa, Nebraska, before entering Hampton Institute in 1879. After he graduated in 1883, he taught a year at the Pawnee Agency and then went to Haskell Institute as disciplinarian and drill master for two years. He went east for more education but was discouraged by the Commissioner of Indian Affairs, who did not approve of higher education. He was sent back to the Pawnee Agency to teach, but the position was filled when he got there, so he took a clerkship instead. He then married and settled down to farming. Murie was described as having "a good mind and an unusual gift for talking and writing." In 1903, he worked at the Field Columbian Museum in Chicago and in later years assisted Erich M. von Hornbostel of Berlin collect material on American Indian music. In 1915, he was president of the newly-formed Indian Farmers' Institute at Pawnee, Oklahoma.

MUSKRAT, RUTH (Cherokee)
Ruth Muskrat, a Cherokee from the Indian Territory, was born about 1897. She attended Carlisle and then the University of Kansas. While a student at the university, she was a delegate to the World's Student Christian Federation Conference at Peking. She was also active as a youth worker in the Y. M. C. A. Her married name was Bronson.

NAPAWAT, MARTHA (Kiowa)
Martha Napawat, from the Indian Territory, was an 1894 grad-

uate of Carlisle. She married Thomas Ahopthoi and lived at Anadarko, Oklahoma.

NARCHO, PABLO (Papago)
Pablo Narcho graduated from Haskell Institute in 1914.

NARSA, MIDA (Pima)
Mida Narsa graduated from the Phoenix Indian School in 1911.

NASON, BERTHA (Chippewa)
Bertha Nason, from Minnesota, attended Carlisle but did not graduate and entered St. Cloud Normal School in 1889.

NATALISH, VINCENT (Apache)
Vincent Natalish (Natailish is a variant spelling) was an 1899 graduate of Carlisle. He became a civil engineer for an elevated railway company in New York. In 1916, he was still living in New York City.

NEAL, DICK (Cherokee)
Dick Neal, from the Indian Territory, was born about 1836.

NEEDHAM, SIMON (Chippewa)
Simon Needham, from the Red Lake Reservation in Minnesota, was born about 1890 and was a 1914 graduate of Carlisle. After graduation, he studied telegraphy at Philadelphia and went to work for the Great Northern Railway Company as a telegrapher at Deere, Minnesota.

NEHOITEWA, ROLAND (Hopi)
Roland Nehoitewa attended the Phoenix Indian School.

NEWASHE, EMMA M. (Sac and Fox)
Emma M. Newashe was born in the Indian Territory about 1891. After graduation from Carlisle in 1912, she attended West Chester Normal School for a short time. In 1914, she married F. A. McAllister, moved to Oklahoma City, and became a housewife.

NICHOLS, JOSEPHINE (Seneca)
Josephine Nichols, born about 1897, graduated from the Phoenix Indian School in 1915.

NICHOLS, ROLAND A. (Potawatomi)
No information is available.

NICOLAR, JOSEPH (Penobscot)
Joseph Nicolar was born in 1827 and died in 1894.

NILES, HERMAN (Stockbridge)
Herman Niles, from Wisconsin, was a 1901 graduate of Carlisle.

NORI, SICENI J. (Pueblo)

Siceni J. Nori, from Laguna Pueblo, was an 1894 graduate of Carlisle. He then graduated from Stuart's Business College, Trenton, New Jersey. He returned to Carlisle as a clerk in the superintendent's office and as a teacher in which capacity he remained for a number of years. Nori married Ida Griffin.

NOTT, ALICE (Maricopa)

Alice Nott was born in 1883 in the Salt River Valley in Arizona. At ten, she entered the Phoenix Indian School where she remained for two years before spending two years in an outing program with a family in Phoenix. In 1897, she reentered the Phoenix Indian School and graduated in 1903. After graduation, she was employed by the school. She married Frank Norton. Mrs. Norton died at Prescott, Arizona, on October 20, 1920.

OCCOM, SAMSON (Mohegan)

Samson Occom was born near New London, Connecticut, in 1723. Converted during the Great Awakening, he studied under Eleazar Wheelock at Lebanon. He became a missionary to the Montauk tribe of Long Island and married one of its members, Mary Fowler. In 1761 and 1763, he was Wheelock's emissary to the Oneidas. In 1765, he went with Nathaniel Whitaker to England and Scotland where he preached and helped raise money for Moor's Indian Charity School conducted by Wheelock. Occom and Whitaker raised about £12,000, which became the financial base for Dartmouth College. After his return to America in 1768, he became an itinerant preacher. He was instrumental in the establishment of Brothertown in New York and removed to there from Connecticut in 1789. He remained there until he died on July 14, 1792.

O'DONNELL, STELLA (Chippewa)

Stella O'Donnell, from Mahnomen on the White Earth Reservation, did postgraduate work at Hampton in 1910. In 1911, she taught at the government school at Bena, Minnesota, and later transferred to the Leech Lake School. In 1914, she completed the business course at Haskell Institute.

O'FIELD, INA (Cherokee)

Ina O'Field was from Kansas, Oklahoma, and graduated from Bacone College in 1923.

OHLERKING, WILLIAM (Sioux)

William Ohlerking, from the Fort Peck Reservation in Montana, graduated from Haskell Institute in 1915.

OLD COYOTE, BARNEY (Crow)

No information is available.

OLIVER, JAMES (Chippewa)

James Oliver, a Fond du Lac Chippewa, was born about 1879. He graduated from the steam fitting and engineering departments of Haskell Institute in 1901 and returned to the reservation.

O'NEAL, MINNIE ELIZABETH (Shoshoni)

Minnie Elizabeth O'Neal, from Wyoming, was a 1915 graduate of Carlisle. After graduation, she attended West Chester Normal School.

OSBORNE, SAMUEL (Pawnee)

Samuel Osborne, from Oklahoma, was a student at Haskell Institute in 1915.

OSICK, ELOISE (Pima)

Eloise Osick graduated from the Phoenix Indian School in 1910.

OSIF, MOLLIE (Pima)

Mollie Osif attended the Phoenix Indian School.

OSKISON, JOHN MILTON (Cherokee)

John Milton Oskison was born at Vinita, Cherokee Nation, on September 1, 1874, the son of John and Rachel Crittenden Oskison. Oskison attended Willie Halsell College at Vinita, where he was a classmate of his lifelong friend, Will Rogers. Oskison also attended Stanford University where he took his B. A. degree in 1899 before going on to do graduate work at Harvard. That year, he won the Century Magazine prize competition for college graduates and launched a long and successful writing career. He worked as an editorial writer on the New York Evening Post and later was associate editor and special writer for Collier's. From 1917 to 1919, Oskison served with the A. E. F. in Europe. He married Florence Ballard Day, the niece of Jay Gould; she divorced him in 1920. He later married Hildegarde Hawthorne. Oskison died in New York in 1947.

OVERTON, BENJAMIN FRANKLIN (Chickasaw)

Benjamin Franklin Overton was born on November 2, 1836, in Mississippi, the son of John Overton and Tennessee Allen, the latter of Chickasaw descent. Orphaned at an early age, Overton received little formal education, only six months at the old Chickasaw Male Academy at Tishomingo. He farmed in Pickens County, Chickasaw Nation, and served in both the Chickasaw House and Senate. Overton was elected to four terms as Governor of the Nation, 1874-1878 and 1880-1884. He died on February 8, 1884.

OWEN, NARCISSA (Cherokee)

Narcissa Owen was born at Webbers Falls in the western Cherokee Nation on October 3, 1831, the daughter of Thomas and Malinda Horton Chisholm. Her father was a chief of the western Cherokees, and her mother was a teacher. In 1853, Narcissa married Robert L. Owen, a planter of Lynchburg, Virginia. After the destruction of their plantation during the Civil War, Owen turned to the railroad business and became president of the Tennessee Railroad. After his death in 1873, Mrs. Owen turned to teaching to support her sons William and Robert (q. v.). Mrs. Owen, whose Indian name was Caulunna, was an accomplished musician and painter. She died at Guthrie, Oklahoma, on July 13, 1911.

OWEN, ROBERT LATHAM (Cherokee)

Robert Latham Owen was born at Lynchburg, Virginia, on February 2, 1856, the son of Robert Latham and Narcissa Chisholm Owen (q. v.). At age ten, he was enrolled in Merillat Institute near Baltimore. He later attended Washington and Lee from which he received an M. A. degree. In the 1870's, the widowed Mrs. Owen returned with her sons to the Cherokee Nation, where Owen taught at the Cherokee Orphan Asylum, practiced law, and served as Secretary of the Board of Education. In 1884, he became owner and editor of the Vinita Indian Chieftain. From 1885 to 1889, Owen was Union Agent for the Five Civilized Tribes. In 1890, he organized the First National Bank of Muskogee. From 1907 to 1925, he was U. S. Senator from Oklahoma. After retirement from the Senate, he kept a law office for a number of years in Washington, D. C. Owen died on July 19, 1947.

OWENS, JOHN K. (Pima)

John K. Owens, from the Gila River Reservation in Arizona, entered the Sacaton School in 1892. He later transferred to a Presbyterian Home Mission Society school in Albuquerque. He worked as an interpreter at Sacaton, disciplinarian at the Phoenix Indian School, and industrial teacher at the Puyallup School at Tacoma. In 1921, he was a merchant at Alicia, Arizona.

OWL, FREL McDONALD (Cherokee)

Frel McDonald Owl, from North Carolina, graduated from Hampton Institute in 1922. He studied as well at Phillips Academy, Andover, Massachusetts.

OWL, GEORGE A. (Cherokee)

George Owl, from North Carolina, was a student at Hampton Institute.

OWL, HENRY M. (Cherokee)

Henry Owl graduated from Hampton Institute and continued his studies at Columbia University. In 1922, he was a teacher at Bacone College.

OWL, LULA (Cherokee)

Lula Owl, from Cherokee, North Carolina, graduated from Hampton Institute in 1914. In 1917, she graduated from the nurses training program at Chestnut Hill Hospital in Philadelphia and entered obstetrics work.

OWL, W. DAVID (Cherokee)

W. David Owl, from North Carolina, graduated from Hampton Institute in 1915 and then attended Y. M. C. A. College in Springfield, Massachusetts. In 1920, he became Y. M. C. A. Secretary among the Pimas, remaining there a year and a half. He returned to Hampton and, in 1923, went to Haskell Institute as Y. M. C. A. Secretary and Director of Religious Studies.

OWL, WILLIAM J. (Cherokee)

William J. Owl, born about 1883, graduated from Carlisle in 1911 and, in 1912, was employed at the Cherokee Indian School in North Carolina.

PABLO, JOSE SAN XAVIER (Papago)
Jose San Xavier Pablo, born about 1888 in Arizona, was a graduate of the Phoenix Indian School. In 1906, he served as disciplinarian at the Tucson Mission School and, in 1912, was treasurer of the Papago Indian Good Government League which at the time represented fifty-eight villages. Pablo was a carpenter, painter, and plumber. He and two other Papagos put up a telephone line between Tucson and the Presbyterian Mission School on the Papago Reservation. When the well-known writer Carl Lumholtz traveled on the reservation, Pablo was his interpreter. In his book, New Trails in Mexico, Lumholtz praised Pablo as a moral man who had read the Bible through twice and was fond of historical works.

PADILLA, POLITA (Pueblo)
Polita Padilla was a student at Haskell Institute in 1901.

PAMBAGO, JOHN B. (Potawatomi)
John B. Pambago, from the Indian Territory, was born about 1853. For many years, he was National Committeeman, or business manager, for the Potawatomis. In 1903, he was also a U. S. Indian policeman.

PAMBRUN, FRANCIS (Piegan)
Francis Pambrun was a 1913 graduate of Carlisle.

PARKER, ANNA (Bannock)
Anna Parker, from Idaho, was a 1904 graduate of Carlisle.

PARKER, ARTHUR CASWELL (Seneca)
Arthur Caswell Parker was born at Iroquois, New York, on April 5, 1881, the son of Frederick Ely and Geneva Griswold Parker. He was educated in the day schools of the Cattaraugus Reservation and at Dickinson Seminary. He also attended Harvard and the University of Rochester. In 1903-1904, he was an ethnologist for the New York State Library; from 1905 to 1925 he was archaeologist for the New York State Museum; and from 1925 to 1946, he was the Director of the Rochester Museum of Arts and Sciences. Parker held a number of editorial positions including ones for the Transactions of the New York State Archaelogical Association (1916-1955), for Museum Service (1926-1946), for Research Records (1926-1946), for The Galleon (1949-1955), and for The Builder (1949-1955). He was as well involved in numerous civic affairs, he was a practicing ethnologist, and he wrote extensively. Parker was married to Beatrice Tahamont and Anna T. Cook. He died on January 1, 1955.

PARKER, ELY SAMUEL (Seneca)
Ely Samuel Parker (or Do-ne-ho-ga-wa) was born near Penbroke, New York, in 1828, the son of William and Elizabeth Parker (Jo-no-es-do-wa and Ga-ont-gwut-turus). He attended Rensselaer

Polytechnic Institute, became Chief of the Senecas in 1852, and represented his tribe in Washington. He was superintendent of construction
for the government at Galena, Illinois, between 1857 and 1862, and
served in the Union Army during the Civil War. He reached the rank
of Brigadier General in 1867 and became Commissioner of Indian Affairs in 1869. He married Minnie Sachett. Parker died on August
31, 1895.

PARKER, ESTHER (Comanche)
Esther Parker, from Indian Territory, was the daughter of
Quanah Parker and his fourth wife Ah-uh-wuth-takum. She attended
Chilocco Indian School. Miss Parker married Charlie Sunrise.

PARKER, FREDERICK E. (Seneca)
Frederick E. Parker resided at New York City and White
Plains, New York, in 1912 and 1913.

PARKER, GABRIEL E. (Choctaw)
Gabriel E. Parker was born at Fort Towson, Choctaw Nation,
on September 29, 1878, the son of John Clay and Eliza Willis Parker.
In 1899, he received a B. A. degree from Henry Kendall College at
Muskogee, Creek Nation. He served as Superintendent of the Spencer
Academy in 1899 and 1900, and as Principal and Superintendent of
Armstrong Academy for Boys in the Choctaw Nation (later Oklahoma)
between 1900 and 1913. He was a member of the Oklahoma Consti-
tutional Convention in 1906-1907 and was Register of the U. S. Treas-
ury, 1913-1915. In 1914, he was appointed Superintendent of the Five
Civilized Tribes in which capacity he served for several years.

PARNELL, ANNIE (Nez Percé)
Annie Parnell, from Idaho, was a 1901 graduate of Carlisle.

PARRIS, CAROLINE (Cherokee)
Caroline (Callie) Parris was the daughter of Moses and Nannie
Thornton Parris. She was orphaned and attended school at the Cher-
okee Orphan Asylum.

PASCHAL, LOUIS (Peoria)
Louis Paschal was born in the Indian Territory about 1890.
The son of Mrs. Florence Lafalier, he attended Chilocco Indian School.

PASCHAL, RIDGE (Cherokee)
Ridge Paschal was born at Van Buren, Arkansas, in July, 1845,
the son of George Washington and Sarah Ridge Paschal. His grandfather, Major Ridge, was a well-known leader of the Treaty Party
Cherokees. Paschal was educated at Wharton College in Austin, Texas, and Virginia Military Institute. Pro-Union during the Civil War,
in 1865 he edited the Republican paper Flake's Bulletin at Galveston.
He then became a law partner in J. R. and G. W. Paschal at San
Antonio where he was associate editor of the San Antonio Express.
In 1869, he served as U. S. Commissioner for the Western District
of Texas and as Supervisor of Internal Revenue for Texas, Arkansas,
and Louisiana. In 1874, he was Collector of Customs at Corpus

Christi. He moved his law practice to Laredo and, in 1880, bought and edited <u>Los Dos Laredos</u>, printed in Spanish and English. In 1884, he moved to Vinita, Cherokee Nation, where he practiced law. In 1890, he was named U. S. Commissioner for the Indian Territory. He married Mrs. Sarah Winston Gasman. Paschal died on February 5, 1907.

PATTERSON, SPENCER (Seneca)
Spencer Patterson attended Carlisle.

PATTON, ALONZO A. (Alaskan Native)
Alonzo A. Patton attended Carlisle.

PAUL, GEORGE (Pima)
George Paul, born about 1894, graduated from the Phoenix Indian School in 1915. He then became a farmer.

PAUL, KENDALL (Alaskan Native)
Kendall Paul graduated from Carlisle in 1899 and then attended school at Mt. Hermon, Massachusetts.

PAUL, MATILDA K. (Alaskan Native)
Mrs. Matilda K. Paul was reared at Killisnoo about eighty miles from Sitka. She lived a traditional life until she was converted as a child and brought up in one of the early mission schools. She and her husband, also a Native, did mission work, first at Chilkat and then at Tongass. When her husband died, Mrs. Paul was then transferred to Sitka, where she continued her work in the early years of the twentieth century.

PAUL, WILLIAM L. (Alaskan Native)
William L. Paul attended the Sheldon Jackson School in Sitka before going to Carlisle, from which he graduated in 1902. He then studied at Banks Business College in Philadelphia before entering Whitworth College at Tacoma, from which he graduated in 1909. After studying law at La Salle University, he was admitted to the bar.

PAWNEE, WILLIAM (Cheyenne-Arapaho)
William Pawnee (or William Redleg) was born in Oklahoma in 1903. He was the son of Crazy and stepson of Joseph Pawnee, whose name he took. He attended the Phoenix Indian School and, in 1917, was attending high school at Geary, Oklahoma.

PEAKE, EMILY E. (Chippewa)
Emily E. Peake, from the White Earth Reservation in Minnesota, was an 1893 graduate of Carlisle. After graduation, she returned to White Earth and married. In 1915, then Emily Robitaille, she was at Carlisle where she edited the Alumni Department of the Carlisle Arrow. The following year she ran "The French Shop," a clothing store in Washington, D. C. In 1917, she reentered government service and helped make the Chippewa per capita payment at White Earth, Minnesota, before returning to Washington to work as a clerk in the War Department.

PERRYMAN, JOSEPH M. (Creek)

Joseph M. Perryman was born in the Creek Nation in 1833, the son of Mayes Perryman. He attended Coweta Mission School and then studied for the Presbyterian ministry, becoming a licensed preacher. During the Civil War, he fought with the Confederate Creek troops and, after the war, served his Nation as Treasurer, Supreme Court Judge, and Superintendent of Public Schools. He married Ellen Marshall.

PERRYMAN, LEGUS CHOUTEAU (Creek)

Legus Choteau Perryman was born at Sodom, Creek Nation, on March 1, 1838, the son of Lewis and Ellen Winslett Perryman. He was educated at Tullahassee Mission School, where he translated Bible history for the Presbyterian mission schools. During the Civil War, he joined the First Confederate Creek Mounted Volunteers, but he later changed sides. After the war, he lived at Coweta and served as Judge of Coweta District and, for a number of years, was a member of the House of Warriors. In 1885, he was a delegate to Washington. In 1887, he was elected Principal Chief, was reelected in 1891, but was impeached in 1895. Perryman was married to Arparye Eshoya. He died on February 5, 1922.

PESHLASKI, FRANK S. (Navajo)

Frank S. Peshlaski was born near the Shaka Mountains in northwestern Arizona. After spending his early years hunting and herding, he entered the Fort Defiance Indian School where he remained for three years. As a trader with a curio company, he attended fairs in Omaha in 1899, Buffalo in 1901, and St. Louis in 1904. He then entered the Phoenix Indian School, from which he graduated in 1907. He then worked as a substitute mail carrier in Phoenix and attended Lamson Business College.

PETERS, BERT (Pawnee)

Bert Peters, from Oklahoma, attended Bacone College.

PETERS, MYRTLE (Stockbridge)

Myrtle Peters attended Carlisle.

PETERS, WILLIAM (Pima)

William Peters, from Gila Crossing, Arizona, graduated from the Phoenix Indian School in 1902. He later graduated from the Charles H. Cook Bible School. He was considered a progressive farmer and preached at the houses of Indians on the Gila River Reservation.

PETERSON, EUNICE (Klamath)

Eunice Peterson was born at Happy Camp, California, in 1886. At age six, she attended public schools for a few months and then went to the Hoopa Valley School. In 1898, she entered the Phoenix Indian School and graduated in 1903.

PETOSKY, CORNELIUS (Chippewa)

Cornelius Petosky, from Petosky, Michigan, graduated from Carlisle in 1902.

PHILLIPS, WALTER (Creek)
Walter Phillips was born in 1896 at Eufaula, Creek Nation, the son of Pahos Harjo and Coosie Phillips. He graduated from Bacone College in 1919.

PICOTTE, CHARLES F., JR. (Sioux)
Charles Picotte (or Miniskuya), from the Yankton Reservation, was born about 1864, the son of Charles F. Picotte. He attended Hampton Institute from 1879 to 1887, when he graduated. He married Marguerite La Flesche (q. v.).

PICOTTE, MARGUERITE LA FLESCHE (Omaha)
Marguerite La Flesche, from Nebraska, was born about 1863, the daughter of Joseph La Flesche. She graduated from Hampton Institute in 1888 and began teaching on the Omaha Reservation. She married Charles Picotte (q. v.).

PICOTTE, SUSAN LA FLESCHE (Omaha)
Susan La Flesche Picotte was born on June 17, 1865, on the Omaha Reservation, Nebraska, the daughter of Joseph La Flesche. She graduated from Hampton Institute in 1886 and then spent three years at the Woman's Medical College in Philadelphia, from which she graduated in 1889. After a year of internship at Women's Hospital, she returned to the Omaha Reservation to practice medicine as the government physician, a position she held for five years. She then entered private practice at Bancroft, Nebraska, and, in 1905, began combining medical practice with missionary work. She married Henri Picotte. Mrs. Picotte died on September 18, 1916.

PIERCE, DELIA (Seneca)
Delia Pierce attended Carlisle.

PIERCE, EVELYN (Seneca)
Evelyn Pierce was born about 1891 and graduated from Carlisle in 1910. She later graduated from the Business Department at Haskell Institute.

PIERCE, MARIS BRYANT (Seneca)
Maris Bryant Pierce, born in 1811, was a Chief of the Senecas. Pierce attended Dartmouth College. He died in 1874.

PIERCE, ROGENE A. (Cayuga)
Rogene A. Pierce, from the Cattaraugus Reservation in New York, attended Hampton Institute, graduating in 1917. She then took stenography courses in Buffalo.

PIKE, ELVIRA (Uintah Ute)
Elvira Pike was a member of the Society of American Indians.

PIKE, MINNIE (Ute)
Minnie Pike attended Haskell Institute.

PITCHER, MARY ELVINA (Cherokee)

Mary Elvina Pitcher attended school at the Cherokee Orphan Asylum. She married Nathaniel Breckenridge Weir.

PITCHLYNN, PETER PERKINS (Choctaw)

Peter Perkins Pitchlynn was born in the Choctaw Nation in Mississippi on January 20, 1806, the son of John Pitchlynn, a white man, and Sopha Folsom Pitchlynn, a Choctaw. Pitchlynn was educated at the Academy of Columbia, Tennessee, and the University of Tennessee. After graduation from the university, he returned to the Choctaw Nation, where he married his cousin, Rhoda Folsom. He was elected to the Choctaw National Council in 1825 and, in 1828, led an exploring and peace-making mission to the Osage country west of the Mississippi. Pitchlynn was active in Choctaw politics throughout his life. He served as Principal Chief from 1864 through 1866 and, after his term of office, stayed in Washington pressing Choctaw claims against the government. He died in Washington on January 17, 1881.

PLATERO, JOSE KIE (Navajo)

No information is available.

POKAGON, SIMON (Potawatomi)

Simon Pokagon was born in 1830 in Pokagon Village in present-day Berrien County, Michigan. His father, Leopold Pokagon, who died in 1840, was Chief of the Potawatomi for forty-two years, was present at the massacre at Fort Dearborn in 1812, and later represented the tribe in negotiations that led to the sale of lands on which Chicago sits. At fourteen, Simon Pokagon entered Notre Dame at South Bend, Indiana, where he remained for three years. He then spent one year at Oberlin and two years in school at Twinsburg, Ohio. As Chief of the Pokagon band of Potawatomis, Simon Pokagon made one of his prime concerns the payment of funds due the tribe for the sale of Chicago and its environs. The claim was finally settled in 1896. When Pokagon learned that the World's Fair was to be held in Chicago in 1893, he tried but failed to organize a congress of American Indians to meet in conjunction with the fair. He was, however, invited to speak at the fair. Pokagon devoted much time during his last years in recording his tribal cultural heritage and history. He died in 1899. Pokagon was married to Lonidaw Sinagaw and Victoria.

PORTER, PETER (Pima)

Peter Porter was a student at the Phoenix Indian School in 1909.

PORTER, PLEASANT (Creek)

Pleasant Porter was born near Clarksville, Creek Nation, on September 26, 1840, the son of Benjamin Edwin Porter and Phoebe, the daughter of Tahlopee Tustennuggee. Porter spent five years in Presbyterian mission schools and obtained the rest of his education through home study. Before the Civil War, he worked as a store clerk and a cattle drover. In the war, he served in D. N. McIntosh's Confederate Creek regiment. After the war, he reorganized

the Creek school system and served as a delegate to Washington.
Later, he was a Captain of the Creek Light-Horse Police, served
four years in the House of Warriors, and was a member of the Creek
commission that negotiated with the Dawes Commission. He served
as Principal Chief from 1899 until his death on September 3, 1907.
Porter was married to Mary Ellen Keys and Mattie L. Bertholf.

POSEY, ALEXANDER LAWRENCE (Creek)
Alexander Lawrence Posey was born near Eufaula, Creek Nation, on August 3, 1873. He was the son of Lewis H. Posey, a Scot
who had been born in Indian Territory, and Nancy Phillips, the full-
blood daughter of Pohos Harjo of the Wind Clan of Creeks. During
his early years, he preferred Creek to English but was forced to
speak English by his teacher at age twelve or fourteen. He attended
Creek public school in Eufaula and then graduated with honors from
the Indian University (Bacone) at Muskogee in 1895. That year, he
was elected to the House of Warriors, the lower house of the Creek
legislature and the next year was appointed Superintendent of the
Creek National Orphan Asylum at Okmulgee. In 1896, he married
Minnie Harris of Fayetteville, Arkansas, a matron at the Asylum.
In 1897, he was appointed Superintendent of Public Instruction of the
Creek Nation, but soon left that office for a career in writing. How-
ever, he later served as Principal at the Creek National High School
in Eufaula and still later at Wetumpka. He edited the Eufaula weekly
Indian Journal, a newspaper in which he published some of his most
successful works. After two years with the Journal, he moved to
Muskogee, where he assisted in editing the Muskogee Times and did
a brief term of government service enrolling Creeks with the Dawes
Commission. In 1905, he served as Secretary of the Constitutional
Convention for the proposed state of Sequoyah. A prolific writer, he
wrote poetry under the name of Chinnubbie Harjo and political satire
under the name of Fus Fixico. He drowned on May 27, 1908.

POWLESS, RICHARD S. (Oneida)
Richard Powless, from Wisconsin, attended Hampton Institute.

PRATT, JENNIE (Pawnee)
Jennie Pratt, from Oklahoma, was a student at Haskell Institute in 1922.

PROCTOR, EZEKIEL (Cherokee)
Ezekiel Proctor was born in the eastern Cherokee Nation on
July 4, 1831, the son of William and Dicey Downing Proctor. He
served as a Union scout during the Civil War and as Cherokee District Sheriff following the war. In 1872, while he was on trial for
the murder of Mrs. Polly Kesterson, Mrs. Kesterson's relatives and
U. S. marshals from Fort Smith, Arkansas, attacked the Cherokee
court while it was in session. The killings that resulted have become known in Cherokee history as the "Tragedy of Going Snake."
Proctor died on February 29, 1907, west of Siloam Springs, Arkansas.

PRUE, ELLEN M. (Sioux)
Ellen M. Prue attended Chilocco Indian School.

QUINNEY, JOHN WAUNNACON (Stockbridge)
John Waunnacon Quinney, a Stockbridge, was born at New Stockbridge, New York, in 1797. He was educated at Yorkton, New York. In 1822, he represented the Stockbridges in negotiations with the Menominees concerning the purchase of lands near Green Bay. Quinney was responsible for bringing constitutional government to his people, he obtained a tribal reserve of 460 acres for them at Stockbridge, and, in 1846, he obtained repeal of an act making the Stockbridges citizens of the United States. In his indefatigable efforts in behalf of his people, he made nine trips to Washington. Quinney married Lucinda Lewis. He died on July 21, 1855.

QUINTANO, SANTIAGO (Pueblo)
Santiago Quintano attended Carlisle.

QUOETONE, FRED J. (Kiowa)
Fred J. Quoetone, from Oklahoma, graduated from the business and printing departments of Haskell Institute in 1920.

RAICHE, MARY (Chippewa)
Mary Raiche graduated from Carlisle in 1915 and later attended West Chester Normal.

RAMONE, JOSEPHINE (Papago)
Josephine Ramone, from Arizona, graduated from Carlisle in 1904.

RAMSEY, JOHN (Nez Percé)
John Ramsey, born about 1888, attended Carlisle.

REDBIRD, SIMON (Ottawa)
No information is available.

RED EAGLE, GRACE (Quapaw)
Grace Red Eagle, born in the Indian Territory about 1874, graduated from Carlisle in 1897. In 1902, she lived in Baxter Springs, Kansas. In 1910, she and her husband, John B. Walker, lived at Quapaw, Oklahoma.

RED EAGLE, LEROY (Quapaw)
Leroy Red Eagle was born about 1885 in the Indian Territory, the son of George and Minnie (or O-gosh-shung) Red Eagle. He attended Carlisle.

REED, ORA V. EDDLEMAN (Cherokee)
Ora Eddleman Reed was the daughter of David J. and Mary Daugherty Reed, the latter of Cherokee descent. In 1898, at age twenty, Ora Eddleman became editor of Twin Territories: The Indian Magazine, established at Muskogee, Indian Territory, in December of that year. The magazine contained a section titled "Round the Center Fire of the Wigwam," in which were published Indian poetry, stories, and folklore. Several Indian writers contributed to the Twin Territories. Miss Eddleman herself contributed numerous pieces to

that magazine and to other publications as well under the pen name of Mignon Schreiber. When Sturm's Statehood Magazine was established at Tulsa, Indian Territory, in 1905, she became editor of the "Indian Department" section, attracting to that journal a number of Indian writers.

REED, THOMAS B. (Alaskan Native)
Thomas B. Reed was born on the Lower Yukon River, about four hundred miles above the coast. He attended Hampton Institute.

REINKEN, OLGA (Alaskan Native)
Olga Reinken attended Carlisle.

RENVILLE, FLORENCE (Sioux)
Florence Renville, a Sisseton, attended Carlisle.

RENVILLE, GABRIEL (Sioux)
Gabriel Renville was born at Sweet Corn's Village at Big Stone Lake, South Dakota, in April, 1824, the son of Victor and Winona Crawford Renville. He was the last Chief of the Sisseton Sioux, appointed by the War Department. He signed the treaty of 1867 as Chief of the Sisseton and Wahpeton Sioux. He received an allotment on the Santee Reservation. Renville died at the Sisseton Agency on August 24, 1902.

RENVILLE, GERMAINE (Sioux)
Germaine Renville, a Sisseton from South Dakota, was born about 1896 and graduated from Carlisle in 1914. She married Peter Eastman (q. v.), and they made their home at Peever, South Dakota.

RHODES, MARIANNA (Maricopa)
Marianna Rhodes, born about 1896, graduated from the Phoenix Indian School in 1915.

RICE, SAMUEL (Mission)
Samuel Rice, from California, graduated from the Phoenix Indian School in 1909.

RICKETTS, HERMAN (Pawnee)
Herman Ricketts, from Oklahoma, was a student at Haskell Institute in 1922.

RIDDLE, JEFF C. (Modoc)
Jeff C. Riddle was the son of Frank Riddle, a white miner, and Winema, the Modoc interpreter for the United States during the Modoc War. From 1874 to 1881, the young Riddle and his parents toured the East with a company performing Winema, a play that told the story of the Modocs.

RIDGE, JOHN (Cherokee)
John Ridge was born about 1800 in the eastern Cherokee Nation, the son of Major Ridge and Susie Wickett Ridge. He attended mission schools at Spring Place, Georgia, and Brainerd, Tennessee,

before going to school at Cornwall, Connecticut in 1819. He married
Sarah Bird Northrup of Cornwall. He was assassinated on June 22,
1839, for having signed the New Echota removal treaty of 1835.

RIDGE, JOHN ROLLIN (Cherokee)
        John Rollin Ridge (Chees-quat-a-law-ny, or Yellow Bird) was
born in the eastern Cherokee Nation in 1827, the son of John Ridge
(q. v.). After his father was killed in 1839 for having signed the
removal treaty, Ridge's family moved to Fayetteville, Arkansas,
where Ridge received a basic education. In 1849, he killed another
Cherokee and fled to Missouri and went the next year to California,
never to return to the Cherokee Nation. There he edited several
newspapers including the Sacramento Bee, the Marysville California
Express and Daily National Democrat, and Grass Valley National. He
founded the Trinity National. Ridge became widely known as a poet
and as the author of the Life and Adventures of Joaquin Murietta. He
died in 1867.

RIGGS, ROLLA LYNN (Cherokee)
        Rolla Lynn Riggs was born at Claremore, Cherokee Nation,
the son of William G. and Ella Riggs, the latter of Cherokee descent.
After high school, Riggs worked for newspapers in Chicago, New
York, and Los Angeles. In 1920, he entered the University of Oklahoma, where he wrote for the University newspaper and magazine.
In the summer of 1922, he toured with a Chautauqua company and
that year taught part time, attended classes, and wrote, mainly poetry. In the fall of 1923, he went to New Mexico for his health and
wrote plays. His first play of significance was Green Grow the Li-
lacs (1930), that later became the Broadway musical Oklahoma! He
went on to write such plays as The Cherokee Night (1933) and Russet
Mantle (1936). Riggs died in New York on June 30, 1954.

RILEY, MARY (Cherokee)
        Mary Riley, from the Indian Territory, attended school at the
Cherokee Orphan Asylum.

ROBERTS, GEORGE (Pawnee)
        George Roberts, from Oklahoma, was a student at Carlisle in
1914.

ROBERTS, VIVIAN (Pawnee)
        Vivian Roberts, from Oklahoma, was a student at Haskell In-
stitute in 1922.

ROBERTSON, ETTA (Sioux)
        Etta Robertson graduated from Carlisle in 1891.

ROBERTSON, NELLIE (Sioux)
        Nellie Robertson went to Carlisle in 1880 and graduated in
1890. She then worked her way through West Chester Normal School
by taking charge of one of the dormitories. After she graduated from
West Chester in 1896, she returned to Carlisle to teach. In 1902,
she was a clerk and assistant in the Outing Program.

ROBINSON, JESSE (Klamath)
No information is available.

RODGERS, THOMAS L. (Cherokee)
Thomas L. Rodgers was a Headman of the Old Settler Cherokees. He operated a salt mill at present-day Spavinaw, Oklahoma.

RODRIGUEZ, FERNANDO (Pueblo)
Fernando Rodriguez graduated from the Phoenix Indian School
in 1910 and then entered public high school in Phoenix. He served
for a time on the Mexican border with the Arizona Regiment, and, in
1917, he was working for Standard Oil Company in Phoenix.

ROGERS, CLEMENT VANN (Cherokee)
Clement Vann Rogers was born at Baptist Mission, Cherokee
Nation, on January 11, 1839, the son of Robert and Sallie Vann Rogers. He attended Cherokee common schools and the Cherokee Male
Seminary. After leaving there, he worked as a drover for a while
before settling down as a rancher at Oolagah. His herd was lost
during the Civil War, during which he served in Watie's Confederate
regiment. After the war, he worked as a freighter until he began
ranching again in 1870, an occupation he followed the rest of his life.
He served his tribe as District Judge, Senator (four terms), and as
a commissioner to meet with the Dawes Commission. In 1896, he
became vice-president of the First National Bank of Claremore. Rogers was married twice, to Mary Schrimsher and Mary Bibles. He
died in November, 1911.

ROGERS, EDWARD L. (Chippewa)
Edward L. Rogers, from the White Earth Reservation, was
born in 1876 in Libby, Minnesota. He entered Carlisle in 1894 and
graduated in 1897. He then studied law at the Dickinson Law School
and then entered the University of Minnesota in 1901. He played
football for the university and spent his summers working in a law
firm in Minneapolis. After graduation in 1904, he returned to Carlisle as the head coach. He then entered law practice at Walker,
Minnesota. He was quite active in Chippewa affairs and served several terms as County Attorney of Cass County. In 1963, he was
named the Outstanding County Attorney in the United States. He retired from practice in 1966.

ROGERS, JOHN (Cherokee)
John Rogers was born in the eastern Cherokee Nation, the son
of John Rogers, a white man, and his Cherokee wife. Rogers emigrated to the western lands in 1817 and later settled at Grand Saline,
near present-day Salina, Oklahoma, where he ran a salt works. He
served as a chief of the Old Settler Cherokees.

ROGERS, ROBERT (Cherokee)
Robert Rogers was born in the eastern Cherokee Nation, the
son of John and Lucy Cordery Rogers. He was one of the signers of
the Treaty of New Echota in 1835. He was married to Mary Ann
Baptiste and Mary Scott Jones.

ROGERS, WILL (Cherokee)
Will Rogers was born William Penn Adair Rogers at Oologah, Cherokee Nation, on November 4, 1879, the son of Clement Vann (q. v.) and Mary Schrimpsher Rogers. He attended Cherokee public schools, Willie Halsell College at Vinita, Cherokee Nation, and Kemper Military Academy at Booneville, Missouri. From 1902 to 1904, he toured England, Argentina, and South Africa. In 1905, he made his debut in vaudeville at Hammerstein's Roof Garden in New York. From 1914 to 1924, he performed in Ziegfeld's Follies and the Night Follies, except for time taken to make motion pictures. He made his home in Beverly Hills, California. After 1922, he traveled widely, wrote newspaper columns, lectured, and published widely. It was on one of his trips that he was killed in a plane crash at Point Barrow, Alaska, on August 15, 1935. Rogers was married to Betty Blake.

ROGERS, WILLIAM (Cherokee)
William Rogers was born in the eastern Cherokee Nation, the son of John and Lucy Cordery Rogers. He was married to Mary Vann Neely and Louisa Reedy.

ROGERS, WILLIAM CHARLES (Cherokee)
William Charles Rogers was born near Claremore, Cherokee Nation, on December 13, 1847, the son of Charles Coody and Elizabeth McCorkle Rogers. He attended tribal school and later took up farming near present-day Skiatook, Oklahoma. He was also a store owner and rancher. He served the Cherokee Nation as a councilman, twice as a member of the Senate, and as the last elected Chief of the Nation. His wife was Nannie Haynie. Rogers died on November 8, 1917.

ROMAN NOSE, HENRY C. (Cheyenne)
Henry C. Roman Nose, born sometime in the 1850's, was one of the prisoners sent to Florida from the Cheyenne Agency in the 1870's. From prison at St. Augustine, he was sent to Hampton Institute in 1878. He was sent to Carlisle when it first opened in 1879 and stayed there two years. He returned to the West and, in 1890, was living in a tent at the agency where he was employed by the government as a tanner. His wife was Standing.

ROMANOSE, OLIVER (Cheyenne)
Oliver Romanose was born about 1895. He was a student at the Phoenix Indian School in 1914.

ROOT, CLARA (Arapaho)
Clara Root was a student at Chilocco Indian School in 1915.

ROSS, AMOS D.
Amos D. Ross, from Wyoming, graduated from Haskell Institute in 1916.

ROSS, DANIEL H. (Cherokee)
Daniel H. Ross was born in the Cherokee Nation in 1848, the

son of Andrew Ross. In 1873, he was a delegate to the Okmulgee Convention, and in 1874, he was one of three people appointed to codify the Cherokee laws. He married Naomi Chisholm and Sarah Halfbreed.

ROSS, DORSIE (Clallam)
Dorsie Ross was born in 1885. She attended local schools and, at the age of fourteen, entered the Tacoma, Washington school, where she remained for two years. She then attended the Phoenix Indian School from which she graduated in 1903. She also graduated from Hampton Institute in 1909 and then did postgraduate work before entering nurse's training in Seattle. In 1912, she was serving as boys' matron at the Tongue River School in Montana. She married E. L. Kearney and in 1921 was living at Kirby, Montana.

ROSS, JOHN (Cherokee)
John Ross (Cooweescoowee) was born near Lookout Mountain, Tennessee, in the eastern Cherokee Nation on October 3, 1790, the son of David and Mary McDonald Ross. He was a veteran of the War of 1812, having served in Andrew Jackson's campaign against the Creeks and held several offices in tribal government: member and President of the Council, Assistant Principal Chief, and Principal Chief (1828-1866). He was instrumental in drafting both Cherokee Constitutions (1827 and 1839) and was bitterly opposed to removal of the Cherokees from the East. He tried to keep his tribe neutral during the Civil War but was finally persuaded to sign a treaty with the Confederacy. He was married to Quatie and to Mary Bryan Stapler. He died on August 1, 1866.

ROSS, JOSEPH C. (Sioux)
Joseph C. Ross attended Hampton Institute.

ROSS, JOSHUA (Cherokee)
Joshua Ross was born in May, 1833, at Wills Valley, Alabama, in the eastern Cherokee Nation, the son of Andrew and Susan Lowrey Ross. He attended Fairfield and Park Hill mission schools in the western Nation. After graduation from the Cherokee Male Seminary in 1855, he attended Emory and Henry College, graduating in 1860. He taught at the Cherokee Male Seminary and, during the Civil War, clerked at a sutler's store at Fort Gibson. He married Muskogee Yargee, a Creek, and, in 1871, moved to Muskogee, Creek Nation, where he opened a store. He was a Cherokee delegate to the Okmulgee Convention from 1870 to 1875 and sat in the Cherokee National Council. He died on February 12, 1924.

ROSS, MARGUERITE (Clallam)
Marguerite Ross graduated from the Phoenix Indian School in 1904 and then entered Hampton Institute. She married George Earl.

ROSS, RUFUS O. (Cherokee)
Rufus O. Ross was born in the Cherokee Nation in 1843, the son of Allen and Jennie Fields Ross. During the Civil War, he was a lieutenant in the U. S. Cherokee Volunteers. He served as a dele-

gate to Washington and for two years as a member of the National Council. Ross married Elizabeth Grace Meigs. He died on May 29, 1877.

ROSS, S. W. (Cherokee)
S. W. Ross was born near Tahlequah, Cherokee Nation, the son of Lewis Anderson and Nellie Potts Ross. He attended private schools, the Presbyterian mission school at Park Hill, and the Cherokee Male Seminary. In his teens, he began working for the Tahlequah Indian Arrow and did newspaper work for a number of years.

ROSS, T. D. (Cherokee)
T. D. Ross was from the Indian Territory.

ROSS, WILLIAM POTTER (Cherokee)
William Potter Ross was born at Lookout Mountain, Tennessee, in the eastern Cherokee Nation on August 28, 1820. He was educated in Presbyterian mission schools, at Greenville Academy in Tennessee, Hamil School in Lawrenceville, New Jersey, and Princeton, from which he graduated with honors in 1842. In 1843, he was elected Secretary of the upper house of the Cherokee Council. In 1844, he became the first editor of the Cherokee Advocate. He served in the Confederate Army during the Civil War. He was a delegate to the Okmulgee Council in 1870, and, in 1873, he was elected Principal Chief of the tribe. He retired from public office in 1875 but maintained interests in newspaper work, including the Indian Journal, the Indian Chieftain, and the Indian Arrow. He died on July 20, 1891, at Fort Gibson, Cherokee Nation.

ROWE, FELIX (Cherokee)
Felix Rowe was from Salina, Oklahoma, and graduated from Chilocco Indian School in 1920.

ROWLAND, EMMA J. (Cheyenne)
Emma J. Rowland, from the Northern Cheyenne Reservation in Montana, was born about 1892 and graduated from Carlisle in 1913. In 1914, she entered government service at the Pine Ridge School in South Dakota. She married George Harris.

RULO, LOUIS (Oto)
Louis Rulo, from Oklahoma, graduated from the Phoenix Indian School in 1911. He took commercial courses at Haskell Institute. He worked at the Mescalero school in New Mexico and served in the Nineteenth Infantry during World War I. In 1921, he was Assistant Disciplinarian at the Santa Fe School.

RULO, ZALLIE (Sioux)
Zallie Rulo, from the Yankton Reservation, was born about 1865, the daughter of Charles Rulo. She entered Hampton Institute in 1881 and graduated in 1885. She married William Campbell.

RUNNELS, LOUIS H. (Sanpoil)
Louis H. Runnels, born about 1885, was a 1911 graduate of

Carlisle. He worked for a short time as a traveling salesman for a Boston firm and then attended school at Keller, Washington.

RUSSELL, INA (Hupa)
Ina Russell, from northern California, graduated from the Phoenix Indian School in 1909.

RUSSELL, SENNAN (Yuma)
Sennan Russell, from the Fort Yuma Reservation in California, graduated from the Phoenix Indian School in 1910 and then entered Hampton Institute. By 1915, he was farming in Arizona.

SAHENTI, MARIE (Yuma)
Marie Sahenti was born on the Fort Yuma Reservation in California. She attended the Fort Yuma School before entering the Phoenix Indian School in 1901. She graduated in 1907.

ST. CYR, JULIA (Winnebago)
Julia St. Cyr, from Nebraska, was born about 1865, the daughter of Michael St. Cyr. She attended Hampton Institute from 1880 to 1885 and during 1887.

SANBORN, JOHN (Gros Ventre)
John Sanborn attended Carlisle.

SANDERSON, HOWARD (Pima)
Howard Sanderson entered the Albuquerque Indian School in 1880. He stayed three years and then became a wagon maker at the school. He then went to work at the Phoenix Indian School. He pursued runaways and helped convince parents of the benefits of education for their children.

SARCOXIE, HENRY B. (Delaware)
Henry B. Sarcoxie was from the Cherokee Nation and attended Bacone College.

SAUNOOKE, NAN (Cherokee)
Nan Saunooke, from North Carolina, was born about 1889. She attended Carlisle.

SCALES, JOSEPH ABSALOM (Cherokee)
Joseph Absalom Scales, whose Indian name was Digadundi, was born near Chattanooga on June 23, 1832. He was the son of the Reverend Nicholas Dalton and Mary Coodey Scales, a niece of John Ross, Chief of the Cherokees. Scales was educated in the Cherokee common schools, the Ozark Institute at Fayetteville, Arkansas, and the Cherokee Male Seminary. He taught one year, engaged in the mercantile trade, and served as Sheriff and Prosecuting Attorney of Canadian District. During the Civil War, he served in the Confederate Army. After the war, he served as Cherokee delegate to the Okmulgee International Council, delegate to Washington, Associate Justice, and Chief Justice of the Supreme Court. Scales died on October 18, 1901.

SCHANADORE, EDWIN (Oneida)
Edwin Schanadore (or Scanadoah), from Wisconsin, graduated from Carlisle in 1889. He entered government service as a teacher and, during the next three decades, taught at various schools, including those at Albuquerque, Carson City, and Riverside, California.

SCHOLDER, FRITZ (Mission)
Fritz Scholder, from San Diego, California, graduated from the business department of Haskell Institute in 1924.

SCRAPER, ETTA JANE (Cherokee)
Etta Jane Scraper, from the Indian Territory, was the only graduate of Bacone College in 1891. She married William Edward Sanders.

SELKIRK, CHARLES (Chippewa)
Charles Selkirk was from the White Earth Reservation in Minnesota.

SELKIRK, GEORGE B. (Chippewa)
George B. Selkirk (Hak-Lak-to-wan), from White Earth, was the son of Henry Selkirk. He lived for a time at Sisseton, South Dakota, but, by 1918, was settled at White Earth where he farmed. In 1923-1924, he served as Secretary of the local council of White Earth Chippewas. After working for a time in the real estate business, he entered the Indian Service as lease clerk at the Yankton Sioux Agency.

SETIMA, MACK Q. (Hopi)
Mack Q. Setima graduated from Chilocco Indian School in 1910.

SHAW, NELLIE (Paiute)
Nellie Shaw, from Wadsworth, Nevada, graduated from the Normal School of Haskell Institute in 1924.

SHAW, ROSS (Pima)
Ross Shaw attended the Phoenix Indian School, graduating in 1916.

SHELTON, WILLIAM (Tulalip)
William Shelton was born about 1869 and grew up on the Tulalip Reservation in Washington. He attended the Tulalip Indian School. He traveled around Washington and collected totem legends.

SHERRILL, WILLIAM (Cherokee)
William Sherrill was an 1897 graduate of Carlisle.

SHIELDS, LIZZIE (Pima)
Lizzie Shields was a student at the Phoenix Indian School in 1909.

SICKLES, MARTHA L. (Oneida)
Martha L. Sickles, from Wisconsin, graduated from Carlisle

in 1898. Her married name was Cornelius, and she and her husband lived at Oneida, Wisconsin.

SILAS, ROGER (Oneida)
Roger Silas, from Wisconsin, attended Carlisle.

SIMON, ELMER (Chippewa)
Elmer Simon, from Michigan, graduated from Carlisle in 1896. He also graduated from the State Normal School at Indiana, Pennsylvania. He taught at Carlisle in 1899. After marrying Bertha Sterling of Trenton, New Jersey, he settled in Johnstown, Pennsylvania, where he was in the hardware business for a time. In 1902, he was a clerk in a furniture store at Windber, Pennsylvania.

SIMPSON, PETER (Tlingit)
Peter Simpson resided at the Cottage Settlement at Sitka, Alaska, a mission enterprise established by the National Indian Association in the late 1890's. In 1902, the Sitka Bay Cannery refused to hire natives. The boys of Cottage Settlement made five fishing boats and under Simpson's leadership sailed to the cannery. When the superintendent refused to hire them, Simpson supposedly said, "You think we are like those Killisno natives, but we are not; we are Christian natives." The superintendent hired them; they built two more boats and had a good season. Simpson attended the Sitka Training School. Besides owning his own boat, he knew the sawmill business, doing seasonal work as a mill foreman. He also received a contract to build a government Native school.

SIOW, BESSIE (Pueblo)
Bessie Siow attended the Phoenix Indian School.

SITTINGBULL, JENNIE (Arapaho)
Jennie Sittingbull was born in Oklahoma in 1902, the daughter of Sitting Bull and Dropping Lip. From Eagle City, Oklahoma, she graduated from Chilocco Indian School in 1923.

SIXKILLER, SAMUEL (Cherokee)
Samuel Sixkiller was born in 1877 in the Cherokee Nation, the son of Samuel and Frances Flora Foreman. After graduation from Carlisle in 1895, he returned to Muskogee. He lived at Afton, Cherokee Nation, in 1895, and later returned to Muskogee again, where he worked as a bookkeeper for the Muskogee Phoenix. In 1915, he was in Del Rio, Texas.

SKENADORE, IDA (Oneida)
Ida Skenadore was from Wisconsin and was a student at Haskell in 1909.

SKIUHUSHU (Blackfeet)
The Rev. Skiuhushu (Red Fox) was General Secretary of the Society of American Indians in 1922.

SKYE, HAZEL N. (Seneca)

Hazel N. Skye, from Bosom, New York, graduated from Carlisle in 1914. She later did hospital work in Buffalo.

SKYE, MAZIE L. (Seneca)
Mazie L. Skye, from New York, was born about 1890 and graduated from Carlisle in 1911.

SLEEPINGBEAR, PAUL (Gros Ventre)
No information is available.

SLINKER, THOMAS DEWEY (Choctaw)
Thomas Dewey Slinker was born at Atoka, Choctaw Nation, in 1898, the son of James and Lizzie Jackson Slinker. He attended Carlisle and served in the Twenty-eighth Infantry, A. E. F., in 1918.

SLOAN, THOMAS (Omaha)
Thomas Sloan, from Nebraska, was born about 1863. He entered Hampton Institute in 1886 and graduated in 1889.

SMALL, MARY T. (Sioux)
Mary T. Small was a student at Haskell Institute in 1922.

SMALLWOOD, BENJAMIN FRANKLIN (Choctaw)
Benjamin Franklin Smallwood was born in the Choctaw Nation in Mississippi in 1829, the son of William and Mary Leflore Smallwood. He attended the common schools and Spencer Academy in the Choctaw Nation. He was a farmer and store owner. Except for the war years, Smallwood held public office from 1847 to 1890, including positions as member of the Choctaw Council, Speaker of the lower house, delegate to Washington, and Principal Chief, to which position he was elected in 1888. His wife was Abbie James. Smallwood died on December 15, 1891.

SMART, LETA V. MEYERS (Omaha)
Leta V. Meyers, from Mountain View, Missouri, attended Hampton Institute. She taught at Mountain View and, in 1915, entered the Indian Service as a teacher at Zuni Boarding School at Blackrock, New Mexico. In the early 1920's, she lived in Washington, D. C., where she was active in Indian affairs for several years. She married Francis G. Smart of Bessemer, Michigan.

SMITH, CALINA (Yokaia)
Calina Smith, from northern California, graduated from the Phoenix Indian School in 1902.

SMITH, CLARENCE (Arapaho)
Clarence Smith, born about 1887, attended Carlisle.

SMITH, DAVID (Pima)
David Smith graduated from the Phoenix Indian School in 1910.

SMITH, ELIJAH B. (Oneida)
Elijah B. Smith of West De Pere, Wisconsin, was born on the

Oneida lands in 1902, the son of Charles and Louisa Smith. He graduated from the high school and engineering departments of Haskell Institute in 1924.

SMITH, FANNIE (Cherokee)
Fannie Smith, from Stilwell, Oklahoma, was born on December 29, 1905, the daughter of Daniel and Lizzie Smith. She graduated from Bacone College in 1925.

SMITH, HARRISON B. (Oneida)
Harrison B. Smith, from Wisconsin, was born about 1890. He attended Carlisle.

SMITH, HENRY E. (Little Lake, or Mitomkai Pomo)
Henry E. Smith graduated from the Phoenix Indian School in 1904 and entered Hampton Institute.

SMITH, HOKE (Apache)
Hoke Smith was a 1905 graduate of the Phoenix Indian School. In 1912, he worked at the Whiteriver, Arizona school. In 1921, he was property clerk there.

SMITH, JAMES (Warm Springs)
James Smith, from California, was a student at Haskell Institute in 1915.

SMITH, JEFFERSON B. (Gros Ventre)
Jefferson B. Smith, from Elbowoods, North Dakota, graduated from Carlisle in 1911. He then attended school in Minneapolis. He married Ruth Packineau, and they made their home at Elbowoods, where he ranched.

SMITH, JENNIE (Cherokee)
Jennie Smith, from Stilwell, Oklahoma, was born on October 3, 1903, the daughter of Daniel and Lizzie Smith. She graduated from Bacone College in 1925.

SMITH, LENA (Klamath)
Lena Smith was born at Ukiah, Oregon, in 1886. She was in a convent briefly before being sent to the Round Valley Boarding School. At the age of twelve, she entered the Chemewa, Oregon, Indian School and later attended the Phoenix Indian School, where she graduated in 1903.

SMITH, MARTHA (Oneida)
Martha Smith, from Wisconsin, was a student at Haskell Institute in 1911.

SMITH, SAMUEL (Cherokee)
Samuel Smith was an early member of the Kee-too-wah Society in the Cherokee Nation. During the Civil War, he was captain of a Union brigade. After the war, he was a National Party leader until 1887, when he joined the Downing Party. Smith served as a delegate to Washington.

SNAKE, JOHN E. (Shawnee)
John E. Snake was a graduate of the Indian school at Shawnee, Oklahoma. In 1907 or 1908, he became an employee of the Shawnee Agency and, in 1918, he was captain of the Indian police at the Indian school.

SNEED, JOSEPH (Pima)
Joseph Sneed attended the Phoenix Indian School.

SNOW, OLIVER LEO (Cherokee-Seneca)
Oliver Leo Snow was from Oklahoma and graduated from Chilocco Indian School in 1924.

SNOW, ROSE THELMA (Seneca)
Rose Thelma Snow, from Farnham, New York, graduated from Carlisle in 1915.

SNYDER, CORA (Seneca)
Cora Snyder, from New York, graduated from Carlisle in 1896. She married William Jones and made her home in Versailles, New York.

SOUCEA, HUGH (Pueblo)
Hugh Soucea graduated from Carlisle in 1894. After he left Carlisle, he went home to farm and later graduated from the normal department of the Indian school at Albuquerque. He then went to Wyoming and took charge of the engineering department at the Wind River School. In 1902, he was disciplinarian at the Santa Fe Indian School. He then moved to Denver, where he worked as a carpenter for several years. In 1914 and 1915, he was at the Shiprock School where he was employed as a carpenter.

SPEARS, JOHN ALBION (Cherokee)
John Albion Spears was from the Indian Territory and served on the Cherokee National Board of Education.

SPLITLOG, CARRIE B. (Seneca)
Carrie B. Splitlog was born in the Indian Territory about 1890, the daughter of Henry B. and Bertha M. Splitlog. She was a student at Haskell Institute in 1917.

SPRINGSTON, JOHN LEAF (Cherokee)
John Leaf Springston was born near Lynch's Mill, Cherokee Nation, in October, 1845, the son of Anderson and Sallie Eliot Springston. He attended Cherokee common schools. Springston served in the Union Army during the Civil War. He was for a time translator and associate editor for the Cherokee Advocate and, in 1894, edited the Tahlequah Morning Sun. He served as clerk of the Cherokee Senate and as translator in the U. S. District Court at Fort Smith, Arkansas. He was twice married, to Sarah E. Moseley and Alice C. Gray. Springston died on January 6, 1929.

STANDING BEAR, HENRY (Sioux)

Henry Standing Bear, from the Pine Ridge Reservation, graduated from Carlisle in 1891. He lived at Chicago for a number of years and worked for the Sears, Roebuck Company before moving to Porch, South Dakota. In 1902, he served as interpreter for the Indian Congress.

STARR, ELLIS (Cherokee)

Ellis Starr was born on Lee's Creek, Cherokee Nation, on June 17, 1853, the son of Leroy Starr. He attended public school until age nine and was then sent to Evansville Academy in Arkansas. At eighteen, he became a clerk in the store of E. E. Starr and, at twenty-two, entered the Cherokee Male Seminary. He served one term as interpreter in the Nation Council, one term as Sheriff of Flint District, and three terms as Prosecuting Attorney of the district. Starr was by profession a farmer and attorney. He married Martha Locust.

STARR, EMMETT (Cherokee)

Emmett Starr was born in Going Snake District, Cherokee Nation, on December 12, 1870, the son of Walter Adair and Ruth A. Thornton Starr. He graduated from the Cherokee Male Seminary in 1888 and from Barnes Medical College at St. Louis in 1891. Starr practiced medicine for five years at Chelsea and Skiatook, Cherokee Nation, but gave up his medical practice to undertake his monumental work on Cherokee genealogy and history. In 1901, he was elected to a term in the National Council. He was a Mason and a Methodist. Starr never married. He died on January 30, 1930.

STARR, EZEKIEL EUGENE (Cherokee)

Ezekiel Eugene Starr was born in the Cherokee Nation on August 11, 1849. He served as the Cherokee National Treasurer and as a Senator from Flint District. He married Margaret Starr. Starr died on October 5, 1905.

STARR, HENRY (Cherokee)

Henry Starr was born in the Cherokee Nation about 1876, the son of Thomas and Clarissa Starr. Starr was a well-known desperado in the late territorial period and was killed during a robbery attempt at a bank in Harrison, Arkansas, on February 22, 1921.

STARR, IDA (Cherokee)

Ida Starr, from the Indian Territory, attended Chilocco Indian School.

STARR, JOHN CALEB (Cherokee)

John Caleb (Cale) Starr was born in Flint District, Cherokee Nation, in October, 1870, the son of James and Emma Rider Starr. He attended public schools and the Cherokee Male Seminary, from which he graduated in 1890. He attended a commercial college in Fort Smith, Arkansas in 1891. He worked as a bookkeeper, a teacher, and clerk of the Cherokee Senate. He married Lillie B. Zimmerman.

STEEPS, GEORGE (Sioux)
George Steeps, a Sioux, was from Kemel, South Dakota.

STEPHENS, SPENCER SEAGO (Cherokee)
Spencer Seago Stephens was born in the Cherokee Nation in 1837, the son of Jess and Malinda Stephens. He attended the Old Baptist Mission School in Going Snake District. Orphaned in 1853, he was taken into the home of Mrs. Lizzie Bushyhead. He graduated from the Male Seminary in 1856. He was for many years Superintendent of Education in the Cherokee Nation and also served as National Auditor. Stephens married Sarah R. Hicks.

STEVENS, AMELIA (Nez Percé)
Amelia Stevens was a student at Haskell Institute in 1909.

STIDHAM, GEORGE WASHINGTON (Creek)
George Washington Stidham was born in the Creek Nation in Alabama on November 17, 1817, the son of Hopaychutke. He emigrated to the West in 1837 and settled at Choska. He was named a delegate to Washington in 1856, a position he held fifteen times. It was during one of his trips to the capital that he met and married Sarah Thornberry. During the Civil War, he served as Chief of the pro-Southern Creeks, represented his town in the House of Warriors, was a delegate to the Okmulgee Council in 1870, and served as Chief Justice of the Supreme Court from 1867 to 1891. For a number of years before and after the war, he operated a store. Stidham died in March, 1891.

STIDHAM, GEORGE WASHINGTON, JR. (Creek)
George Washington Stidham, Jr., was born in the Creek Nation on March 17, 1859, the son of George Washington and Sarah Thornberry Stidham. He attended neighborhood schools and then went to Henderson Masonic Institute, Henderson, Tennessee, Louisville School of Medicine, and Vanderbilt University. He practiced medicine in the Creek Nation for only a short time before entering the mercantile business and finally becoming a stockman. He also served as Clerk of the House of Kings and as private secretary to Principal Chiefs Samuel Checote and Ward Coachman. Stidham married Hallie Buckner.

STINSON, LIZZIE M. (Cherokee)
Lizzie M. Stinson, from the Indian Territory, attended school at the Cherokee Orphan Asylum.

STRONG, NATHANIEL T. (Seneca)
Nathaniel T. Strong, from New York, was a Chief of the Senecas.

STRONG WOLF (Chippewa)
Strong Wolf was the Assistant Business Manager for the American Indian Association in 1922.

STUART, MARIE (Cherokee)

Marie Stuart, from the Indian Territory, was a student at the Cherokee Female Seminary in 1854.

SUIS, GEORGE (Crow)
George Suis, from Montana, graduated from Carlisle in 1895 and attended Dickinson College in Carlisle, Pennsylvania. In 1902, he was a government employee at the Crow Agency.

SULLIVAN, NAPOLEON BONAPARTE (Creek)
Napoleon Bonaparte Sullivan attended Tullahassee Mission School, where he translated various works from English into Creek.

SUNCHIEF, STARRY (Pawnee)
Starry Sunchief, from the Indian Territory, graduated from the Phoenix Indian School in 1904 and entered Hampton Institute.

SUTTON, HENRY P. (Seneca)
Henry P. Sutton, born about 1893 in New York, was a student at Carlisle in 1914.

SWAMP, JOEL (Oneida)
Joel Swamp, from Wisconsin, graduated from Haskell Institute in 1910.

TABISCHADDIE, IRENE (Apache)
Irene Tabischaddie, from the San Carlos Reservation, was born in 1885. She attended the San Carlos School before attending the Santa Fe Indian School for two years and mission school for a third year. In 1900, she entered the Phoenix Indian School, from which she graduated in 1903. She also graduated from Hampton Institute in 1909 and went to Haskell Institute as a teacher. She then taught at the Phoenix Indian School. Her married name was Besaw. She died of influenza on December 1, 1919.

TAHAMONT, ROBERT J. (Abnaki)
Robert J. Tahamont, born about 1890, graduated from Carlisle in 1911, after which he lived in Newark, New Jersey.

TALAVENKA, CLARA M. (Hopi)
Clara M. Talavenka attended the Phoenix Indian School. Her married name was Keshotewa.

TATIYOPA, HENRY (Sioux)
Henry Tatiyopa, from South Dakota, graduated from Carlisle in 1903.

TAYLOR, JOHN M., JR. (Cherokee)
John M. Taylor, Jr., lived in the Indian Territory.

TAYLOR, RICHARD (Cherokee)
Richard Taylor was born in the eastern Cherokee Nation on February 16, 1788. He was a veteran of the War of 1812, and he served his nation as delegate to Washington and as Assistant Principal

Chief (1851-1855). He was married to Ellen McDaniel and Susie Fields. Taylor died at Tahlequah, Cherokee Nation, on June 15, 1853.

TEHEE, HOUSTON BENGE (Cherokee)
Houston Benge Tehee was born on October 14, 1874, in Sequoyah District, Cherokee Nation, the son of Stephen and Rhoda Benge Tehee. He attended Cherokee common schools and the Male Seminary and went one term at Fort Worth University. He served as Clerk of Tahlequah District for ten years and, in 1906, became cashier of a bank. Meanwhile, he studied law, specializing in oil and gas matters. In 1910, he served as Mayor of Tahlequah and was elected to the Oklahoma State Legislature in 1910 and 1912. From 1914 to 1919, he served as Register of the U. S. Treasury, and, in 1926-27, as Assistant Attorney General. He was vice-president, treasurer, and general manager of the Continental Asphalt and Petroleum Company of Oklahoma City. Tehee died on November 19, 1938.

TEMPLE, JACKSON (Klamath)
Jackson Temple graduated from the Phoenix Indian School in 1905 and was accidentally shot and killed in northern California as he was on his way back to the reservation.

TENIJIETH, SILAS (Apache)
Silas Tenijieth, from the Fort Apache Reservation, attended the Phoenix Indian School.

TEQUAWA, BERT (Apache)
Bert Tequawa was born about 1898. In 1913, he made a trip to the East. At the time, he was a student at the Phoenix Indian School.

THAYER, WILLIAM JOSEPH (Chippewa)
William Joseph Thayer was born at Shell Lake, Wisconsin, on July 25, 1894, the son of Henry and Mary Thayer. He attended the public schools at Hayward, Wisconsin, and entered Carlisle in 1912, graduating in 1915.

THOMAS, ALBERT L. (Pima)
Albert Thomas graduated from the Phoenix Indian School in 1910 and died that same year.

THOMAS, DANIEL (Pima)
Daniel Thomas graduated from Hampton Institute in 1916 and became disciplinarian at the government school at Fort Hall. He left after a year and then taught printing in New Orleans. He died about 1920.

THOMAS, FANNIE (Cherokee)
Fannie Thomas lived in the Indian Territory.

THOMAS, MYRTLE (Chippewa)
Myrtle Thomas, born about 1891, attended Carlisle.

THOMPSON, JOSEPH FRANKLIN (Cherokee)
Joseph Franklin Thompson was born on Beatties Prairie, Cherokee Nation, on May 21, 1841, the son of James Allen and Martha Lynch Thompson.   He attended the Cherokee common schools, the Cherokee Male Seminary, Cane Hill College in Arkansas, and Cumberland University of Lebanon, Tennessee, from which he graduated in 1861.   During the Civil War, Thompson joined the Seventh Tennessee Infantry (Confederate) and later fought with the First Arkansas Cavalry and Watie's First Cherokee Regiment, reaching the rank of Colonel.   After the war, Thompson taught school and served on the Cherokee Board of Education.   He was also superintendent of the Cherokee Female Seminary, Asbury Manual Labor School in the Creek Nation, and the Cherokee Orphan Asylum (1882-93, 1897-1901). Thompson also served as National Auditor and delegate to Washington. He was a Methodist preacher and was married three times: to Mary Ellen Adair, Mary Fannie Adair, and Mrs. Sarah Lovett.   Thompson died on November 9, 1922.

THOMPSON, MARTHA (Tuscarora)
Martha Thompson, from New York, graduated from the home economics department of Haskell Institute in 1920.

THOMPSON, WALTER A. (Cherokee)
Walter A. Thompson was born in 1866, the son of Joseph Franklin Thompson (q. v.).   He was well-educated and taught for a number of years at the Cherokee Male Seminary.

THREE STARS, CLARENCE (Sioux)
Clarence Three Stars went to Carlisle from the Pine Ridge Reservation in 1879 and stayed nearly five years.   He returned to the Pine Ridge Agency and, after working for a trader for a time, entered government service.   He taught for many years in the day school at Pine Ridge and for a time was a merchant there.   In 1912, he was elected County Attorney of Bennett County, South Dakota. Three Stars married Jennie Dubray.

TIAOKASIN, JOHN (Sioux)
John Tiaokasin (or Looks-into-the-Lodge), from the Standing Rock Reservation, was born about 1865, the son of Porcupine.   He attended Hampton Institute from 1881 to 1884 and from 1885 to 1889. He married Rosa Pleets.

TIBBETTS, JESSE (Chippewa)
Jesse Tibbetts attended Haskell Institute.

TIBBETTS, LUZENIA E. (Chippewa)
Luzenia E. Tibbetts, from the Leech Lake Reservation in Minnesota, graduated from Carlisle in 1901 and spent the next two years at Bloomsburg Normal School.   Her married name was Isham, and she lived in later years at Bena, Minnesota.

TIGER, EUNAH J. (Creek)
Eunah J. Tiger was born at Wetumka, Creek Nation, in 1901, the son of Barney and Katie Tiger.   He attended Bacone College.

TIGER, HELEN MAY (Creek)

Helen May Tiger was born at Okmulgee, Creek Nation, in 1901, the daughter of George W. and Susan H. Tiger. She graduated from Bacone College in 1920.

TIGER, IDA R. (Creek)

Ida R. Tiger was born at Sharpe, Creek Nation, in 1892, the daughter of George W. and Rose Tiger. She graduated from Bacone College in 1916.

TIGER, MARY J. (Creek)

Mary J. Tiger was born at Catoosa, Creek Nation, in 1899, the daughter of Thomas and Nicey Tiger. She attended Bacone College.

TIGER, MOTY (Creek)

Moty Tiger was born in the Creek Nation in 1842, the son of Tulsa Fixico and his wife Louisa. He was a Methodist preacher and served as a member of the Creek National Council for twenty years. In 1875, he was also captain of the light-horse police. In 1907, he was appointed Principal Chief upon the death of Pleasant Porter (q. v.), and he served as Chief until his death in 1917. Tiger's first wife was a fullblood, and his second was Mrs. Kizziah Lewis Shaw.

TOWNSEND, HARVEY (Pueblo)

Harvey Townsend was from San Filipe Pueblo in New Mexico.

TOWNSEND, SAMUEL (Pawnee)

Samuel Townsend, from the Indian Territory, attended Carlisle from 1879 to 1892 and then attended Marietta College in Ohio. He then returned to Oklahoma, where he attended Chilocco Indian School. From there he went to Guthrie, the capital, where he worked as the night foreman for the Daily Oklahoma State Capital. Earlier, he had worked as a printer at the White Earth, Minnesota, Boarding School, leaving there in 1903 to become an industrial teacher at the Potawatomi School in Kansas.

TRACY, CALVIN BRADLEY (Chickasaw)

Calvin Bradley Tracy, from Oklahoma, was born in 1901. He graduated from the high school department of Haskell Institute on 1923.

TRIPP, DORA (Klamath)

Dora Tripp was born in California in 1883. She attended school on the Hoopa Reservation and then entered the Phoenix Indian School, graduating in 1903.

TROTT, WILLIAM LAFAYETTE (Cherokee)

William Lafayette Trott, a Cherokee from the Indian Territory, was born about 1844, the son of James Jenkins and Rachael Pounds Adair Trott. He was married to Malinda Stover and Louise Moore.

TSATOKE, MONROE (Kiowa)

Monroe Tsatoke, from Oklahoma, was born on September 29, 1904, the son of Tsa-to-kee (Hunting Horse) and Poetomah. He attended local schools and Bacone College where he took up painting. After Bacone, he farmed and continued his study of art in the early 1920's at the Fine Arts Club at Anadarko, organized by Susie Peters for Indian students. He was then chosen to enter the experimental art program at the University of Oklahoma that began a revival in Plains Indian Art. Tsatoke became an internationally-known artist. He died at Lawton, Oklahoma, on February 2, 1937. He was married to Martha Koomsataddle.

TUTTLE, THOMAS W. (Sioux)
Thomas W. Tuttle (or Standing Holy), from the Yankton Reservation, was born about 1865, the son of One Ear. He attended Hampton Institute from 1881 to 1884. He married Susan Kill Many.

TWISS, FRANK W. (Sioux)
Frank W. Twiss, from the Pine Ridge Reservation in South Dakota, attended the Genoa, Nebraska, Indian School, where he worked before entering Carlisle, which he left in 1884. In 1892, he was a clerk in a store on the reservation. He married Adelia Lowe and lived at Porcupine, South Dakota.

TWOGUNS, EVELYN R. (Seneca)
Evelyn R. Twoguns was from Brent, New York. She graduated from Hampton Institute in 1909. In 1915, she worked as assistant nurse at White Earth, Minnesota, and, in 1920, was matron at the government hospital in Winnebago, Nebraska. In 1923, she was a nurse at Rochester, New York.

TWOGUNS, SELINA (Seneca)
Selina Twoguns, from New York, was born about 1887 and graduated from Carlisle in 1910. She then entered the Indian Service as boys' matron at the boarding school in Greenville, California.

UPSHAW, ALEXANDER B. (Crow)
Alexander B. Upshaw, from St. Xavier, Montana, was born about 1875, the son of Crazy Pend d'Orielle. He graduated from Carlisle in 1897 and he then attended Bloomsburg State Normal School. He worked as an industrial teacher at the Genoa, Nebraska, Indian School. In 1901, he helped survey the Crow Reservation, and he later farmed in the Pryor Valley, sixteen miles north of old Fort C. F. Smith. In 1906, he became associated with Edward S. Crutis, assisting him in gathering information for his works on the North American Indians, and, with Curtis, toured the northwest coastal area in 1909.

VALENZUELA, JUANA (Pima)
Juana Valenzuela attended the Phoenix Indian School.

VALENZUELA, KATHERINE (Pima)
Katherine Valenzuela was born at Lehi, Arizona, the daughter of Mrs. Encarnacion Valenzuela. She graduated from the Phoenix

Indian School in 1904. After graduation, she worked at the St. Louis Exposition. She then entered the Indian Service. In 1911, she was appointed boys' matron at the Whiteriver, Arizona, Boarding School. Her married name was Luna.

VALENZUELA, MYRA (Pima)
Myra Valenzuela, from Lehi, Arizona, was the daughter of Mrs. Encarnacion Valenzuela. A 1909 graduate of the Phoenix Indian School, she married John Dodson. In 1914, she became seamstress at the Fort Apache School, Whiteriver, Arizona.

VALENZUELA, THOMAS (Pima)
Thomas Valenzuela, from Lehi, Arizona, was the son of Mrs. Encarnacion Valenzuela. After graduation from the Phoenix Indian School in 1909, he returned to Lehi.

VANN, CLEMENT NEELEY (Cherokee)
Clement Neeley Vann was born in the Cherokee Nation, the son of David (q. v.) and Martha McNair Vann. Before the Civil War, he served as a Senator from Saline District. During the war, he was a colonel in the Second Cherokee Confederate Regiment. After the war, he served as clerk of the Council, Treasurer of the Nation, delegate to the Okmulgee Council, and delegate to Washington for the Southern Cherokees.

VANN, DANIEL WEBSTER (Cherokee)
Daniel Webster (Webb) Vann was born in the Cherokee Nation on October 12, 1845, the son of James and Elizabeth Eaton Vann. He was educated in the Cherokee public schools. During the Civil War, he served with the First Cherokee Cavalry (Confederate). He was a farmer and stockman and served as a member of the National Council for ten years. He was married twice, to Tookay Riley and Clerinda Rowe. He made his home at Pryor Creek.

VANN, DAVID (Cherokee)
David Vann was born in the eastern Cherokee Nation on January 1, 1800, the son of Avery and Margaret McSwain Vann. Before the Civil War, he served four terms as National Treasurer, and during the war, he ran a salt works on Dirty Creek until he was killed on December 23, 1863. Vann was married to Jennie Chambers and Martha McNair.

VAUGHN, GERALD (Yuma)
Gerald Vaughn graduated from the Phoenix Indian School in 1909. In 1915, he was working for the Southern Pacific Railroad.

VENNE, ALFRED M. (Chippewa)
Alfred M. Venne was born in 1880 of Chippewa and French parentage on the Fort Totten Reservation. He spoke only his native language and French until he was twelve. At age thirteen, he entered the Fort Totten School and finished the elementary grades. He remained there as disciplinarian and bandmaster for four years. From 1901 to 1904, he was at Carlisle, where he was Assistant

Physical Director while he was a student. After graduation, he became Physical and Athletic Director for the school and remained at that post for five years. In 1909, he was transferred to Chilocco as Disciplinarian and band leader, Athletic Director, and Y. M. C. A. Secretary. He took summer courses at the School of Physical Education at Lake Chatauqua, New York, and at Kansas State University. In 1912, he worked briefly at Haskell Institute and then returned to Chilocco. Venne married Sara Williams.

VENNE, ERNESTINE (Chippewa)
     Ernestine Venne, born about 1891, graduated from Carlisle in 1912.

VERIGAN, FRANCIS (Tlinget)
     Francis Verigan graduated from Carlisle in 1918. He then attended Hampton Institute and Phillips Academy at Andover, Massachusetts.

WAITE, AGNES V. (Serrano)
     Agnes V. Waite, from California, was born about 1889 and graduated from Carlisle in 1912, after which she attended high school at Glendale, California. After graduating in 1914, she entered the Indian Service as a teacher at the Indian School at Fort Yuma.

WALKER, BERTRAND N. O. (Wyandot)
     Bertrand N. O. Walker, who wrote under the name of Hen-Toh, was a Wyandot of the Big Turtle Clan. Born in Wyandot County, Kansas, on September 5, 1870, he was the son of Isaiah and Mary Walker and a descendant of a number of important men in Wyandot history dating back to Colonial times. In 1874, Walker's family moved to lands assigned the Wyandots in extreme northeastern Indian Territory, southwest of Seneca, Missouri. He attended the Friends Mission School near present-day Wyandotte, Oklahoma, and public schools and a private academy at Seneca. Walker taught school for several years and served as an Indian Service teacher and clerk in the Indian Territory, Kansas, Oklahoma, California, and Arizona. He also maintained the family farm, which was on his allotment. He read widely and talked to older Indians of various tribes about traditions, legends, myths, customs, and manners. From 1917 to 1924, he wrote, publishing a book of legends and a volume of poetry. In 1924, he became clerk at the Quapaw Agency at Miami, Oklahoma, and served until his death on June 27, 1927.

WALKER, GEORGE (Creek)
     George Walker, from the Indian Territory, entered Bacone College in 1917 and graduated in 1923.

WALKER, JOHN G. (Navajo)
     John Walker graduated from Hampton Institute in 1898 and became a businessman in Arizona. In 1912, he went to Los Angeles to study law.

WALKER, LILLIAN (Ottawa)

Lillian Walker, from Mt. Pleasant, Michigan, was born about 1894 and graduated from Carlisle in 1915.

WALKER, WISEY (Creek)
Wisey Walker, a Creek from Oklahoma, was the son of Bettie Walker. He was a student at Haskell Institute in 1915.

WALKINGSTICK, SIMON RALPH (Cherokee)
Simon Ralph Walkingstick was born in the Cherokee Nation in 1896. He graduated from Bacone College in 1914 and entered Dartmouth, but left in 1918 without taking a degree. He was the first Secretary for Indian Work under the State Committee of the Y. M. C. A. of Oklahoma and spent two years as War Work Secretary of the Y. M. C. A. with the British Expeditionary Force in India and Mesapotamia. In the 1950's, Walkingstick made his home in Syracuse, New York.

WALLACE, RICHARD (Crow)
Richard Wallace attended Carlisle.

WANNEH, GAWASA (Seneca)
No information is available.

WARD, J. L. (Cherokee)
J. L. Ward lived in the Cherokee Nation and served as Judge of Delaware District.

WARD, ROBERT J. (Choctaw)
Robert J. Ward was born at Scullyville, Choctaw Nation, in July, 1850, the son of Jeremiah and Eliza Leflore Ward. He attended neighborhood schools until 1861 and returned to school after the Civil War. In 1873, he became Sheriff of Scullyville County, after which he worked as a store clerk for a time before becoming Sheriff again. He also served as a member of the Choctaw Light Horse Police, county and district clerk, Senator, and delegate to Washington. He raised livestock and owned a store at Melton, Indian Territory. Ward married Ida Barker, a Cherokee.

WARDEN, ROBERT J. (Choctaw)
Robert Warden of Geary, Oklahoma, graduated from Chilocco Indian School in 1920.

WARREN, WILLIAM WHIPPLE (Chippewa)
William Whipple Warren was born at La Pointe, Wisconsin, on May 27, 1825, the son of Lyman M. Warren, a New England fur trader and his French-Chippewa wife Mary Cadotte. He grew up on Madeline Island and attended La Pointe Indian School and Mackinaw Mission School before going to Clarkson and the Oneida Institute in New York. He returned to the West and, in the 1840's, interpreted for the agent at La Pointe. He then settled at Crow Wing, Minnesota, and, in 1850, was elected to the state legislature. Fluent in Chippewa, he was interested in the history of his people. He began writing sketches that eventually became a history of the Ojibways, completed

in 1852. He was unsuccessful in getting it published during his lifetime. He died at St. Paul on June 1, 1853. His wife was Matilda Aitkin.

WATERMAN, CHARLES E. (Seneca)
Charles E. Waterman, from New York, attended Carlisle.

WATERMAN, LEILA (Seneca)
Leila Waterman, from Gowanda, New York, was born about 1894 and graduated from Carlisle in 1913.

WATSON, D. C. (Creek)
D. C. Watson lived in the Creek Nation and did extensive work as a translator.

WATTA, VENTURA (Mission)
Ventura (or Ben) Watta, from California, graduated from the Phoenix Indian School in 1905. He worked as a ranch hand and was Grand Secretary of the Mission Indian Federation at San Jacinto, California.

WEBB, EMMA (Pima)
Emma Webb graduated from the Phoenix Indian School in 1909.

WEBBER, DOTTIE (Pima)
Dottie Webber graduated from the Phoenix Indian School in 1914.

WEBSTER, CYNTHIA (Oneida)
Cynthia Webster, from Wisconsin, was born about 1875, the daughter of Simeon and Electa Webster. She graduated from Carlisle in 1896. After graduation, she took a teaching position at Nadeau, Kansas. She returned to Wisconsin in 1900, and, in 1902, taught at Lac du Flambeau. She then settled at Kaukauna. Her married name was Moore.

WELCH, JAMES (Chippewa)
James Welch, from the Lac Court Oreilles Reservation, was born about 1892. He attended Carlisle.

WELCH, WILSON (Cherokee)
Wilson H. Welch, from North Carolina, graduated from Carlisle in 1898.

WELLINGTON, JOSEPH E. (Pima)
Joseph E. Wellington was a graduate of Sherman Institute in Riverside, California. In 1909, he lived in Scottsdale, Arizona, and did missionary work.

WEST, BESSIE (Creek)
Bessie West received her early education at Tullahassee Mission in the Creek Nation. She left there in 1881 for Carlisle, from which she graduated. She returned to the Indian Territory and, in 1888, worked at Nuyaka Mission in the Creek Nation.

WEST, LUCY (Pawnee)
Lucy West was from the Indian Territory.

WHEELOCK, DENNISON (Oneida)
Dennison Wheelock, from Wisconsin, was born about 1871, the son of James A. Wheelock, a noted leader of the tribe. He graduated from Carlisle in 1891 and entered Dickinson Preparatory School and studied law. In the late 1890's, he returned to Carlisle as a teacher and, in 1901, succeeded his brother James (q. v.) as assistant band director. While there, he set "Pawnee Religious Song" to music and worked on his own compositions including "Indian Suite" and "Indian School Band March." He left Carlisle and lived briefly in De Pere, Wisconsin, and, in 1902, served as disciplinarian and band master at Flandreau, South Dakota. In 1903, he became band director at Haskell Institute, but shortly returned to De Pere and entered law practice. He served as Green Bay City Attorney and was admitted to practice before the Wisconsin Supreme Court in 1911 and before the U. S. Supreme Court in 1919. Wheelock married Louisa La Chapelle.

WHEELOCK, JAMES RILEY (Oneida)
James R. Wheelock was born about 1876, the son of James A. Wheelock, one of the leading men of the Oneidas in Wisconsin. He graduated from Carlisle in 1896. He remained at Carlisle as a printer, assistant band director, and conductor. In 1903, he traveled to England and Germany and studied music in the latter country. He returned to Philadelphia to pursue a music career, but he later reentered the Indian Service, becoming band leader and assistant superintendent of industries at Sherman Institute, Riverside, California. In 1916, he resigned at Sherman and became an orchestra leader in Philadelphia. Wheelock married Emma Everson.

WHEELOCK, JEMIMA (Oneida)
Jemima Wheelock, from Wisconsin, was an 1890 graduate of Carlisle. She returned to Wisconsin and taught at South School at the Green Bay Agency. She married Simon Webster and lived at Oneida, Wisconsin.

WHEELOCK, LIDA O. (Oneida)
Lida O. Wheelock, from Wisconsin, was born about 1891 and attended Carlisle. After graduation in 1913, she was employed briefly as a substitute in the domestic department at Carlisle before taking a position at the Truxton Canyon School at Valentine, Arizona.

WHEELOCK, MARTIN F. (Oneida)
Martin F. Wheelock, from Wisconsin, was born about 1874, the son of Abram Wheelock. He was a 1902 graduate of Carlisle.

WHIPPER, DALLAS (Sioux)
Dallas Whipper, from South Dakota, graduated from the home economics department of Haskell Institute in 1921.

WHIPPER, ROSE (Sioux)
Rose Whipper, from South Dakota, was born about 1886 and

graduated from Carlisle in 1914. After graduation, she briefly attended Wesleyan College in Mitchell, South Dakota, and then entered government service as a girls' matron at the Cheyenne River Boarding School. She later held a similar post at Browning, Montana.

WHITE, JOHN (Mohawk)
John White, born about 1886, attended Carlisle.

WHITE, MINNIE (Mohawk)
Minnie White, from the St. Regis Reservation in New York, was born about 1888 and graduated from Carlisle in 1911. She returned to New York and taught at the reservation school at Hogansburg, her home town.

WHITE, RENA S. (Chippewa)
Rena S. White, from the Bad River Reservation in Wisconsin, was born in 1905, the daughter of James and Cecilia White. In 1922, she was a student at Haskell Institute.

WHITEBULL, JAMES (Sioux)
James Whitebull was a student at Haskell Institute in 1915.

WHITEWOLF, HOWARD (Comanche)
Howard Whitewolf, from the Indian Territory, attended Carlisle. He returned to the Indian Territory and for a number of years after 1900 was a prominent church leader and interpreter for the Comanche mission of the Reformed Church in America at Fort Sill.

WHITMAN, ATALOYA (Pima)
Ataloya Whitman graduated from the Phoenix Indian School in 1905. She worked for a number of years in Phoenix and married John Rogers.

WILKIE, MICHAEL (Chippewa)
Michael Wilkie, from the Turtle Mountain Reservation in North Dakota, graduated from Carlisle in 1915.

WILLIAMS, ELEAZER (Mohawk)
Eleazer Williams was born in May, 1788, at St. Regis, New York, the son of Thomas and Mary Ann Rice Williams. He attended school at Long Meadow, Massachusetts, and, from 1809 to 1812, studied at East Hampton to become a missionary. During the War of 1812, he was appointed Superintendent General of the Northern Department of Indian Affairs. In 1812, he was elected Sachem by the Iroquois Council at Caughnawaga. Williams conducted effective work until he became involved in land schemes in the 1820's related to the removal of New York tribes to Wisconsin. He lived for a time among the Oneidas in Wisconsin until they repudiated him in the 1830's. He then dropped from sight until 1852, when he made news by claiming to be the Lost Dauphin of France. Williams was married to Mary Magdeline Jourdain. He died in New York on August 28, 1858.

WILLIAMS, EMMA LOWREY (Cherokee)

Emma Lowrey Williams was the daughter of William and Annie Wolf Williams. She attended the Cherokee Female Seminary, from which she graduated in 1856. She married George Washington Gunter.

WILLIAMS, GEORGE (Pueblo)
George Williams graduated from Chilocco Indian School in 1910.

WILLIAMS, JAMES P. (Ponca)
James Williams, from Oklahoma, studied at Haskell Institute and other Indian schools.

WILLIAMS, JOHNSON (Puyallup)
Johnson Williams taught at Cushman Indian School, Tacoma, Washington.

WILLIAMS, JULIA (Chippewa)
Julia Williams graduated from Carlisle in 1897.

WILLIAMS, LEWIS (Nez Percé)
Lewis Williams, from Idaho, graduated from Carlisle in 1895.

WILLIAMS, S. F. (Seneca)
S. F. Williams attended Carlisle.

WILLIS, JAMES (Choctaw)
James Willis, a Choctaw from Oklahoma, was a student at Haskell Institute in 1915.

WILLIS, LILLIE (Choctaw)
Lillie Willis, from Oklahoma, attended Haskell Institute.

WILMETT, ANTOINE (Potawatomi)
Antoine Wilmett, from Kansas, graduated from the business department of Haskell Institute in 1921 and was employed as clerk at the Osage Agency in Oklahoma.

WILSEY, FREDERICK (Concow, or Konkau)
Frederick Wilsey was born at Covelo, California, on March 2, 1890. He began school in 1895. He attended the Round Valley Day School from 1895 through 1896 and from 1898 to 1906. In the fall of 1906, he entered the Phoenix Indian School, from which he graduated in 1908.

WILSON, MARIE (Delaware)
Marie Wilson was from Copan, Oklahoma, and graduated from Chilocco Indian School in 1920.

WILSON, PETER (Cayuga)
No information is available.

WILSON, WILLIAM (Cherokee)
William Wilson was born in the eastern Cherokee Nation on October 14, 1811, the son of George and Ruth Springston Wilson. He

married Malinda Horton Chisholm, Mary Sanders Thornton, and Eliza
Hyles.   Wilson died on June 20, 1897.

WINNEMUCCA, SARAH (Paiute)
    Sarah Winnemucca was born near Humboldt Lake, Nevada, in
the mid-1840's, the daughter of the Paiute leader Winnemucca.   She
was an interpreter, taught on the Malheur Reservation and at Van-
couver Barracks, was a guide and interpreter for General Howard
during the Bannock War of 1878, served as a delegate to Washington
in 1879-1880, and lectured in the East in 1881.   She married three
times, to Edward Bartlett, to a Paiute, and to an officer named
Lambert H. Hopkins.   She died in Montana on October 16, 1891.

WISTAR, MARY (Ottawa)
    Mary Wistar attended Haskell Institute.

WOLF, JONAS (Chickasaw)
    Jonas Wolf was governor of the Chickasaw Nation from 1884
to 1886 and from 1892 to 1894, when he died in office.

WOLFCHIEF, JOHN (Arapaho)
    John Wolfchief, from Cantonment, Oklahoma, attended mission
school and the Phoenix Indian School.   He then entered high school in
Phoenix, graduating with honors in 1906.

WOLFE, JOE (Papago)
    Joe Wolfe, from Arizona, graduated from the Phoenix Indian
School in 1910.   He worked as a tailor in Phoenix for a short time
and then moved to Los Angeles to follow his trade.

WOLFE, KATHRINE E. (Cherokee)
    Kathrine Wolfe, born about 1885, attended Carlisle.

WOLFE, LIZZIE (Papago)
    Lizzie Wolfe, from Arizona, graduated from the Phoenix Indian
School in 1911.

WOLFE, MICHAEL (Chippewa)
    Michael Wolfe, from the Lac Court Oreilles Reservation in
Wisconsin was a teacher at Hampton Institute in 1913.   In 1914, he
taught at the Rainey Mountain School among the Kiowas but the next
year became disciplinarian at the Rosebud Boarding School at Mission,
South Dakota.   In 1917, he went to Reserve, Wisconsin, where he
fought the American Public Utilities Company that wanted to build a
dam that would flood the eastern part of the reserve.   He also wrote
for eastern newspapers, discussing some of the problems facing Indians.   Wolfe married Emma Sherer.

WOLFE, REUBEN (Omaha)
    Reuben Wolfe, from Nebraska, was an 1892 graduate of Car-
lisle.

WOLFE, RICHARD MURRELL (Cherokee)

Richard Murrell Wolfe was born in the Cherokee Nation on November 16, 1849, the son of John H. and Elizabeth Saunders Wolfe. Although he had limited formal education in the national schools as a youth, he was self-educated and attended public schools after adulthood. He served his nation as clerk of the lower house of the Council, a member of the Senate, a delegate to Washington, a Supreme Court Judge, and Attorney for the Nation. His wife was Susan E. Shirley.

WOODWARD, KATHLEEN CONNER (Osage)
Mrs. Kathleen Woodward (or To-wam-pah) was the daughter of William Conner. She lived at Pawhuska, Oklahoma.

WOOLWORTH, ROSE (Arapaho)
Rose Woolworth, from Oklahoma, graduated from the commercial department of Haskell Institute and took a position in the office of the superintendent of the Genoa, Nebraska, Indian School.

WRIGHT, ALLEN (Choctaw)
Allen Wright was born in the Choctaw Nation in present-day Attala County, Mississippi, in November, 1826, the son of Ishtemahilvbi and Ahepat. He went by the name of Kiliahote until 1834 when he entered the Choctaw school at Bok-tuk-lo in the western Choctaw Nation. He later attended Pine Ridge School and Spencer Academy in the nation and then went on to Delaware College and Union College at Schenectady, New York, where he graduated with an A. B. degree in 1852. He then entered Union Theological Seminary, from which he received an M. A. in 1855. Allen returned to the Choctaw Nation where he served his people in various capacities: Principal of Armstrong Academy, member of the National Council, National Treasurer, Superintendent of Schools. He was Principal Chief from 1866 through 1870. Allen was a scholar. In 1872, he translated Choctaw laws from English to Choctaw, in 1883-1884, he translated the Psalms from Hebrew to Choctaw, and in 1885, he was editor and translator for the Indian Champion at Atoka. He was an ordained Presbyterian minister and a Mason. His wife was Harriet Mitchell, a white woman. Allen died on December 2, 1885.

WRIGHT, ALLEN, JR. (Choctaw)
Allen Wright, Jr., was born on October 6, 1867, at Boggy Depot, Choctaw Nation, the son of Allen (q. v.) and Harriet Mitchell Newell Wright. He attended Choctaw neighborhood schools and Kemper Military Academy, Booneville, Missouri, from which he graduated in 1889. He then attended Union College, Schenectady, New York, graduating in 1893. He returned to the Choctaw Nation, read law at Atoka, and was admitted to the bar in 1895. In 1897, he was appointed U. S. Commissioner at South McAlester. He later practiced law at McAlester.

WRIGHT, MURIEL HAZEL (Choctaw)
Muriel Hazel Wright was born at Lehigh, Choctaw Nation, in 1889, the daughter of Eliphalet Nott and Ida Belle Richards Wright. She graduated from East Central Oklahoma Normal School at Ada and

did graduate work at Columbia University. She taught school and then became the high school principal at Wapanuka, Oklahoma, and, later, rural schools principal for Coal County. She then became a writer, writing numerous works on Oklahoma history. From 1943 to 1955, she was associate editor of the Chronicles of Oklahoma and was editor of that historical quarterly from 1955 until her death in 1975.

YANDELL, MINNIE (Bannock)
    Minnie Yandell, from the Fort Hall Reservation in Idaho, was an 1894 graduate of Carlisle. Her married name was Le Sieur (or Lecier), and she made her home at Ross Rock, Idaho.

YELLOW BIRD, FRANCIS (Sioux)
    Frank Yellow Bird (or Zitkanazina), from the Fort Berthold Reservation, was born about 1859, the son of Hunkenisni. He attended Hampton Institute from 1878 to 1880. He then served as drillmaster at St. Paul's Episcopal School on the Yankton Reservation. He died in November, 1884.

YELLOWROBE, CHAUNCEY (Sioux)
    Chauncey Yellowrobe was born about 1870 near Rapid City, South Dakota, the son of Yanktonai Sioux parents, Tasi Nagi (Yellow Robe) and Tahcawin (The Doe). In 1890, he was in Washington, translating for the Indians traveling with Buffalo Bill's Wild West Show. He entered Carlisle in 1891 and graduated in 1895. He became disciplinarian at the Genoa, Nebraska, Indian School and then at the Fort Shaw School, where he introduced football. In 1897, he returned to Carlisle as assistant disciplinarian. In 1903, he became disciplinarian at the Rapid City School and remained in that position for many years. Yellowrobe took an active interest in Indian affairs. He died on April 6, 1930.

YELLOWTAIL, ROBERT (Crow)
    Robert Yellowtail, from Montana, attended Carlisle. He later graduated from Sherman Institute at Riverside, California. He then returned to the Crow Reservation in Montana, improved his allotment, became a successful farmer, and played an active role in tribal affairs.

YOUNGBULL, TYLER (Arapaho)
    Tyler Youngbull, from Oklahoma, graduated from Bacone College in 1923.

YUCKKU, LEMUEL (Hopi)
    Lemuel Yuckku graduated from the Phoenix Indian School in 1916.

YUPE, SUSIE (Shoshoni)
    Susie Yupe graduated from Carlisle in 1900. She returned to Idaho and taught at the Fort Hall School for one year. Her married name was Green, and she made her home at Fort Hall.

INDEX OF WRITERS BY
TRIBAL AFFILIATION

(Underlines indicate pseudonymous
writers listed in Part II.)

ABNAKI
  Tahamont, Robert J.

ABSENTEE SHAWNEE see SHAW-
  NEE

ALASKAN NATIVE
  Brown, Margaret Jeane
  Cushing, George
  Patton, Alonzo A.
  Paul, Kendall
  Paul, Matilda K.
  Paul, William L.
  Reed, Thomas B.
  Reinken, Olga
  Simpson, Peter
  See also HAIDA, TLINGIT,
    TSIMSHIAN

APACHE
  Apache, Antonio
  Davis, Gilbert
  Ethelba, Kay
  Gilmore, Gus (San Carlos)
  Goody, Ida
  Heyl, Richard D.
  McIntosh, Robert (San Carlos)
  Montezuma, Carlos (Pinal)
  Natalish, Vincent
  Smith, Hoke
  Tabischaddie, Irene (San Carlos)
  Tenijieth, Silas (Fort Apache)
  Tequawa, Bert

ARAPAHO
  Coolidge, Sherman (Northern)
  Friday, Moses
  Medicinegrass, Lucy
  Mountain, Thirza
  Root, Clara
  Sittingbull, Jennie (Southern)
  Smith, Clarence
  Warden, Robert

Wolfchief, John (Southern)
Woolworth, Rose (Southern)
Youngbull, Tyler (Southern)

ARICKARA
  Bear, Stell V.
  Dawson, Anna

ASSINIBOIN
  Gregg, Clark
  Mitchell, Charles
  Murdock, Wesson

BANNOCK
  La Vatta, Emma
  Parker, Anna
  Yandell, Minnie

BLACKFOOT
  Clarke, Malcolm (Piegan)
  Hamilton, Joseph H. (Piegan)
  Hamilton, Robert J. (Piegan)
  Pambrun, Francis (Piegan)
  Skiuhushu

CADDO
  Dale, William
  Finley, Minnie
  Hazlett, Malcolm

CATAWBA
  Harris, David A.

CAYUGA
  Bishop, William C.
  Pierce, Rogene A.
  Wilson, Peter

CAYUSE
  Minthorn, Aaron

CHEHALIS
  Jackson, Robert

315

CHEROKEE
"A"
A
Achillahcullaghee
Ada
Ada May
Adair, B. K.
Adair, Hugh Montgomery
Adair, J. W.
Adair, John Lynch
Adair, Lena Harnage
Adair, Walter
Adair, Washington
Adair, William Penn
Ah-sto-la-ta
Alberty, Elias Cornelius
Alberty, John Wright
Alice
Anderson, Hellen Rebecca
Anderson, Mabel Washbourne
Athome
"Aunt Susan"
B. W. A.
Ballard, W. H.
Balloa
Bean, J. S.
Bear, Johnson
Beck, John H.
Beck, Stacy
Bell, Lucien Burr
Bell, Mattie
Bell, Oregonia
Bell, William Watie
Belle
Benge, Samuel Houston
Bessie
Big Creek Scribe
Big Indian
"Big Injin"
Bill
Black Fox
Blackburn, Cyrus Leonidus
Bood Guy
Boudinot, Elias
Boudinot, Elias Cornelius
Boudinot, Elias Cornelius, Jr.
Boudinot, Franklin Josiah
Boudinot, William Penn
Brown, David J.
Bryant, Charlie
Buffington, Ezekiel
Buffington, Thomas Mitchell
Bushyhead, Dennis Wolfe
Butler, George O.
"Canadian"
"Captain Jack"
Carey, James
Cawlahnah Oonakah

CHEROKEE (cont.)
Cha-lah-gee
Cha-wah-yoo-kah
"Cherokee" [used by several writers]
Cherokee by Blood
A Cherokee Farmer
A Cherokee Indian
"Chicamauga"
Choate, Robert M.
Choon-noo-lus-ky
Choon-stoo-tee
Chouteau, Edmond
A Citizen
Clod Hopper
Cochran, Jesse
Comingdeer, John
Coodey, William Shorey
Cook, William Tuttle
Cookson, Edley Levi
Corrinne
"Cornsilk"
Coyote
Crutchfield, Joseph Vann
Cunningham, Jeter Thompson
Dah-lo-ne
Dick, Coffee
Dick, John Henry
Dick Clod Hopper
Downing, Lewis
Duncan, De Witt Clinton
Duncan, Emma
Duncan, J. C.
Duncan, James W.
Duncan, Jennie
Duncan, Walter Adair
Eaton, Rachel Caroline
Edith
Edmondson, Bula
Eubanks, William
Fanny
Fields, Richard
Fields, Richard H.
Foreman, Harrison
Foreman, Stephen
French, William
Full Blood
Fullblood
Ga-yu-ga
George, Dahney E. (North Carolina)
Going Snake
Gourd, Louis B. R.
Grace
Gray, Stand Watie
Green, Flora
Greenway, Minnie
Gritts, Daniel
Gu-la-tsi

CHEROKEE (cont.)
Haide
Half Breed, Richard
Harris, Colonel Johnson
Harris, George
Hastings, William Wirt
Hattie
Henderson, William Penn
Hendricks, George
Hendricks, William
Hicks, Clara
Hicks, Elijah
Hicks, William
Hors de Combat
Icy
Ida
"Indian"
Indian
Inez
Injun
I-no-li
Ionia
Isabella
Israel, Ella
Ivey, Augustus E.
Jones, Abraham Linkum
Jordan, John W.
Justice
Justice
Ka-ya-kun-stah
Kah-Too
"Kate"
Kaw-la-nah
Kenah Tetlah
Kepler
Kingfisher
Kitty
Landrum, Elias M.
Landrum, Hiram Terrell
Lee, Lilly
Lelia
"Len-oh-pee"
Leonora
Letilla
"Lone Tree"
Long, Sylvester (North Carolina)
Lowrey, George
Lusette
McCoy, John Lowrey
McLemore, Gussie
Martin, John
Martin, Joseph Lynch
Mayes, Joel Bryan
Mayes, Samuel Houston
Melton, Anna
Miller, Iva
Morgan, Gideon
Mumblehead, James

CHEROKEE (cont.)
Murrel
Muskrat, Ruth
Na-Li
Native
Native
Neal, Dick
Ne-wo-ta-ka
Oakfuskie
Observer
"Oc"
"Oceola"
Oconestota
O'Field, Ina
Old Injin
Oo-da-sa-tih
Oo-na-kah-tuh
Oogalah
Ooh-la-nee-ter
Oolagah
"Or-gun-stau-tah"
Oskison, John Milton
Owen, Narcissa
Owen, Robert Latham
Owl, Frel McDonald (North Carolina)
Owl, George A. (North Carolina)
Owl, Henry M. (North Carolina)
Owl, Lula (North Carolina)
Owl, W. David (North Carolina)
Owl, William (North Carolina)
Parris, Caroline
Paschal, Ridge
Pedagogue
Pewter Dick
Pitcher, Mary Elvina
Poo Injun
Procter, Ezekiel
Qua-tsy
Quale-u-quah
Raven
Redbird
Reed, Ora V. Eddleman
Ridge, John
Ridge, John Rollin
Riggs, Rolla Lynn
Riley, Mary
Rodgers, Thomas L.
Rogers, Clement Vann
Rogers, John
Rogers, Robert
Rogers, Will
Rogers, William
Rogers, William Charles
Ross, Daniel H.
Ross, John
Ross, Joshua
Ross, Rufus O.

CHEROKEE (cont.)
  Ross, S. W.
  Ross, T. D.
  Ross, William Potter
  Rowe, Felix
  Sah-le-gu-ge
  Saline
  "Sa-loo"
  Sapsucker
  Saunooke, Nan (North Carolina)
  Scales, Joseph Absalom
  Scraper, Etta
  Sherrill, William
  Sixkiller, Samuel
  Ska-quah
  Skiatook
  Sleeping Rabbit
  Slimkins Joner
  Smith, Fannie
  Smith, Jennie
  Smith, Samuel
  Snow, Oliver Leo [Cherokee-
    Seneca]
  Spears, John Albion
  Spectator
  Springston, John Leaf
  Starr, Ellis
  Starr, Emmett
  Starr, Ezekiel Eugene
  Starr, Henry
  Starr, Ida
  Starr, John Caleb
  Stephens, Spencer Seago
  Stinson, Lizzie M.
  Stuart, Marie
  Taylor, John M., Jr.
  Taylor, Richard
  Tecumseh
  Tehee, Houston Benge
  Thomas, Fannie
  Thompson, Joseph Franklin
  Thompson, Walter A.
  Tickanooly
  Too Stoo
  Toy-ah-nee-tah
  Tree-tee
  Trott, William LaFayette
  Turtle
  U-na-kuh
  Utaletah
  "V"
  Vann, Clement Neely
  Vann, Daniel Webster
  Vann, David
  Veritas
  Vidoco
  Voter
  Wah-le-ah

CHEROKEE (cont.)
  Wah-lie
  Walkingstick, Simon Ralph
  Ward, J. L.
  War-too-hee
  Weewah
  Welch, Wilson H. (North Carolina)
  Wenonah
  White Arrow
  White Horse
  Williams, Emma Lowrey
  Wilson, William
  Wolfe, Kathrine E.
  Wolfe, Richard Murrell
  Woochee Ochee
  The Woodpecker
  Yellow Hammer
  Young Beaver

CHEYENNE
  Balenti, Michael R. (Southern)
  Balenti, William M. (Southern)
  Blackbear, Joseph (Southern)
  Davis, Richard (Southern)
  Hart, Homer
  Hauser, Anna
  Hawkins, Edna (Southern)
  Hawkins, Kish (Southern)
  Kingsley, Llewellyn
  Merrick, Richenda
  Pawnee, William [Cheyenne-
    Arapaho] (Southern)
  Roman Nose, Henry C. (Southern)
  Romanose, Oliver (Southern)
  Rowland, Emma J. (Northern)

CHICKASAW
  Burney, Benjamin Crooks
  Byrd, William Leander
  Carter, Charles D.
  Chickasaw
  Colbert, Daugherty
  Colbert, Humphrey
  Full Blood
  Gitchie Manitou
  Guy, James Harris
  Harkins, George W.
  Harris, Cyrus
  Harris, Robert Maxwell
  Hayes, Joseph William
  Hughes, Eula
  Johnston, Douglas Henry
  Land, Vernola
  Overton, Benjamin Franklin
  Tracy, Calvin Bradley
  Wolf, Jonas

CHIPPEWA
  Agosa, Robert D.
  Arteshaw, Marie
  Ashmun, H. C. (Bad River)
  Azure, Ovilla (Turtle Mountain)
  Baldwin, Marie L. B.
  Beaulieu, C. H. (White Earth)
  Beaulieu, Clarence (White
    Earth)
  Beaulieu, Gustave (White
    Earth)
  Beaulieu, Theodore (White
    Earth)
  Beauregard, Margaret
  Bebeau, Genevieve
  Bellanger, Alice
  Bellecourte, Charles James
    (White Earth)
  Bender, Charles A. (Bad Riv-
    er)
  Bender, Fred (Bad River)
  Blackwood, Margaret O.
  Bluesky, Louise
  Bourassa, Rosa
  Boutwell, Leon (White Earth)
  Bracklin, Edward (Lac Court
    Oreilles)
  Bradley, Estelle (Isabella)
  Bresette, Francis (Bad Riv-
    er)
  Broken Wing Bird
  Broker, Frederick (White
    Earth)
  Broker, Joseph Henry (White
    Earth)
  Brunette, William (White
    Earth)
  Butterfield, Angeline (Bad
    River)
  Cajune, Frank (White Earth)
  Caswell, Benjamin
  Chapman, Arthur (White Earth)
  Cloud, Elizabeth Bender (Bad
    River)
  Copway, George
  Davis, Oscar DeForest (White
    Earth)
  Denomie, Antoine (Bad River)
  Denomie, S. F. (Bad River)
  Denomie, William (Lac Court
    Oreilles)
  Doherty, John J. (Bad River)
  Enmegahbowh (White Earth)
  Frechette, Julia
  Gordon, Philip B.
  Gouge, Joseph J. (Fond du
    Lac)
  Greensky, Naomi Evelyn

CHIPPEWA (cont.)
  Grumboise, Emma
  Hamlin, George (White Earth)
  Hazen, Bessie
  Holmes, Frank (Bad River)
  Isham, Ira O. (Lac Court Oreilles)
  Jackson, Charles
  Jerome, Elmira
  Jerome, Marcelle
  Jordan, Peter Joseph
  Kah O Sed, E. C. (White Earth)
  Ke-Wa-Ze-Zhig
  King, Louis
  Lariver, Frank
  Merrill, George
  Miller, Mary
  Morrin, Alvis M. (Red Cliff)
  Morrisette, Fred William
  Morrison, Carrie
  Morrison, Joe (White Earth)
  Morrison, John George, Jr. (White
    Earth)
  Nason, Bertha
  Needham, Simon (Red Lake)
  O'Donnell, Stella (White Earth)
  Oliver, James (Fond du Lac)
  Peake, Emily E. (White Earth)
  Petosky, Cornelius
  Raiche, Mary
  Rogers, Edward (White Earth)
  Selkirk, Charles (White Earth)
  Selkirk, George B. (White Earth)
  Simon, Elmer
  Strong Wolf
  Thayer, William Joseph (Lac Court
    Oreilles)
  Thomas, Myrtle
  Tibbetts, Jesse
  Tibbetts, Luzenia E. (Leech Lake)
  Venne, Alfred
  Venne, Ernestine
  Warren, William Whipple
  Welch, James (Lac Court Oreilles)
  White, Rena S. (Bad River
  Wilkie, Michael (Turtle Mountain)
  Williams, Julia
  Wolfe, Michael (Lac Court
    Oreilles)

CHOCTAW
  Alexander, John C.
  Anderson, Alice
  Choctaw
  Colbert, Ben H.
  Cole, Coleman
  Conlan, Czarina M.
  Durant, Will
  Folsom, Don D.

Folsom, Israel
Folsom, Joseph P.
Full Blood
Garvin, Isaac L.
Hattak Sipokini
Hopisahubbee
James, Alice
Kully Chaha
Leflore, Campbell
Locke, Victor M.
McCurtain, Ben F.
McCurtain, David Cornelius
McCurtain, Edmond
McCurtain, Green
McCurtain, Jackson Frazier
McGilberry, Charles W.
McKinney, Thompson
Old Timer
Parker, Gabriel E.
Pitchlynn, Peter Perkins
Slinker, Thomas Dewey
Smallwood, Benjamin Franklin
Sope Stix
Tuskahomma
Ward, Robert J.
Washakshihoma
Willis, James
Willis, Lillie
Wright, Allen
Wright, Allen, Jr.
Wright, Muriel Hazel

CLALLAM
Ross, Dorsie
Ross, Marguerite

COLVILLE
Arcasa, Alexander

COMANCHE
Coffey, Robert
Parker, Esther
Whitewolf, Howard

CONCOW see MAIDU

CREEK
Alexander, Jacob
Arna-waky
Cain, Archibald
Callahan, Sophia Alice
Carr, Robert L.
Checote, Samuel
Childers, Ellis Buffington
Childers, Robert C.
Coachman, Ward
Cosar, Galvos

CREEK (cont.)
Echo-hutka
Emarthla
Este Maskoke
Fisher, Henry Clay
Fisher, William
Fix-e-co
Freeman, Theodore R.
Gibson, Charles
Grayson, George Washington
Grayson, George Washington
Harris, William
Hayes, Henry Horace
Herrod, Mary
Hodge, David McKillop
An Indian
Istechule
Jones, John
Kanard, Bettie
McCombs, William
McDermott, Jesse J.
McGilbra, Sanford
McIntosh, Albert Gallatin
McIntosh, Jeanetta
McIntosh, Luke G.
McKellop, Albert Pike
Mahia
Moharjo
Perryman, Joseph M.
Perryman, Legus Chouteau
Phillips, Walter
Poor Lo
Porter, Pleasant
Posey, Alexander Lawrence
Stidham, George Washington
Stidham, George Washington, Jr.
Sullivan, Napoleon Bonaparte
Tiger, Eunah J.
Tiger, Helen May
Tiger, Ida R.
Tiger, Mary J.
Tiger, Moty
Tustenuck Emarthla
Walker, George
Walker, Wisey
Watson, D. C.
West, Bessie

CROW
Chiefchild, Delia
Frost, Alice
Leider, Carl
Old Coyote, Barney
Suis, George
Upshaw, Alexander
Wallace, Richard
Yellowtail, Robert

DALLES
    Johnson, Victor H.

DELAWARE
    Adams, Richard Calmit
    Duckworth, M. Zoe
    Gaddy, Virginia
    Gibbs, Adin C.
    Miller, Sadie (Delaware-
        Cherokee)
    Sarcoxie, Henry B.
    Wilson, Marie

DIGGER
    James, Fremont
    Mason, Marie

FLATHEAD
    Lassa, Nicholas

FOX see SAC AND FOX

GROS VENTRE
    Sanborn, John
    Sleepingbear, Paul
    Smith, Jefferson B.

HAIDA
    Davis, Samuel G.

HOPI
    Chooro, Emma
    Chooromi, John
    Coochasnema, Jessie
    Gashoienim, Nora (Oraibe)
    Kate, Clara M.
    Nehoitewa, Roland
    Setima, Mack Q.
    Talavenka, Clara M.
    Yuckku, Lemuel

HUPA
    Russell, Ina

IOWA
    Leary, Evelyn

IROQUOIS
    Garen, Mary

KANSA
    Curtis, Charles

KAW see KANSA

KICKAPOO
    De Peltquestangue, Estaiene M.

KIOWA
    Aitsan, Lucius Ben
    Doyeto, Morris
    Given, Joshua H.
    Lone Wolf, Delos
    Napawat, Martha
    Quoetone, Fred J.
    Tsatoke, Monroe

KLAMATH
    Ball, Joseph
    Bussell, Clara
    Dedrick, Edith
    Drew, Harvey
    Ferris, George
    George, Lewis
    Jackson, Emma
    Kenney, Louisa
    Kirke, Clayton
    Kirke, Seldon
    Knudson, Elizabeth E.
    Merrill, Susie
    Peterson, Eunice
    Robinson, Jesse
    Smith, Lena
    Temple, Jackson
    Tripp, Dora
    Valley of Mountains

KONKAU see MAIDU

LITTLE LAKE see POMO

LUMMI
    Lane, Helen

MAIDU
    Anderson, Phenia (Concow, or
        Konkau)
    Clements, Luther (Michopdo)
    Wilsey, Frederick (Concow, or
        Konkau)

MARICOPA
    Johns, Lillian
    Nott, Alice
    Rhodes, Marianna

MASHPEE
    De Grasse, Alfred

MENOMINEE
    Brunett, Joseph M.
    Brunette, Cecelia
    Chickeney, Charles W.
    Greenbrier, Adeline

Greenbrier, Carlysle
Kershaw, William J.
Keshena, Elizabeth
Maquimitis, Mitchell

MIAMI
Aveline, Frank D.

MICHOPDO see MAIDU

MISSION
Alis, Herman
Anderson, Paquala
Calac, Claudina
Calac, Georgia E.
Coleman, Charles F.
Costo, Martin
Costo, Nattie
Hoxie, William
Largo, Anthony
Lugo, Francisco
Lugo, Patricio
Rice, Samuel
Scholder, Fritz
Watta, Ventura

MODOC
Clinton, Mary L.
McCarty, Adam
Maddox, Sarah
Riddle, Jeff C.

MOHAVE
Davidson, Hal O.
Harris, Arthur T. (Mohave-
Apache)
Kelton, Homer
Kennawa, Herb
Mott, Seward (Mohave-
Apache)

MOHAWK
Bruce, Louis
Jocks, Joseph
White, John
White, Minnie
Williams, Eleazer

MOHEGAN
Occom, Samson

MUNSEE
Jones, Flora E.

NAVAJO
Baker, Lillie
Beale, Grace Henrietta
Damon, Nellie

Denetsouenbega, Manuelito
Green, Tzulko
Peshlaski, Frank S.
Platero, Jose Kie
Walker, John G.

NEZ PERCÉ
Axtell, Obed
Carter, Caleb
Complainville, Lillian T.
Hayes, Noah
McFarland, David
Montieth, Sara
Parnell, Annie
Ramsey, John
Stevens, Amelia
Williams, Lewis

NOAMLAKI
Hoxie, Sara

OMAHA
Barada, Mitchell
Barnaby, Josephine
Chase, Hiram
Chase, Hiram, Jr.
Fontenelle, Eugene
Freemont, Henrietta R.
Fuller, Elsie
LaFlesche, Francis
LaFlesche, Susette
Levering, Levi
Picotte, Marguerite LaFlesche
Picotte, Susan LaFlesche
Sloan, Thomas
Smart, Leta V. Meyers
Tibbles, Susette
Wolfe, Reuben

ONEIDA
Archiquette, Martin
Cooper, Electa
Cornelius, Brigman
Cornelius, Chester Poe
Cornelius, E. L.
Cornelius, Electa
Cornelius, Lilly
Cornelius, Nancy O.
Doxtator, Margaret
Elm, Cora
Hillman, Levi
James, Julia
Kellogg, Laura Minnie Cornelius
King, Birdie
King, Marie
Metoxen, Anna
Metoxen, Daisy
Metoxen, Evelyn

Metoxen, Iva
Metoxen, Joe
Metoxen, Malinda
Powless, Richard S.
Schanandore, Edwin
Sickles, Martha L.
Silas, Roger
Skenadore, Ida
Smith, Elijah B.
Smith, Harrison B.
Smith, Martha
Swamp, Joel
Webster, Cynthia
Wheelock, Dennison
Wheelock, James
Wheelock, Jemima
Wheelock, Lida O.
Wheelock, Martin F.

ONONDAGA
Doxon, Charles

OSAGE
Kohpay, Harry
Woodward, Kathleen

OTO
Rulo, Louis

OTTAWA
Blackbird, Andrew J.
Cooke, Clifford
Ettawageshik, J. William
Kewaygeshik, Mary Wonita
Redbird, Simon
Walker, Lillian
Wistar, Mary

PAIUTE
Brazzanovich, Flora
Foster, Wimmie
Shaw, Nellie
Winnemucca, Sarah

PAPAGO
Antonio, Jose
Jose, Magela
Lewis, Jose
Maristo, Martin
Narcho, Pablo
Pablo, Jose Xavier
Ramone, Josephine
Wolfe, Joe
Wolfe, Lizzie

PAWNEE
Adams, Alex
Fields, Arthur

Murie, James R.
Osborne, Samuel
Peters, Bert
Pratt, Jennie
Ricketts, Herman
Roberts, George
Roberts, Vivian
Sunchief, Starry
Townsend, Samuel
West, Lucy

PENOBSCOT
Nicolar, Joseph

PEORIA
Dagenett, Charles Edwin
Paschal, Louis

PEQUOT
Apes, William

PIEGAN see BLACKFOOT

PIMA
Allen, Josiah
Anton, Florence
Anton, Wallace
Antone, Lola
Antonio, Hal
Breckenridge, John C.
Breckenridge, Mary
Burke, Joseph
Burke, Robert
Cheerless, Luciana
Clark, Emma P.
Colt, Lewis
Easchief, Annie
Easchief, Manuel
Easchief, Oldham
Emerson, Calvin
Enas, Lasalle
Enos, Johnson
Howard, Barney
Hughes, Martha
Jackson, Alfred
Jackson, Helen
Jackson, Thomas
Johnson, Eliza
Juan, Jose
Kalka, Jose
Lewis, Annie
Lewis, Robert
Lewis, Simon
McAfee, Johnson
McArthur, Nellie
Manuel, Victor
Martin, Joe
Micha, Lizzie

PIMA (cont.)
  Mills, Inez
  Mollie, Alma
  Mollie, Ossie
  Moore, Annie T.
  Narsa, Mida
  Osick, Eloise
  Osif, Mollie
  Owens, John K.
  Paul, George
  Peters, William
  Porter, Peter
  Shaw, Ross
  Shields, Lizzie
  Smith, David
  Sneed, Joseph
  Thomas, Albert L.
  Thomas, Daniel
  Valenzuela, Juana
  Valenzuela, Katherine
  Valenzuela, Myra
  Valenzuela, Thomas
  Webb, Emma
  Webber, Dottie
  Wellington, Joseph E.
  Whitman, Ataloya

POMO
  Busch, Elmer
  Crabtree, Mary (Little Lake, or
    Mitomkai)
  Doolittle, Ottowell (Little Lake,
    or Mitomkai)
  Fulwilder, Penrose (Little Lake,
    or Mitomkai)
  Smith, Calina (Yokaia)
  Smith, Henry E. (Little Lake,
    or Mitomkai)

PONCA
  McDonald, Louis
  Williams, James P.

POTAWATOMI
  Cooper, Stella
  Goulette, Emma D. Johnson
    (Citizen Band)
  Ignatius, Joe Mack (Prairie)
  James, Otwin (Potawatomi-
    Kansa)
  Kakaque, Mary
  Moose, Joseph (Prairie)
  Nichols, Roland A.
  Pambago, John B.
  Pokagon, Simon
  Wilmett, Antoine (Prairie)

PUEBLO
  Avalos, Cipriana
  Avalos, Juan B.
  Goyitney, Annie
  Hudson, Frank (Laguna)
  Hunt, Evelyn
  Kendall, Henry J.
  Leeds, Yamie
  Lolorias, John
  Lujan, Max
  Madrid, Savannah
  Montion, Carmen
  Morton, Annie M. (Laguna)
  Nori, Siceni J. (Laguna)
  Padilla, Polita
  Quintano, Santiago
  Rodriquez, Fernando
  Siow, Bessie
  Soucea, Hugh
  Townsend, Harvey (San Filipe)
  Williams, George

PUYALLUP
  Bastian, John
  Brewer, Ella
  Kalma, Francis
  Williams, Johnson

QUAPAW
  Red Eagle, Grace
  Red Eagle, Leroy

ROGUE RIVER see TUTUTNI

SAC AND FOX
  Battice, Cora Melbourne
  Battice, Walter C.
  Ellis, Estella W.
  Harris, Frances
  Ingalls, Sadie M.
  Jones, Frank
  Jones, William
  Keokuk, Fannie
  McCoy, Pauline
  Miles, Thomas J.
  Newashe, Emma M.

SANPOIL
  Runnels, Louis H.

SAUK see SAC AND FOX

SEMINOLE
  Brown, John F.

SENECA
  Bearskin, Cora
  Bishop, Albert

Bluesky, Bertram
Cornplanter, Edward
Crowe, Janie
Dye, Bertha E.
Hardy, James Ora
Hardy, Percy
Hill, Jesse
Jamison, Jacob M.
Johns, Della May
Johnson, A. Ella
Johnson, Ruth Adelia
Kennedy, Alvin
Lay, Theresa
Nichols, Josephine
Parker, Arthur Caswell
Parker, Ely Samuel
Parker, Frederick E.
Patterson, Spencer
Pierce, Delia
Pierce, Evelyn
Pierce, Maris Bryant
Skye, Hazel N.
Skye, Mazie L.
Snow, Rose Thelma
Snyder, Cora
Splitlog, Carrie
Strong, Nathaniel T.
Sutton, Henry P.
Twoguns, Evelyn R.
Twoguns, Selina
Wanneh, Gawasa
Waterman, Charles E.
Waterman, Leila
Williams, S. F.

SERRANO
Gabriel, Christiana
Waite, Agnes V.

SHAWNEE
Alford, Thomas Wildcat (Absentee)
King, John (Absentee)
Snake, John (Absentee)

SHOSHONI
Dodson, John
La Vatta, George
La Vatta, Isabel
La Vatta, Philip
McAdams, James C.
O'Neal, Minnie Elizabeth
Yupe, Susie

SIOUX
Archambeau, Lorena (Yankton)
Arrow, Arthur
Barse, Alcesta

SIOUX (cont.)
Baskin, Samuel (Santee)
Bear, Joseph L.
Bearface, Rosa (Standing Rock)
Beaulieu, Irene Campbell (Santee)
Blackbear, Thomas (Pine Ridge)
Bonnin, Gertrude Simmons (Yankton)
Bonser, Harry
Bow, Claude (Standing Rock)
Bowker, Mabel
Brave, Benjamin (Lower Brule)
Brown, Harry (Cheyenne River)
Brown, Irene M. (Sisseton)
Buck, George (Fort Peck)
Buck, Mabel (Fort Peck)
Bush Otter, George (Yankton)
Carlin, Walter
Carter, Minot
Cash, A. Warren
Cetan Sapa
Cloud, Benedict D.
Conger, Lucille (Yankton)
Conroy, Harry (Pine Ridge)
Cook, Charles Smith (Pine Ridge)
De Fond, Samuel C. (Yankton)
Deitz, William
Deloria, Ella Cara (Yankton)
Demarrias, Frances
Drapeau, Agnes
DuBray, Joseph (Yankton)
Eastman, Charles Alexander (Santee)
Eastman, Peter (Sisseton)
Estes, Joseph Folsom (Standing Rock)
Fire Thunder, Ella (Lower Brule)
Fish, Charles L. (Lower Brule)
Flood, Henry J.
Freeman, Albert B.
Gardner, Lucie
Garvie, James William (Santee)
Hare, DeWitt
Hawley, Alvin (Fort Peck)
Henderson, Kate (Fort Peck)
Higheagle, Robert P.
Hodjkiss, William D. (Cheyenne River)
Jones, Stephen (Santee)
Kealear, Charles H. (Yankton)
King, Kenneth (Fort Peck)
Knocksofftwo, Henry (Rosebud)
Kollenbaum, Lillian (Fort Peck)
Lamoureaux, Calvin
Long Wolf, Hattie (Pine Ridge)
Lyman, Annie (Yankton)
McGaa, Agnes
McLaughlin, Marie L.

SIOUX (cont.)
McLean, Samuel
Means, Hobart W.
Ohlerking, William (Fort Peck)
Picotte, Charles F., Jr. (Yankton)
Prue, Ellen M.
Renville, Florence (Sisseton)
Renville, Gabriel (Sisseton)
Renville, Germaine (Sisseton)
Robertson, Etta
Robertson, Nellie
Ross, Amos D.
Ross, Joseph
Rulo, Zallie (Yankton)
Small, Mary T.
Standing Bear, Henry (Pine Ridge)
Steeps, George
Tatiyopa, Henry
Three Stars, Clarence (Pine Ridge)
Tiaokasin, John (Standing Rock)
Tuttle, T. W. (Yankton)
Twiss, Frank W. (Pine Ridge)
Whipper, Dallas
Whipper, Rose
Whitebull, James
Yellowbird, Francis (Fort Berthold)
Yellowrobe, Chauncey

SKAGIT
Lang, Henry

STOCKBRIDGE
Leicher, Fred
Miller, Artie E.
Niles, Herman
Peters, Myrtle
Quinney, John W.

TLINGIT
Verigan, Francis L.

TSIMSHIAN
Marsden, Edward
See also ALASKAN NATIVE

TULALIP
Shelton, William

TUSCARORA
Cusick, David
Gansworth, Howard
Gansworth, Leander
Garlow, William
Hewitt, John Napoleon Brinton
Johnson, Elias
Mt. Pleasant, Edison
Mt. Pleasant, Mamie
Thompson, Martha

TUTUTNI
Bagwell, Amy T.

UTE
Pike, Elvira (Uintah)
Pike, Minnie

WALAPAI
Clarke, Francis

WARM SPRINGS
Smith, James

WASHO
Lowry, Katherine
McInnis, John

WICHITA
Campbell, Joseph

WINNEBAGO
Baptiste, John
Bear, John
Cloud, Henry Roe
De Cora, Angel
Hunter, Lucy E.
Kingsley, Nettie Mary
Lamere, Oliver
Londrosh, Cecelia
St. Cyr, Julia

WYANDOT
Choteau, Luzena
Clarke, Peter Dooyentate
Crotzer, Grace
Gordon, Jane Zane
Johnson, S. Arthur
Walker, Bertrand N. O.

YOKAIA see POMO

YUCHI
Gregory, James Roane

YUKI
Anderson, Arthur

YUMA
Dorchester, Daniel
Flame, Sylvester

Hammond, James P.
Jackson, Bernard S.
Jaeger, Agnes R.

Russell, Sennan
Sahenti, Mary
Vaughn, Gerald

Acorn bread 481
Adair, Brice (Cherokee) 1243
Adair, E. M. (Cherokee) 4056
Adopted citizens, among the Cherokees 62; rights of 62
Adoption 94, 252, 1751; dance 1283
Advertising 2618
Agreements, Cherokee 910, 911, 930, 931, 968, 977, 1067, 1068; Creek 874; see also Treaties
Agricultural associations 77, 78
Agriculture 11, 522, 1267, 1517, 1800, 2008, 2064, 2071, 2072, 2130, 3946; see also Farming
Airplanes 1675
Alaska 2111-2113, 2115, 2118, 2119
Alaska Native Brotherhood 2970
Alaskan Natives, conditions of 2968-2970
Alcohol 681, 1549, 1615, 1952; effects of 1320; see also Liquor; Prohibition; Temperance
Alcoholism 1880; fight against 564
Algonquins, last of 1156; legends of 3051; in New York 2932
Allotment 57, 376, 561, 715, 1256, 1834, 1930, 3030, 3709, 3829; Cherokee agreement on 99; among the Cherokees 857, 983, 1033, 1035-1038, 1709, 3535, 3719, 4102, 4116, 4146, 4164, 4165, 4286; among the Choctaws 2030; among the Creeks 2080, 3840; among the Pimas 1870; among the Shawnees 116
Allotments, removal of restrictions on 3769; sale of 2760, 2763, 2767
Alluwee, Oklahoma 3768
Aluminum 2713
American, duty of the 4003
American Aboriginal Association 2842

American Character 1327
American Indian Club 3780
American Indian Day 649, 650, 2873, 2874, 3664
American Indian Magazine 2354
Amusements 1999, 2568
Animal dance 2172
Animals 431, 1368, 1371; fables about 3119, 3120, 3121; legend about 537; stories of 1130, 1133, 2703; see also names of specific animals
Anishinabwe Enamiad 1597, 1600
Anti-Horse Thief Association 2092
Apaches 2695; Christmas among 3812; education among 3698; hunting among 2708
Apple trees 1317
Apples 2705
Arabs 2107
Arapahoes, land claims of 1031; and mescal 3963; myths of 1273, 1274
Archaeology, method in 2933; in New York 2918, 2923, 2927, 2929, 2931, 2932
Arizona, Indians in 2706; statehood for 2782, 2788
Arkansas, backwoods of 1318; poem about 3216, 3217; political activities in 355-360, 363
The Arkansian, editorial policy of 362, 364
Arrowheads 1249, 2914, 2938; poems about 3900, 3905
Art, Native American 771-775, 786, 3652, 3653
Artisans, Indian 3846
Artists, Indian 3846
Asia 1812
Assimilation 1828, 2906
Astronomy 1211
Athletics 1674, 3966
Atlantic Cable 3357
Autobiography 98, 160, 210, 303, 590-592, 653-655, 658, 661, 776, 1127, 1146, 1170, 1179, 1931, 2109, 2201, 2734, 2943, 3974

Automobile 570

Bacone College 826, 2076, 3074, 3838
Baking 1779, 1785
Ball game, Cherokee 4006, 4007
Ball play, Creek 4304; poem about 3078
Bank, Indian 2512
Banking and Currency 2799-2808, 2826, 2827, 2828, 2830
Banner Stones 2923
Baraga, Bishop 1595
Baseball 3647
Basketry 187; Pima 2604, 2605
Bear, story of 3771
Bear Star, legend of 2964
Beaulieu, Gustave (Chippewa) 2402, 2403
Beauty 3783
Beaver Medicine, story of 1627
Beck, John H. (Cherokee) 9, 10; charges against 262
Belgians 2716
Bells 998
Betatakin 2712
Beverly Hills, California 3447
Big Dipper, legend of 3690
"Big Stick" policy 3191
Biology 2665
Birch tree 3275
Birds, stories about 2849; see also names of specific birds
Black Hills, legend of 170
Black snake, legend of 2171
Blacks 1236; Cherokee citizenship of 252; in the Cherokee Nation 639, 972, 973, 2160, 4075, 4201; among the Creeks 1407, 1775, 3092, 3099, 3108, 3193, 4163, 4340; story of 1356
Blizzards 769
Bluejay, legend of 201, 202; poem about 3105
Bob white, poem about 3104, 3132, 3197
Boilers 3871
Bolshevism 2725
Books 3834
Bows and arrows 1946
Boy Scouts of America 1163
Brainerd Mission 343
Bread 1290, 1785, 2001
British Columbia 2114
Broadway 665
Brooklyn Indian Association 2608

Bryan, William Jennings 3489, 3492, 3494
Buffalo, Creek hunting of 1386; legend of 233
Buffalo Bill 2346
Buffington, Thomas Mitchell (Cherokee) 406
Bunch, Rabbit (Cherokee) 3716, 3799, 3800
Bureau of Indian Affairs 2722, 2724; complaints about 3633; criticism of 2332, 2344, 2347, 2353, 2358, 2359, 2360, 2405, 2426, 2434, 2435, 2442, 2448, 2460, 2465, 2467, 2478, 2482, 2484, 2487, 2489, 2492, 2498, 2500-2501, 2510, 2513-2516, 2519, 2527, 2528-2532, 2535, 2540, 2546, 2549, 2551, 2553, 2900, 3683; object of 3293; officials of 579, 582; opposition to 1594
Bureaucracy 223, 1365
Burial customs, Iroquois 3855
Bushyhead, Dennis Wolfe (Cherokee) 423
Business, success in 2169
Butter 1290

Cactus 2183, 2657
Caddo 2194
Calendars 3728
Calumet 1751; legend about 3932; poem about 3906
Campfire Girls 1163, 1663
Camp meeting, Creek 2995
Camping 3327
Capache Ematha (Creek) 1478
Carlisle, Pennsylvania 1975
Carlisle Indian Industrial School 1268, 1293, 1914, 1980, 1992, 2173, 2462, 2464, 2468, 2476, 2972, 3874, 3916, 3937, 3951, 3976; graduates of 177
Carpentry 1908, 3863
Carter Bill 2437
Casa Grande, Arizona 1825
Catawbas 1702, 2846, 2847
Catechism 1990
Catfish, legend of 1902
Catherine's Town 1751
Catholicism 1590
Cattlemen 4177
Cayuse 2193
Centipedes 1334
Champlain, Samuel de 2926
Cherokee Advocate 412; editorial

policy of 3, 5, 516, 517, 546
Cherokee Citizenship Association
  4117
Cherokee Nation, adopted citizens
  of 62, 252, 402, 860, 981,
  1109, 1110; affairs of 1, 2,
  4, 6-8, 12-15, 16, 21-25, 27-
  39, 46, 50, 51, 53-63, 65-71,
  72-75, 80-82, 99-101, 104,
  209, 244-247, 249-259, 261,
  263, 267, 347-349, 351, 353,
  354, 367-378, 381-393, 398,
  400-405, 415-418, 420-422,
  465-471, 473-475, 485-487,
  489-495, 497, 498, 501-503,
  506-512, 628-630, 637-641,
  734-741, 796-801, 802, 813-
  815, 857, 861-873, 875-879,
  882-906, 908-911, 918-924,
  927-931, 933-950, 957-973,
  1000, 1002-1004, 1007, 1035-
  1038, 1040-1056, 1059, 1062-
  1082, 1087-1103, 1224, 1225,
  1610, 1662, 1681-1690, 1692-
  1697, 1709-1711, 1713, 1760-
  1764, 1766, 1767, 2000,
  2127, 2129, 2131, 2135,
  2136, 2139-2141, 2148-2168,
  2562, 2609-2617, 2747, 2748,
  2751-2754, 2961, 2962, 3335-
  3342, 3357, 3381, 3386,
  3506-3512, 3520-3529, 3531-
  3541, 3543, 3545, 3548-3574,
  3579-3581, 3586-3594, 3596-
  3598, 3600, 3601, 3626-3628,
  3705-3707, 3718, 3719, 3731,
  3799-3803, 3806, 3808, 3809,
  3823, 3848, 3849, 3853, 3864,
  3866-3870, 3929, 3930, 4012-
  4017, 4051, 4052, 4054-4062,
  4065, 4067-4069, 4072, 4076,
  4078, 4079, 4081, 4082, 4090-
  4092, 4101, 4102, 4105-4108,
  4110-4119, 4124-4144, 4157,
  4158, 4202, 4221, 4233, 4236,
  4239, 4243-4246, 4257, 4265,
  4292, 4305, 4308, 4326, 4337,
  4342, 4343; black citizens of
  972, 973; blacks in 2160,
  4282; Canadian District in
  1863; changes in 463; citizenship in 1089, 1090, 2144, 4117,
  4144, 4293, 4294; civil strife
  in 3569; claims of 848; constitution of 42, 411, 1214,
  1260, 3519, 3625; Cooweescoowee District in 4072, 4295;
  definition of 4128, 4129; Dela-

Cherokee Nation (cont.)
  ware lands in 86; delegates from
  4077; destruction of 1219; dissolution of 4147; economic affairs
  of 1225; education in 3525, 3741-
  3746, 3822, 4081, 4090, 4238,
  4240, 4241, 4258, 4259, 4307,
  4317, 4335; Female Seminary in
  4161; financial affairs of 76, 738,
  739, 741, 1041, 1042, 1045, 1047,
  1049, 1682, 1683, 3525, 4143,
  4197; geology in 1001; and Georgia 3553, 3554, 3558, 3563,
  3564, 4095; and Georgia laws
  346-348, 1762; history of 847,
  1712; improvements in 420; insane asylum in 2131; intruders
  in 2739; land title of 844-846,
  984-986; lands of 54-57, 1002,
  1027-1031, 1033, 4225, 4270,
  4330, 4369; law and order in
  4234; laws of 12, 18, 42, 409,
  411, 414, 1214, 1699, 2613, 3259,
  3519, 3625, 4218, 4237; natural
  resources of 4082; Orphan Asylum in 1008-1010, 1012, 1232;
  outlaws in 4148; passing of 1082;
  penal system of 4235; permit
  laws of 4250; politics in 53, 61,
  101, 255-259, 268, 513, 514, 639-
  641, 836, 859, 919, 920, 923,
  1238, 1239, 3716, 3799-3803,
  4106, 4113-4115, 4231, 4288,
  4291, 4363, 4364, 4368; and railroads 841, 975, 984, 985, 4285;
  seminaries of 47, 48, 1187; status of 869, 871-873, 1050; stories
  about 2660, 2661, 2663, 2664,
  2672; town sites in 863, 867,
  882, 896, 902; towns in 961, 962;
  travels in 4360; treaties with
  866, 957, 960, 970, 971, 1699,
  2141; western lands of 4269,
  4271, 4272, 4276, 4327, 4365,
  4366; see also Cherokees, Eastern
  Band
Cherokee Outlet 56, 393, 852, 853,
  2740, 2741; funds from 1047,
  1049; lease of 56, 400, 597, 738,
  741, 1027-1028, 2962, 4272; sale
  of 244, 261, 1682
Cherokee Phoenix, and Indians' Advocate, editorial policy of 335, 337,
  338, 340, 1765; prospectus for
  335, 337
Cherokee Rose, legend of the 2581,
  3582
Cherokees 1660, 3576, 3584, 4252;

advice to 4254; agriculture among 11; antiquities of 1023; cattle owned by 4130; character of 4196; in Civil War 60, 367, 3357, 3570; claims of 1713, 3761; condition of 334; education among 47, 48, 76, 125, 341, 343, 832, 850, 978, 1000, 1008-1010, 1014-1017, 1021; history of 995, 1105, 1698, 1700, 1955, 3729, 3730, 4103, 4109, 4344-4359, 4362; lands of 8, 15, 597, 1076, 1079, 1081, 1088; legends of 1218; literature of 851; livestock of 12; lore of 1265, 1266, 1648, 3729, 3730; lost 1091; migration of 2666; mythology of 3299; name for 1746; names of 1998; Old Settler 413, 528, 854, 1737, 2014-2016, 3379, 3385, 3726, 3995-3997; orphan asylum for 102, 103; per capita payments to 50, 51, 4125, 4207, 4209, 4274, 4275; plight of 3338; poverty among 50, 51; removal of 3559, 4320, 4371; rights of 4095; secret societies among 191, 1310-1312; in Texas 3865; Texas claims of 64, 85; traditions of 3298; treaty with 3559; in the West 1223; and whites 4306

Cherokees, Eastern Band (North Carolina) 2841, 3524, 2527, 3534, 3949, 4017, 4120, 4281; claims of 75

Cheyennes, land claims of 1031

Chicago 1546

Chickasaw Nation 2746; affairs of 480, 519-521, 601, 1664, 1679, 1701, 1705, 1706, 1831, 1832, 2729, 2733, 3020, 3022, 3033, 4000-4002; agreement of 743; cattlemen in 4177; citizenship in 1832

Chickasaws 3297; per capita payment to 2822; traditions of 2965, 3324

Child rearing 1157, 1247, 1351, 1680, 3639, 3919

Childhood 4336

Chilocco Indian Industrial School 757, 3710, 3993

Chinookan family 4005

Chipeta 316

Chipmunks 1126

Chippewas 227, 286, 288, 1596,

3873, 3972, 3984; beliefs of 292; disturbances among 1196; removal of 1196; see also Ojibways

Chippewas (Minnesota) 236-239, 700, 1196, 2451, 2496, 2569, 3831; general council of 239, 2567

Chippewas (Wisconsin) 792-794, 804-808; affairs of 518; Lac Court Oreilles 1795

Chisholm, Jesse (Cherokee) 1532

Chitto Harjo (Creek) 3180, 3247

Choctaw Nation, affairs of 295-302, 601, 603-614, 1294, 1973, 1974, 2020, 2022-2025, 2027-2042, 2044-2058, 2093, 2094, 3020-3039, 3676, 3677, 3931, 4022-4025, 4122, 4123, 4296, 4301; agreement of 743; claims of 1974, 2025, 2746, 3032, 3036, 3039; coal in 2027, 4298; constitution of 606; education in 4300; laws of 1260, 1261; minerals in 4297; permit law of 2053

Choctaws 2065, 3282, 3296; citizenship for 3029; education among 295, 297, 300-302; life style of 4215; per capita payment to 2822; rights of 4299; traditions of 1258, 1259, 3019

Christianity 436, 437, 578, 580, 826, 1195, 1287, 1758, 1981, 2334, 2630-2645, 2991, 3575, 3955, 3977, 3978, 4136; among the Cherokees 333, 3583, 4210; among the Chickasaws 602; effects of 2209; among the Kiowas 98; at Lower Brule 436; among the Ojibways 653-655; among the Pequots 161, 162; among the Pimas 2102, 2102, 3691, 3692; among the Winnebagoes 590, 592; see also Catholicism

Christmas 114, 166, 176, 427, 430, 458, 626, 770, 788, 1234, 1273, 1306, 1307, 1799, 1948, 1969, 2010, 2105, 2106, 2852, 3258, 3373, 3439, 3675, 3787, 3825; among Apaches 3812; among California Indians 1809; Indian celebration of 3333; for Indian youth 3973; among the Nez Percé 532, 533; among the Oto 3606; among the Pawnees 3372; among the Pimas 477, 3815; story about 439, 457, 1966

Citizenship, Cherokee 245, 246, 252, 262, 263, 4057, 4058

Citizenship, U. S. 332, 767, 829,

1164, 1177, 1278, 1279, 1553,
1588, 1873, 2453, 2945, 2950,
2994, 3003, 3029, 3642, 3651,
3832, 3960, 3999; debated 194;
for the Omahas 193, 194
Civil Service 2458
Civil War 1301, 1560; Cherokees
in 60, 367, 1421, 3570;
Creeks in 1653, 1656, 3160,
3185; Delaware losses during
94; Indian participation in 728,
3357; story of the 1404
Civilization 542; effects of 3784;
Indian 1669
Clans, Cherokee 343
Claremore, Oklahoma 2735
Claremore Mound 3582, 3804,
3805
Clothing 1114
Cloture 2817, 2818
Clown, Indian 1314
Coal 2796; in Choctaw Nation
2027
Columbia, State of 4160
Columbus, Christopher 3656
Columbus, Ohio 3938
Colvilles, Christmas among 166
Comanches 186
Commerce 1910
Concrete 2108
Congress 3465, 3469, 3773; Indi-
an representation in 376
Conservation 1114, 1115
Coolidge, Calvin 3441, 3466,
3486
Coolidge, Sherman (Arapaho)
2894
Cooper, James Fenimore 671,
702
Corn 2071, 2176, 2177, 3607,
3621; legends of 1866, 1867
Cornstalk (Shawnee) 2196
Cornwall Seminary 1300
Cotton 1912
Council Hill, Oklahoma 1417
Courts, Cherokee 4060
Courts, U. S. 376, 1430, 3753,
4247; in Indian Territory 1689
Cowboys 3304
Coyote, legend of 535, 536, 3861,
3862
Creation myths 214, 215, 283,
1189, 1192, 1273, 1819, 1820,
1983, 2600, 2602, 3053; Mo-
have 763; Papago 156
Crawling Stone Lake 171
Creek Nation 3292; affairs 501,
552-554, 596, 1231, 1619,

1633, 1634, 1639, 1773-1775,
2082-2085, 2087, 2089, 2090,
2973-2978, 2980, 2982-2985, 3060-
3062, 3064, 3065, 3069, 3070,
3540, 3785, 3841, 4162-4165,
4192, 4193; blacks in 1775, 3193,
4163, 4340; conditions in 1611;
constitution of 2088; council of
the 1541; future of the 1472;
internal strife in 1527, 1528;
lands of 1322, 1329, 1335, 1346,
1352, 1383, 1426, 1438, 1455,
1465, 1471, 1474, 1490, 2084;
laws of 2088, 2091, 2979, 2981,
3940-3942; livestock in 1442;
novel set in 526; politics in
1495, 1616, 2082, 2086, 3165,
3170; schools in 1738; Snake
movement in 3180; story set in
3281; treaty with 1319, 1324,
1339, 2090; visit to 4216
Creek National Council, rules of
2086
Creeks, camp meetings among 2995;
child rearing among 1351; in the
Civil War 1653, 1656, 1775;
claims of 2769, 3160, 3185; condition of 2059; early history of
3595, 3599; education among
1250, 1252, 1345, 1512, 2077-
2079; full-blood 3212; Hichitee
1658; legends of 4256; lore of
the 1302-1307, 1309, 1321, 1323,
1326, 1328, 1330, 1342-1344,
1351, 1360, 1361, 1405, 1408,
1410, 1411, 1413, 1414, 1417,
1428, 1432, 1433, 1437, 1460,
1462, 1475, 1488, 1493, 1500-
1504, 1508-1510, 1523, 1524,
1527, 1534, 1563, 1654, 1655,
1657-1659, 1661, 3213; noted
3312; origin of 1344; Snake movement among 1567, 1569; Spokogee
1313, 1400, 1405, 1411, 1657;
towns of 1347; as war refugees
1775
Crime 633, 634, 2026, 2092, 4149
Croatan Indians 1894
Crow Reservation 4043
Crow Wing, Minnesota 220
Crows (birds), legends about 1792,
1793
Crows (tribe) 2410, 3701; tradition
of 1297-1299
Cuba 696, 3081
Cubans 2205
Curtis Act 879, 881, 890, 897, 940,
941, 944, 947, 1069, 2378, 2744,

2745, 4213
Custer, George Armstrong 1125

Dairying 2850; among the Oneidas 3789
Dakotas 3720; amusements of 1999; legend of 233, 575, 576
Dalles tribe 1828
Dances 309, 530, 762, 1283, 1645, 1786, 1869, 1888, 1895, 2097, 2172, 3265, 3668
Dancing 2997
Daughters of the Confederacy 3319
Dawes, Anna 216
Dawes, Henry 523
Dawes Act 3382, 3953; see also General Allotment Act
Dawes Commission 1092, 3722, 3735; Cherokee negotiations with 2151
Deaf and blind, among the Cherokees 4052
Debates 1727
Debating society 1200
Deer, Charmed 1361
Deerskin, story of 1963
Delawares, Cherokee citizenship of 252; citizenship of 1043; in Civil War 94; claims of 91, 93, 94, 96, 875; legends of 84, 89; picture writing of 90; religion of 87; Texas claims of 85; war claims of 93, 94, 96
Deluge, The 2066; legend of 155, 3645
Descent, Creek law of 1342
Desert 1253, 3329; plants of 3859; poem about 3885
Desks 3632
De Soto, Hernando 1750
Devil, story of the 1354
Dialect 1560
Dickens, Charles 135
Digger Indians 1811
Diplomats 3460
Disease 569, 2170; see also names of specific diseases
Dissipation 4096
District of Columbia, money lending in 746; see also Washington, D. C.
Ditch work 2992
Dog feast 1508, 1509
Dogs 3820

Domestic science 1821
Dreams 673
Dressmaking 3613
Drinks 1875
Dustin, Oklahoma 1463

Eads, Captain James 1976
Eagle, legends of 784, 785; story of 2198
Eagles Mere 3952
Easter 148, 179
Economics 2678, 2688, 2691, 2696-2698, 2702, 2781, 2799-2808, 2826-2828, 2830
Edison, Thomas Alva 174, 2716
Education 106, 113, 120, 121, 177, 181, 158, 159, 199, 205, 207, 279, 304, 443, 444, 455, 483, 524, 543, 551, 555, 567, 577, 585, 587, 593, 620, 651, 717, 719, 731, 757, 759, 803, 816, 817, 819, 821-823, 826, 828, 832, 850, 925, 978, 1000, 1008-1010, 1014-1017, 1021, 1024, 1044, 1108, 1117, 1118, 1120, 1141, 1155, 1174, 1187, 1190, 1193, 1220, 1222, 1248, 1250, 1252, 1254, 1270, 1272, 1284, 1345, 1379, 1512, 1585, 1586, 1604, 1605-1607, 1609, 1632, 1663, 1672, 1673, 1719, 1722, 1724, 1725, 1728, 1729, 1730, 1738, 1752, 1768, 1778, 1784, 1803, 1804, 1807, 1817, 1821, 1884, 1906, 1907, 1914, 1915, 1918, 1920, 1922, 1927, 1931, 1954, 1959, 1980, 1991, 1992, 1994, 1995, 2002, 2003, 2011, 2017, 2060, 2077-2079, 2081, 2098, 2100, 2173, 2174, 2178-2180, 2186, 2187, 2199, 2200, 2201, 2207, 2208, 2337, 2557, 2564, 2580, 2590, 2592-2594, 2619, 2628, 2652, 2685, 2686, 2851, 2944, 2946, 2954, 2958, 2967, 2987, 2999, 3002, 3015, 3260, 3271-3273, 3325, 3330, 3331, 3525, 3584, 3594, 3604, 3608, 3612, 3616-3618, 3631, 3654, 3655, 3657, 3671, 3674, 3688, 3689, 3691, 3692, 3696-3700, 3703, 3714, 3717, 3741-3746, 3790, 3821, 3827, 3838, 3843, 3858, 3874, 3875, 3913, 3916, 3937, 3956, 3967, 3976, 3983, 3993, 4034; among the

Cherokees 1044, 3586, 3594, 3741-3746, 3822, 4054, 4055, 4081, 4090, 4190, 4240, 4241, 4238, 4258, 4254, 4335; among the Choctaws 4027, 4030; domestic 732, 1289; higher 277, 293, 456, 1788, 1789, 3011; industrial 461, 819, 821, 822, 1726, 1962, 2892; influence of 3943; monolingual 3956; among the Pimas 3691, 3692; practical 3760; tribal systems of 76, 102, 103, 125, 297, 300-302, 341, 2077-2079, 3525, 3586, 3594, 4027, 4030, 4054, 4055; vocational 2601, 3717, 3910, 3991

Educational systems, tribal 47, 48
Egotism 621
Elk Horn Butte 212
Emigration, Cherokee 4246; see also Removal
Engineering 2621
English, need to study 832
Erie village 2856
Ethnology, teaching of 1752
Eufaula, Oklahoma 1487; development of 1473; economic development of 1550; federal court in 1430; improvements in 1332; landmarks in 1359
Eureka Springs, Arkansas 123
Europe, observations on 664; sketches of 710
Exploitation 6279

Fairs 3635; agricultural 77, 78; among the Cherokees 1230; Indian 1011, 1019; among the Kansas Potawatomies 2560; among the Pimas 2009
Farmers' Alliance 11
Farming 697, 1183, 1199, 2696-2698, 2700, 2701, 3607; Indians and 168, 211
Fasting 813
Feathers 2096
Federal Reserve Act 2821, 2834
Federal Reserve Bank 2799
Fencing, wire 1957, 4059
Fine arts 687
"Fire water" 3791, 3792
Fish, killing of 1447; legend of 529
Fishing 3880; on the Yukon 3322

Five Civilized Tribes 374; affairs of 452, 1695, 3058, 3059, 3537, 3538, 4012; condition of 373, 2955; land titles of 2795; and railroads 519, 4012, 4013
Five Nations, constitution of 2912, 2919
Flag, U. S. 1369, 1977, 2522, 2538, 4011
Fletcher, Alice C. 1945
Flowers 683
Flying Canoe, story of the 1629
Flying machines 1987
Food 1875
Football 2208, 3383, 3384, 3957
Foreign exchange 2829, 2834
Fort Arbuckle, poem about 1665
Fort Dearborn, massacre at 3049
Fort Gibson 136, 141, 144, 3724, 3755
Fort McDowell Reservation, conditions on 2526, 2530, 2531
Fort Phil Kearney, massacre at 2941
Fort Smith, Arkansas 1427, 4099
Four-leaf clover 3547
Fourth of July 4361
Fox, fables about 1885; story of the 3771
Fox Indians 1854, 1856-1858
Fraud 262, 331, 2683, 2688, 3774
Freemasonry 4153, 4154; among Indians 2925
Friendship 1350
Fuller, Mary Tenny 3807
Funerals 1362, 1364

Game, protection of 1385; state laws regarding 2428
Games 2717, 2859, 2860; see also Sports; names of specific sports
Gardening 4220
General Allotment Act 715, 1834; see also Dawes Act
Gentlemen, qualities of 4046
Geology 1001
George, Lloyd 3390
Georgia, Cherokee relations with 346-348, 1762, 3553, 3554, 3558, 3563, 3564, 4095
Geronimo (Apache) 1587
Gettysburg, Pennsylvania 1794
Ghost Dance 1844
Goingsnake (Cherokee) 4093
Gold, in Georgia 46; myth about 1205, 1206

Graft 1094
Grammars, Chippewa 288; Ottawa 288
Grand Council of the Indian Territory 278; see also Okmulgee Council
Grant, Ulysses Simpson, character of 2942; Indian policy of 410
Grasshopper war, legend of 3793
Great Doctor, legend about 3944
Green Corn, legend of 3669; origin of 3670
Green Corn Dance 1888; poem about 1645
Green Leaf, Cherokee Nation 1266
Green Peach War 1527, 1528
Gros Ventre 3701
Guaxule 1750

Hall, Robert 2508
Hampton Institute 443, 1248, 2590; graduates of 577
Handicrafts 3914
Handsome Lake (Seneca) 2879
Harris, Colonel Johnson (Cherokee) 4
Harrisburg, Pennsylvania 1909
Haskell Institute 651, 789, 1254, 1962, 2594, 3967
Hawaii 2655
Hayden Bill 2424
Health 795, 1167, 1169, 1194, 1221, 1671, 2170, 2623, 2682, 2789, 2854, 2990; national program for 2780; see also Public Health Service
Health education 787
Heroes 173; Indian 1173
Hewitt, John Napoleon Brinton (Tuscarora) 183
Hitchcock, Ethan Allen 1111
Holidays 26; see also names of specific holidays
Hollywood, California 3469
Home building 445, 3515
Homemaking 184, 240, 273, 825, 2179, 2574, 3624
Homestead entries 2771
Hoover, Herbert Clark 2726, 2727
Hopi 566, 627, 1876; beliefs of the 565; customs of the 3795; history of the 4049; legends of the 3796, 3797; story of the 1295

Horses 755, 4278, 4279
Horseshoeing 3992
Hotgun (Creek) 3218, 3225, 3228
Household hints 4070
Housekeeping 2197, 4008; see also Homemaking
Housing 451, 1671, 1723, 2119, 3004
Howie, Tom 395
Hoyt, Squirrel (Choctaw) 2026
Humboldt River, poem about 3346, 3347
Hummingbird, poem about 3080
Humor 2132-2134, 2137, 2138, 3133, 3135-3192, 3194-3196, 3201, 3202, 3204-3211, 3215, 3219-3224, 3226, 3388-3438, 3440-3505, 3585, 4065, 4067-4069, 4075, 4078, 4080, 4124, 4125, 4131-4135, 4137, 4138, 4140, 4201, 4260, 4261, 4278, 4279, 4282, 4283, 4309-4316, 4318, 4321-4325, 4363, 4364
Hunting 1305; Apache 2708; Creek 1309, 1326, 1386, 1466, 1469
Hupas, story of 515
Hurons 679
Hymns 1712, 2635, 2637, 2638, 2641

Ice making 3332
Iceland 2182
Imperialism 952
Indian, American 1780, 3921; appropriations for 1714, 2415; as athlete 3966; attitudes toward 459, 1497, 2339, 2342, 2351, 2361, 2362, 2369, 2370, 2483; awakening of 2883, 2885, 2886, 2890; beliefs of 3836; betrayal of 2214; celebrations of 1921; characteristics of 1129, 1154, 1349, 1372, 1376, 1378, 1391, 1510, 1519, 1537, 1542, 1544, 1548, 1552, 2123; "civilization" of 1131, 2189, 2211, 2212, 2373, 2571, 3629, 3753, 3852, 4168, 4169, 4172; competence of 2401; condition of 172, 235, 289, 369, 370, 440, 581, 645, 887, 1013, 1168, 1216, 1219, 1308, 1331, 1388-1390, 1395, 1398, 1429, 1435, 1441, 1443, 1467, 1540, 1576, 1577, 1580, 1618, 1781, 1898-1901, 1905, 1949, 2075, 2204, 2206, 2209-2211, 2213, 2220-2230, 2490, 2507, 2518-2521, 2526, 2528,

Indian, American (cont.)
2530, 2531, 2544, 2552, 2554, 2607, 2626, 2667, 2668, 2674, 2676, 2704, 2706, 2887, 2949-2952, 3041-3045, 3048, 3066-3068, 3269, 3514, 3577, 3649, 3959, 3987, 3994, 4009, 4087, 4205; cultural contributions of 200, 319, 321, 327, 810, 1161, 1162, 1166; customs of 559, 1165, 2648, 2998, 3659; defended 230; definition of 2450, 2461, 2523; demoralization of 2477, 2480, 2481, 2488; domination of 2332; duty of 644; and the earth 3928; equality for 2956, 3661; exploitation of 2374, 2379, 2397, 2401, 2406, 2431, 2520, 2526; festival of 1123; festivities of 1328; future of 595, 781, 1511, 1883, 1951, 2217, 2990, 3750, 3751, 3981, 4047, 4370; games of 2717; handicrafts of 1135; hate for 1886; history of 3857; historical significance of 2067; home life of 588; independence of 2389; languages of 1739-1741; legal status of 2871, 2882, 2894, 2899; legends of 308, 311, 1984, 2192, 2603, 3047, 3702, 3711, 4048; legislation affecting 560, 942, 948, 2506; origin of 152, 2068, 2880, 2889, 2891, 4152; outlook of 3920; passing of 780, 996, 1355, 1363, 1374, 1377, 1388, 1391, 1464, 1465, 1468, 1526, 1537, 1542, 1544, 1548, 1552, 2709, 3071, 3307, 3310, 3637; past life of 1934; and politics 1517, 1521; problems of 4042, 4280; progress of 276, 538, 558, 623, 624, 716, 721, 1707, 1729, 1986, 1996, 2875, 2893, 2898, 2906, 2907, 3986; rights of 464, 505, 616, 618, 945, 1176, 1269, 1598, 2226-2230, 2347-2353, 2372, 2374, 2381, 2385, 2392, 2393, 2397, 2405, 2406, 2411, 2416, 2417, 2420, 2423, 2425, 2427, 2453, 2454, 2456, 2458, 2471, 2496, 3634, 3678, 3679, 3682-3686, 3740, 3872, 4044, 4191; social condition of 2903; stories of 3311, 3704, 3890, 3906, 3907; traditions of 2625; treatment of

Indian, American (cont.)
1979, 2534, 2537, 2548, 4089; as warrior 3926; and whites 4200; and wild west shows 4038; see also Indians, American; specific tribal names
Indian Affairs 27, 834, 835, 888, 2940; see also specific tribal name, "affairs of"
Indian Chieftain, editorial policy of 19
Indian International Fair 77, 78
Indian policy 2380, 2388
Indian Progress, prospectus for 380
Indian Territory, affairs in 278, 3133, 3135-3192, 3194-3196; beauty of 3765, 3766; changes in 3186; crisis in 2742; government proposed for 371, 372, 375, 376-378, 386-390, 814, 837, 1054, 1055, 1100, 1681, 1773-1774; Indians of 2019; opening of 1756; passing of 830, 831; proposed 660; statehood for 849; territorial status of 21, 67
Indian tribes, confederation of 692
Indians, American 713, 714, 1285, 3315; Alaskan 3322; in America 322, 328, 548, 549; in Arizona 2706; attorneys for 2494; business training for 1817; conference of 2469, 2511, 2525, 2876, 2877; council of 2872, 3518; famous 3303; in Indian service 2391; insane asylum for 1379; lands of 1322, 1329, 1335, 1346, 1352; leadership among 280, 2722-2724, 2843; money for 2399; in New York 3006, 3777-3779; observation powers of 1893; occupations for 818, 2897; orphans home for 3314; in the professions 2692; professions for 175; public opinion of 1882; renaming 1138; self-help urged for 1879, 2390, 2398; as soldiers 643; success for 764, 3274; successful 2845; supernatural power of 2620; and U. S. government 3856; and work 758, 3694; see also specific tribal names
Indians and Their Friends 2876, 2877
Industriousness, debated 2366; urged 2491; need for 1353, 1781
Industry 2711
Initiative and referendum 2765, 2772, 2778
Insane asylum 1381, 2131

Insurgency 2775, 2776
Intercourse laws 4022
Intruders, on Cherokee Lands
344, 345, 2739, 3760; in
Creek Nation 1612, 2083
Iowa, politics in 833
Iroquois 189, 2865, 2870;
burial customs of 3855;
ethnology of 1751; festival
of 733; history of 1742, 1743,
language of 1739, 1740; laws
of 1824; league of 1755, 3014;
legends of 282, 1824, 1958,
3936; maize used by 2864;
myths and legends of 2857,
2862, 2863; origin of 2904,
2908; peace policy of 2868,
2869; prehistoric 2924; silversmithing by 2861, 2866, 2867;
towns of 1751; traditions of
1824; tree myths of 2878; wars
of 679
Isparhecher (Creek) 1460, 1483,
1485, 1638

Jackson, Andrew, policies of
1763
Japanese 2485
Johnson, Senator Edward S. 2486
Judiciary, federal 2783, 2785,
2797, 2825

Kachina dance 1786
Kansa Reservation 1813
Kansas City 550
Karma 4155
Keetoowah Society 1005, 1310-
1312
Keokuk, Moses (Sac and Fox)
1896, 1897
Kickapoos 1859; tales of 1860
Kindergarten 2017
Kindness 4185
King Philip 164
Kiowas 188
Klamaths 290; ways of 3847

Lake Mohonk Conference 2673
Lancaster County, Pennsylvania
3964
Lands, Cherokee 393, 421, 422,
597, 877, 3738, 3739, 3754,

4251, 4330; Cherokee cession of
391; Cherokee claims to 1076,
1079, 1081; Delaware claims to
91; Indian 82, 1002, 1027-1031,
1033, 1383, 1401, 1438, 1455,
1465, 1471, 1474, 1490, 2084,
2374, 2425, 2760, 3183, 3738,
3739, 3754, 4225; Indian claims
to 85, 86; Indian coal 2796;
Indian title to 453, 844-846, 877,
984-986, 2795; Osage 2784; sale
of 2760; surveying 2120; see also specific tribal name, "lands of"
Language, Algonquin 1851; Fox
1854, 1857; sign 3969; study of
4180
Languages 832, 2077; Çegiha 1925;
Choctaw 4026, 4028; Indian 1426,
1739-1741, 1776, 3052, 3956
La Pointe, Wisconsin 218
Laurel Hill Cemetery (Philadelphia)
4249
Law, Indians under 549
Lawyers, Indian 2503
League for the Extension of Democ-
racy to the American Indians
2427, 2433
League of Nations 2832, 3836
League of Peace 3922
Legislative Reference Bureau 2815
Library of Congress 2809
Lincoln, Abraham 1624, 1625, 2960
Lion, story of 1470
Liquor 997; suppression of 2812;
see also Alcohol; Prohibition
Literary societies 1911, 1276, 3604
Literature 698
Little Big Horn 1125
Little Lake Indians 1280
Little Water Medicine Society 724
Livestock 1442; laws regarding 12
Lodge, Henry Cabot 2831
Love 4329

McIntosh, D. N. (Creek) 3117
McIntosh County, Oklahoma 1556
Magazines, Indian 2354, 2377, 2432
Magnetism 1207
Maize 2864; discovery of 1940;
see also Corn
Manitou 1852, 1853
Maple sugar 274
Maple trees 462, 1808
Marshals, U. S. 1531, 4100
Mascots 3811
Mashpees 163

Massachusetts, Indians in 163
Mayes, Joel Bryan (Cherokee)
253, 1240, 4113
May-zhuck-ke-ge-shig (Chippewa)
238
Mechanics 818
Medical care 3005
Medicine 1382, 2572, 3622, 1302,
1769, 1823, 1929, 1933, 1935,
2991
Medicine dance 1895, 3668
Medicine societies 2858
Medicine worship, legend of 674
Meno, legend of 1904
Menominees 2103
Merchant Marine 2816
Mescal 3963
Meteorites 1208-1210
Methodism 3955
Mew-seu-qua 95
Mexico 3445; affairs in 2814
Michigan 1286
Milk 3860
Mineral leases 1070, 1071, 1073;
in Cherokee Nation 404
Minerals 893
Minnesota, history of 220
Minnesota Point 2565
Mission Indians 619, 729, 730;
festival of 525
Missionaries 557, 591, 703,
3583; among the Cherokees
348; Indian 3575
Missions 2458; education through
343
Modoc War 2012, 3334
Modocs 290; story of the 2012
Mohave-Apache, removal of 2219
Mohaves 2530, 2531; customs and
beliefs of 1887; legends of 763;
poem about 3884, 3889
Mohawks 2575, 2576; legends of
3971
Mohonk Conference 3270
Mole, legend about 151, 3911
Money lending 746
Monopolies 856
Montana 1978
Moody's Summer School 4034
Mormonism 1025, 1026
Morning and evening stars, legends
of 1274, 2971
Mosquito, legend of 2573
Mound builders 1584
Mounds 6, 3374
Mt. Shasta 3363, 3364
Munsees 1816
Murieta, Joaquin 3344, 3360

Music 1924, 1926, 3837, 3838,
4021, 4208; Indian 3975; Indian
fondness for 3854
Muskmelons 1333
Muskogee, Oklahoma 1535
Muskogee Institute 4303
Muskogee language, dictionary of
1776

Names 2060, 4198; Cherokee 1998;
Indian 632, 1138, 1746, 2988,
2989, 3046, 4088
Na-ne-bosho 435
National defense 2835
Natural resources 843
Nature study 1267
Navajos 182, 208, 3040, 3912; poem
about 3887, 3896; thrift of 3915
Navy 2714, 2718; history of 2719
Negroes see Blacks
New Hope Seminary (Choctaw) 4027
New Metlakahla, Alaska 2113
New Mexico, statehood for 2782,
2788
New Orleans Exposition 1617
New Year's Day 720, 1890; among
the Oneidas 2175
New Year's festival 733
New York 1965, 3513; Indians in
2927, 2929-2932, 2935, 2936,
3006
Newspapers 4121, 4184; Arkansas
362, 364; Cherokee 3, 5, 19,
335, 337, 381, 412, 516, 517,
1765, 3546; Indian 1591, 1592,
1597, 1600
Nez Percé 2957, 3268; athletic train-
ing among the 534; Christmas
among the 176, 532, 533
Night Hawk Ketoowah Society 191
North Carolina Cherokees see Cherokees, Eastern Band
Nursing 795, 1652

Occupations 175
Ocean City, Maryland 1720
Oglalas 631
Oil industry 3448, 3450, 3451, 3453-
3457
Oil leases 1070
Oil scandal 3450, 3454-3457
Ojibways 653-655, 658, 659, 661,
662, 679, 711-713, 1150; customs
and traditions of 236; handicrafts

of 1152; history of 3933; tales
of 1861; texts of 1862; see
also Chippewas
Oklahoma 3585, 4182-4184; at-
tempts to establish 67, 375,
386-390, 505, 838, 839, 840,
1679, 3588-3590, 3597, 4242;
constitution for 2563; encyclopedia of 3727; fraud in 331;
history of 4031; Indians of
2018; land rush in 1370; politics in 44, 1495, 1517, 1798,
2761, 2762, 2791-2794, 3224,
3810, 4029; prohibition in
1529; statehood convention for
563; statehood for 987, 1040,
1046, 1048, 1052, 1085, 1087,
1099, 1448, 1459, 1492, 1557,
1577, 1620, 1864, 2756, 2963,
3163, 3175, 3196, 3757-3759,
3764, 3770, 3772, 4071, 4141,
4253, 4367
Oklahoma Historical Society 625
Okmulgee Council 1678, 3057,
3587, 4178; see also Grand
Council of the Indian Territory
Old Hickory 1406
Omahas 1936, 1938, 1947, 1948,
1950, 3005; bow and arrow
makers of 1946; Buffalo Medicine Men of 1924; citizenship
for 193-194, 3003; condition
of 195, 198; funeral customs
of 1937; music of 1926
Oneidas 720, 1751, 3954; attack
on 2926; dairying among 3789;
Methodism among 3955; New
Year's Day among 2175
Onondaga Indian Welfare Society
824
Onondagas 1751; towns of 1751
Opeche, legend of 3605
Opossum 1188
Oratory 260, 2013
Orphans 102, 103, 1008-1010,
1012, 1232, 3314, 3316, 3748
Osages 127, 4206, 4289; cere-
monies of 1942, 1943; lands
of 2784; origin of 3970; sym-
bolic men of 1944
Ottawas 286-288
Outing system 1191, 2656, 3656
Outlaws 1336, 1338, 1341
Owen, Robert Latham (Cherokee)
963, 965
Owls, legend about 527,
574

Pacific States Telephone and Tele-
graph Company 2786
Pacifism 222
Painters (artists) 139
Painting (as occupation) 118, 1116,
1989, 3817
Panama Canal 478, 2811
Papagos 2104, 3267; Christmas
among 2105, 2106; legends of
156, 2600, 2602; life style of
1868; myths of 1983
Paternalism 558
Patriotism 2715, 3968, 4040
Paul, Moses 2630-2634, 2636, 2639,
2640, 2642-2645
Pawnees, ceremonies of 2595;
Christmas among 3372; Creek
war with 1655; legends of 213,
1866, 1867; societies of 2596,
2597
Payne, David L. 840
Peace 699
Peace Pipe 1941, 2966; see also
Calumet
Peaches 1113
Penmanship 4212
Pensions 742, 747
Permit laws 2053
Peyote 599, 2913
Phoenix Indian School 1117, 2967;
graduates of 181
Philadelphia, Pennsylvania 2146
Philippinos 1316
Phillips, Colonel W. A. 4337
Pickering Treaty 2937
Picnic 1668
Picture writing 3969
Pilgrims 3660
Pimas 441, 2558, 3056, 3267, 3733,
3818; agriculture among 3946;
allotments for 3709; basketry of
2604, 2605; beliefs of 3644;
building construction by 2126;
Christianity among 2101, 2102;
Christmas among 477, 3815;
community work among 2848;
customs of 3819; fairs among
2009; home life of 1902; legends
of 556, 1197, 1198, 2654, 3816;
life of 3945; progress of 1806
Pitchlynn, Sophia C. (Choctaw) 3925
Pocahontas 1475
Poets, English 3377
Political parties, Cherokee 255-258
Political satire 1564; see also Humor
Politics, American 2819, 3436,
3441, 3444, 3449, 3465-3497; the

Indian and 1521
Poncas 3982; legend of 1941
Pond lilies, legend of 1626
Pontiac, poem about 3886
Popular rule 2764, 2777, 2779, 2810, 2831
Posey, Alexander Lawrence (Creek) 1570, 1571, 3317, 3320, 3895
Post Office, U. S. 2787
Postage stamps 3842
Postal savings 2781
Potawatomies 1751, 2853; legend of 1815, 3053
Potawatomies (Prairie) 1790, 2559-2561
Potlach 768
Pottery 187, 3323
Powhatan 323
Powhatan (tribe) 1589, 1593
Powhohatawa 2653
Pow-wow 1304, 1434, 1450, 2413, 2418, 2440, 2449, 2457, 2473, 2499
Pratt, General Richard H. 1953, 1968, 2524, 3875
Prayers 3839
Prejudice 1237, 1757, 2454
Press Association, in Indian Territory 3154
Prince of Wales 3502, 3503
Printing 2184, 2986; Indians in 83
Prison reform 2611
Prisons 4099, 4235
Probation system 2770
Procrastination 3775
Prohibition 1529, 4331-4333; see also Alcohol; Liquor
Proverbs 615, 1476, 1481; Indian 3302
Public Health Program 2780, 2798
Puckered Moccasin, people of the 2646
Pueblos 1972, 2627, 2694; celebration of 2005; Christmas among 2852
Pushmataha (Choctaw) 4338, 4339

Rabbit, legend about 1892; story of 1498
Raccoon 1188; story of 1371
Races, origin of 1819, 1820
Racial segregation 3958
Railroads 4285; in Cherokee Na-
tion 841, 975, 984, 985; and the Cherokees 3531, 3534; and the Five Civilized Tribes 452, 519; Indian lands granted to 82, 398; in Indian Territory 3058, 3059, 4012, 4013
Rain-in-the-face (Sioux) 1140
Ration system 284
Ream, Vinnie 132
Recall 2783, 2785, 2797
Recreation 1184, 1630
Red bird 3123
Red Cross 458, 1969, 3825
Red Fox (Blackfoot) 2419
Red Jacket 3297, 3300, 3306
Red Stick War 1414
Reform organizations 2419, 2427, 2430, 2876, 2877
Relics, Creek 1488, 1493
Religion 676, 1059, 1213, 1408, 1502, 1503, 1744, 1745, 1747-1749
Remington, Frederic 1839
Removal 351, 928, 1325, 1677, 1763, 4320, 4371
Reservation System 2221-2223, 2477
Reservations 3630, 4043; Cherokee 3560; conditions on 1877, 1878; economic aspects of 583, 584; leaders on 1837; social aspects of 583, 584
Responsibilities 3786
Restrictions, removal of 2763, 2767
Returned students 113, 620, 759, 1193, 1607, 2628, 2851, 3331
Revenge 1417
Ridge, John Rollin (Cherokee) 146
Riggs, Alfred Longley 591
Roads 805, 807; condition of 1384
Robin, poem about 3102, 3128, 3131, 3200, 3235; story of 2188
Roosevelt, Theodore 1399, 2386; and the Indian 2667
Rose 4066
Ross, Carrie 1057
Ross, John (Cherokee) 60, 185, 1186; reply to 353, 354
Ross, William Potter (Cherokee), reply to 371
Russia 2579

Sabbath 4063
Sacs and Foxes 204, 207, 1896, 1897; condition of 2185; culture-hero myth of 1850
Sanitation 2854

Sarcoxie, Henry (Delaware) 3103
Sauks see Sacs and Foxes
Scalping 265
Schools, day 1768; federal Indian
  1606, 2337, 2462, 2464, 2468,
  2476, 2944, 3260, 3272, 3273;
  Indian 2017; reservation 207
Science 1222
Sehon Chapel 1020
Sells, Cato 2429, 2510, 2513,
  2516; Indian policy of 2380,
  2388
Seminoles 1439, 1642, 4223; passing of the 3310
Senate rules 2817, 2818
Senecas 2879; archaeology related
  to 2927; condition of 3012,
  3013; dance of 1888; fiction of
  1753, 1754; games of 2859,
  2860; legends of 725, 1753, 1754,
  1833; medicine societies of 2858;
  myths and folk tales of 2934;
  stories of 1772; tales of 1112;
  traditions of 3007-3009; in the
  War of 1812 2901, 2910
Sequoyah (Cherokee) 248, 1083,
  1084, 1108, 1712, 1955, 3072,
  3073, 3723, 3725, 4214; poem
  about 446, 447, 449, 900; monument to 913
Sequoyah Statehood Convention
  3196
Serrano Indians, festivals of 1281;
  stories of 1282
Sewing 3965
Shakespeare, William 3712
Shawnees 108-111, 2196; Cherokee
  citizenship of 252; conditions
  among 116, 117; Texas claims
  of 85
Sheldrake duck, story of 2073,
  2074
Sherman, William Tecumseh 481
Shiprock, legend of 791
Shoshoni 2007
Silversmithing, Iroquois 2861,
  2866, 2867
Sioux 1121, 1125, 1127, 1128,
  1142, 1143, 1144-1148, 3967,
  4039, 4041; condition of 1172;
  folktales of 1143, 1181, 1182;
  justice for 1175; mythology of
  1119; myths and legends of
  2095; progress of 3798; stories
  of 1148; see also names of
  specific bands and tribal divi-
  sions
Sioux Outbreak of 1862 2915

Sitka, Alaska 2115
Situwaka (Chilcat) 3923, 3924
Six Nations 751-754
Skunk 1565
Sky Cha-cul-la 1323
Slander 1237
Slavery, among the Indians 2583
Snake, legend about 1964, 2649
Snake dance 1869
Snake root 1382
Snow, legend of 1903
Snow-snake 2859, 2860
Society of American Indians 647-649,
  777, 2356, 2375, 2408, 2414,
  2474, 2508, 2525, 2536, 2547,
  2881, 2884
Soil, Indian relation to 1961
South America 3387
South Canadian River, poem about
  3126, 3203, 3231, 3237, 3242
Spanish American War 3063
Spavinaw, Oklahoma, traditions of
  128, 129, 137, 142
Sports 1732, 1736, 1818, 1913,
  2181
Spring 1666, 3276, 4181
Squirrels 1466
The Star 4121, 4186
Starr, Tom (Cherokee) 880, 3736
Stars 4176; origin of 3378
States' Rights 4245
Steam engines 1801
Stockbridges 3261-3263
Stones, origin of 105
Storekeeping 1960
Storms, Indian protection from
  1872
Sugar, beet 4004; cane 1988
Sugar bush 442
Sun, legends of the 760, 761
Sun myths, Iroquois 2862, 2863
Sunday School 4210
Superstition Mountains 3643
Sweat bath 2572

Tacquish, legend of 3881, 3882
Tahlequah 4284, 4359; poem about
  45
Taos, Pueblo de 3883
Tardiness 4074
Tariffs 748, 749, 2759
Teachers 3638, 3744, 3947; Indian
  305, 2999
Teaching 2077, 3745; in Indian Ter-
  ritory 2186
Tecumseh (Shawnee) 95, 579, 686

Teedyuscung 3794
Teeth, care of 153
Temperance 1615, 2953, 4179, 4277
Tepees 3313
Territories, U. S. 744, 745
Texas, Cherokee claims in 64, 3865; description of 1452; Indian claims in 85
Thanksgiving 531, 994, 1579, 2006, 2555, 2577, 2578, 3948, 4341; among the Cherokees 472, 488, 496, 499, 500, 504, 1691, 2147
Theosophy 1034, 1213
Three Sisters, legend of 1958
Thrift 2707
Thunder, legend of 242, 243, 266, 685; origin of 3830
Thunderbird, legend of 431-433, 1708
Timber industry 718
Tinsmithing 2996
Tipi Order of America 2419
Tobacco 2072
Toloman Mountain 3611
Tosas, story of the 1622
Totems 768, 2195; legends of 3640, 3641
Towns, in Cherokee Nation 961, 962; Indian 1347
Two Cousins, legend of 689
Travel 204, 688, 779, 1122, 1452, 1458, 1546, 2111, 2114-2118, 2121, 2122, 2146, 2589, 2659, 2663, 3513, 3530, 3619, 3788, 3813, 3845, 3938, 3952
Treaties 684, 808, 866, 903, 904, 957, 960, 1085, 1063, 1319, 1324, 1339, 2090, 2141, 2349, 2937, 3022, 3026, 3032, 3038, 3559, 3737; breaking of 2021; rights under 368; see also Agreements
Treaty, with Cherokees 368, 3737; with Chickasaws and Choctaws 601, 3022, 3026, 3032, 3038
Tree myths 2878
Trees 783
Tuberculosis 569
Turkey, legend of 3623
Turtles, legends about 725, 3917
Tuscaroras 1751, 2575, 2576; history of 1824; towns of 1751

United Daughters of the Confederacy 138
Utes 314, 3016

Village improvements 804
Village life 3983
Vinita, Oklahoma 132

Wachache (Creek), the prophet 1462
Wakachee 1413
Walking 667
Walking Purchase 1771
Wampum, poem about 3901, 3903
War bonnet 4018
War of 1812, Indians in 2901, 2910, 3054
War whoop, Creek 1360
The War-Whoop, editorial policy of 1591, 1592
Washbourne, Edward Pason 139
Washington, George 811
Washington, D. C. 2589, 3788; see also District of Columbia
Washington's Birthday, celebration of 26
Wassaja 2377, 2432
Watie, Stand (Cherokee) 149, 1421
Wheelock Seminary (Choctaw) 4030
Whipoorwill, poem about 3077
White Canoe, legend of the 3667
White Cloud (Chippewa) 237
White Earth Reservation 2451
Whitehead, Major James 220
Whitesides, G. W. 2736
Wichitas 2746
Wild Cat (Seminole), story of 1425, 1431, 1533
Wild Rice 1153
Wild west shows 2110, 4037, 4038
Wildcat, legend of 2070
Williams, Eleazer 1751
Williams, Robert L. 2813
Williams, Thomas (Caughnawaga) 3979
Wilmington, Delaware 3845
Wilson, Woodrow 3449
Wind 4073
Wind River Reservation 1877, 1881
Winnebagoes 778
Winnebagoes (Nebraska) 1787
Winter, legend of 2099
Wit, Indian 3301
Witchcraft 2190, 2591
Wolf, story of the 1498
Women 1733; attitudes toward 709;

equal suffrage for 2773; health education for 787; ideal 3835; Indian concept of 3666; influence of 4263; National Organization of 2766; proper dress for 1783; proper conduct for 3665; rights of 2757; role of 790; work of 3962

Women, Indian 1139, 3609, 3646, 3717; Cherokee 4227; education of 1607, 1609; home economics for 2179; occupations for 167, 184, 795, 2556; role of 154, 240, 241, 1821, 2197, 2574; as teachers 3947; and World War I 3516

Wool 1731

Worcester, Samuel Austin 3583

Work 568; Indians and 758, 1917, 1919, 2586, 2624, 2651, 3693

World War I 222, 2191, 2823, 2824, 2826, 2836-2839, 3388; Indian attitudes toward 3516; Indians in 545, 1608, 2411, 2467, 2493, 2495, 2844, 2916, 2917, 2920, 2921, 2922, 4044; veterans of 3442

World's Fair 992, 993, 4036

Wren, legend of 1927, 1928

Writers, Indian 3294, 3846

Writing 690, 695

Wyandots 572, 3888, 3899; history of 3894; poem about 3897, 3898, 3904

Wyoming 3828

Xuala 1750

Yankton Sioux 544

Yellow fever 2789

Yosemite Valley 2658

Young Men's Christian Association 1287, 1758

Younger's Bend, Indian Territory 1336, 1338; story about 2669

Youth, advice to 1226-1228, 1241, 1244, 1245, 1796, 4097

Yuchi 1659

Yumas, advancement of 3614; legends of the 3615